TRANSMISSION IN MOTION

How can various technologies, from the more conventional to the very new, be used to archive, share and understand dance movement? How can they become part of new ways of creating dance? What does this tell us about the ways in which technology shapes how we think?

Well-known choreographers and dance collectives, including William Forsythe, Siobhan Davis, Merce Cunningham, Anne Teresa De Keersmaeker, Emio Greco | PC and BADco., have initiated projects to investigate these questions. In so doing, they have inaugurated a new era for dance archives, education, research and creation. Their work draws attention to the intimate relationship between the technologies we use and the ways in which we think, perceive and make sense.

Transmission in Motion examines these extraordinary projects 'from the inside', presenting in-depth analyses by the practitioners, artists and collectives involved in their development. These projects are framed by scholarly reflection, illuminating their significance in the context of current debates on dance, the (multimedia) archive, immaterial cultural heritage and copyright, embodied cognition, education, media culture and the knowledge society.

Maaike Bleeker is a professor in the Department of Media and Culture Studies at Utrecht University.

TRANSMISSION IN MOTION

The technologizing of dance

Edited by Maaike Bleeker

LONDON AND NEW YORK

First published 2017
by Routledge
2 Park Square, Milton Park, Abingdon, Oxon OX14 4RN

and by Routledge
711 Third Avenue, New York, NY 10017

Routledge is an imprint of the Taylor & Francis Group, an informa business

© 2017 Maaike Bleeker

The right of the editor to be identified as the author of the editorial material, and of the authors for their individual chapters, has been asserted in accordance with sections 77 and 78 of the Copyright, Designs and Patents Act 1988.

All rights reserved. No part of this book may be reprinted or reproduced or utilised in any form or by any electronic, mechanical, or other means, now known or hereafter invented, including photocopying and recording, or in any information storage or retrieval system, without permission in writing from the publishers.

Trademark notice: Product or corporate names may be trademarks or registered trademarks, and are used only for identification and explanation without intent to infringe.

British Library Cataloguing-in-Publication Data
A catalogue record for this book is available from the British Library

Library of Congress Cataloguing-in-Publication Data
Names: Bleeker, Maaike, editor.
Title: Transmission in motion : the technologizing of dance / edited by Maaike Bleeker.
Description: New York, NY : Routledge, 2016. | Includes bibliographical references and index.
Identifiers: LCCN 2016009866| ISBN 9781138189430 (hardback) | ISBN 9781138189447 (pbk.) | ISBN 9781315524177 (ebook)
Subjects: LCSH: Dance and technology. | Dance—Data processing.
Classification: LCC GV1588.7 .T73 2016 | DDC 792.8—dc23
LC record available at https://lccn.loc.gov/2016009866

ISBN: 978-1-138-18943-0 (hbk)
ISBN: 978-1-138-18944-7 (pbk)
ISBN: 978-1-315-52417-7 (ebk)

Typeset in Bembo
by Swales & Willis Ltd, Exeter, Devon, UK

CONTENTS

List of illustrations viii
Notes on contributors xi
Preface xvi
Introduction xviii

PART I 1

1 Movements across media: twelve tools for transmission 3
   Maaike Bleeker and Scott deLahunta

2 Not fade away: thoughts on preserving Cunningham's *Loops* 16
   Paul Kaiser

3 Steve Paxton's *Material for the Spine*: the experience of
   a sensorial edition 32
   Florence Corin

4 William Forsythe's *Improvisation Technologies* and beyond:
   a short design history of digital dance transmission
   projects on CD-ROM and DVD-ROM, 1994–2011 41
   Chris Ziegler

5 *A Choreographer's Score*: Anne Teresa De Keersmaeker 52
   Bojana Cvejić

6 Archiving the dance: making *Siobhan Davies Replay* 62
   Sarah Whatley

7 Searching movement's history: *Digital Dance Archives* 70
   Rachel Fensham

8 The *Dance-tech* project: how like a network 80
   Marlon Barrios Solano in collaboration with Rachel Boggia

9 *Double Skin/Double Mind*: Emio Greco | PC's interactive installation 91
   Bertha Bermúdez Pascual

10 *Synchronous Objects*: what else might this dance look like? 99
   Norah Zuniga Shaw

11 Wayne McGregor's *Choreographic Language Agent* 108
   Scott deLahunta

12 BADco. and Daniel Turing: *Whatever Dance Toolbox* 118
   Nikolina Pristaš, Goran Sergej Pristaš and Tomislav Medak

13 *Motion Bank*: a broad context for choreographic research 128
   Scott deLahunta

PART II **139**

14 Making knowledge from movement: some notes on the
   contextual impetus to transmit knowledge from dance 141
   James Leach

15 Dancing in digital archives: circulation, pedagogy, performance 155
   Harmony Bench

16 Digital dance: the challenges for traditional copyright law 168
   Charlotte Waelde and Sarah Whatley

17 Between grammatization and live movement sampling 185
   Sally Jane Norman

18 What if this were an archive? Abstraction, enactment and
   human implicatedness 199
   Maaike Bleeker

19 Indeterminate acts: technology, choreography
    and bodily affects in *Displace* 215
    Chris Salter

20 Newman's note, entanglement and the demands of
    choreography: letter to a choreographer 228
    Alva Noë

Index *237*

ILLUSTRATIONS

2.1	Annotated code script for first version of *Loops*, 2001. Courtesy of the OpenEndedGroup.	24
2.2	Excerpt of *Loops Score*, 2004. Courtesy of the OpenEndedGroup.	26
2.3	Conceptual diagram, 2008. Courtesy of the OpenEndedGroup.	27
2.4	Conceptual diagram, 2008. Courtesy of the OpenEndedGroup.	28
2.5	Conceptual diagram, 2008. Courtesy of the OpenEndedGroup.	28
2.6	Conceptual diagram, 2008. Courtesy of the OpenEndedGroup.	29
4.1	*The Loss of Small Detail* (1994) showing William Forsythe, Dana Caspersen. Photos © Dominik Mentzos. Screenshots by Chris Ziegler.	42
4.2	*Self Meant to Govern* (1995) showing Christine Bürkle, Francesca Harper, Andrea Tallis, Ana Catalina Roman, Emily Molnar, Jill Johnson, William Forsythe. Screenshots by Chris Ziegler.	43
4.3	*William Forsythe: Improvisation Technologies. A Tool for the Analytical Dance Eye*, (1999) showing Noah D. Gelber, William Forsythe, Thomas McManus. Screenshots by Chris Ziegler.	45
4.4	*That's Kyogen!* (2001) showing Mansaku and Mansai Nomura. Screenshots by Chris Ziegler.	46
4.5	*NAGARIKA 1 Bharatanatyam* (2006) showing V.P. Dhananjayan, Prof. C.V. Chandrashekhar, Deepti Rajesh of Bharatakalanjali, Shantha Dhananjayan. Screenshots by Chris Ziegler.	48
4.6	*NAGARIKA 2 Kalaripayatthu* (2010), showing G. Sathyanarayanan Gurukkal, Rajesh and Sreejesh of Hindustan Kalari. Screenshots by Chris Ziegler.	49

7.1	Sample of the 65 pose search queries tested in the *Digital Dance Archives*. Screenshot by John Collomosse.	76
8.1	The dance-tech.net home page featuring the video *Pathfinder* by and with Mio Loclair. Photo by Ragnar Schmuck. Image by Marlon Barrios Solano, 2015.	83
8.2	A page of dance-tech.net with videos tagged with "cognition" featuring conversations with Lisa Nelson, Alva Noë, William Forsythe and Glenna Batson. Image by Marlon Barrios Solano, 2015.	85
8.3	The home page of dance-tech.tv. Image by Marlon Barrios Solano, 2015.	86
8.4	Collage of screenshots taken during work sessions and creative projects during Meta-Academy@Bates 2013. Images by Marlon Barrios Solano, collage by Rachel Boggia.	88
9.1	*Double Skin/Double Mind*, the installation. Photo by Thomas Lenden, 2009.	92
9.2	The *Double Skin/Double Mind* glossary as it appears as part of the installation manual. Courtesy of the artists.	93
9.3	*Double Skin/Double Mind* showing choreographer Emio Greco giving instructions. Photo by Thomas Lenden, 2009.	94
9.4	*Double Skin/Double Mind* showing Bertha Bermúdez Pascual in the installation. On screen choreographer Emio Greco giving instructions. Photo by Thomas Lenden, 2009.	95
10.1	Opening interface online for *Synchronous Objects*. Courtesy of the artists William Forsythe, Maria Palazzi and Norah Zuniga Shaw.	100
10.2	The Data Fan object from *Synchronous Objects* created using choreographic cueing and alignment data from William Forsythe's *One Flat Thing, reproduced*. Courtesy of the artists William Forsythe, Maria Palazzi and Norah Zuniga Shaw.	101
10.3	Image from *Synchronous Objects: Reproduced* video installation at PACT Zollverein Essen, Germany, August 2010. Curator Andreas Broeckmann. Courtesy of the artists William Forsythe, Maria Palazzi and Norah Zuniga Shaw.	106
11.1	The left and right screens of the Choreographic Language Agent. Courtesy of the OpenEndedGroup & Wayne McGregor|Random Dance.	113
11.2	Experimental sketching of a new movement sequence (left), followed by dance exploration of the geometry created (right). Dancer is Jessica Wright. Photos: Luke Church.	113
12.1	Screenshot of *Matching Positions*. Image courtesy of BADco.	119
12.2	Screenshot of *Inertia*. Image courtesy of BADco.	120

12.3 Zrinka Užbinec using the *Capture/Replay* tool. Image courtesy
of BADco. 121
12.4 *Whatever Dance Toolbox* set-up. Image courtesy of BADco. 126
13.1 Video still from digitally rendered overlay of twenty-one versions
of the solo adaptations of *No Time To Fly* (dancers/choreographers:
Jeanine Durning, Juliette Mapp and Ros Warby). Deborah Hay
took this video as an inspiration for a new work commissioned
by the Cullberg Ballet, *Figure a Sea*, which premiered in
September 2015. Video still credit: Motion Bank. 135

CONTRIBUTORS

BADco. is a Zagreb-based theater collective. The collective shares interests in choreography, dramaturgy, and philosophy, and currently consists of Ivana Ivković, Ana Kreitmeyer, Tomislav Medak, Goran Sergej Pristaš, Nikolina Pristaš, and Zrinka Užbinec. Founded in 2000, BADco. has systematically focused on theater and dance performance as a problem-generating rather than problem-solving activity—questioning established ways of performing, representing, and spectating. BADco. approaches the theatrical act as an unstable communicational exchange: a complex imaginary that challenges the spectator to look beyond the homogenizing image of reality presented by the media, and reclaim her or his freedom of spectating. For the *Whatever Dance Toolbox*, BADco. collaborated with Daniel Turing, a software developer with an interest in human–machine interfaces.

Marlon Barrios Solano is a Venezuelan interdisciplinary artist, educator, and researcher with an interest in consciousness, embodied awareness, human-knowledge networks, and contemporary choreographic practices. He has a hybrid background in movement, new media arts, organizational development, and cognitive science. He creates platforms for open knowledge production and distribution among trans-local artistic communities and organizational contexts. He is the creator/producer/curator of dance-tech.tv, dance-tech.net, and the dance-tech interviews and views. Marlon is a research associate at HZT Berlin (Germany) and an international Vipassana meditation facilitator. He holds an MFA in Dance and Technology (2004) from The Ohio State University, USA.

Harmony Bench is Assistant Professor in the Department of Dance at The Ohio State University, where she teaches in the areas of Dance, Media/Digital Humanities, and Performance Studies. Her writing can be found in *Dance Research Journal*, *The International Journal of Performance Arts and Digital Media*, *Participations*, and *The International Journal of Screendance*, for which she serves as co-editor. She is currently working on a book manuscript tentatively entitled *Dance as Common: Movement as Belonging in Digital Cultures*, as well as a digital humanities and database project focused on the performance engagements of early twentieth-century dance companies.

Bertha Bermúdez Pascual (MA in Dance and Choreography) is a PhD student at the Amsterdam School for Heritage and Memory Studies. A former dancer at Frankfurt Ballet, Compañia Nacional de Danza, and Emio Greco | PC, she turned towards research on dance documentation and notation. She coordinated and contributed to various research projects under the umbrella of ICK Amsterdam, including *Capturing Intention* (2005–2008), *Inside Movement Knowledge* (2009–2011), and *Pre-choreographic Elements* (2009–2014), and *Intangible Traces* (2006–present) with Las Negras Productions where she currently works as artistic director and researcher.

Maaike Bleeker is a professor in the Department of Media and Culture Studies at Utrecht University. She graduated in Art History, Theatre Studies, and Philosophy, and obtained her PhD from the Amsterdam School for Cultural Analysis (ASCA). She was the organizer of the 2011 world conference of Performance Studies international (PSi) *Camillo 2.0: Technology, Memory, Experience* and president of PSi (2011–2016). She has published extensively in international journals and edited volumes and edited several books, including *Anatomy Live: Performance and the Operating Theatre* (AUP 2008) and *Performance and Phenomenology: Traditions and Transformations* (Routledge 2015). Her monograph *Visuality in the Theatre. The Locus of Looking* was published by Palgrave (2008).

Rachel Boggia is a multidisciplinary dance artist whose work explores digital media, performance, collaboration, and documentation. With Marlon Barrios Solano, she co-leads Meta-Academy, an experiment in collaborative online learning focused on embodied and performance practices. Boggia is an Assistant Professor of Dance at Bates College in Lewiston, Maine, USA. See http://www.rachelboggia.com.

Florence Corin trained as an architect and is now working as a video artist, choreographer, and publisher. She works mainly in the field of dance and multimedia. Since 1998, she has worked for Contredanse which she is now in charge of editing and publishing. For Contredanse, she co-realized the DVD-ROM *Material for the Spine, Steve Paxton* (best publication award, CORD 2010), and the DVD-ROM *Anna Halprin. Dancing Life/Danser la vie*. Parallel to this, she creates interactive performances and installations with her association Mutin (www.mutin.org). She also organizes workshops and gives lectures about her work, digital technologies, and relations to architecture.

Bojana Cvejić is a performance theorist and performance maker based in Brussels. She studied musicology and holds a PhD in philosophy from Centre for Research in Modern European Philosophy in London. Cvejić has made many theater and dance performances since 1996 as (co)director or dramaturg, and has published several books, most recently *Choreographing Problems: Expressive Concepts in Contemporary Dance and Performance* (Palgrave Macmillan, 2015), *Public Sphere by Performance*, (with Ana Vujanović, Bbooks, 2012), and *Drumming & Rain: A Choreographer's Score* (with Anne Teresa De Keersmaeker, Mercatorfonds 2013). She has taught at contemporary dance school P.A.R.T.S. in Brussels since 2002, and is member of TkH collective.

Scott deLahunta has worked as writer, researcher, and organizer on a range of international projects bringing performing arts with a focus on choreography into conjunction with other disciplines and practices. He is currently a Senior Research Fellow at the Centre for Dance Research, Coventry University (UK) and Deakin Motion.Lab, Deakin University (Australia). He is co-directing the Motion Bank Institute based in Frankfurt, DE with Florian Jenett. See http://www.sdela.dds.nl.

Rachel Fensham is Professor of Dance and Theatre Studies at the University of Melbourne. Her current research focuses on theater spectatorship, costume histories, and digital archives, with recent publications in *Scene*, *Dance Research Journal*, and *Design History*. She is the author of *To Watch Theatre: Essays on Genre and Corporeality* (Peter Lang 2009), *Dancing Naturally: Nature, Neo-classicism and Modernity in Early Twentieth Century Dance* (co-edited with Alexandra Carter, Palgrave 2011), and *The Dolls' Revolution: Australian Theatre and Cultural Imagination* (co-authored with Denise Varney, Australian Scholarly Publishing 2005). She is also co-editor of the Palgrave book series *New World Choreographies*.

Paul Kaiser is a digital artist and writer who has created a body of work for stage, gallery, screen, and public space, crossing many disciplinary borders. Much of his work has been in collaboration with others, primarily with OpenEndedGroup colleague Marc Downie (and formerly with Shelley Eshkar), but sometimes extending to such collaborators as Merce Cunningham, Trisha Brown, Bill T. Jones, and others. In 1996, Kaiser was the first digital artist to receive a Guggenheim Fellowship; in 2008 he received the John Cage Award from the Foundation for Contemporary Arts. In 2015, MoMA acquired eight OpenEndedGroup 3D films, including *Loops*.

James Leach is a social anthropologist who has worked in Melanesia, undertaking fieldwork in Papua New Guinea since 1993. He is a member of the CREDO (Centre for Research and Documentation of Oceania) at Aix-Marseille University, as a Directeur de Recherche with the CNRS. James's education was at Manchester University in the UK. He has held research and teaching positions at Cambridge and Aberdeen Universities. See http://www.jamesleach.net.

Alva Noë is Professor of Philosophy at the University of California, Berkeley, where he is also a member of the Institute for Cognitive and Brain Sciences and the Center for New Media. He is the author of *Strange Tools: Art and Human Nature* (Hill and Wang 2015), *Varieties of Presence* (Harvard 2012), *Out of Our Heads: Why You Are Not Your Brain and Other Lessons from the Biology of Consciousness* (Hill and Wang 2009), and *Action in Perception* (MIT 2004). He has been philosopher-in-residence with The Forsythe Company and has collaborated with Deborah Hay on a lecture-performance project called *Reorganizing Ourselves*. Noë is a 2012 recipient of a Guggenheim fellowship, and is a weekly contributor to National Public Radio's science blog *13.7: Cosmos and Culture*.

Sally Jane Norman is a New Zealand/French theater historian and theorist of performance studies (Doctorat d'état, Paris III), whose practice-informed research addresses relations between art and technology, and the ways we stage evolving notions of liveness. Sally Jane has instigated, collaborated, and published on creative digital initiatives spanning several decades, institutions, and countries. After serving as founding director of Culture Lab, an interdisciplinary digital research hub at Newcastle University, then as Professor of Performance Technologies and director of the Attenborough Centre for the Creative Arts, a major arts refurbishment program at the University of Sussex, Sally Jane is now Co-Director of the new Sussex Humanities Lab, where she leads the Digital Technologies/Digital Performance research strand. See http://www.sussex.ac.uk/shl.

Chris Salter is an artist, University Research Chair in New Media, Technology and the Senses at Concordia University, and Co-Director of the Hexagram network for Research-Creation in Media Arts, Design, Technology, and Digital Culture, in Montreal. He studied philosophy and economics at Emory University and completed a PhD in directing and dramatic criticism at Stanford University where he also researched and studied at CCRMA. He collaborated with Peter Sellars and William Forsythe and the Frankfurt Ballet. His work has been shown at the Venice Architecture Biennale, Vitra Design Museum, HAU-Berlin, BIAN 2014 (Montreal), LABoral, Lille 3000, CTM Berlin, National Art Museum of China, Ars Electronica, Villette Numerique, Todays Art, Mois Multi, Transmediale, and EXIT Festival (Maison des Arts, Créteil-Paris), among many others. He is the author of *Entangled: Technology and the Transformation of Performance* (MIT Press 2010), and *Alien Agency: Experimental Encounters with Art in the Making* (MIT Press 2015).

Charlotte Waelde is Professor of Intellectual Property at the Centre for Dance Research (CHDaRE), Coventry University. Her research interests center on the role of IP law within the cultural sector and digital environment. Her research includes sole and co-authored articles with cross-disciplinary intersections published in a range of national and international journals. She has participated in a number of funded projects examining the role of IP law in the cultural sector including the AHRC project *InVisible Difference: Dance, Disability and Law* (see http://www.invisibledifference.org). She has advised national and European policy makers on a range of IP and culture matters, and chairs the UK Intellectual Property Office Unregistered Rights Research Expert Advisory Committee.

Sarah Whatley is Professor of Dance and Director of the Centre for Dance Research (C-DaRE) at Coventry University. Her research interests include dance and new technologies, dance analysis, somatic dance practice and pedagogy, and inclusive dance practices; she has published widely on these themes. The AHRC, the Leverhulme Trust and European Union fund her current research. She led the AHRC-funded Siobhan Davies digital archive project, *Replay* and continues to work with Davies on other artist-initiated research projects. She is also editor of the *Journal of Dance and Somatic Practices* and sits on the editorial boards of several other journals.

Chris Ziegler is a director, digital artist, and architect of numerous international interdisciplinary projects in dance, performing, and new media arts. Currently he holds a position as Assistant Professor for Interactive Media at Arizona State University (ASU) where he is researching and developing immersive environments for the stage. He is Associate Artist of ZKM Karlsruhe, lecturer, teacher, and researcher at SINLAB Lausanne, the Amsterdam School for the Arts (AHK) and the International Choreographic Center in Amsterdam (ICK Amsterdam), the Art University of Linz "Interface Cultures," LaSalle University Singapore and also at the School of Creative Media, City University of Hong Kong.

Norah Zuniga Shaw is an artist and scholar focusing on choreographic ideas as the locus for interdisciplinary and intercultural creativity. She is known for her award-winning collaborations with William Forsythe and Maria Palazzi integrating art and science research. Zuniga Shaw tours her work internationally and gives public lectures for a broad range of audiences including such venues as the Chicago Humanities Festival, Spring Dance, Sadler's Wells, and Taipei Arts Festival. Since 2004 she has been Director for Dance and Technology at The Ohio State University Department of Dance and Advanced Computing Center for the Arts and Design (ACCAD) where she is a tenured professor teaching courses in intermedia, creative research, theories of the body, dance improvisation, and digital literacy.

PREFACE

It has taken many years to develop this volume and over these years a great number of wonderful people were involved in the various projects represented on these pages. It would be impossible to mention them all. Therefore I will have to limit myself to mentioning only a few who have played a crucial role in how these projects have come together on the pages that follow. These are first of all Marijke Hoogenboom, whose vision and vigor as professor of Arts Practice and Development at the Amsterdam School of the Arts has been, and is, a driving force behind many important research projects in the arts, including the *Inside Movement Knowledge* (IMK) project that provided the context for the first phase of this book project. IMK brought together participants from dance company Emio Greco | PC, the Netherlands Media Art Institute, the Department of Media & Culture at Utrecht University, and the dance program of the Amsterdam School of the Arts. Thank you all for the inspiring discussions and explorations. IMK also provided me with the opportunity to collaborate with Laura Karreman, which was an incredible pleasure. Together we thought up the outline for this volume and she did much of the practical work that laid the foundations for its growth during the years that followed. The Dance Engaging Science working group of the *Motion Bank* provided a second context that has been of great importance to the further development of this project. Thank you Bettina Bläsing, Dana Caspersen, Emily Cross, Patrick Haggart, David Kirsch, James Leach, Alva Noë, Liane Simmel, Michael Steinbusch, Kate Stevens, Guido Orgs, Freya Vass-Rhee, Elisabeth Waterhouse, and Riley Watts for thinking (and moving) together. Thank you Talia Rodgers, Ben Piggott, and Kate Edwards of Routledge for your trust in this book project and for all your support in making it become an actual book.

Finally, this book would not have been here without Scott deLahunta. As project leader of both the *Inside Movement Knowledge* project and the Dance Engaging Science working group, he set the stage for both the first and the second phases of the development of this book project. As collaborator in and/or (co)organizer of many projects discussed in this volume he has been an incredible informant, matchmaker, and co-thinker. As (co)organizer of many more projects beyond the scope of this book he has most generously included me in collaborations that have inspired and challenged me for more than fifteen years already. I am deeply grateful for this and I am much looking forward to new projects in the time to come.

INTRODUCTION

Maaike Bleeker

One of the characteristics of the transformations brought about by the rise of digital and networked media, Wolfgang Ernst (2013) observes, is that the traditional separation between transmission media and storage media becomes obsolete. "When we talk about maximized computer memory capacities, this discourse continues an old occidental obsession that culture depends on storage (historic architectures, libraries, museums). But media analysis indicates that in the future cultural emphasis will be rather on permanent transfer" (98). The modes of operating of what Mark Hansen (*Feed Forward*) describes as twenty-first-century media are those of continuous transmission in which storage becomes transfer across temporal distance.

This volume engages with these transformations from the perspective of dance. The premise of this volume is that dance as a practice of doing, thinking, and transmitting movement has most relevant expertise to offer with regard to transmission in motion as afforded by various new and older media. Dance makers eagerly explore the potential of technological possibilities of capturing, storing, processing, and transmitting, and incorporate these in their practice. Easy to use technologies like digital cameras and weblogs are widely used to capture and disseminate finished works, to document and share creation processes, as mediators in new modes of (self) reflection about these processes, as means to mediate in future processes of understanding creations and to anticipate their future historicity, as well as to relate to creations from the past in new ways. These explorations make available a wealth of material while also allowing for new modes of interacting with this material, navigating through it, understanding it, selecting and recombining it, pulling information from it, and putting it to new (creative) uses.

These explorations are informative not only with regard to the possible usage of technologies in dance practice and research, but also with regard to the ways in which these technologies afford new ways of relating to and doing things with movement. Furthermore, the ways in which technologies are being incorporated in practices of creating, sharing, and making sense of dance draws attention to the ways in which more generally modes of perceiving, sense making, and thinking are intertwined with technology. We think through, with, and alongside the media we use, observes Katherine Hayles (2012). This is what she and other media theorists call *technogenesis*: the co-evolution of humans and technology. From the first attempts at noting down information, to high tech digital information storage and retrieval systems, technologies have mediated our psychic organization and reshaped our consciousness. What we know and how we think therefore cannot be understood separately from the technologies we use to process, store, and transmit information.

A major step in this co-evolution with technologies of various kinds occurred with the invention of writing and print. The impact of these inventions, Walter Ong (1989) famously observes, is not merely a matter of having a means to store spoken language by writing it down, but manifests itself in major transformation in modes of understanding, thinking, and imagining, including the emergence of new ways of knowing and new conceptions of what knowledge is. Key to what the technology of writing brought about is how it transformed language from an aural transitory phenomenon directly connected to a speaker and place of utterance into a visual spatial phenomenon that exists independent from a speaker and place of utterance. The *technologizing of the word* (Ong) set the stage for new ways of handling and organizing information, as well as for ways of thinking and knowing in which defining the meaning of something begins with subtracting movement from the picture. Writing captures and fixates language and is co-constitutive of modes of thinking in which movement, to speak with Massumi (*Parables*), has been bracketed out and has been subordinated to the positions it connects.

This general positionality, as Massumi terms it, is now at odds with developments in a wide variety of fields that point to meaning as something that is performative and comes into being rather than is, that transforms, is relational, and emerges from the interplay between our cognitive perceptual practices and the technologies used to produce, store, and transmit information. A great number of more recent technological developments—from finger gestures on the iPhone, to the physically moving control of the Wii, to Microsoft's gestural games interface Kinect—allow for movement to become increasingly part of modes of interaction between bodies and technologies. Modes of interaction and of handling information and knowledge afford users to navigate through information by means of gesture. More radical than that, new information technologies make possible a shift towards movement (actual or imagined) as means of apprehension. Brian Rotman (2008) points to an increased focus on the importance of physical activity and bodily mechanisms within all forms of learning, from new developments in serious gaming (interactive gaming technology used, among other things for learning purposes) to abstract mathematical thinking. Hansen (in *Bodies in Code*) observes that with the convergence of physical and virtual spaces informing today's corporate and entertainment environments, researchers and artists have come to recognize that motor activity—not representationalist verisimilitude—holds the key to fluid and functional crossings between virtual and physical realms. Furthermore, the shift from nineteenth- and twentieth-century media towards what Hansen (*Feed Forward*) proposes calling twenty-first-century media fundamentally modifies the scope and operation of recording as well as that of the archive. Characteristic of "twenty-first-century media" is that they do not record human experience but data. In this context, Hansen observes, mediation can no longer be understood to name the technical inscription of human experience but rather mediation describes "the task of composing relations between technical circuits *and* human experience" (43).

These new technologies are rapidly becoming the standard in a wide variety of fields. Yet many questions concerning their implications and potential are still to be researched. This volume explores these implications, and in particular what the technologizing of dance may help to understand about much broader cultural transformations. The title of this volume resonates with that of earlier publications titled *Meaning in Motion. New Cultural Studies of Dance* (edited by Jane Desmond, 1997) and *Knowledge in Motion. Perspectives of Artistic and Scientific Research in Dance* (edited by Sabine Gehm, Pirkko Husemann, and Katharina von Wilcke, 2007). This volume aims to continue the important work done by these earlier publications while also to shift attention from meaning and knowledge as part and parcel of dance practice towards dance as partner in dialogue in a rethinking of meaning and knowledge from the perspective of permanent transfer rather than storage.

William Forsythe (USA/Germany), Merce Cunningham (USA), Siohban Davis (UK), Emio Greco | PC (The Netherlands), Steve Paxton (USA), Wayne McGregor (UK), Anne Teresa De Keersmaeker (Belgium), BADco. (Croatia): all well-known dance makers or dance companies who are (or, in the case of Cunningham, was until recently) prominently present in the field of contemporary dance, and all of them are investing considerable amounts of time, effort, and money to create tools to make, capture, archive, disseminate, and study dance. Many more dance makers are considering similar projects or are in the process of developing them. The first part of this book presents an in-depth analysis of a selection of their projects at the intersection of dance and various media, some of them very old, like writing, many of them much newer and even very new. These projects are presented "from the inside," that is by authors who have been closely involved in developing them. They introduce the history of the projects (aims, preparations, starting point, trajectory, "bottle-necks," current state, collaborators), possible uses, and potential future developments. These introductions are illustrated with instructive images and documentary material, and framed by a comparative analysis (Chapter 1) of the projects, illuminating important similarities and differences with respect to the aims and scope of the projects, the aspects of dance addressed by them, as well as potential uses and users.

This selection of projects is precisely that: it is a selection and not an exhaustive overview. More projects exist or are being developed at the moment of writing, and likely more again will be initiated after the completion of this text. Each in their own way, these projects explore the potential of various technologies (from the old technology of writing to the latest possibilities for motion tracking and movement steered interfaces) to become how we create, make sense, and share. Together these projects offer a complex image of knowledge cultures in transformation. The ways in which they explore the potential of various media from the perspective of dance reflects broader transformations in practices of knowledge transmission and raises questions like: how do these developments transform our relationship to current as well as historical practices of knowledge transmission? What might these projects contribute to current debates on the preservation and reconstruction of immaterial cultural heritage? How might new technological possibilities change our understanding of archival practices and the relationship between the archive and creative practice? What implications does this have for the practice of teaching and learning? These and other questions are subject of the second part of this book. This second part consists of seven chapters that further elaborate and contextualize questions and issues that emerge from the project descriptions in Part I.

James Leach in his chapter "Making knowledge from movement: some notes on the contextual impetus to transmit knowledge from dance" offers a contextualization of what he calls "the impetus to transmit knowledge from dance," and on the prominence of the concept of knowledge in many of the projects represented in Part I of this volume, as well as the discourse around them. He points to relationships between initiatives from within the field of dance to develop new ways of transmitting and circulating knowledge about dance, and the broader context within which this happens, in particular the context of what is referred to as "knowledge economy." In this context, he observes, there is an understandable desire to re-present skill and creativity in contemporary dance as a specific process of "thinking," and the outcome, a form of knowledge.

Harmony Bench too points to the relationship between modes of circulating dance made possible by digital and networked media and the broader context of what she refers to as neoliberal information economy. Digitalization contributes to a situation in which the circulation of choreographies and dance movements happens less via body to body interaction and increasingly through direct interfacing of dancers with the archive. This opens up new possibilities for circulation but also raises important questions about authorship, ownership, and exploitation. Bench shows how a closer look at the ways in which digitalization redirects and reconceives dance pedagogy may contribute to further our understanding of the role of technology in the transmission of knowledge, and how this is not only a matter of what can be captured (or not) by various technologies (as it has dominated the discourse about dance and performance documentation) but also of what kind of interaction is afforded by the technology. In this context, documentation and the archives themselves become sites of performance.

Charlotte Waelde and Sarah Whatley (in their chapter titled "Digital dance: the challenges for traditional copyright law") point to a tension between the practice of dance and copyright protection as it is currently based on single authorship and fixation of the object of protection. The emergence and popularization of digital technologies seem to allow for a more dynamic approach to capturing and storing dance, as well as a more democratic approach to what will be stored and preserved. Yet, in this situation the tension between the laws of copyright and the practice of dance become all the more prominent. In this context, they argue, dance and the scholarship around it may provide a useful partner in dialogue for a more general rethinking of the assumptions and parameters underlying the practice of copyright protection.

Sally Jane Norman's chapter "Between grammatization and live movement sampling" provides a historical perspective on contemporary explorations of the potential of digital technologies that elucidates how the potential of modes of notating and capturing to transmit movement is not only a matter of the technologies used, and what they are capable of capturing or notating, but also of how perceivers respond to the affordances of the technologies. An important potential of the transformations brought about by new digital technologies seems to be how they appeal to our muscular intelligence in new ways. These developments draw attention to the fundamental relationship between movement as object of knowledge and intuitive knowledge of what it means to move. Furthermore, these new technologies present the promise of combining in new ways what seem to be opposed ways of knowing movement as essentially indivisible and endlessly divisible.

My own chapter ("What if this were an archive? Abstraction, enactment and human implicatedness") shows how projects like *Synchronous Objects*, *Loops*, and *Double Skin/Double Mind* point to transformations in the functioning of the archive brought about by digitalization and networked media. This is a shift from a logic based on storage towards a logic of continuous (re)generation through what Alva Noë (2004) describes as enactment and what Massumi (*Semblance and Event*) refers to as lived abstraction. Dance has a history of dissatisfaction and discomfort with the traditional archive. This resistance is not resolved by digitalization. Rather, dance's resistance to fixation and how this inspires alternative approaches to knowledge transmission draws attention to mediality and performativity as fundamental aspects of how knowledge is transmitted, and also to how transformations brought about by digitalization highlight the intimate connection between conceptions of what it means to know and the media we use to store and transmit knowledge.

Chris Salter (in his chapter "Indeterminate acts: technology, choreography and bodily affects in *Displace*") introduces (after Foucault) the concept of "technologies of sense" to describe instruments and procedures that operate in tandem with bodies to produce perceptions and understanding. He too refers to Noë's enactive approach to perception and in particular his insight that bodies are actively engaged in processes of skillful probing in interaction with what they encounter. He also shows how dance has a history of exploring the potential of technology and systems of rules to intervene in such sense making practices in order to generate movement in ways independent from human intention and demonstrates the relevance of this history for designers of media and architectural systems and processes that engage with how users and visitors navigate specific technical-architectural conditions.

Finally, Alva Noë offers a poetic and philosophical reflection about what he learned about choreography from the many dance makers who invited him into their studios. Noë's work on enactive perception has been, and is, a source of inspiration for many of the artists and theorists represented on these pages. He was involved in different ways in various projects discussed in Part I of this volume. In his own contribution to this volume he observes that choreography shares with philosophy that it is a reorganizational project unveiling the ways in which our ordinary, habitual modes of coping and engaging make us what we are. In philosophy, the technology of writing plays an important role in supporting reflection on patterns of organization and habits of doing and thinking. Philosophical writing is like creating scores to disrupt, and disorganize and so allow for reorganization. Similarly, choreography is a practice of remaking ourselves. The interaction of choreography with technology brings to the fore this shared characteristic of choreography and philosophy and supports choreography as practice of reorganization.

References

Desmond, Jane. *Meaning in Motion: New Cultural Studies of Dance*. Durham and London: Duke University Press, 1997.

Ernst, Wolfgang. *Digital Memory and the Archive*. Edited and with an introduction by Jussi Parikka. Minneapolis: University of Minnesota Press, 2013.

Gehm, Sabine, Pirkko Husemann, and Katharina von Wilcke, eds. *Knowledge in Motion: Perspectives of Artistic and Scientific Research in Dance*. Bielefeld: Transcript Verlag, 2007.

Hansen, Mark. *Embodying Technesis: Technology Beyond Writing*. Ann Arbor: University of Michigan Press, 2000.

—— *Bodies in Code: Interfaces with Digital Media*. New York and London: Routledge, 2006.

—— *Feed Forward: On the Future of Twenty-First Century Media*. Chicago and London: University of Chicago Press, 2015.

Hayles, Katherine N. *How We Think: Digital Media and Contemporary Technogenesis*. Chicago and London: University of Chicago Press, 2012.

Massumi, Brian. *Parables for the Virtual: Movement, Affect, Sensation*. Durham and London: Duke University Press, 2002.

—— *Semblance and Event. Activist Philosophy and the Occurrent Arts*. Cambridge, Mass.: The MIT Press, 2011.

Noë, Alva. *Action in Perception*. Cambridge, Mass.: The MIT Press, 2004.

Ong, Walter. *Orality and Literacy: The Technologizing of the Word*. London and New York: Routledge, 1989.

Rotman, Brian. *Becoming Besides Ourselves: The Alphabet, Ghosts and Distributed Human Being*. Durham and London: Duke University Press, 2008.

PART I

1
MOVEMENTS ACROSS MEDIA
Twelve tools for transmission

Maaike Bleeker and Scott deLahunta

The twelve individual projects represented in this first part of *Transmission in Motion* each in their own way engage with something that may be called dance knowledge. Yet what kind of knowledge this is and how the transmission of such knowledge is mediated, stimulated, or redirected, varies considerably per project. A project might be based entirely on the work of an individual choreographer (like William Forsythe in *Improvisation Technologies* and *Synchronous Objects*, Steve Paxton in *Material for the Spine*, Merce Cunningham in *Loops*, Emio Greco | PC in *Double Skin/Double Mind*, Siobhan Davies in *Replay*, or Anne Teresa de Keersmaeker in *A Choreographer's Score*) or be conceived of as a platform for more than one choreographer (*Motion Bank*), or a project may be more broadly related to the history and development of dance (*Digital Dance Archives*), or to networking across the dance community (the *Dance-tech* project). Some projects aim to transmit knowledge embedded within movement practices (*Improvisation Technologies*, *Material for the Spine*, *Double Skin/ Double Mind*), others within choreographies (*Replay*, *Motion Bank*, *Loops*), dance knowledge as constituted in archives or community networks (*Digital Dance Archives*, the *Dance-tech* project), or within modes of creating (*Replay*, *A Choreographer's Score*). Many of them aim to actively contribute to making dance, by offering insight in movement practices (*Improvisation Technologies*, *Material for the Spine*, *Double Skin/Double Mind*), tools for creating choreographies (*Whatever Dance Toolbox*, *Choreographic Language Agent*), or a platform for exchanging "movement arts" research (the *Dance-tech* project). Many of the projects also, implicitly or explicitly, raise questions about how dance can be known, how such knowledge can be transmitted, and more broadly, what knowledge is, what dance can tell us about the relation between knowledge and movement, and about the potential of various media technologies in the transmission of knowledge. While each individual project and its stated aims, both implicit and explicit, offers diverse perspectives on these questions, the goal of this volume is also to enable questions from other perspectives (in Part II) to be asked, not always explicitly about dance knowledge, but knowledge more generally, relations between movement and meaning, and the potential of various media technologies to transmit knowledge. The goal of this chapter is to offer a comparative overview of the twelve individual projects in Part I, and some points of connection with the other chapters in Part II.

The intrinsic diversity across the projects is reflected in the different writing styles of the authors and their different approaches to introducing their projects. Although points of connection can be observed (in terms of aims and goals, challenges, collaborators) each of these projects developed in its own unique way. Nevertheless, some recurring tendencies can be observed as well, points of connection between the motivations and needs of each project, and what was encountered in the process toward outcomes, both planned and unforeseen. The goal of this chapter is to provide observations that may support grasping the specificity of each individual project as well as points of connection between them. And also, to support grasping connections not only across the separate projects, but also in relation to the chapters in the second part of this volume. It is important to note that what the chapters in this first part offer is not the projects themselves (all are accessible via their own form of publication), but stories of how they came to be, what was discovered in the process, and reflections on what that has brought. Our discussion in the pages that follow contains many references to these stories which are told in the next twelve chapters. All page numbers mentioned refer to pages elsewhere in this volume.

Motivations and needs

A closer look at what motivated the development of these projects reveals that in most cases they were motivated by very concrete needs in combination with the perceived potential of a particular medium to fulfill these needs. Chris Ziegler describes how what would become the CD-ROM *William Forsythe: Improvisation Technologies* developed out of the need to circulate recordings of performances of Forsythe's creations among the dancers. Because Forsythe never stopped changing his creations, after its premiere every performance was documented on video. This video archive helped new members of the company learn movements of past productions. To allow them to better prepare for rehearsals, the company handed out portable video players to dancers so they could learn the movements from home. Constant play and rewind of these analog videos caused wear and tear on the tapes. Digitalization promised a more sustainable approach. Eventually the video-documentation trajectory resulted in the annotation tool called Piecemaker, a software that assists in scoring video recordings of dance and sharing this information with others developed by David Kern (see also page 43). What would become the *Improvisation Technologies* CD-ROM with 65 small lectures from Forsythe and demonstrations from dancers became its own trajectory.

Many other projects as well were motivated by a need for ways to capture and transmit dance knowledge that threatened to get lost when, for example, particular works would no longer be performed, or could no longer be performed the way they had been performed, or makers would cease to be active. Paul Kaiser describes how one of the motivations for *Loops* was "to convey Merce's intricate timing when he was no longer able to perform it" (22). Bojana Cvejić explains how the idea for the scores was triggered by De Keersmaeker's observations that this would probably be the last time she would be performing these works herself, and the observed importance of a retrospective exploration of De Keersmaeker's legacy. Sarah Whatley describes how as a researcher, she became increasingly aware of the difficulties of accessing records of dance in performance. The development of *Siobhan Davies Replay* responded to the need to make the oeuvre of this choreographer and more broadly, the history of contemporary British dance, as well as Davies' role in shaping that history, accessible and visible.

In several projects the aim was not (or not only) to transmit knowledge about particular creations but (also) about modes of working and creating. *Siobhan Davies Replay* not only offers access to recordings of past performances, but also insights into materials that inspired creation and into how dance is formed. For Emio Greco | PC, interactive technology held the promise of the possibility of a virtual version of a workshop with which dancers can familiarize themselves with the specificities of Emio Greco | PC's movement language. Steve Paxton's many years of research he called "material for the spine" aimed to create "a strong technical approach to the processes of improvisation" characteristic of Paxton's Contact Improvisation (32). And although the first phase of the development of *Improvisation Technologies* focused on transmitting knowledge about one specific creation (*Self Meant to Govern*), in a later stage the aim shifted towards the creation of a "digital dance school" that would introduce Forsythe's ideas for creating movement material. BADco. and Wayne McGregor, recognizing the potential of technological agents to extend their choreographic methods, set out to develop technological aids to enhance their creative processes.

In most cases, the reasons for embarking on these projects include the desire for new and different ways of sharing dance knowledge, critically, creatively, and disruptively. Cvejić explains that the reasons for her to design a "choreographic score" stemmed from her discontent with dance education "privileging the technical import of what it means to dance a bodily movement cut from the historical, contextual and poietical aspects integral to the actual dance form and technique" (53). The scores are meant as "tools to emulate the choreographic thought" rather than showing them what to imitate (53). The development of *Replay* seeks to afford active ways of engaging with the materials available by means of, among others, virtual scrapbooks, which allow users to collect and reflect on their searches. Similarly the *Digital Dance Archives* aim to enhance user interaction. The project was designed to encourage students and artists to create their own "scrapbooks" of images as a research repository arranged into folders, displayed, tagged, annotated, stored, and shared (74). *Motion Bank* wants to be an interdisciplinary research environment for dance, a broad context for research into choreographic practice, but is also focused on the development of digital documentation and design to record and share aspects of dance. The *Dance-tech* project is meant as a tactical media project that intervenes in the knowledge distribution systems of contemporary performance and their contexts by means of a networked environment that is open for sharing, telling, and retelling.

For many projects, the motivation to create them included the desire to communicate with a broader community of peers as well as the desire to reach out to new contexts, beyond dance. Cvejić observes an urge "to reflect on their methods and tools and share them with a larger readership outside the discipline," and the importance of claiming a different status and position for dance (53). The aim to bring new viewers to dance who might discover dance by searching for other artists, compositions, and literary sources informed the construction of *Siobhan Davies Replay* from the very beginning. The *Synchronous Objects* project also had the ambition from the outset to attract as diverse an audience as possible on the basis that the content in dance can be made accessible to experts outside the field of dance whose areas of interest intersect with dance not as art or performance perhaps, but as complex organizational structures and interaction patterns that are objects of study for other fields. Making choreographic ideas and processes available for study by other research domains was one of the aims of *Motion Bank* from its very beginning.

Process and development

The process phase of each project is where motivations and ideas had to be turned into concrete practices to develop that which the project aimed to create. In many cases this involved working along two lines of research and inventing ways of bringing these together: on the one hand, the material that the aimed-for tool or platform was intended to transmit (modes of working of choreographers or companies, knowledge embedded in or about specific creations, or more broadly, knowledge of and about dance) and, on the other hand, the technological possibilities available to do so. For example, developing the *Digital Dance Archives* required on the one hand developing insight in the materials that were made to be accessible by the archives and on the other hand insight into metadata schemes and in how website design would function across different search engines. In addition, the *Digital Dance Archives* experimented with more analytic problems, such as how a non-linear cultural history might be meaningfully exposed through a new "visual search" method that allows the visitor to look for similar movements or poses in the material across different dance styles and periods. Cvejić describes how making De Keersmaeker's choreographic knowledge accessible meant first of all externalizing this knowledge, which involved extensive preliminary research and two phases of interviews. The next step was reconstituting choreography in writing, and combining this writing with synthetic schemes, diagrams, and drawings, annotated by the choreographer, photos from the performances and rehearsals, and additional photography made for the purpose of illustrating the verbal explanation in concrete detail, program notes, reviews, notes from De Keersmaeker's notebooks, and letters. She also describes how even though the media used were not new, this did involve a reconsideration of their use, a reinvention of what writing is: "how could choreographic parameters be rearticulated as a matter of writing, *écriture* in the poststructuralist sense? How to investigate and conceive that choreographic writing *in a score*?" (53). Corin describes how the choice for the medium of DVD-ROM presented them with the positive challenge of how to use the possibilities of this medium to give a sense of movement through image and sound and expand the ways one perceives movement. "We had intuitions and desires, but we did not know yet how to make them real. With time, through filming sessions, this project would teach us to fine-tune our point of view" (36). In the case of the *Double Skin/Double Mind* interactive installation, Bertha Bermúdez Pascual, a former Emio Greco | PC performer, did extensive work developing a tightly structured framework of keywords and descriptions—a glossary—to serve as "the conceptual inside" to the artistic practice. Having already embodied on a deep level an understanding of Emio Greco | PC's work and modes of working, the creation of the glossary served as a bridging device helping bring the other members of the interdisciplinary team closer to "the logic of the body" of the artist. The *Siobhan Davies Replay* project worked with Deborah Saxon, a dancer who has worked with Davies for many years, to select and edit where necessary, particularly when it concerned the more sensitive material that was being made public for the first time. At the same time, others worked on questions around the organization and editing of content, data management, digitization, and interface design. Many of the diverse results of these projects can be attributed not only to the different artists involved, but also to the expertise of these others involved.

The descriptions of these projects coming into being testify to how the ways in which they took shape are intertwined with the emergence of new technological possibilities they could draw on. The move from hard drives to CD-ROM to DVD-ROM as described by Ziegler followed the technological trends of the time that continue today; increasing storage space on smaller and smaller media. With regard to *Synchronous Objects*, Zuniga Shaw writes that "when we started in late 2005, YouTube was a new phenomenon (. . .), HD-DVD and Blu-Ray were in a format war (. . .) and the potential for sharing great quality video online was still emerging" (104). What she doesn't say explicitly is that in the earliest days of the project it was originally conceived of as a DVD-ROM; but she makes it clear that developments in technology—making great quality video online possible—inspired their decision to take *Synchronous Objects* onto the net. Barrios Solano describes how emergent modes of articulation, circulation, expression, and affiliation afforded by digital social media networks provide the context within which the *Dance-tech* project could emerge. The web allowed him to take a step beyond the dance and technology listserv that the community had been using to communicate. Later on newer technological developments like augmented reality apps set the stage for new additions to the *Dance-tech* project. Evolving technology is reflected in Kaiser's observation that

> [i]n 2000 we'd realized that motion-capture techniques had advanced far enough that we could capture Merce's hand movements with the same accuracy as we had recorded his dancers' full body dancing. And so we captured Merce performing *Loops*, and when he was done he declared this performance to be definitive, his final and finest expression of the dance.
>
> Data in hand, though, Shelley and I at first did nothing. We put it in a drawer, so to speak, waiting to see if a future possibility might bring it to the life we were starting to imagine for it.
>
> *(22)*

It was only when they got to know Marc Downie and were introduced by him to the possibilities of artificial intelligence that the project entered its next phase. By that time, their aim changed as well:

> At the same time Shelley and I had started to dream of a live and ever-changing version of the work, one that improvised itself in the same way that Cunningham did in his dance. At no time did we think of such a piece as documentation of the original but rather as an autonomous artwork that would exist—almost *live*—in parallel to it.
>
> *(23)*

Kaiser's observations on *Loops* also illustrate the importance of interdisciplinary collaborations for these projects and how the shape these projects took is intimately intertwined with the collaborators involved. Corin phrases it beautifully, observing that "This project is what it is because it is made of who we are" (38). "We" were an interdisciplinary team consisting of, alongside Steve Paxton himself, editors, artists, architects, and movement artists. The collaborators contributing to *Synchronous Objects* included members of the Forsythe Company as well as a large interdisciplinary team of students, faculty, and staff researchers in the US and Europe, including architects, statisticians, cognitive psychologists, philosophers, visual artists, designers, animators, geographers, dancers, and computer scientists. In case of Wayne McGregor's *Choreographic Language Agent* a collaborative interdisciplinary research project titled *Choreography and Cognition* (2003–2004) was set up to draw on the field of cognitive science to enhance understanding of the choreographic process. This laid the groundwork for conversations with specialists working in the field of AI and related areas and for exploring the computational relationship between software and choreographic structure. *Siobhan Davies Replay* was developed in a long term collaboration between Davies' dance company and

Coventry University. The *Digital Dance Archives* are a collaboration between the University of Surrey, the National Resource Centre for Dance in the UK and Coventry university. These projects took shape within a strong and relatively stable institutional context, which is very different from, for example, the *Dance-tech* project, that lacks such context and depends on the creative effort of Barrios Solano to develop online and on-site platforms for interdisciplinary interactions through a great number of (often only very temporary) collaborations with festivals and other events, venues, and individuals at very different places. The context for the development of the *Double Skin/Double Mind* interactive installation was partly provided by dance company Emio Greco | PC and partly by (shorter term) interinstitutional collaborations that set the stage for (among others) the *Inside Movement Knowledge* research project around the installation.

Often these collaborations had a history prior to the actual development of the project. BADco.'s collective project *Whatever Dance Toolbox* developed from a long-standing collaboration with Daniel Turing, a "human-machine interface developer and artist," a specialist in the computer vision techniques that serve to provide the "real time video analysis of human motion" (118). Bermúdez Pascual and Saxon had worked as performers for many years with Emio Greco | PC and Siobhan Davies respectively before embarking on the projects described here. Kaiser and Shelley Eshkar had worked previously with Merce Cunningham on another motion capture project resulting in the installation *Hand-Drawn Spaces* (1998).

The descriptions in the chapters that follow also reveal many connections between the projects in terms of collaborators. Ziegler was a key design contributor to a history of CD/DVD-ROM projects and also a core collaborator on the development of the *Double Skin/Double Mind* installation. Marc Downie, who worked on the development of the *Choreographic Language Agent*, was also one of the main artists working on the *LOOPS* project. Scott deLahunta, who has contributed two of the chapters in Part I (about the *Choreographic Language Agent* and the *Motion Bank*), worked also as a researcher on *Replay*, *Synchronous Objects*, and *Inside Movement Knowledge* (the research project around the *Double Skin/Double Mind* installation of Emio Greco | PC).

How these projects took shape was not only a matter of possibilities opened up by technologies, but also of limitations imposed by the amount of time and resources available, as well as by technology and copyrights. Whatley explains how from the beginning of developing *Replay*, there needed to be pragmatic decisions. With limited time and resources they decided to purchase a proprietary system for asset management because the open source alternatives at that time would have needed considerable specialist work, which was beyond the team's capacity. Furthermore, they were confronted with issues of copyright and ownership. The complexities of dealing with authorship in dance, multi-media rights issues, and how projects like *Replay* confront us with the limitations of how copyright is accounted for, is further elaborated in her and De Waelde's chapter in Part II. Unresolved copyright issues are also the reason that only the second part of the *NAGARIKA* project by Ziegler and Jayachandran Palazhy is available to the public.

Both Whatley and Barrios Solano mention the challenge of sustainability: of finding the funding necessary to maintain projects and their digital infrastructure, and to update and revise them in relation to new developments. This is a problem not only for them. Ziegler observes that at the time of writing *Improvisation Technologies* is now more easily accessible via unauthorized uploads on YouTube than via the CD-ROM that is available for purchase. Resources on CD-ROM and DVD-ROM, like *Improvisation Technologies* and *Material for the Spine*, have to be upgraded to new operating systems with each new release. The question is what will happen to these resources when CD and DVD get replaced by newer media. Online resources face similar problems when operating systems are no longer supported. In the case of *Loops*, the very practical given that technology ages quickly and data formats and storage media change, as a result of which data quickly become unreadable, informed the choice to approach preserving *Loops* in a radical new way, namely as a thing whose form is permanent but whose materials are perishable—perishable but replaceable. These issues around digital sustainability are not only reflected at the level of each individual project, they are features of larger changes and cultural funding, in particular in the area of performing arts, seems often to be lacking sufficient knowledge or the means to take this into account.

The exploratory nature of these projects also meant that insights would change during the process of development. Corin describes how, at first, Steve Paxton was hesitant to focus on the past and did not agree to be filmed because he did not want to appear as a model, as someone who should be imitated. As the project proceeded, however, "it seemed important to see him practice *Material for the Spine* in person, to contemplate his body as the very place which holds the memory of many years of research, and makes the principles of movement so visible" (34). Most of the time these changes were anticipated as part of an iterative design process. Ziegler describes how they tried various animated graphics for the *NAGARIKA Bharatanatyam* DVD-ROM, but these were left out in the end to highlight temporal and not visual structures. Bermúdez Pascual observes that during developing *Double Skin/Double Mind*, they were confronted with additional research questions like:

> What is it exactly that we do in our attempts at capturing dance? How do we deal with its ephemeral nature? Which are the existing systems for its documentation? How do these systems deal with qualities and intentions? How may motion capture and new media developments allow not only for a quantitative capturing of movement but also for an analysis of its qualities? And how may this help us to develop further understanding of the specificities of the knowledge that is dance?
>
> *(91)*

Products and outcomes

The projects have resulted in a variety of products: archives, online platforms, CD and DVD-ROMs, installations, books, and tools for creation. These products afford new modes of researching and knowing dance, new ways of engaging with dance and dance knowledge, and new modes of creating dance.

In several cases, new insights that emerged during the process of developing the project changed the outcomes. In Ziegler's project description we discover that the original motivation for *Improvisation Technologies* was to provide information to the dancers in the company, not to a general readership. Only in a later stage it was decided to develop the project into a CD-ROM for a wider audience. BADco.'s *Whatever Dance Toolbox* followed a similar line of development from something made for creative use within the company to a public release. McGregor's *Choreographic Language Agent* was also created as a digital sketching environment for in studio use, but was redeveloped as an autonomous installation offering stimulus to the rehearsal process and providing insight into choreographic creativity for visitors to the Wellcome Collection during a six-week exhibition titled *Thinking with the Body*.[1] The *Double Skin/Double Mind* installation of Emio Greco | PC was developed for use in the company. During its creation and being tested it became clear that the installation might also serve educational purposes and could be used to enhance and enrich the experience of dance audiences. This resulted in the development of a "light" version that can provide non-dancers with an insight into some of the principles of the work of Emio Greco | PC.

Projects also resulted in additional outcomes that build on what was developed and take this in new directions. The *Improvisation Technologies* CD-ROM attracted a lot of attention, including that of the Japanese TV producer Tokyo Media Connections (TMC) who recognized the potential of the CD-ROM not only to transmit Western avant-garde dance technique but also as an attractive digital tool to reconnect younger audiences to the old Japanese performance tradition of Kyogen. This project in its turn was followed by two projects in India where the technology developed was made productive for the transmission of Bharatanatyam and Kalaripayatthu dance practice. Zuniga Shaw was invited to re-imagine the screen-based *Synchronous Objects* project as a series of site-specific video installations for venues in Europe, the US, and Asia. *Synchronous Objects* was also the pilot project for the first phase of *Motion Bank* based in Frankfurt, Germany. The *Double Skin/Double Mind* installation became a case-study for a large-scale knowledge transfer research project in the Netherlands titled *Inside Movement Knowledge*. During this two-year project new outcomes materialized including a model for documentation of live performance developed by a new media institute and the development of a new curriculum using the project inside of dance education. Once launched, *Replay* also gave rise to new related funded projects, including one embedding the concept of archive in a university dance education curriculum. But perhaps of equal significance is the impact *Replay* has had on the artist herself. Davies has begun to collect and digitize far more of her process material than before to include in the *Replay* framework. McGregor's *Choreographic Language Agent* project is also one that has moved through several iterative stages over a period of a decade; imagined at the outset was that engagement in making creative tools for dance should produce new insights into that process. What was unforeseen was that the collaborative relationships with the scientists would generate a "rich landscape of concepts, vocabulary, descriptions and models" (109); and as such a valuable collection of non-digital tools for understanding and transmitting choreographic practice. And Ziegler describes how that what started as a digital archive documenting changes of a production over time and providing access to rehearsal material eventually became a "digital dance school" (43). The *Dance Engaging Science* working group that was part of the development of *Motion Bank* continues to initiate research and collaborative events also beyond the group's existence as part of the first phase of the development of *Motion Bank*.

Observations and conclusions

Each in their own way operating at the intersection of dance and various technologies, these projects together outline a unique field of research lying at the intersection of theory and practice, the digital and the corporeal, technology and thinking, meaning and movement, creative practice and the archive. Many more such intersections could be added. The aims, interests, and modes of operating of this field of research overlap with evolving theory around practice-based research and increased interest in embodied and tacit knowledge in a variety of fields, and is in line with a general tendency towards international and cross-institutional resourcing from research, education, and culture. Operating from or on these intersections, these projects themselves act as interfaces: in their ways of operating they connect and make possible modes of navigating between fields, disciplines, and practices, and in new collaborative modes of working. They are testing grounds for new modes of radically interdisciplinary ways of working that challenge existing practices of doing research as well as our understanding of what the outcome of such practices is or can be. Projects like *Dance-tech*, *Synchronous Objects*, and the *Motion Bank* also challenge more traditional distinctions between research and publication.

Although these projects differ in many respects and represent a wide range of possibilities, there are also important similarities and shared concerns. All of them aim to make dance knowledge available to new audiences, and in ways that allow for unique types of interaction with this knowledge. Even though many of them work with "captured" dance and provide means to store this and make it accessible, many of them explicitly resist the idea of merely looking back to the past. New and innovative uses are emphatically part of many of the projects. They provide tools that can be used for creative ends, as well as novel applications of digital technology.

Exploring the potential of various technologies to make possible new ways of using and producing knowledge about dance, they also invite reflection on our modes of understanding dance: how we (think we) know dance and what it means to know it. Forsythe's CD-ROM *Improvisation Technologies*, developed as a tool to demonstrate his approach to movement to his dancers, provides fresh insights into ways of thinking movement underlying his compositions and, by extension, to what dance is about and how it can be known. The website *Synchronous Objects* shifts attention from movement of dancing bodies to transformations in spatial organization and how this organization might be analyzed according to a variety of parameters. Understanding dance here involves active engagement with the rather abstract principles underlying the choreography as a four dimensional spatio-temporal construction. The multimedia installation *Double Skin/Double Mind* facilitates a somatic understanding of the aesthetic logic of Emio Greco's movement language through active and immersive involvement. Paxton's DVD-ROM *Material for the Spine* also aims to evoke a new understanding of dance movement, in this case through an analytical approach supported by novel filming ideas to demonstrate the logic of muscle movement. Other projects like the website *Siobhan Davies Replay* and the *Digital Dance Archive* take the shape of online archives that allow users to navigate through a variety of performance related materials (including "scratch tapes" from rehearsals) and explore the making process.

Although all of these projects were initiated from the field of dance, dance does not so much frame these projects as provide a kind of "Archimedean point" from where these projects open towards a diversity of other directions. This means they have no proper place. They are unstable and peculiar objects of study pointing toward and oscillating between various positions of interest and attention. Unstable and peculiar, yet timely and most relevant with regard to how they make space for investigations that engage with fundamental transformations in practices of capturing, storing, and transmitting information. Many of these projects raise questions or provide answers beyond the field of dance. They explore new approaches to organizing large amounts of digital material, of connecting human ways of searching and organizing to computer and computational logic, and of connecting the moving body to the logic of the new, digital archive. They experiment with multi-sensory interfaces, with non-linear modes of thinking, and with the possibilities and implications of big data research and new ways of data visualization. They point to the intimate connection between the virtual and the material world and to how technologies mediate in renegotiations between past, present, and future.

Reflecting on the development of *Replay*, Whatley observes how they found themselves confronted by questions like "What does it mean for an artist to create, and be the subject of, a digital archive of their work? Does distributing the work online change how the work is 'read' and might new meanings emerge because of having easy access to what were previously 'lost' dances? And what impact will this have on dance makers, performers, viewers; and on students, researchers and our cultural institutions?" (63). In her chapter in Part II of this volume ("Dancing in digital archives: circulation, pedagogy, performance"), Harmony Bench observes that, particularly for a younger generation, digitalization contributes to a situation in which "archives no longer preserve the past for the future, but serve as generative repositories of the present and recent past for contemporary audiences" (156). Digital technologies, she argues, "have redirected the archive's social, political, and historical purposes and achievements, prioritizing circulation over preservation" (156).

The circulation of dance through media like YouTube draws attention to how this situation raises questions about authorship, ownership, and copyright, and to how, as Derrida already observed, the technological structure of archiving also determines the form of the archivable content. Waelde and Whatley, in their chapter "Digital dance: the challenges for traditional copyright law," further elaborate the complicated relationship between dance and existing practices of copyright protection. Choreography as an object of digitization highlights how our understanding of objects is grounded in fixation and how this is reflected in laws of copyright, and, we might add, these laws in their turn reflect a more general and pervasive understanding of what objects are.

In her account of the development of *Material for the Spine*, Corin describes how they had "to balance together the videos of real bodies, superposed graphics, images put together by association, virtual representations etc., in order to express at their best the sensations, the movements, the exercises, and the thoughts of Steve Paxton. We worked towards the distillation of an object addressing its user both mentally and physically (. . .)" (39). Similarly, *Replay*, the *Digital Dance Archives* and *Synchronous Objects* point to how new technological means afford new objects to be distilled from that what is captured and collected as a result of how technological developments afford what Barrios Solano describes as new couplings of human cognition with computational networked systems. *Motion Bank*, with its focus on the potential of computation for exploring patterns in the digital recordings of choreographic works, is pushing the boundaries of what it means to document and translate dance into digital form through development of open software systems and dance-related databases. These couplings and the new objects emerging from them are the subject of Maaike Bleeker's chapter ("What if this were an archive? Abstraction, enactment and human implicatedness"), in which she shows how explorations of new modes of transmitting and archiving dance invite a reconsideration of the relation of the object of knowledge in terms of movement.

The ways in which movement, dance, and choreography appear as new objects of knowledge is not a matter of digital technology per se but part of more general transformations in perceiving, understanding, and thinking that are brought about by the widespread incorporation of digital technologies in our daily practices. *A Choreograper's Score*, for example, uses the old medium of writing in new ways to produce De Keermaeker's choreographies as objects of knowledge in ways that reflect what Sally Jane Norman describes as "the growing importance of annotation and metadata—i.e. notes, commentaries, or other such resources previously considered secondary or superfluous to core data—translates heightened recognition of contexts as an essential if not determinant part of usefully transmissible information" (195) typical of the rise of digital culture.

In her chapter "Between grammatization and live movement sampling," Norman traces a range of historical examples of writing, recording and capturing movement to set the projects described in the chapters that follow in a wider historical and conceptual context. This overview helps to understand that crucial to how media transmit movement is not only what of movement is captured but also how different modes of transmission present an appeal to our bodies' sense of movement, and how in this way they can be considered what Chris Salter proposes calling "technologies of sense." Projects like *Improvisation Technologies*, the *Whatever Dance Toolbox*, the *Double Skin/Double Mind* installation, and the *Choreographic Language Agent* demonstrate the potential of new technologies to act as frameworks within which perception, movement, and (self)understanding take shape as a result of bodies responding to what they encounter, and also to interfere in these modes of responding. Understood as technologies of sense, they present demonstrations and explorations of perception and thinking unfolding from the entanglement of humans and technological apparatuses.

Making choreographic ideas and processes available for study was an important aim of *Motion Bank* from its very beginning. Many of the projects described in the following chapters share a similar aim. They also share a tendency to describe what they aim to share in terms of dance knowledge. James Leach (in his chapter "Making knowledge from movement: some notes on the contextual impetus to transmit knowledge from dance") points to connections between what these projects aim to do and the context of the so-called knowledge economy in which knowledge is a product of a specific currency. In his text, Leach shows how the framing of the aims and goals of these projects in terms of knowledge and the framing of dance as a knowledge making enterprise runs parallel to contemporary tropes around the social and economic value of knowledge, transmission, and utility characteristic of the the current political economy. At the same time this claim may be taken as an invitation to consider how these projects from the field of dance may change our conception of what knowledge is, and contribute to understanding how technological developments pave the way for such new conceptions of knowledge to become conceivable.

Note

1 http://wellcomecollection.org/thinkingwiththebody/?video=5, accessed May 19, 2016.

2

NOT FADE AWAY

Thoughts on preserving Cunningham's *Loops*

Paul Kaiser

Descent

Following the death of his father, Rainer Maria Rilke discovered among his effects a daguerreotype that he'd not seen since a child. As a young man his father had sat still for the camera's long exposure, dressed in his imperial officer uniform; now the son's gaze was drawn to his father's youthful hands, which rested on the hilt of his sword.

The poem he wrote in meditation on this portrait ends with the beautifully recursive lines: "O quickly fading photo/in my more slowly fading hand."[1]

Remains

Of the things Rilke describes in the poem, the hands of the father and of the son, and the photograph that links them, these are fated to decay in short order—but the steel sword will persist. Metal outlasts both paper and flesh, and the sword will speak to remote descendants even if they have no prior knowledge of such a weapon.

In taking hold of a sword it's natural to slip your hand into the sword's grip, and the sharpness of the blade and the thrust it suggests will tell you what deadly purpose you might once have put it to.

Enshrined

On my first visit to Merce Cunningham's loft, he showed me the little nook where John Cage had once worked, the space nearly filled with Cage's desk. There, perched at a window above Sixth Avenue, Cage would compose his music and his texts, often letting chance dictate his decisions as he tried eluding his habits and his tastes. (This having long since *become* Cage's habit, I wondered how well it could still have worked.)

In the last years of his life Cage had given pride of place on this desk to a computer, on which he could run simple programs written for his use to generate chance operations faster than he could with the old throw of the dice. Now only six years later, this PC was already a relic.

Not unusual for a desk to be left just as it was when a great writer dies; in St. Petersburg, for example, one can find Dostoevsky's desk untouched. And so it seemed natural to me at the time to find Cage's desk in the same state as when he left it, and slightly startling when several years later it was not: the computer now gone. I never asked Merce why, but I imagine it was for completely practical reasons: the machine, left idle and quickly outmoded, would no longer have run.

(Of course another possibility, not to be ruled out, is that a museum or even a collector had acquired and enshrined it, its uselessness perhaps its selling-point.)

Lost transmission

Even with the manpower and funding of a government agency it's hard to evade this process of information obsolescence; NASA can no longer read some of its own space exploration data dating back only to the 1970s, so quickly and irreversibly have data formats and storage media changed in the few intervening decades.

Imagine a science fiction story in which the alien messages so eagerly sought a decade later by the SETI Institute (Search for Extraterrestrial Intelligence) had been received and recorded but never recognized in the 1970s, and were now forever irretrievable in NASA's decaying data-sets. Perhaps Stanislaw Lem could have done this justice, a small companion piece to his novel *His Master's Voice*.

Now think whether this might really be the case in many human communications, where for example in a dance concert the audience may not yet have the eyes with which to take in something radically new. Since live performance is in some sense unrepeatable, this means that these signals too are gone for good.

Last run

On the week these sentences are being written, the Cunningham Dance Company is performing certain works for the last time ever here in New York City.

Not long before his death, Merce had decided that his company would undergo one last farewell tour in his absence and then fold its tent, disbanding forever. The choreography itself will continue to survive as other dance companies license, learn, and perform it, but never again will the pieces be danced by a group overseen by Cunningham himself and without doubt these works will begin to deviate from the originals.

As in the children's game of telephone, I imagine that the signal initiated at one end of the chain will eventually re-emerge almost unrecognizable at the other.

No resurrection

This deviation was a complaint even when Cunningham was alive and could direct the revival of his older dances. Those aficionados who could recall Merce's own dancing would shake their heads when they watched even the best-trained and most naturally gifted dancers try to resurrect his roles. No one could match the original, and only much later did Merce explain to me why, not that the answer hadn't dawned on me long before. It was an open secret of *Loops*.

Flung or cast

One of the pieces performed this week was *BIPED*, the best-known of Merce's later works and one that he kept in his repertory right up from its creation in 1999 to now. This was the dance for which Shelley Eshkar and I had created the visual decor in the form of huge projections, and seeing it for the last time made me think.

At the time we were conscious that Merce, having collaborated with us first on our terms (the triptych installation *Hand-drawn Spaces*, 1998), had now invited us to collaborate on his, the dance stage; and so Shelley and I were intent on merging our non-dance sensibilities with the dance tradition that Merce had opened up so wide.

Hand-drawn Spaces had had us working with Merce much more closely than normally allowed in the Cage/Cunningham practice of parallel rather than intersecting collaborations. This was necessitated by our using a beta form of software that we all thought would be an interesting new way for Merce to create the virtual choreography we needed; since this was software he could not master on his own, we all worked together at the same screen.[2]

During our sessions, we were surprised when Merce brought out a small collection of many-sided dice of a kind I recognized from my days as a schoolteacher in the 1980s—for these were the same dice I saw kids using to play the elaborate role-playing game of Dungeons and Dragons. Merce explained that he'd discovered that such dice were considerably faster to employ than the yarrow sticks traditionally cast by readers (perhaps better termed *users*?) of the Chinese *Book of Changes* as they determined which of 64 ideograms to consult next. It had been this ancient practice of divination and reading that had first inspired Cage's use of chance operations.

This image of flung sticks remained with Shelley and me, so we created one of the virtual figures in *BIPED* to embody it. Constructed entirely of short straight lines, when this figure leaped it would fling its lines up into the air and then gather them back in on landing again. Up to then, Shelley and I had taken pains to limit our virtual figures to the constraints of human anatomy; this was our first step toward more abstract body systems that while remaining true to the underlying human movement propelling them managed to express that movement more freely. This abstracted anatomy took us a first step toward *Loops*.

Tools determinism

In watching the *BIPED* projections twelve years after creating them, I recognized with a touch of chagrin that a few elements of certain sequences came almost straight out of the box—the box in question being the commercial animation program 3DS Max. This Autodesk package contained as one of its plug-ins the biped figure animation software we'd been using since before its release, developed by close friends in the proverbial Silicon Valley garage before being acquired by the huge software company; the package also included the renderer with which we output our frames.

Some of these, as I said, bore the unmistakable imprint of the tool we'd made them with, more naively than I had remembered. I was surprised only because this inevitable consequence was one I was now seeing in my own work; I'd long ago spotted it in others. Oh, I'd say to myself, there's that MaxMSP patch triggered again, and over there that seamless masking of layers proclaims its AfterEffects origin; as for that sleek mapping of data, that can only be Processing.

Later my colleague Marc Downie would give this effect a name: *tools determinism*.

Three asides

1. If dancers are shaped by training and practice into human tools for their choreographers' use, then this kind of tools determinism is evident, sometimes sadly, in the work of ex-company dancers—a post-Cunningham or post-Forsythe creation is often unmistakably (and unshakably) stamped by the original, even to the point of unwitting parody.
2. Cannot the same misfortune befall even the original artist who sticks too rigidly to a method or style?
3. Not necessarily a misfortune, though, because sometimes it is turned into the very opposite, a windfall, the market actually rewarding what we might deplore as a limitation. Repetition and consistency, after all, are the hallmarks of commercial branding.

Blurred distinction

A point of confusion, never quite clarified, arose in the public mind (and in ill-informed critics') between Merce's use of software and our own. When in old age Merce's feet and ankles gave out and he could no longer create his phrases by dancing them, he had turned to a software program, then called LifeForms, to help generate these instead.

This proved to be an irresistible story, lapped up by many journalists and given prominent play: the grand old man of the avant-garde was in fact ever-young, always poised on the cutting edge. Perhaps abetted by publicists, some critics could later hardly resist attributing *BIPED*'s projections to Merce himself, blurring him with two younger unknowns.

Mechanisms of movement

This blurring obscured the fact that what Merce was seeking in the computer was the opposite of what we sought, no doubt because of the very different places we started out from—Merce from the body, we from the screen. To take Merce's case first:

Trying to remove himself from the too-easy instincts and habits of the warm socialized human body, Merce embraced the colder schemes suggested to him by the rather primitive calculations of LifeForms. This program provided a very crude model of the body (with no inverse kinematics), and so its solutions were often anatomically impossible. Merce however delighted in having his dancers try adapting themselves to some of these unreachable poses, ones sometimes so implausible as to be beyond even his wide range of imaginings.

When I first started going to see Merce's work—new to dance, I did not begin until the mid-90s—the tools determinism of LifeForms was in full effect (by the time of *BIPED* it had receded). In works like *CRDSPCR* (its name betraying its computer origin), the grace and flow ordinarily sought in dance were subverted by visibly artificial operations that directed the dancers' motions in mechanical ways. It was a wrenching thing to watch, no doubt Merce's intention, in particular because each dancer was rendered more cog or function than individual being. I remember being struck by the dancers' sexlessness, again a quality rarely encountered in dance.

Interchangeability

I once wrote:

> A curious thing about *Hand-drawn Spaces*: The movements we captured were truly detached from the dancers who had so brilliantly performed them, Jeannie Steele and Jared Phillips. The differences between the two in size and sex and style were annulled as Merce combined their captured phrases freely, making long passages in which one dancer's movements alternated frequently with the other's, both mapped to the same hand-drawn figure. Psychology and intention were absent from this choreographic process, for Merce used chance operations to see what phrase went next.

"Warming up the pixels"

This was Shelley's humorous phrase, used to describe what we sought to do to the computer—in contrast to the computer's computational chilliness that Merce had embraced. Cold perfection came easily to the computer, as did artificiality, and while new and exciting to Merce, these were old and oppressive to us.

What we wanted was what he had as a given in dance: the warmth of human presence, the individuality of human touch, the irregularity of human motion.

And so we pursued what we called the hand-drawn line instead of the simple geometrical one, and we chose to motion-capture humans dancing rather than simulating flawless approximations of the same.

Bystander

In the motion-capture sessions for *Hand-drawn Spaces* and *BIPED,* Merce as dancer was reduced to a bystander's role: he was there as choreographer only, supervising his dancers from a seat on the sidelines. This was an unacknowledged tragedy, for in his prime Cunningham had commanded the dance stage as no one else ever would.

Even in old age Merce would shuffle onto the stage for cameo appearances in company events. With his halo of white hair and expression of sage benevolence, he looked the part of the legend he'd become, which was enough to hold his audience not only rapt but rapturous. The trouble was that the solo movements he would then perform with his hands were hard to see clearly at a distance, especially with the other dancing going on all around him, so it was on faith that one took his solo to be great.

That this dance of the hands *was* great was one impetus behind our making *Loops* the digital artwork. We all silently aimed it at posterity.

Loops the dance

In 1971 Cunningham created *Loops* as a dance solo for himself; when he designated it as a "solo event," he meant that its form was to continually adapt to the requirements of occasion and venue. Thus *Loops* had no fixed choreography, but was instead an improvisation—though this was a term that both Cunningham and Cage shied away from, perhaps because it implied the easy indulgences of informality and self-expression rather than the formal rigor they always sought.

Cunningham first performed *Loops* at the Museum of Modern Art in New York City, where he danced in front of the Jasper Johns painting entitled *Map (after Buckminster Fuller's Dymaxion Air Ocean World).*

Loops got its name, Merce once told me, from the circular movements he could do with his wrists. Originally the piece was not restricted to the hands, but instead took different body parts through their variations one at a time—feet, head, trunk, leg, shoulder. He sometimes set this order by chance, but only "if I had time enough to learn it. Because when you use chance, as you probably know, it dislocates your memory, so you have to start all over again."

As Merce's age advanced and his mobility diminished, he channeled the intricate movements of *Loops* into his fingers, hands, and arms alone.

In this form *Loops* became the signature solo work of Merce's later career, one that he was never to set on any other dancer. He told us he wanted to keep it "my little secret."

A larger secret

Loops is a markedly *different kind* of choreography from that which Cunningham set on his company dancers: its timing has an amazing intricacy not to be found elsewhere. (I've long been surprised that to my knowledge—admittedly limited—dance critics and scholars haven't exclaimed over the difference between Cunningham's solo and group choreography.) In my last extended conversation with Merce (in June 2007), I pressed him to account for this difference, which struck me as crucial.

Merce began by explaining that *Loops* is "not teachable." This, he said, has to do with the particularity of any dancer—"everyone's rhythm is different." In *Loops*, he described ten movements happening at once, which you cannot perform by thinking them through on a given beat. Instead, he said, you have to skip all that somehow and simply *do* them in the interval you've given yourself. His unspoken implication was that other dancers couldn't manage this—which made the dance unteachable.

Merce went on to explain that when setting choreography on his dancers, he'd found long ago that he had to teach to a beat, which "becomes a language to talk about time." This accounted for something I'd found exceedingly odd in his company rehearsals. While I'd been expecting either silence or the sort of meter-less electronic music common in his performances, I was surprised to discover that in his classes a pianist would play old-fashioned show tunes that kept very simple time. The beat enabled his dancers to coordinate with one another as well as to memorize their movements more easily. As a consequence, their movements remained rhythmically much simpler than those Merce could conceive and perform himself.

So this provided another impetus to our project: how to convey Merce's intricate timing when he was no longer able to perform it?

Motion capture

In 2000 we'd realized that motion-capture techniques had advanced far enough that we could capture Merce's hand movements with the same accuracy as we had recorded his dancers' full body dancing. And so we captured Merce performing *Loops*, and when he was done he declared this performance to be definitive, his final and finest expression of the dance.

Data in hand, though, Shelley and I at first did nothing. We put it in a drawer, so to speak, waiting to see if a future possibility might bring it to the life we were starting to imagine for it.

Cat's cradle

Inspiration often comes to me from children's games and activities. I think childhood is a resource we can continue to draw upon, for the possibilities that we close off for ourselves as we grow up and take the particular forks in our roads are still wide open in childhood, accessible to us not only through our individual memories but also by simply watching children at play.

For *Loops* I wanted to push the idea of abstracted identities that we had just started to explore in *BIPED*, and I started picturing the way the children's game of cat's cradle sets up fluctuating networks of string between the opposing fingers of each hand. So rather than just tracing the normal hierarchy of Merce's hands from joint to joint, I wondered about a web of connections arising between the points of those hands.

At the same time Shelley and I had started to dream of a live and ever-changing version of the work, one that improvised itself in the same way that Cunningham did in his dance. At no time did we think of such a piece as documentation of the original but rather as an autonomous artwork that would exist—almost *live*—in parallel to it.

ID/entity

In 2000, the Kitchen in New York partnered with the MIT Media Lab to commission a series of new media works that would link artists in New York to engineers in Cambridge. The title of the show was to be *ID/entity: portraits for the 21st century*—the slash punctuation mark too cleverly postmodern for my liking at the time, though I must admit that on examining it now I see that the singling out of *entity* proved oddly prophetic in the case of *Loops*.

At the Lab, Shelley and I were introduced to Marc Downie, then a doctoral student there; by no means an engineer only, he was both artist *and* scientist. At our first meeting, I went on in vague and visionary mode about our perhaps impossible desire for the piece—which was to have each point of Merce's hands treated as its own dancer of sorts, with the choreography between them emerging cat's-cradle-style from their fleeting cross-connections. To which fanciful notion Marc merely nodded. He was currently programming AI frameworks for the emergent behavior of virtual wolves in a virtual wolf pack, and this proposal seemed a natural extension of that work.

Creatures

Marc's word for artificially intelligent entities was *creatures*, and so that's how we started designating the 48 moving points that comprised the motion capture data of Merce's hands. Our creation of the artwork entailed setting up the conditions for these creatures' decisions as they tracked the underlying motion; that is, we relinquished direct control in favor of emergent behavior.

Rather than looking at the collection of movements as a whole, Marc showed me that since aggregate behavior percolated up from each individual creature's choices, it was best to imagine the array of choices it faced at any given moment. These included:

- *how to shape its body*: as expressed by the lines by which it could connect to other points. This meant its picking a topological rule to follow—to reconstruct the hierarchy of the hand, or to grab points as they came close in space, or to connect to a corresponding point on the opposite hand, and so on.

─────────────── LOOPS — EXCERPTS FROM THE SCORE ───────────────

```
public class LoopsScript
    implements Updateable
{
    Script s;
    public LoopsScript()
    {
        s = new Script();
        s.new LoopingRealTimeBase
            (mins(10.6), true);
        
        // cats cradle
        s.new Event(0.1).add(new String[]{
            "s_pureCatCradle=100",
            "s_cameraTime=0.6",
            "s_timeFlow=2",
            "point'Trans=0.3"
        });
        
        // a little of "xray"
        s.new Event(30).add(new String[]{
            "s_xrayContent=5"
        });
```
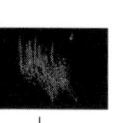
```
        // scribble (by sampling motion forward in time)
        s.new Event(45 + 30 + 25).add(new String[]{
            "s_onlyPoints=0",
            "s_forwardSampling=10",
            "s_xrayContent=0"    //???
        });
```
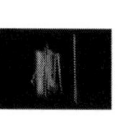

whiteGia refers to a rendering style that we found reminiscent of the line quality of Giacometti's portraits.

```
        // back away (make the transition tentative)
        s.new Event(35).add(new String[]{
            "s_xrayContent=0"
        });
        
        // mixed state — some "xray", some "cat's cradle"
        s.new Event(40).add(new String[]{
            "s_xrayContent=5",
            "s_pureCatCradle=5"
        });
        
        // force a transition into "xray"
        s.new Event(45).add(new String[]{
            "s_xrayContent=100"
        });
        
        // thin out density and show points
        s.new Event(46).add(new String[]{
            "s_nothing=10000",
            "s_forwardSampling=0",
            "s_accPointSize=1",
            "pointTrans=0.2"
        });
```

```
        // complicate matters by introducing some "whiteGia"
        s.new Event(45 + 30 + 45).add(new String[]{
            "s_whiteGia=20",
            "s_nothing=1",
            "s_accPointSize=0",
            "point'Trans=0.0001"
        });
        
        // move camera towards hands
        s.new Event(45 + 30 + 45 + 20 + 20).add(new String[]{
            "s_forwardSampling=10",
            "s_nothing=0",
            "s_cameraTime=0.47"
        });
        
        // transition to "whiteGia" complete
        s.new Event(45 + 30 + 45 + 20 + 25).add(new String[]{
            "s_whiteGia=100",
            "s_nothing=0",
            "s_forwardSampling=2",
            "s_timeFlow=1"
        });
        
        // propagate force messages between creatures
        s.new Event(45 + 30 + 45 + 20 + 25 + 20).add(new String[]{
            "s_doForceFlare=100"
        });
        
        s.new Event(45 + 30 + 45 + 20 + 25 + 25).add(new String[]{
            "s_doForceFlare=10"
        });
        
        s.new Event(45 + 30 + 45 + 20 + 25 + 35).add(new String[]{
            "s_doForceFlare=0"
        });
        
        // thin out "whiteGia"
        s.new Event(45 + 30 + 45 + 20 + 25 + 45).add(new String[]{
            "s_nothing=1",
            "s_point'Trans=0.2"
        });
        
        s.new Event(45 + 30 + 45 + 20 + 25 + 47).add(new String[]{
            "s_nothing=0"
        });
    });
```

forward sampling randomly elongates the point creatures bodies along the animation material. The result is often similar to inverted comet trails.

force propagation refers to the virtual dispersive medium that the point creatures are 'embedded in'. Creatures can inject force into what is in essence a simple cloth simulation, to perturb and flatten the geometry of nearby creatures.

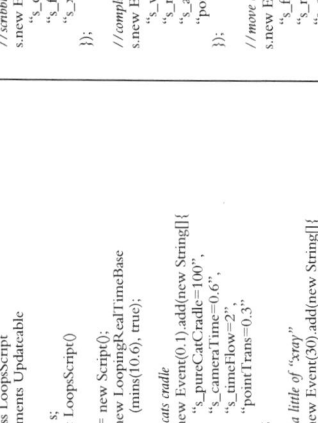

throughout the script there are references to terms such as "**xRay**" or "**amoeba**". These are names that the artists used to talk about the basic stylistic vocabulary built for the piece. They refer to behavioral tendencies, connection topologies and/or rendering styles. These common labels became increasingly important as the piece's stylistic vocabulary developed.

the creatures are responsible for showing how they are connected to other points. Sometimes they choose to connect themselves to points that are make sense in a traditional joint hierarchy. However, they can choose to produce complex 'cat's cradles' or sparse points.

FIGURE 2.1 Annotated code script for first version of *Loops*, 2001. Courtesy of the OpenEndedGroup.

- *how to move:* in relation to the motion capture data: shall it lead or trail the motion, or cut corners, or preserve imaginary physical momentums?
- *how to communicate:* by sending signals out into the colony of points and attempting to exert persuasive influence ("be like me")—which could cause rapid shifts of behavior and appearance, sometimes leading to local patches of agreement and coordination.
- *how to appear:* by picking from a blended continuum of line rendering styles, tuned, selected, and named (as "adjectives") by the three of us, the artists.

To structure the visual flow of *Loops*, Marc then created a scripting interface that allowed us to adjust its visual styles and AI decision making in real-time. But again, our adjustments were not in the form of direct commands; instead, we shifted tendencies within the artwork's autonomous system, where decisions were probabilistic rather than fixed. Among other things, we would adjust tolerances of boredom—which by our raising or lowering would influence the rate of change in the piece, not by fixed duration or rhythm but simply by *proclivity*.

This was for me very odd, for in order to think this through, I had had to posit that each creature had its own *desires*—And that their desires were perhaps no more precisely determined by their programming (but also no less) than were my own by genetic code.

Recall

I learned long ago in working with children how telling it can be to pair voice with virtual drawing; but when I requested that Merce retell certain stories he'd told us in previous conversations, he demurred, saying it might sound too much like John Cage's *Indeterminacy* and other pieces. A week or so later, however, Merce came back to me with a different idea—to read from the diary he'd kept over the three days of his first visit to Manhattan at age 17, a series of open-eyed snapshots of the city.

How fascinating it is to hear a young man's earnest impressions read aloud in his own voice, but a voice some sixty years older and wiser. You get Manhattan then and now, the man then and now—and you're as struck by the continuity as by the difference in each pairing.

Well, both are now gone, now gone in *this* now—the one fading away more slowly but no less certainly than the other.

Merce speaks, Cage listens

Since we had Merce talking, we then thought of John Cage listening, or perhaps his ghost. This gave rise to the second version of *Loops* in 2004, for which we created a live score. Our idea was to propel the intonation patterns of Merce's reading into a virtual version of Cage's prepared piano, which would trigger unexpected notes, often percussive.

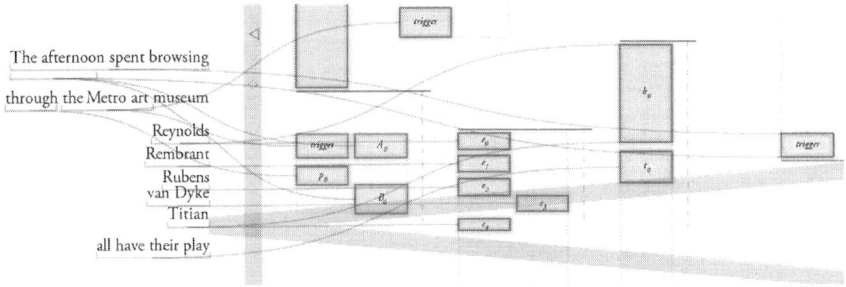

FIGURE 2.2 Excerpt of *Loops Score*, 2004. Courtesy of the OpenEndedGroup.

We sought structures in the text that had both musical and linguistic functions, and were halfway between forms found in music and in language. Such forms included lists; comparisons; spatial relationships; and markings of time passages. We coupled our analysis of the narrated text to the sound of the narration by marking the onset and offset of each word in the voice recording.

This fragment of the score illustrates the time periods during which the "sound creatures" could listen for opportunities. Each creature could then draw upon its vocabulary of possible actions that correspond metaphorically to the kinds of structures that trigger them:

- *list-actions* repeat their triggering elements while searching for a stable rhythm inside the elements;
- *comparison-actions* state their elements and then emphasize the differences between them;
- *passage-actions* state their first element and then continue to look for material that is sonically related until the close of their marked passage;
- *return-actions* compress material from their triggering element all the way back to where they "came from."

In doing all this, the sound creatures must pay attention to each other as they opportunistically align, modify, and perhaps even fight for space and relationships "on output."

From the start Merce wanted his voice not to dominate the score, but rather for it to merge at times as rhythm and timbre with the music, and this was the effect we achieved. It occurred to me recently that listening to the *Loops* score is a bit like walking in a busy city, where your thoughts are often overtaken by, and then submerged in, a wash of new impressions.

Cultural ecology, endangered species

It is a convenient fiction that completed artworks exist in perfect and isolated purity, framed for eternity. But the truth is more entangled than that, for artworks both grow from, and survive within, what we might call a cultural ecology. And this ecology is itself a changing environment—it is an intricate system of balances and inter-dependencies that evolves (or devolves) over time.

The cultural ecology for *Loops* is a good case in point for it is under constant threat. As a dance, can it somehow last now that its sole performer has died? As a digital artwork, can it survive the rapid and inevitable obsolescence of its hardware and software?

Figures 2.3, 2.4, 2.5 and 2.6 show how we diagrammed the cultural ecology of *Loops* in 2008. Figures 2.4–2.6 expand upon the nodes illustrated in Figure 2.3.

Living wills

In 2008, with support from the Mellon Foundation, we analyzed and confronted these problems directly. Our intent was not only to preserve and document the dance and the digital artwork, but also to create "living wills" for the choreography and the software that would allow their perpetuation—and propagation—far into the future.

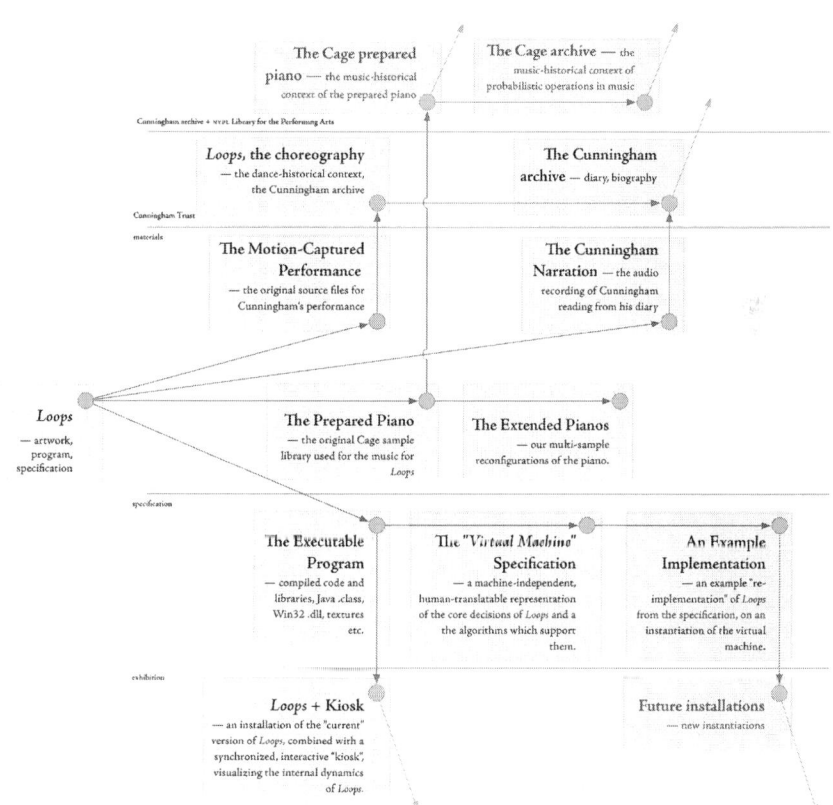

FIGURE 2.3 Conceptual diagram, 2008. Courtesy of the OpenEndedGroup.

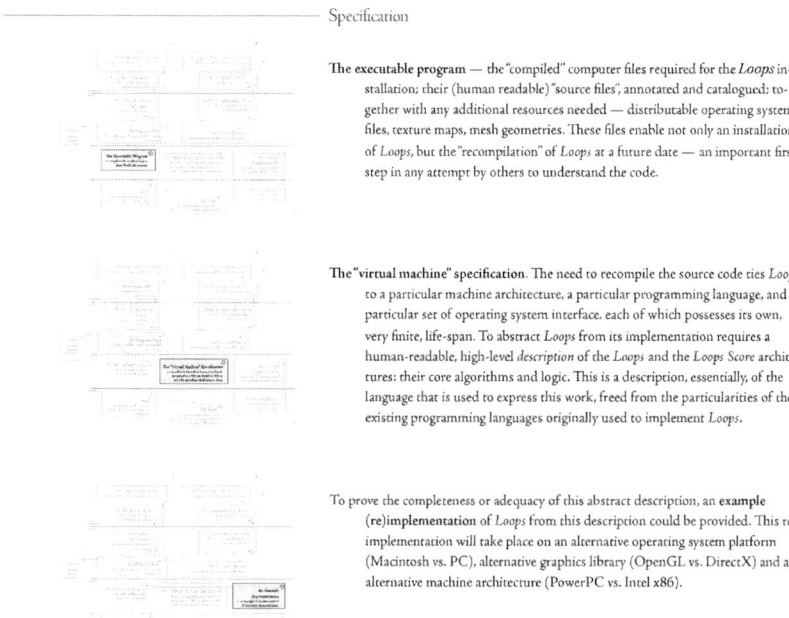

Specification

The executable program — the "compiled" computer files required for the *Loops* installation; their (human readable) "source files", annotated and catalogued; together with any additional resources needed — distributable operating system files, texture maps, mesh geometries. These files enable not only an installation of *Loops*, but the "recompilation" of *Loops* at a future date — an important first step in any attempt by others to understand the code.

The "virtual machine" specification. The need to recompile the source code ties *Loops* to a particular machine architecture, a particular programming language, and a particular set of operating system interface, each of which possesses its own, very finite, life-span. To abstract *Loops* from its implementation requires a human-readable, high-level *description* of the *Loops* and the *Loops Score* architectures: their core algorithms and logic. This is a description, essentially, of the language that is used to express this work, freed from the particularities of the existing programming languages originally used to implement *Loops*.

To prove the completeness or adequacy of this abstract description, an **example** (re)implementation of *Loops* from this description could be provided. This reimplementation will take place on an alternative operating system platform (Macintosh vs. PC), alternative graphics library (OpenGL vs. DirectX) and an alternative machine architecture (PowerPC vs. Intel x86).

FIGURE 2.4   Conceptual diagram, 2008. Courtesy of the OpenEndedGroup.

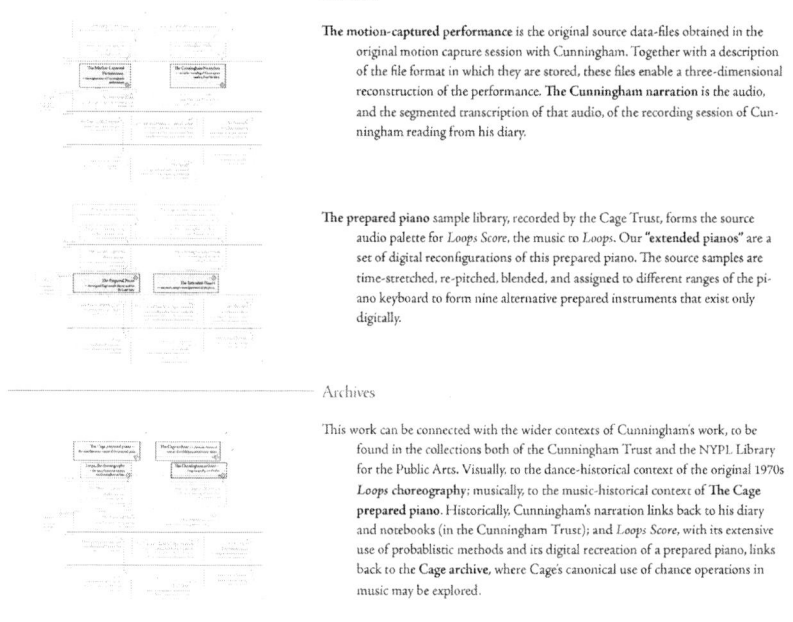

Materials

The motion-captured performance is the original source data-files obtained in the original motion capture session with Cunningham. Together with a description of the file format in which they are stored, these files enable a three-dimensional reconstruction of the performance. The **Cunningham narration** is the audio, and the segmented transcription of that audio, of the recording session of Cunningham reading from his diary.

The prepared piano sample library, recorded by the Cage Trust, forms the source audio palette for *Loops Score*, the music to *Loops*. Our **"extended pianos"** are a set of digital reconfigurations of this prepared piano. The source samples are time-stretched, re-pitched, blended, and assigned to different ranges of the piano keyboard to form nine alternative prepared instruments that exist only digitally.

Archives

This work can be connected with the wider contexts of Cunningham's work, to be found in the collections both of the Cunningham Trust and the NYPL Library for the Public Arts. Visually, to the dance-historical context of the original 1970s *Loops* choreography; musically, to the music-historical context of **The Cage prepared piano**. Historically, Cunningham's narration links back to his diary and notebooks (in the Cunningham Trust); and *Loops Score*, with its extensive use of probablistic methods and its digital recreation of a prepared piano, links back to the **Cage archive**, where Cage's canonical use of chance operations in music may be explored.

FIGURE 2.5   Conceptual diagram, 2008. Courtesy of the OpenEndedGroup.

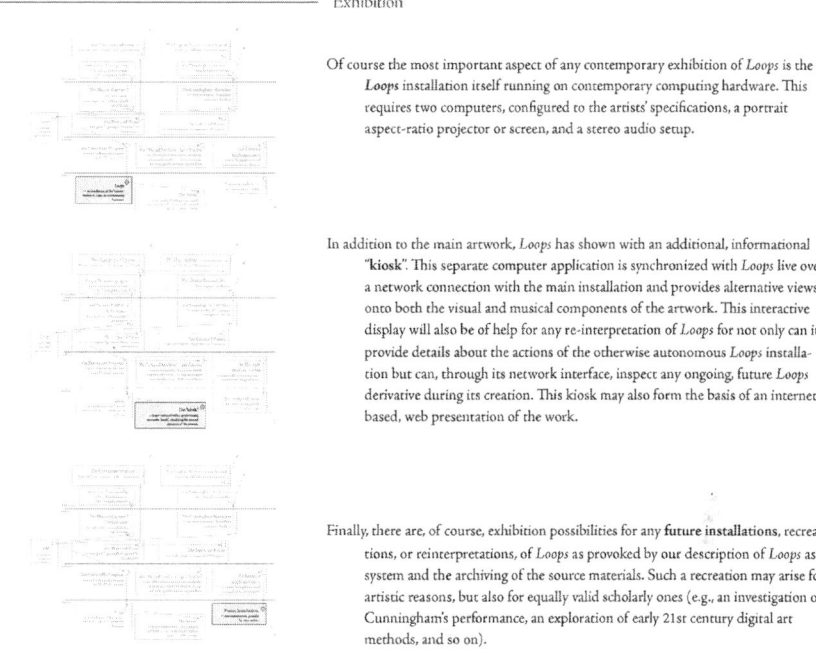

Exhibition

Of course the most important aspect of any contemporary exhibition of *Loops* is the *Loops* installation itself running on contemporary computing hardware. This requires two computers, configured to the artists' specifications, a portrait aspect-ratio projector or screen, and a stereo audio setup.

In addition to the main artwork, *Loops* has shown with an additional, informational "kiosk". This separate computer application is synchronized with *Loops* live over a network connection with the main installation and provides alternative views onto both the visual and musical components of the artwork. This interactive display will also be of help for any re-interpretation of *Loops* for not only can it provide details about the actions of the otherwise autonomous *Loops* installation but can, through its network interface, inspect any ongoing, future *Loops* derivative during its creation. This kiosk may also form the basis of an internet-based, web presentation of the work.

Finally, there are, of course, exhibition possibilities for any **future installations**, recreations, or reinterpretations, of *Loops* as provoked by our description of *Loops* as a system and the archiving of the source materials. Such a recreation may arise for artistic reasons, but also for equally valid scholarly ones (e.g., an investigation of Cunningham's performance, an exploration of early 21st century digital art methods, and so on).

FIGURE 2.6 Conceptual diagram, 2008. Courtesy of the OpenEndedGroup.

Our approach resembled that of the Variable Media Initiative devised almost a decade ago by the Guggenheim Museum, the Pacific Film Archive, the Walker Art Center, the Franklin Furnace, and others. We shared their belief that artists need to start defining artworks independently of specific media, at least for preservation purposes. Our project, however, was considerably more complex than the existing variable media case studies, for we were to create strategies for preserving both a complex dance and a complex computer program—and for coordinating the two.

We had two goals: first, to enable both works to survive long into the future; and second, to allow students, scholars, and artists to examine both works with an unprecedented level of precision and with a rich awareness of context.

Dance data

Cunningham agreed to make his choreography of *Loops* available for non-commercial use under a Creative Commons license. And so we released video documentation of his performance as shot from multiple cameras—and, more crucially, the digital motion-capture files themselves. These make it possible to examine Cunningham's motion from any angle and from any distance, to speed up or slow down playback to any rate, to measure joint angles and their correlations, and even to perform sophisticated statistical analysis of the movement.

Open source code

At the same time we released as open source both the specific code for the 2008 implementation of *Loops* as well as the much larger programming environment, Field, that we have relied upon not only to create *Loops* but also all our other artworks since about 2001. This enables the study of the digital artwork not only by watching the runtime version, but also by examining its underlying code.

Our thought was that such an approach would also address the practical problems of keeping the work running. After all, since we cannot foresee future formats, programs, computers, operating systems, displays, and so on, we must accept that all present equivalents will be obsolete in very short order.[3]

Our further idea was to allow future (and even contemporaneous) programmers to update the work as well as to create their own derivative artworks. We would enable them to forge creative reinterpretations of *Loops* in a fashion that went far beyond the present-day practice of "remixes," which operate only on the surface rather than on the structure of the original work.

We're entrusting the future preservation and perpetuation of *Loops* to unforeseen hands.

Data

One way to make a thing that can last through the ages is to make it out of nearly indestructible materials, as in the example of the ceremonial sword we considered earlier. We can also work to safeguard the material existence of the thing, as for example in museum conservation, where precious manuscripts and paintings are protected from heat, light, humidity, and touch.

A different approach is to make a thing whose form is permanent but whose materials are perishable—perishable but replaceable. Such is the case for certain sacred structures in Japan made out of wood. As the wood decays, it can simply be replaced. As Alexander Stille puts it:

> Just as our bodies replace their old cells with new ones while we remain "ourselves," the buildings would be constantly regenerated, remaining forever new and forever ancient.[4]

And so none of the materials of the Ise Temple have ever been in place for more than twenty years, yet the Japanese can rightly regard the building as being thirteen hundred years old.

We have entered an age where many material things are vanishing into digital bits. Such bits, being merely an arrangement of ones and zeros, are in theory imperishable and infinitely reproducible; but not so in practice. Their environment—the computers and storage devices, the operating systems and programs on which they depend—keeps changing, causing disruptions much more severe than those brought on by rain, snow, wind, and sun.

Even so, our only hope for preserving digital artworks lies with this idea: that we are true to their form rather than to their materiality.
(2012)

***

Loops has existed in four versions. In 2001, it was commissioned by the M.I.T. Media Lab for the *ID/Entity* show; in 2005 its sound score was remade for Ars Electronica; in 2007 it was re-created in tryptich form and its underlying code released as open source; and in 2011 it was recreated in its definitive version in cinema-resolution for the New York Film Festival.
See: http://openendedgroup.com/artworks/loops.html.

***

I wrote this account of *Loops* in December 2011. Now, on the eve of this book publication, we're creating yet another version of the work, this time in virtual reality. VR is a perfect medium for the work, and I only wish Merce were alive to experience *Loops* in this radically new way.

Notes

1 From Rainer Maria Rilke's "Youthful Portrait of My Father." Author's translation adapted from Gass, William, *Reading Rilke: Reflections on the Problems of Translation*, Knopf, 1999.
2 The beta software was called *biped*, which was also the term for its kinematic figures. The following year this gave Merce the title for *BIPED* (often mis-written in title case rather than all-caps).
3 We have already encountered several obsolescences in the ten-year life of *Loops* to date; indeed, every time the work is exhibited, its code must be carefully adjusted to accommodate even small updates in commercial display drivers.
4 Alexander Stille. *The Future of the Past*, Picador, 2003.

3

STEVE PAXTON'S *MATERIAL FOR THE SPINE*

The experience of a sensorial edition

Florence Corin with very special thanks to Baptiste Andrien (translation by Vincent Rafis)

In 1986, dancer Steve Paxton began examining the spine he had observed in the practice of Contact Improvisation, a duet movement form he had instigated in 1972, in which the torsos of the dancers are especially interactive. In 2008, Contredanse Editions (Brussels) released the four hour DVD-ROM *Material for the Spine: A Movement Study* containing audiovisual essays, motion capture sequences, and extracts from lectures, classes, and performances that together present an extensive introduction to Paxton's modes of working and thinking.

In Paxton's own words:

> With Material for the Spine, I am interested in creating a strong technical approach to the processes of improvisation. It is a system for exploring interior and exterior muscles of the back. It aims to bring consciousness to the dark side of the body, that is the "other" side, or the inside, those sides rarely seen, and to submit sensations from them to the mind for consideration.
>
> *(Paxton in* Material for the Spine*)*

The project was born from an encounter between Patricia Kuypers[1] and Steve Paxton. They met in Brussels in 1985 during Paxton's creation of *Ave Nue*, set in a former fire station. Through the years, Kuypers, who performed in *Ave Nue*, remained influenced by this dance master. While initiating projects like Contredanse (a small association promoting reflection and collaborations around dance which would later become a dance-specialized documentation center and publishing house), Patricia Kuypers started developing the idea of publishing a monograph on Steve Paxton's work. For many years and on several occasions, she asked for his contributions.

In January 2004, on the occasion of a performance in Ghent, Paxton agreed to discuss this idea with Contredanse. Paxton, Kuypers, and I—a newcomer at Contredanse—met at an Asian restaurant to talk about the project. Several concepts were thrown on the table: people at Contredanse wished to publish a DVD-book in order to bring together a text and moving images; Steve Paxton, however, was not keen on a "historical" overview of his work. While the idea of evoking Steve Paxton's background, works, and thoughts was not swept aside, two axes of research were then proposed: one on gravity, with the slightly absurd idea of parabolic flights; the other on motion capture.[2]

What follows is a series of emails and phone conversations whose aim was to reach an agreement on the material to be used.

From Patricia—September 2004

(. . .) First we would like to know if you agree to collaborate on this, and for that I try to give you here a view on the ensemble we have in mind at the moment. We perhaps won't have the possibility to realize the whole, but for sure we are going to publish this DVD-book at least and try to feed it with as many experiences and events we can produce in this period of time (and with the money we can find).

I send you here the planning Flo made, so you have an idea about the general events we want to organize, this is for sure subject to changes and you can interfere by giving us feed-back. We will send you also later the list of writings of or about you that we have, so you can complete it if you want. We will begin also to collect film documents and if you can help that's great.

Steve Paxton, book and DVD – deadline : spring 2007

Project[3]:

Book:
Around different concepts:
Spherical space
Walking studies
Helix and rolls and puzzles
Anatomical principles which underlie the movement
Around different works:
PA RT,
Ave Nue,
Goldberg Variations.

DVD:
Around concepts :
puzzles of movement (base of Contact Improvisation)
technical bases of the exploration of the improvised movement
Material For the Spine (MfS)

> Around exploration:
> gravity to no-gravity: spherical space in parabolic flight - microgravity, in water, with gyroscope, . . .
> Motion capture of some specific movements of the spine/pelvis
>
> *From Steve*—September 2004
>
> I agreed to the project because it was adventurous to work in our present tense, and a big relief from the continuous maintenance of the past which workshops, books, normally require.
>
> As for me, I hoped the project would become a vehicle for investigating gravity. Thus the Toulouse flights would tie into the motion capture of Material for the Spine, the personal body's way of coping set beside the absence of the forces it works with.
>
> Anyway, lets talk between us about what to do and why to do it, and really to what end. I suspect that between us we can produce some very interesting research and proceed to publish with plenty of material.

These conversations led us to refine our thinking and to adjust our editorial plans according to Steve Paxton's wishes. We allowed ourselves to dream, to think outside of the box in order to avoid the content being limited by its form; even though, later, reality would come to reframe all of it. At first, Paxton did not want to focus on the past. He refused the use of archives and he did not agree to be filmed. He did not want to appear as a model, as someone who should be imitated. He wanted to vanish and let the principles which underlie the movement speak for themselves. Little by little, however, it seemed important to see him practice Material for the Spine in person, to contemplate his body as the very place which holds the memory of many years of research, and makes the principles of movement so visible. Eventually, some "historical" excerpts of his work would appear and reinforce his thinking in "present tense."

Moreover, early on, the questions and topics which are at the core of the publication were debated in our emails.

> *From Florence*—March 2005
>
> Well then the central question is what do we want to explore? What do we want to research? And how do we want to express that?
>
> We have talked about two axes of reflection, one based on your research on gravity and the other on Material for the Spine. To report and to research on these subjects.
>
> Actually, on this side of the sea, we need more information of what you have in mind, what is your desire, to see what elements are relevant. How is the best way to transmit that on which media.

From Steve—March 2005

Your final question below has been driving this project, in that we want to create products, not just do research. The one product we cannot create however is the only one I use, which is the sensations of the body. All very well in the workshop world, but not translatable from the person to the screen or text.

To focus our minds, I propose this theoretical question. If we were to research the effect of Tai Chi on the spine, how could it be done? That is, not the steps and moving of arms, but how forces used in the movement are supported by the spine, initiated in the pelvis, etc. Central skeleton research. . . .

I am a bit dismayed by the time limitation. Are we really doing research, or just trying to get material together to publish by a certain time? I have been looking at Material for the Spine since 1986. That seems to me to suggest research on the body's development relative to a proposition.

So. the research may not be trying to find new forms of movement, but instead would be into ways to present research already done.

We have two foci: MfS, and gravity.

On "research": I take the word seriously. Mocap and weightless flights are experiments. Research does require experimentation, we know, but publishing research requires a thesis, demonstrations, and evidence. So I feel that even research on modalities such as texts or videos, should support or deny governing ideas.

I am very happy and grateful for your input, insight and invention, Florence. This project comes from you and Patricia, and in the grind to produce this publication I'm sure I have to try to overcome my long-term disregard for anything but the sensations and senses, and you have a responsibility, actually, to engage me in arguments and inspire the best work we can do.

I think the very least we can aspire to is not to be boring, visually or verbally. So the illustration of the materials have to be apt, well edited, and informative.

In 2008, what do you want to be seeing when you look at the DVD or book?

Here Paxton gave details on the two major themes that would later structure the publication: "MfS (Material for the Spine), and gravity." He also defined how we would proceed: what was at stake was not "just" research, but the exploration of how to display an already-existing experimentation on "the body's development." Paxton wondered how to translate the sensations of the body to a medium other than the body: how could they be approached by the reader/viewer of a book/DVD? These questions echoed those consistently addressed by Contredanse: how can we, through editorial projects, bind together theory and practice in order to stay as close as possible to the body and its experience? The challenge of publishing a DVD which would give a sense of movement through image and sound was also a contribution to expanding the ways one perceives movement. We had intuitions and desires, but we did not know yet how to make them real. With time, through filming sessions, this project would teach us to fine-tune our point of view.

From Florence—May 2005

During the stay of Lisa[4] (and Scott Smith) in Brussels, we had the occasion to speak a little about how it is possible to share sensations of the body through a visual medium. Actually, this is the question for the entire project—book and DVD—as you write in your last email: how to express through text or through image your knowledge of the sensations of the body?

It is a challenging question.

And in the discussion, we thought that we could add to the videos (conventional videos or videos with comments and representations of what is acting on the movement) some other video images which express the "image" of the sensation of the movement. Videos working as analogy. I'm thinking that is also a possible way to enrich the sensations for the readers/viewers.

From Steve—May 2005

One question left hanging in my mind from the beginning: who is the camera person for the video we plan?

From Florence—May 2005

About the person for the camera, actually I am very much interested to do this myself. I know that you don't know how I'm filming or working. But these questions—how to film dance, how to express something in the movement, the question of representation—really interest my personal work and I'm working a lot with video and image.

Filming was ready to start. We were lucky enough to be partnered with the Spanish association L'animal a l'esquena, which invited us to start shooting on their site. Steve Paxton had been there for weeks in a writing residency when Patricia Kuypers and I joined him for a week of filming and interviews on the nature of his work. Two of Paxton's collaborators/practitioners of MfS were also there: Scott Smith and Charlie Morrissey. During that time, we mostly shot the basic movements of MfS—crescent rolls, helix rolls, undulations—often performed on a glass table:

L'animal diary—Steve—December 2005

When I go into L'animal, the 2x2 m glass is on the frame, at 1 m height.

It is still quite cold from its trip to the studio. There is no sense of fragility under full body, so I stand. I walk gingerly. It is able to carry 100 kilos at its center, but on this first try it is difficult to let my weight down. I try to lift it off the glass.

Charlie Morrissey seems to assess the glass differently. He gets up on it casually, rolls around, and stands without being tentative. Later, he will take small soft jumps on the center.

Lighting concerns take much of the day. The sun hits this position twice a day, from high upper windows. At these moments we are working on the surface of the body touching the glass, however, so natural strong light is not welcome. When weight comes onto the lower surface of the body, the skin changes color, toward a yellow. Charlie's feet, which have thick calluses, look almost lemon compared to his high arches, which are pink.

During this first week we shot and recorded a lot of material, which allowed us to have a first sense of what we wanted to see and what, according to us, would convey a sensation. We also got to know each other better. Steve Paxton would discover our way of working, while we would further explore material that we mostly knew theoretically through his writings and interviews. Following this, Paxton invited us to learn more about the teaching and practice of MfS and to film a workshop he was to give in September 2006 in Seattle. Growing busy with her own creations, Patricia Kuypers could not attend, so we decided to hire a new person in order to realize this large-scale project. Baptiste Andrien was our ideal choice: a dancer specialized in Lisa Nelson's *Tuning Score*, as much as a video and martial artist, he had previously contributed to the *Body-Mind Centering* DVD edited by Contredanse.

Later on, we organized a series of two workshops—one in Brussels with the collaboration of Charleroi/Danses, the other in Paris with the collaboration of the Centre National de la Danse. Filmed and recorded, these workshops usually provide our publications with the experiences of the dancers involved, and as such, fully contribute to Contredanse's editorial policy. As publishers and directors, the moments spent in the studio also allow us to move from a theoretical knowledge to a technical observation, and finally to a corporeal experiment. During those days of training, we also motion-captured some dancing and interviewed Steve Paxton for a few extra hours. His thinking became more and more clear to us.

We were lucky enough to work at Paxton's place in Vermont during the year 2007. Those moments proved to be very beneficial, since at that time we were involved in editing all the material that we had previously gathered. Being next to Paxton while we were trying to structure our thoughts helped us develop a common lexicon. We had not chosen yet between a DVD and a DVD-ROM.

But once we approached the complexity of Paxton's thinking, we figured out that the ramified navigation of a DVD-ROM would be a better option than the linear reading of a DVD. The DVD-ROM[5] could also work as a pedagogical tool, encouraging the viewer to be active. There again, we wanted to put body and thoughts into action in order to stay as close as possible to sensation. We also wanted the interface to be ergonomic and sleek, while revealing the content through its design. Using a spiral shape was a natural choice, offering a graphic representation for what, quintessentially, is MfS. Emeric Florence, a flash artist who had previously collaborated with us on a digital publication,[6] executed this concept.

This project is what it is because it is made of who we are. It was conceived around and grateful to Paxton, of course, but also as a result of the variety of our backgrounds: editors, artists, architects with their distinct sensibilities, and movement artists. I remember Baptiste Andrien and I practicing MfS throughout the realization phase. It was very important for us to test the theories of Paxton physically in order to convey his research through our sensations. It was obvious from early on that we would have to feel the transformations in our body (like, for instance, the spirals around our spine) in order to translate them visually. We would have to integrate this knowledge both physically and mentally in order to transmit it. Thus, not only would the structure of the DVD-ROM echo Paxton's research; it would also be the reflection of what we were taught by his techniques and thinking. Being accompanied by Paxton while we were doing this made the project particularly unique.

From Baptiste—August 2006

Oh, the floating balls . . . I remember this basic imagery, quite blurry. I could only relate to ischia through the sensation of sitting on them and feeling the flesh moving around, so I had no clue about the relationship of the ischia to the skeleton, and that basic sensation gave me an image of floating balls. I couldn't even name the ischia. But if it's not named yet, I still had sensations from where to name. And I remember my movements at that time were not named in detail, which means I was moving with less articulation. Looking at dance as a language, I found these early movements close to shouting, primary speech. So step by step, new words, new articulations, other speeches. And now, breathing, just looking at it seems to change it, so it needs time. I found the question of how to touch with attention delicate.

From Steve—January 2007

So cool, I got your email at the library parking lot, so I could immediately check the website. I am grateful to be working with you and Baptiste. I get a big shot of optimism whenever I see your inventions.

> Visuals: the helix is excellent. Would it be possible to make it walk?
>
> The fine-line energy illustrations are beautiful, a big leap from our first tries. They work much better without the body distracting from the geometry. Because MfS. is so based in geometry, these are very useful mental implants, but at the same time they are complex. I think they should be visually built for the viewer, to draw them in slowly in order that the final visuals can be better appreciated.

Therefore, from mid-2007 to the end of 2008, the shaping of the project demanded that we re-unite our memories and the physical sensations that we had stored. We had to balance together the videos of real bodies, superposed graphics, images put together by association, virtual representations, and so on, in order to express in the best way the sensations, the movements, exercises, and thoughts of Steve Paxton. We worked towards the distillation of an object addressing its user both mentally and physically, whoever this user may be: professional dancer, dance researcher, or amateur. Finally, we formalized the initial question: how to reveal the physical research of an artist through imagery conveying its very essence, through both content and form.

> *From Lisa*—August 2008
>
> The new version is a terrific job. A real shift to wholeness. I was surprised, I can't say why, to realize the DVD IS about Material for the Spine—what it is, what it looks like, what it's for, where it came from. I get the impression from the DVD that it's the technical work/discovery of an artist, that it's a special KIND of technical training ("normal to formal"!) that albeit specific in its movements, is foremost learned through imagery and practice with awareness. Something akin to yoga, which theoretically and ultimately is not about achieving asanas, but rather, achieving awareness.

For Contredanse, for Baptiste Andrien, and for me, this project was a big step towards learning about audiovisual editing of dance. It brought us to deepen and clarify how to develop means for transmitting the thinking of an artist on a sensorial level. It allowed us to acknowledge the importance of integrating praxis before translating it into words and images. Working with Steve Paxton opened us up to further collaborations with great artists whose knowledge leads to improve choreographic culture. Hopefully, we will keep contributing in a relevant and unique way. We learned a lot through this journey, and were enriched by Paxton's humanity, physical practice, and invaluable thinking. I believe that the mutual trust and the common language we developed led to a creative freedom which illuminated this project.

***

Material for the Spine: A Movement Study was realized by Baptiste Andrien and Florence Corin (for Contredanse) and Steve Paxton, and edited and produced by Contredanse Editions (Brussels) in collaboration with the cooperation of L'animal a l'esquena (Celra, ES) and le Centre National de la Danse (Pantin, FR), 2008.

The project was initiated by Patricia Kuypers. Artistic advisors: Patricia Kuypers, Lisa Nelson. Camera, video editing, graphics, 3D, layout, and subtitles: Baptiste Andrien and Florence Corin. DVD-ROM development: Emeric Florence. Soundtrack: Yvan Hanon. Transcriptions: Agnès Benoit-Nader. Translation: Denise Luccioni. Motion Capture: Mocap.be. Testing DVD-ROM: Contredanse.

Notes

1 Patricia Kuypers is a dancer, an improvisational artist, and a dance researcher. She founded Contredanse in the 1980s and the journal *Nouvelles de Danse* in the 1990s. She is currently developing a writing and residence project dedicated to improvisation.
2 Motion capture is a technique designed to register in a time-based 3D sequence the movements of real objects in order to re-use them in a virtual environment.
3 This list of concepts and ideas is based on a conversation between Steve Paxton, Patricia Kuypers, and Florence Corin which took place in January 2004.
4 A dancer, video artist, and editor of *Contact Quarterly* journal, Lisa Nelson is a friend and artistic collaborator of Steve Paxton.
5 During the conception of the DVD-ROM, it appeared that the ambition of the project made it necessary to separate the book and the DVD-ROM. They would eventually be published separately.
6 "Interagir avec les technologies numériques," *Nouvelles de Danse* 52, Brussels (2004).

4

WILLIAM FORSYTHE'S *IMPROVISATION TECHNOLOGIES* AND BEYOND

A short design history of digital dance transmission projects on CD-ROM and DVD-ROM, 1994–2011

Chris Ziegler

In 1994, William Forsythe approached ZKM Karlsruhe through digital artist Paul Kaiser, who at that time was working on a CD-ROM about Robert Wilson's stage works in New York. Forsythe requested ZKM Karlsruhe to design an interactive installation for the tenth anniversary of the Frankfurt Dance Company. Later he changed his mind and supported a research project instead on digital tools for dance transmission, which resulted in the production of the digital archive *The Loss of Small Detail* (1994); the first "digital dance school" *Self Meant to Govern* (1995), which was used inside the company and the published CD-ROM *William Forsythe: Improvisation Technologies. A Tool for the Analytical Dance Eye* four years later. This CD-ROM became the model for several other CD-ROM and DVD-ROM projects including one about Japanese Kyogen Theater (in 1999) produced right after the release of the Frankfurt Ballett CD-ROM. NAGARIKA, a DVD-ROM series on Indian classical dance Bharatanatyam and Kalaripayathu. The series was created 2006 and 2010 together with Jayachandran Palazhy, the artistic director of Attakkalari, Bangalore. 2000 at a dance workshop at Arizona State University I introduced him to the newly released CD-ROM *William Forsythe: Improvisation Technologies*.

Analog to digital transfer—*The Loss* . . .

When Forsythe started working at the Frankfurt Ballet, the company began to meticulously record rehearsals and stage productions on video. Forsythe never stopped changing his creations after the premiere and therefore every performance was documented on video. A continuous series of productions resulted in an extensive video archive documenting rehearsals, performances and their changes over time. This video archive helped new members of the company to learn movements of past productions. To allow them to better prepare for rehearsals, the company handed out portable video players to dancers so they could learn the

42   Chris Ziegler

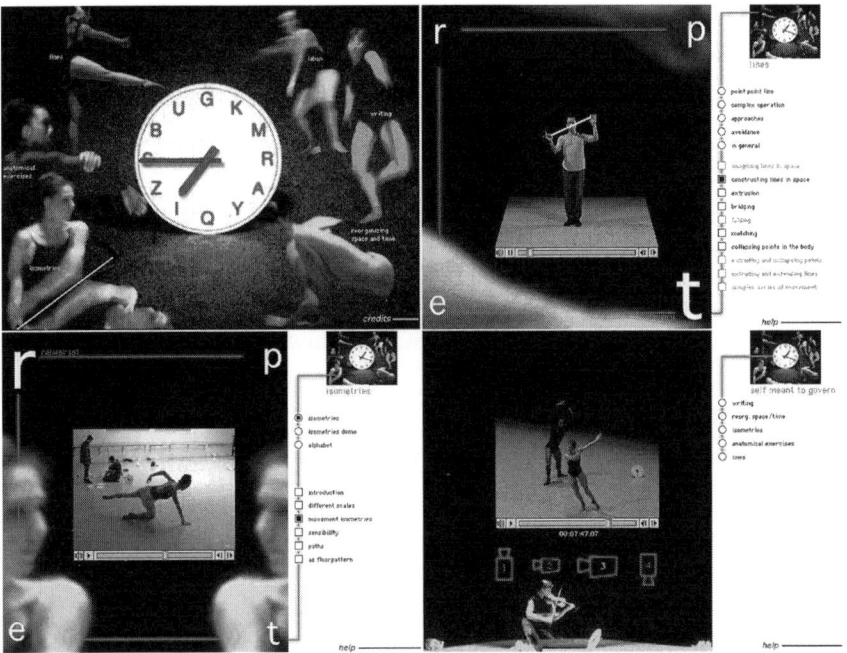

FIGURE 4.1   *The Loss of Small Detail* (1994) showing William Forsythe, Dana Caspersen. Photos © Dominik Mentzos. Screenshots by Chris Ziegler.

movements from home. Constant play and rewind of these analog videos caused wear and tear on the tapes. Digitizing the existing archive was important to help restore and preserve precious movement material.

Forsythe's *The Loss of Small Detail* gave the impetus to a digital movement archive created in an attempt to try to NOT lose any small detail. This creation had been performed for almost four years when we started the archiving project. Forsythe continuously changed movement instructions and repositioned props in order to keep the dancers alert. The dancers themselves kept developing the piece as well. Therefore, when a dancer had to be replaced, the knowledge of the piece that had to be transmitted to new dancers was not only what was initiated by the choreographer. Each dancer leaving the production had to teach his/her own part to the one replacing him or her, including all changes that were made over time. The process of change could now be digitally recorded and reconstructed.

In addition to recordings of the performance, we incorporated an interface that linked excerpts of rehearsals to the timeline. An interactive cursor in playback of the performance provided access to the rehearsal history of certain scenes, complimented by Forsythe's sketches and verbal comments on the development of the piece as a whole. The viewing angles can be switched from front to side whilst watching the performance. The recordings from the side of stage were almost entirely shot by Forsythe himself.

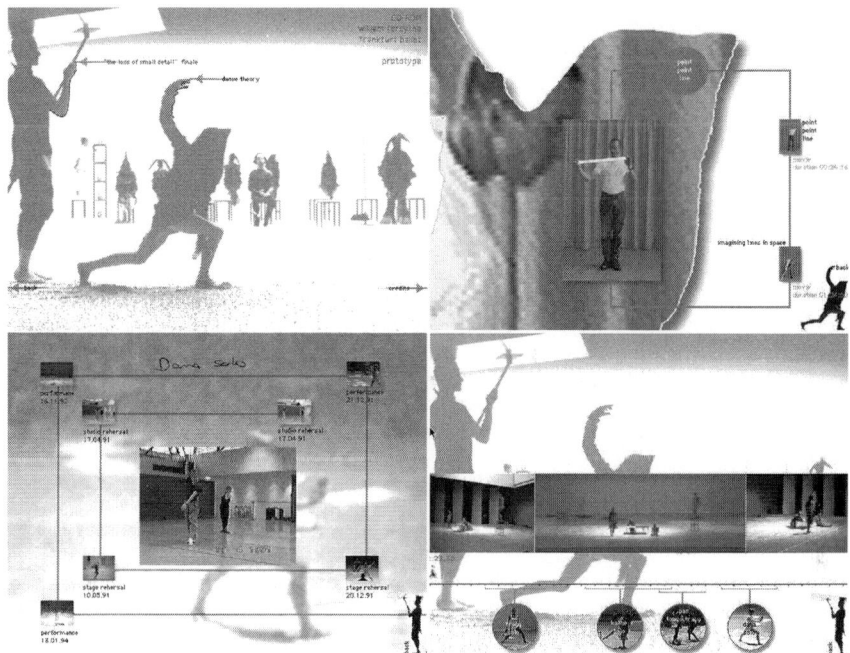

FIGURE 4.2 *Self Meant to Govern* (1995) showing Christine Bürkle, Francesca Harper, Andrea Tallis, Ana Catalina Roman, Emily Molnar, Jill Johnson, William Forsythe. Screenshots by Chris Ziegler.

1995—Self Meant to Govern

The Loss of Small Detail digital archive documents changes of a production over time and provides access to rehearsal material. In *Self Meant to Govern*, video lectures, movement demonstration material, and excerpts of the *Self Meant to Govern* production on stage created a "digital dance school" merging video archiving with a teaching tool for movement techniques. The first generation of dancers in the company were involved in developing what would become Forsythe's Improvisation Technologies as a technique for "self governed" movement generated during rehearsals. At the same time, David Kern, one of the dancers of the company, began developing a rehearsal software named Piecemaker, which would later be used in the Forsythe Ballet research project *Motion Bank*, also represented in this volume in Chapter 13 (for more on Piecemaker, see page 133).

The performance *Self Meant to Govern* was performed only once on stage. The piece was a choreography with improvisation elements on stage and demonstrated Forsythe's Improvisation Technologies. *Self Meant to Govern* was professionally recorded with four cameras on stage. The dancers also made recording of themselves during rehearsal, movement "selfies" used as movement sketches. We also recorded demonstration lectures by Forsythe, explaining and demonstrating the Improvisation Technologies in front of the camera.

The project began three months after Forsythe's wife and leading dancer of the company Tracy-Kai Maier passed away with cancer. Her death had a tremendous impact on the company and the members who worked on the project. The somber mood created a reflective situation and I felt a sense of holding back. The focus shifted to documentation, archiving work and dance techniques rather than dynamically producing new work. Although *Self Meant to Govern* was never performed again, the material was later developed into the first part of *Eidos: Telos* (1995).

The amount of footage shot for *Self Meant to Govern* was approximately 4GB, which made it impossible to fit it onto one CD-ROM. Hence the entire workstation with the application was placed into Forsythe's office at the Ballet Frankfurt. In 1995, only a few dancers had laptops or access to computers, so dancers came to his office (adjacent to the stage) to use it to learn Forsythe's Improvisation Technologies. The first movement lesson actually was to teach dancers how to use a mouse! Forsythe told me during the project that he considered his computer the most precious tool for a choreographer: a time saver.

T E R P interface

During the design process I learned from Nik Haffner (one of the dancers and also an editor for our production), how dancers incorporate new movements. Armed with this information, I developed a design that involved four stages[1]:

1. **t** heory (verbal explanation)
2. **e** xample
3. **r** ehearsal
4. **p** erformance.

t (theory) shows Forsyth's lecturing and teaching dance both verbally and by demonstration. Links from **t** (theory) lead to **e** (example), which is a short excerpt of the performance recording showing a specific movement of the final performance. The creation starts in **r** (rehearsal), showing oral and physical dialogues between the dancer and the choreographer. **p** (performance) has four video streams of different camera angles—all linked to the lectures of **t** (theory). This interface made it possible for dancers to learn movement ideas either from theory to practice or vice versa.

1999—Improvisation Technologies

In 1997, the hard drives containing all video material of *Self Meant to Govern* were stolen from the Frankfurt Ballet. Only one more copy of the application and recordings was still kept in the German Dance Archive in Cologne. We decided finally to use the opportunity not only to reconstruct the old version that was stolen but also

William Forsythe's *Improvisation Technologies* 45

FIGURE 4.3 *William Forsythe: Improvisation Technologies. A Tool for the Analytical Dance Eye*, (1999) showing Noah D. Gelber, William Forsythe, Thomas McManus. Screenshots by Chris Ziegler.

to enhance it to develop a new update. This theft was the push we needed to finally produce the first publically available digital dance knowledge CD-ROM.

This CD-ROM does not focus on one specific stage production, but on the Improvisation Technologies as a dance technique developed by Forsythe and the company over the years. Some (wrongly) assumed that Forsythe was releasing a CD-ROM providing insights into ways on how to create dance productions. This was not the case. Instead the CD-ROM titled *William Forsythe: Improvisation Technologies. A Tool for the Analytical Dance Eye* is designed to help dancers generate movement material. The CD-ROM is also (as indicated in the second part of the title) a tool that explains how to look at Forsythe's dances.

Some chapters were omitted to streamline the application for public use. I was not happy to see these chapters removed, especially the one about Laban, since it provides links to the notation systems on which the Improvisation Technologies technique is based. However, the CD-ROM had limited capacity and therefore it was necessary to remove some of the materials of the full installation version which was designed for a specific use inside the company to prepare classical trained dancers for rehearsal in Frankfurt Ballett.

The original four chapters of the learning cycle were reduced to two. **t** (theory) and **e** (example) were kept, chapters **r** (rehearsal) and **p** (performance) were

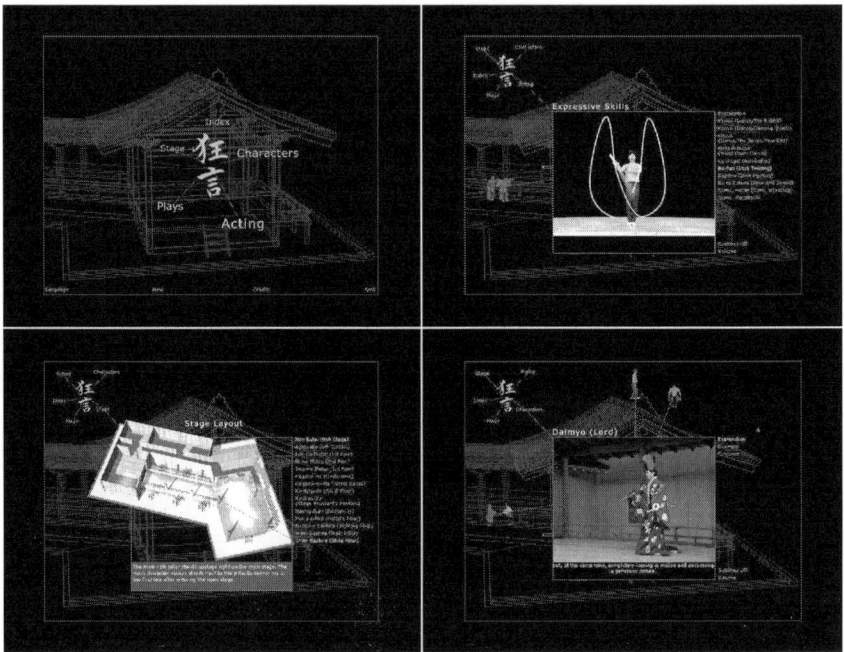

FIGURE 4.4 *That's Kyogen!* (2001) showing Mansaku and Mansai Nomura. Screenshots by Chris Ziegler.

removed. Movement examples can be found in chapter **e** (example), showing demonstrations of the technologies for improvisation. Christine Bürkle demonstrates how to develop new movement material on the basis of a "non-improvised theme." After demonstrating the movement, she unfolds, flips, and reverses the movements to reorganize the material. Noah D. Gelber demonstrates "room writing" by moving quickly through a visual narrative, creating and deleting imagined objects. He shows how this results in executing a precise physical storyboard. Crystal Pite and Thomas McManus demonstrate various other principles to re-organize movement. The CD-ROM also includes *Solo*, a dance film project of Forsythe filmed in 1997 by Thomas Lovell Balog. This film demonstrates the result of a choreographic process.

2001—That's Kyogen!

Improvisation Technologies became a big seller in Japan. It probably was the popularity of martial arts (Tai Chi and others) which generated this interest. TV producer Tokyo Media Connections (TMC) recognized the potential of what we developed as a means to document the traditional performing art form of Kyogen and partnered with Waseda University in Tokyo and ZKM Karlsruhe to produce the DVD-ROM *That's Kyogen!*[2].

Noh dramatic theater productions are long performances with short half-hour inserts of Kyogen comedies. Kyogen has been practiced for over 500 years and details had only been captured in writings. The way Kyogen is performed has not changed since then. Younger audiences have problems understanding the old dialect and lost interest in an old theatrical form, which was very popular in past generations.

TMC's goal was to develop a digital application that could raise the interest of a younger generation. A unique collaboration was established with the Mansaku/Mansai family, one of the two families that has passed on the tradition of Kyogen for many generations. This collaboration meant a break from old traditions because our project meant opening up family knowledge to the public. This also meant we had to invent how to teach Kyogen outside the traditional family situation. Becoming a Kyogen actor is a life-long learning process. One literally grows into different roles. The older an actor becomes, the more challenging the acting becomes. For this DVD-ROM, we had to change the traditional holistic way of teaching. Chapters and subchapters were established to create a learning cycle from theory to practice, and vice versa. In *Improvisation Technologies* there were no links from stage performance to theory but *That's Kyogen!* was entirely based on this feature.

NAGARIKA

In summer 2000, during the CELLBYTES digital dance workshop at Arizona State University, I met Jayachandran Palazhy, the artistic director of Attakkalari, the Centre for Movement Arts and Mixed Media in Bangalore. Since then we have collaborated on various projects for the stage as well as on *NAGARIKA*, a series of DVD-ROMs based on traditional Indian dance teaching techniques. *NAGARIKA* is a heritage preservation project using digital technology for transmission. The initiative received support from the Daniel Langlois Foundation in Canada, the Goethe Institute, the Art Foundation in Japan, and the Ford Foundation in India. Palazhy formed a small interactive media design and development team that included Japanese media artist Matsuo Kunihiko, programmer Junji Koyanagi, local videographers, editors, and myself. *NAGARIKA 1* (2006), introduces the practice of Bharatanatyam and *NAGARIKA 2* (2010) introduces the Kalaripayatthu dance. Due to legal issues only the second DVD-ROM is available to the public.

2006—NAGARIKA 1: Bharatanatyam

The first *NAGARIKA* DVD-ROM is about Bharatanatyam dance. Indian dance training has always been strictly oral, transmitted through spoken instructions, supported by vocal singing and beats of clapping hands. Therefore we designed the *NAGARIKA* project around verbal instruction given by six masters and teachers. Palazhy himself had been a dance student to some of the senior teachers and *NAGARIKA* is a tribute to his teachers. The DVD-ROM contains recordings of teachers from various schools with introductions to and perspectives on Bharatanatyam technique, explaining movements, time, rhythm, and the role of music in demonstrating the movements.

48 Chris Ziegler

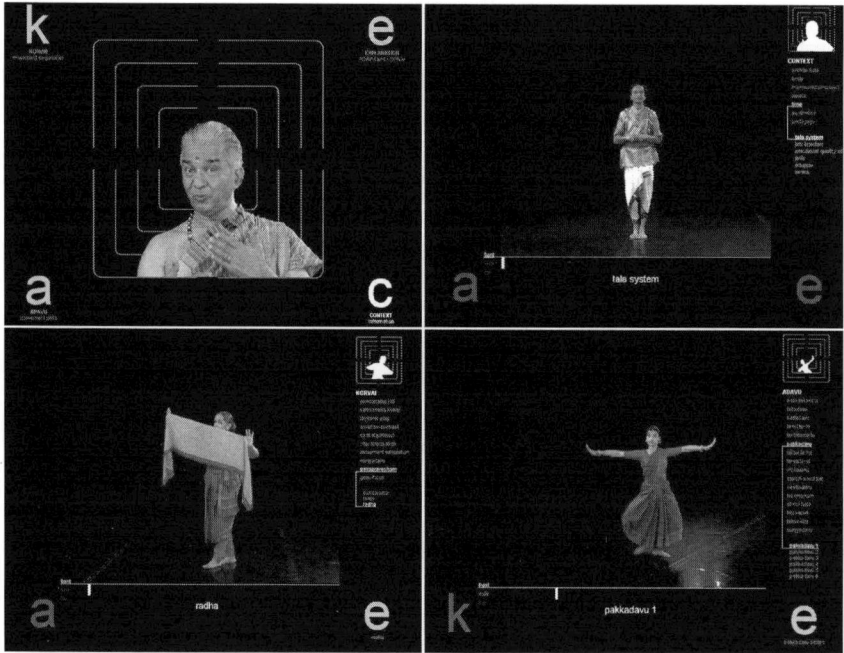

FIGURE 4.5   *NAGARIKA 1 Bharatanatyam* (2006) showing V.P. Dhananjayan, Prof. C.V. Chandrashekhar, Deepti Rajesh of Bharatakalanjali, Shantha Dhananjayan. Screenshots by Chris Ziegler.

The design of the title screen of the DVD-ROMs relates to floor patterns of Indian temples (the *Bharatanatyam* DVD-ROM) and the *Kalaripayatthu* training pit (the *Kalaripayatthu* DVD-ROM), both training spaces in which areas are dedicated to rituals and ceremonies. Palazhy considered these floor plans an appropriate metaphor for dance and how it is located in Indian traditions. During the days that India was colonized by the British, traditional Indian dance was banned. *Bharatanatyam*, a dance by women, was considered sexually explicit. Many *Kalaripayatthu* schools had to close down and "Kalari Pits" were destroyed because the dance has its roots in medieval martial arts fight training traditions for soldiers and such training was deemed a threat to the British.

The interface designed for the *Bharatanatyam* DVD-ROM was similar to the basic layout of the Forsythe's *Improvisation Technologies* CD-ROM, linking short lectures to movement sequences. They are different however in terms of complexity. The *Bharatanatyam* DVD-ROM includes short lectures with movement demonstrations and explanations of movement techniques. Each movement demonstration is divided into short movement units (Bharatanatyam/Kalaripayatthu: ADAVU) and movement sequences (Bharatanatyam: KORVAI/Kalaripayatthu: MURA). Next to oral introductions of each movement technique there is also a context section. Lectures were divided into two parts: "explanations" of movement and "context" of dance. Both are linked to excerpts of short movement units and longer sequences. Although teachers sometimes gave recurrent context introductions to Bharatanatyam, each of the teachers' individual way of explaining movement ideas were unique, reflecting the manifold character of Indian movement culture. On the *Bharatanatyam* DVD-ROM space was allocated for context explanations on architecture and the view on body, time, and the space, remarks on aesthetics and the pedagogy of dance training. On the *Kalaripayatthu* DVD-ROM the "Context" chapter presents three Kalari schools, founded in the Southwest of India in different traditions and thoughts on oral commands in the practice of Kalaripayatthu.

We discussed the possibility of visually highlighting expressive gestures and facial communications, eyes and head movement and many other expressive body skills by adding graphics to video, similar to *Improvisation Technologies*. In an opening scene of *Bharatanatyam* a dancer very often "creates" the stage by eye movement from left to right, followed by a panning arm movement. The audience "reads" this combined gesture as the opening of a scene like raising an imagined curtain. In *Improvisation Technologies* we used rotoscoping techniques, animating lines on top of video images as a tool to follow movements, constructing space over time. On the *Bharatanatyam* DVD-ROM we tried a similar approach, using graphics on top of movement gestures. Palazhy however argued that the key to understanding Indian dance is to start from its temporal structure. These rhythm exercises are expressed by singing and hand gestures. Indian dance also involves the knowledge

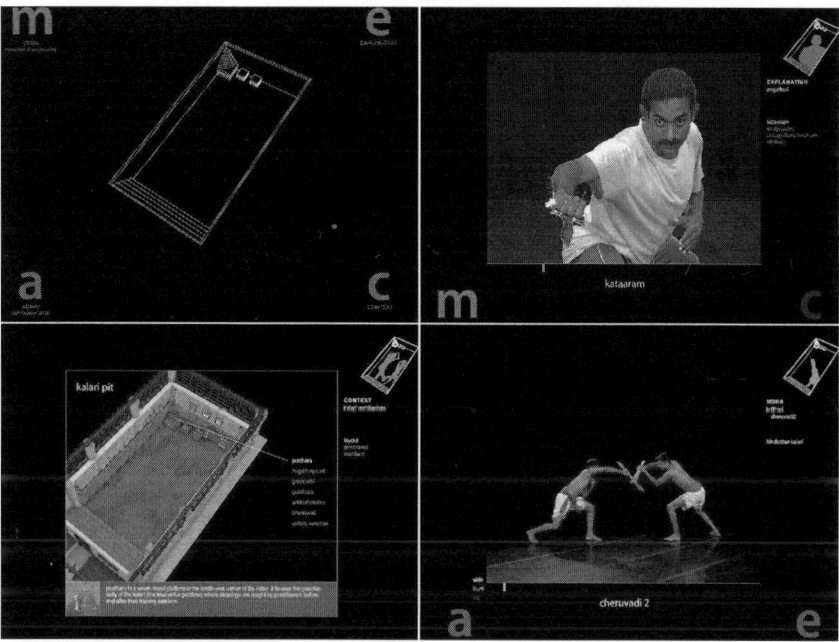

FIGURE 4.6   *NAGARIKA 2 Kalaripayatthu* (2010), showing G. Sathyanarayanan Gurukkal, Rajesh and Sreejesh of Hindustan Kalari. Screenshots by Chris Ziegler.

of different non-linear time scales. In order to understand the complex temporalities it is necessary to practice the vocalization of beats. Teachers use singing, hand gestures, and finger clapping to recall very complex temporal structures. We designed watches with different graphic scales layered on top of each other. The results however were not satisfactory, because the temporal layers, and the variations in Indian music and the dance traditions, were too complex to explain with a simple graphical metaphor. Hence we decided to not work with graphics.

2010—NAGARIKA 2: Kalaripayatthu

Kalaripayatthu dance is one of the world oldest movement art forms. It was developed around the eleventh century as a training and healing practice for soldiers. It was taught in many schools in Kerala, a southwestern Indian state. Buddhist monks moving north across the Himalayas brought the training to new areas. Taekwondo and other forms of martial arts evolved from it.

Movements in Kalaripayatthu are derived from mimicking animal movements. The aim is to inherit their qualities, like the strength of the elephant, the speed of the serpent, and the agility of the tiger. Learning animal movements improves flexibility and invited the spirits of the animals into the bodies of the soldiers improving their strength. The dancers also learn to fight using a long wooden stick before they use metal swords. The ultimate weapon in martial arts however is to fight with bare hands. Training happens in a training pit. The architecture of the pit sets the training below earth level. There is no ceiling, which allows for air circulation and works like an air conditioner system. In the corners and on the walls there is space for religious objects and weapons.

The training pit is the basis for the design of the DVD-ROM. A stylized wireframe image shows a traditional Kalaripayatthu training pit. Each corner of the screen provides entry points into chapters, connecting two practice chapters on the left side to the two theory chapters on the opposite side of the screen. *Adavu* and *Korvais* movement units and complex movement examples were linked to verbal explanations and context information. Several teachers of various schools provide introductions to the art of training in Kalaripayatthu, some in their native language, Malayalam, with English subtitles. The verbal commands and instructions given to the dancers executing long phrases of movement sequences in the training sessions were set as chapter titles. For example, "kai nivarthi kootti thozhuthu madakki nettikku pidichu amarnnu" is a chapter which explains the "meipayattu randaam mura/methari" movement, following the Hindustan Kalari School tradition in Kerala next to movements demonstrated by Choorakkody Kalari and CVN Kalari. All these schools are based in the north or the central area of Kerala in the southwest of India.

New interfaces

Improvisation Technologies was the first digital publication of dance knowledge and became a point of reference and inspiration for many other projects—including

Forsythe's own *Synchronous Objects* and *Motion Bank*. Between 1994 and around 2011, many more CD-ROMs and DVD-ROMs appeared on the market, illuminating the complex relations between theory and practice in the work of different dance makers and dance traditions.

As member of the Academia Mobile Group of Emio Greco | PC dance company 2006–2007 I worked with dancer and researcher Bertha Bermúdez Pascual and Fréderique Bévilaqua of the IRCAM (Paris) on the DVD-ROM *Double Skin/Double Mind*. We used Gesture Follower algorithms, which later were used in the *Double Skin/Double Mind* interactive installation discussed in Chapter 9 of this volume.

At the time *Improvisation Technologies* was created internet data transfer was too slow for transmitting videos. CD-ROMs and DVD-ROMs provided easy access to comprehensive video based interactive knowledge systems in dance. Today, access to this material is easier now. Unauthorized uploads of *Improvisation Technologies* on YouTube can be accessed online from everywhere in the world. Web resources are more dynamic and can be updated, whereas the content of a CD-ROM or DVD-ROM is much more fixed and the production is more costly. It took almost five years to decide on the final release of the *Improvisation Technologies* CD-ROM. But the object character of CD-ROM or DVD-ROM publication generated a final and reliable knowledge base for research on movement systems in younger history.

***

William Forsythe: Improvisation Technologies. A Tool for the Analytical Dance Eye (CD-ROM) Produced at ZKM, Karlsruhe. Distributed by Hatje Cantz Publishers (ISBN 978-3-7757-2184-4). First release 1999, technical updates released 2003 and 2012.

Mansaku & Mansai: That's Kyogen (DVD-ROM). Initiated by Waseda University and Tokyo Media Connections. Produced by Karlsruhe: ZKM/Zentrum für Kunst und Medientechnologie Karlsruhe, 2001. Published by Kadokawa Shoten Publishing Co. LTF, Tokyo Japan (ISBN 04-906225-9).

Kalarippayattu—An Interactive DVD (in the series *NAGARIKA—An Integrated Information System on Indian Physical Traditions*). Produced by Attakkalari Centre for Movement Arts, Bangalore, directed by Jayachandran Palazhy, supported by Ford Foundation.

See: http://www.nagarika.attakkalari.org.

Notes

1 In the production also involved were Volker Kuchelmeister (programming) and Yvonne Mohr (graphics).
2 Again with Volker Kuchelmeister (programming) and Yvonne Mohr with Andreas Kratky (graphics) joining the team.

5

A CHOREOGRAPHER'S SCORE
Anne Teresa De Keersmaeker

Bojana Cvejić

Prior to establishing the ground for the (already realized) three-volume series titled *A Choreographer's Score*, the initial idea for the project of setting Anne Teresa De Keersmaeker's choreographies into scores was sparked by a question De Keersmaeker addressed to me. I'll paraphrase: "I am reviving my four early works in which I myself will dance for the last time. Is this an occasion to write these choreographies down?" *Fase, Four Movements to the Music of Steve Reich* (1982), *Rosas danst Rosas* (1983), *Elena's Aria* (1984), and *Bartók/Mikrokosmos* (originally called *Mikrokosmos*, 1987) were to be performed in a row for the first time, thus enabling a certain genealogical insight into four distinct strands in the substantial oeuvre of De Keersmaeker and her dance company Rosas, each of which stems from these four "early works."[1] *Fase* stands out as a programmatic manifesto of post-minimalist, post-Judson formal-abstract "concert of dance."[2] Apart from blending daily movements and gestures and putatively "pure" dancing into an idiom emblematic of Rosas in the 1980s, *Rosas danst Rosas* introduces a novel synthesis of rigorous formal-structural composition and dramaturgical development of an evening-long piece into European dance. *Elena's Aria* points to the theatrical strain close to Pina Bausch's Tanztheater, and the choreography to Bartók's String Quartet no. 4 unravels De Keersmaeker's most distinctive contribution to contemporary dance: a serious choreographic commitment to modern and contemporary music in times when the structural partnering between dance and music is no longer self-evident. Beyond the self-reflective quest of coherence in a single oeuvre, the retrospective inquiry intended to explore De Keersmaeker's legacy of advancing four seminal directions in European contemporary dance (rigorous choreographic formalism, structural relationship to music, a method of dramatization and theatrical expression). This would be my rationale for the choreographer's primary motivation for initiating this project.

However, the reasons that prompted me to undertake the role of a dance researcher who will combine the competencies of musicology, practical dramaturgy, and performance theory in order to design a "choreographic score" stem from my discontent with dance education. The transmission of dance repertoire is still much too "technocentric," privileging the technical import of what it means to dance a bodily movement cut from the historical, contextual, and poietical aspects integral to the actual dance form and technique. For reasons of specialism and efficiency, the oral-mimetic regime in learning dance repertoire prevails, harking back to the tradition of the classical dance "masterclass": dancers imitate and repeat movements from the ideal ("authentic") image represented by the choreographer or licensed dancer. Observing the transmission of repertoire by Rosas, Trisha Brown Company, and William Forsythe at P.A.R.T.S., the school founded in 1994 and run by De Keersmaeker, I wondered whether, in the case of studying the choreographies of Rosas in the close vicinity of the choreographer herself, the technical instruction of dance movement could be supplemented with a more comprehensive inquiry into the choreography of these performances. Scoring De Keersmaeker's early works in particular held an additional advantage in store: the students might better learn from how the choreographer taught herself as an autodidact; in a word, they would do better were they given tools to emulate the choreographic thought, instead of mainly imitating the aesthetic attributes of a style. From this wager, two questions followed which framed this project as research: what constitutes choreography in these particular works and how could choreographic parameters be rearticulated as a matter of writing, *écriture* in the poststructuralist sense? How to investigate and conceive that choreographic writing *in a score*?

More than a self-rotating wheel, dance

Before I unfold the method, format, structure, and material of *A Choreographer's Score*, a few more remarks about the resonance of these questions in a broader context of this project are necessary. Over the last decade, which has also been characterized by the "educational turn" in the arts (Rogoff), a keen interest in developing modes of documenting, archiving, and transmitting contemporary dance emerged in Europe and North America in concert with new digital technologies. Three projects (all three of them also represented in this volume) were referential for *A Choreographer's Score*: William Forsythe's *Improvisation Technologies* (CD-ROM, 1999), Emio Greco | PC's *Inside Movement Knowledge* (2008), and *Synchronous Objects* (2009) by Forsythe and his collaborators. What resonated with De Keersmaeker's intentions was an urge among her peers to reflect on their methods and tools and also share them with a larger readership outside of the discipline, as can be observed in the following remark Forsythe made: "Perhaps our practices are outdated or can be improved. How can we doubt our own processes and question our own methods?" (in DeLahunta "Talking about Scores", 136).

De Keersmaeker belongs to the generation of choreographers from the 1980s who for a long time have mistrusted the theoretical incursion of interpretative discourses, as if words threatened to "dirty" their dance, as Pina Bausch once famously said (Bausch in Huxley and Witts, 57). Therefore, her wish and readiness now to formulate all she could remember and convey about the creation and choreography of her performances, attests to a mature awareness of the importance of disseminating knowledge about dance beyond its hermetic specialism. Perhaps it is time that choreographers and dancers who have been drawing on the sources of other arts and sciences contributed with their specific practices—choreographic ideas and techniques about the body, movement and time—to other disciplines. However, dance, in comparison to music, visual arts, theater, and cinema, suffers, for that matter, from a significant lack of self-reflective writing that would illuminate choreography as an authorial poietics, and eventually mediate between mute video-recordings of dance practitioners' technical know-how. Dance would then be more than a "wheel that turns on itself"—a visual metaphor Alain Badiou uses to describe dance's autonomy as self-referential closure (Badiou, 58). This may be said more bluntly: in order for dance to be "taken seriously," it needs to take itself seriously. The more *amateurs de danse*, scholars, and artists from a variety of disciplines can learn from choreographers and dancers about their notions and methods, the more complex, sophisticated, discriminating, or adequate their experiences and thoughts about dance might become. It is perhaps the duty of dance specialists to provide or facilitate a comprehensive access into, as well as a transfer of, their own poietics and praxis.

Method for a "choreographic score"

The creation of *A Choreographer's Score* began with an attempt to conversationally exhaust the knowledge surrounding the construction of the choreography of De Keersmaeker's first piece, *Fase*. My first task was to draft questions for this interview on the basis of my analysis of the work as well as my research of the archival documentation. I examined all available documents about the given work—the abundant archive of Rosas that not only encompasses working materials, numerous notebooks containing sketches, drawings, schemes, and all kinds of notes, program brochures, reviews, technical lists, budget calculations, letters to cultural officials, but also offers a slice of private life in the margins of the work, as in diary notes and personal letters. The "archeological" findings unraveled problems or clues pointing to what was invisible in the work alone. Hence they helped me formulate questions about the genealogy of the project, about aborted ideas, discarded materials, tasks to achieve, unresolved problems, and dilemmas. These questions triggered a dialogue in which De Keersmaeker and I tried to lay out the work in everything that constitutes it. A pronounced yet unspectacular setup akin to a lesson—a triangle of two chairs and a blackboard on which De Keersmaeker made her drawings and schemes—enabled me to persistently ask questions and the choreographer to burst into dancing at ease, demonstrating movements that I could re-identify while watching the performance several times, both in recordings and live.

The first interview generated the method that we subsequently followed in the process of scoring eight choreographies in all three volumes. The first step consisted in my mapping out the choreographic parameters according to an analysis of the performance, including the information I derived from exhaustive notes and documents from the archive. The first interview comprises the choreographer's first answers to these questions. It is also the moment when De Keersmaeker recollects not only the exact circumstances that precipitated her decisions, but also the feelings, moods, events, places, people, and stories that make up the life-fabric of processes of creation. After reexamining the result of the first interview together with my analysis of the choreography, I conceived the script for a second interview. Then follows the second interview, in which the conversation is classified into thematic sections by those topics that prove to be relevant for the examined choreography. This is also the moment when the choreographic structure is "scored" as it unfolds in a chronological order of sections from the outset to the end of the performance. Both conversations are taped, and eventually the second interview provides the base for a video. In the editing of the video, dancers' demonstrations and excerpts from the performance recordings together with any relevant documentary footage are interpolated to supplement practical demonstrations of De Keersmaeker's account.

In the next step, the two interview transcripts provide the basis for reconstituting choreography in writing. In order for this text to become a written score, it is checked for its accuracy and reedited for comprehensibility. Secondly, the choreographer and I prepare synthetic schemes, diagrams, and drawings with which the choreographer annotates the text in her own pen. We also select photos from the performances and rehearsals, and eventually have additional photography made for the purpose of illustrating the verbal explanation in concrete detail. Each chapter is appended with a selection of documents from the archive: program notes, reviews, notes from De Keersmaeker's notebooks, letters. This aspect of documentation is inspired by Yvonne Rainer's *Work 1961–1973*, in particular, her principle of radically juxtaposing heterogeneous elements: "categories of things" that "have varying degrees of emotional load" (unknown reference). The result is a book-cum-video (in DVDs), or an expanded hybrid publication which reconstitutes the work of dance from a choreographic point of view. It is comprised of a narrative account about the creation process, a presentation of main choreographic and dramaturgical ideas, compositional principles and dance techniques, linear formal analysis of the entire work abounding in technical detail about the choreographic structure, photography, drawings, documentary materials, and video.

What renders this publication a choreographic score, and as what kind of score does it qualify? Firstly, the main text with photographs and drawings enables one to *read* the choreography on its own terms (i.e., in a language that clarifies its own rules). As a score, it doesn't provide the full-fledged notation of the dance from instant to instant in the ways that Labanotation aspires to do. In other words, it would be impossible to reconstitute *Fase* from the *Choreographer's Score* alone, without recourse to the video recording of the work or precise instructions about how to embody the movement itself given by a dancer who has performed the piece. Being just one of the three elements required to reconstitute the dance (next to video and studio instruction), the publication is nevertheless a score, one that could be compared to the idiosyncratic writing of twentieth- and twenty-first-century contemporary music. Composers from Anestis Logothetis to Helmut Lachenmann have devised scores tailored in individual works to experimentation with sound material and instrumental techniques. Secondly, *A Choreographer's Score* is comparable to a familiar format for publishing music in print: the "critical edition" of a musical work. The scholarly or critical edition employs careful scholarship—historical knowledge, deductive skills, and artistic practice—in an attempt to edit music as closely to the so-called composer's original intentions as possible, and to reconstruct the contextual margins that are missing from the composer's manuscript. Critical editions of music often include footnotes or critical reports that describe discrepancies between various editions or performance practices. My footnotes don't try to diverge from the main text by all means possible; instead they appear in order to clarify a phrase or a reference regarded as common or tacit knowledge, or inform about the people and places that contributed to the creation of the works, or offer more specialist accounts about topics of reference (for instance, on the origin of Ars subtilior in musicology, see note 9 in *En Atendant & Cesena: A Choreographer's Score*.

In search of a choreographer's poetics

A Choreographer's Score seems to respond to two aims identified in the projects discussed in this book. Firstly, it documents each work in a thoroughly analytical and interpretative manner from the perspective of the choreographer as its "chief" author. Secondly, it develops choreographic parameters from the studied choreographies, and hence produces generative tools which can be tested and implemented beyond De Keersmaeker's oeuvre. Yet, it isn't a manual of choreographic craftsmanship or a handbook of practical exercises designated for dance students and artists. Beyond this project's pedagogical and historical missions lies the goal of formulating De Keersmaeker's choreographic poietics: a reflection on the choreographic thinking that motivates and comprehends the creation of dance in an oeuvre that in this case entails the logos of structural methods. By choreographic poietics I mean the art of making dance performances in analogy with the poietics of composers in twentieth-century modern music, as in the canonical examples of Igor Stravinsky (*Poétique musicale*, 1942) or Arnold Schoenberg (*Fundamentals of Musical Composition*, 1967 and *Style and Idea*, 1975). There are, exceptionally, only a few specimens of this genre in dance literature, such as Rainer's aforementioned *Work*,[3] that could be compared with composers' writings on poietics. Therefore, I considered my own function to be the articulation of De Keersmaeker's methods and intuitions into a poietics, a more or less coherent set of ideas, concepts, and methodological parameters, which I will briefly outline next.

The order and variety of the concepts and parameters change in each of the three volumes, attesting to an evolving conception of choreography throughout three distinct periods: "early works" (1981–1986), which focuses on the self-learning of an autodidact choreographer; *Drumming* (1998) and *Rain* (2001), which mark the mid-point of a mature choreographic *écriture*; and *En Atendant* (2010) and *Cesena* (2012), which feature De Keersmaeker's most recent exploration of counterpoint in music and dance, among other choreographic concerns. These concepts and parameters fall under three temporally consecutive categories: the horizon of initial ideas, intentions, and constraints prior to the creation; the choreographic structure of the dance (in its development and its finished shape); and "post-hoc dramaturgy" concerning the performance, its interpretation, and retrospective consideration.[4]

The first category concerns identifying *the heuristic mission* in the creation of each performance: De Keersmaeker elaborates her primary intention through a task of producing constraints that will drive the creation toward overcoming an initial difficulty. For example, in the case of *Violin Phase*, her goal was to learn to choreograph by herself with the compositional tools that she would develop by exploring Reich's composition while dancing to it. In *Drumming*, it was the challenge of composing a dance to a more than hour-long piece of contemporary music, operating like a relentless machine. In *En Atendant* and *Cesena*, the problem was more complex and multifaceted: how to set the highly sophisticated polyphonic style of early renaissance music into a dance, whereby dancers and musicians are both dancing and singing outdoors in natural light. De Keersmaeker, like any other author, wasn't all alone in her choreographic decisions. Hence the parameter that involves tracing the choreographer's *intercesseurs*, to borrow Gilles Deleuze's term for his collaboration with Guattari as a mediator who helps discover one's "unknowns" (Deleuze, 125). For instance, the composer Thierry De Mey, whom De Keersmaeker dubs her "musical dealer," not only helped her develop her compositional methods in the early works but also directed her attention to the musics she could explore in future; or the dramaturge Marianne Van Kerkhoven was responsible for metanarrative frameworks and literary materials; or Björn Schmelzer, director of *GraindelaVoix*, encouraged a heterodox contemporary approach to old period music; or one could also note the more remote presence of conceptual personae like Trisha Brown, whose *Set and Reset* unraveled the power of monothematic architectonics in dance. In all these cases, it wasn't only significant to reveal the voices of those numerous others who are indispensable to the enterprise of each project, despite its strong single authorship. It was equally necessary to show the role of intertextual and contextual specifics in forging De Keersmaeker's *technē* while becoming an author.

Most of the choreographic parameters are to be found in the second category, the first set of which pertains to *macrostructural decisions*: the decisions that determine the global frame of the dance. In the first place, these include the choice of music, which apart from more specific aspects of that musical composition entails defining its function (structural, dramaturgical, narrative etc.) and formal presentation (live performance in concert, played back or appropriated); and the *spatial design*, rooted in a geometrical framework which is either static, or more often evolves in the dynamic of the choreographic organization of the perception of the space.⁵ Analogous to the spatial development is the *timeline plan* of the whole, which regulates the distribution of levels of intensity in the experience of the duration of choreography: a composition of a curve of attention, indicating peaks and anticlimaxes, moments of contrast or of recapitulation. The fourth set of macrostructural decisions relates to the *main working method* or the logos of the composition: is the choreography constructed on the basis of one formal principle, (e.g., a basic phrase informing many other parameters, such as vocabulary, syntax, counterpoint, and spatial design)? Such logic of the method qualifies for an integral, monothematic composition, as in *Drumming*, in which the phrase acts as a veritable *pars pro toto*. Or, alternatively, is the piece composed in divergent sections according to other criteria (e.g., through a metanarrative background of hidden stories or images as in *Cesena*, whose music secretly recounts the history of the calamitous fourteenth century)?

The next three parameters treat the formal aspects of dance movement. *Genesis of movements* describes the most intriguing quest for (an often opaque) origin of movements, not only in how the vocabulary was devised, but with what mindset it was conceived. Hence, a great difference can be noted from the peculiar blend of daily movements, gestures, and formal abstract dancing that is emblematic of an early Rosas intent on dancing their "feminine selves" in the 1980s, to the recent choreographies' rearticulation of bodily schema according to three centers of motion (head, torso, and pelvis) inspired by Leonardo's Vitruvian man.

After genesis of movement, *syntax* is another vital parameter, the importance of which is often misrecognized in reconstructions.⁶ Understanding how movements connect and what determines their flow is probably the most difficult technical aspect to studying dance, simply because it isn't merely technical. What fills the gap between two movements or makes them flow uninterruptedly as one bound motion is a matter of desire, belief, and a choreographic unconscious; what is often referred to as "energy" is no less than ideology's stake in a movement. This is why discerning the structural principles of the movement syntax—for example, the distinctions between a "series" and a "phrase" in early works, or the principles "my walking is my dancing" and "my talking is my dancing" in the recent works—requires an intricate analysis from which a more conceptual understanding of how a movement is to be performed can arise.

After syntax, *counterpoint* is a key element of composition at which De Keersmaeker excels. It details the effect of the distribution of movements among dancers upon the "texture" of the dance, combining the musical technique of superimposing divergent lines (of voices or parts, that is, bodies, polyphony) with the geometrical patterns appearing from many bodies dancing together as if to form a fabric. Again, the insight into the three series of choreographies demonstrates a development from more didactic principles of the so-called strict counterpoint (superimposition of the same material, as in canons) to a more complex apparatus of the vocal-kinetic three-part counterpoint derived from the music of the late fourteenth century that a simultaneously singing and walking body produces.

Two poietic parameters intervene in the making of a choreography, yet are reflected a posteriori. In most of the works studied by *A Choreographer's Score*, dramaturgy reveals a metanarrative component: an imaginarium that "nourishes" the formal-structural framework. De Keersmaeker is reluctant about sharing it with an audience for whom the narrative background remains hidden. While in some of the early works, as well as in those performances that acted as theatrical laboratories of excess from which abstract and formally stringent, condensed and unified pieces of pure dance were distilled (*Drumming* and *Rain* after *Just Before*, 1997 and *In Real Time*, 2000), narration emerged through textual utterances. Whereas in the later works, as well as in the reworked versions of *Bartók Aantekeningen* (1986), text is altogether omitted, as if it would reveal the mark of past times and outdatedness. Transforming text into a compositional tool, the choreographer provides a pragmatic rationale for its function. In a large-scale setup of these choreographies, not every moment or point can be set. A way to set up a game by which the whole space will choreograph itself is meant to provide dancers with a framework of rules and tasks they can apply at their discretion. Narrative indications and images motivate formal tasks with additional character and provide consistency to dancers' behavior. At best, they might suggest intensity or color of movement. Or they might flash in a tableau emerging from a more abstract configuration of movement. The concrete meaning of their vividness remains with the dancers, while their form may animate spectatorial imagination.

Such explanation links the tool with the *material* unfolded in the documentary appendix to the text of the score. The term "material" has had a peculiar status in choreographic and performance methodology, since performance makers understand each other well when they operate with a notion that appears so underdetermined and jargonized. The usage defines the term here. De Keersmaeker's materials range from concepts to things, from bodily movements to literary, philosophical and theoretical texts, from music to films, from clothes to furniture. They are materials in the sense that they look back and give material resistance to actions; they may not make it into the composition, yet they shape its imaginarium, a zone of influence which is not only felt, but also retraceable in the material.

The other post-hoc parameter addresses the role of dancing and the *performance-style* aspects in choreographic poietics. The co-creative role of individual dancers is recognized for shaping idiosyncratic movement idioms, and the choreographer demonstrates how she composes *with* the dancers, on the basis of their materials. Another element of the performance-style is the relationship between the working process and the final product: the spectrum of ways that the performance mirrors the rehearsal. Lastly, the choreographer observes the differences in transmitting some of these performances to new casts of Rosas or other dance ensembles.

Practicing *A Choreographer's Score*

Until now, the three volumes have been probed in both academic scholarship and dance practice programs. The books with DVDs have been included in the curricula of dance and performance studies programs in which they are studied as part of the history of contemporary dance as well as literature on choreographic poietics.[7] In master programs of dance, they have been the focus of methodological inquiry in workshops in which dance students exercise their own appropriation and adaptation of De Keersmaeker's choreographic procedures. What remains to be further investigated is a dancer's score of De Keersmaeker/Rosas choreographies. This would not only complement (and probably diverge from) *A Choreographer's Score*, but it would also enable access for further, "external" interpretation of the oeuvre of Rosas, relativizing the ontological priority of choreographer's insight as a kind of first-hand knowledge with respect to theoretical "second-hand" readings.

De Keersmaeker and I have been offering numerous public sessions as part of the tour of performances, in which the books are presented with the choreographer dancing with a spoken commentary, or with the Rosas dancers showing a fragment of the piece with De Keersmaeker's live commentary. In those talks, usually moderated by a local *intercesseur* of De Keersmaeker's work, a lay audience is initiated into the intricacies of choreography. Wouldn't it be a rewarding achievement if one day dance were to attain an audience that could also read and reason about, and not just fetishistically admire, the sublime bodies of dance?

***

Anne Teresa de Keersmaeker and Bojana Cvejić

- *A Choreographer's Score: Fase, Rosas Danst Rosas, Elena's Aria, Bartók*. Brussels: Rosas & Mercatorfonds, 2012.
- *En Atendant & Cesena: A Choreographer's Score*. Brussels: Rosas & Mercatorfonds, 2013.
- *A Choreographer's Score: Drumming & Rain*. Brussels: Rosas & Mercatorfonds, 2014.

Notes

1 De Keersmaeker's oeuvre under the name of her dance company Rosas comprises more than forty works made since 1981.
2 Dance concert is a conventional American term for an evening of several shorter dance performances by one or more choreographers in the 1960s and 1970s.
3 Doris Humphrey's book *The Art of Making Dances* (1957) is the most notable self-reflective piece of writing about modern dance by a contemporary of Stravinsky and Schoenberg. However, it is a technical guide to choreographic composition and contains too few indices of the poietical or aesthetic concepts of that choreographer, or of modern dance in general.
4 I'm adapting the term "post-hoc dramaturgy" from the theatermaker Goran Sergej Pristaš as an opportunity to immediately reflect on how initial ideas, problems, or fantasies are resolved in certain compositions and then how these compositions continue to operate *after* the works have been completed.
5 Throughout the three volumes, the development of the spatial aspect of choreography can be traced from a minimalist structural viewpoint in the early works to the ideas of order

rooted in "sacred geometry" and Taoism (the ideal proportions in the Fibonacci sequence and the golden section, Platonic solids, "the magic square," etc.).
6 Reconstructions based on photographic sources often suffer from arrested movements, static poses and animated tableaus that lack the life of motion, just as words without the grammar of a syntax would impede or obscure the meaning of a sentence. This is evidenced in Milicent Hodson's reconstruction of Vaslav Nijinsky's *Rite of Spring*.
7 Performance Studies program at New York University, Tisch School; Master in Choreography and Performance at the Institute for Applied Theater Studies at the University of Giessen.

References

Badiou, Alain. *Inaesthetics*. London: Verso, 2005.
Bausch, Pina. "Not How People Move but What Moves Them," *The Twentieth-Century Performance Reader*. Ed. Michael Huxley and Noel Witts. London: Routledge, 1996. 53–60.
DeLahunta, Scott (ed.) *Capturing Intention: Documentation, Analysis, and Notation Research Based on the Work of Emio Greco | PC*. Amsterdam: Emio Greco | PC and AHK/Lectoraat, 2007.
DeLahunta, Scott, Rebecca Groves, and Norah Shaw Zuniga. "Talking About Scores: William Forsythe's vision for a new form of dance 'literature'," *Knowledge in Motion*. Ed. Sabine Gehm, Pirkko Husemann, and Katharina von Wilcke. London and New Brunswick: Transaction, 2007. 91–100.
Deleuze, Gilles. *Negotiations*. Trans. Martin Joughin. New York: Columbia University Press, 1990.
Forsythe, William, and Christine Bürckle. *William Forsythe Improvisation Technologies: A Tool for the Analytical Eye*. Special issue, 2nd ed. Karlsruhe and Ostfildern: ZKM and Hatje Cantz Verlag, 2003.
Rainer, Yvonne. *Work 1961–1973*. Halifax: Press of the Nova Scotia College of Art and Design, 1974.
Rogoff, Irit. "Turning". *e-flux* #0 (2008/11), available at http://www.e-flux.com/journal/turning/, accessed April 2015.
Schoenberg, Arnold. *Fundamentals of Musical Composition*. New York: St. Martin's Press, 1967.
—— *Style and Idea*. Ed. L. Stein, trans. L. Black. New York: St. Martin's Press, 1975.
Stravinsky, Igor. *Poétique musicale*. Paris: Flammarion, 1942/2000.
Synchronous Objects for One Flat Thing, Reproduced (2009), available at http://synchronousobjects.osu.edu, accessed April 2015.

6

ARCHIVING THE DANCE

Making *Siobhan Davies Replay*

Sarah Whatley

Siobhan Davies Replay is the first digital dance archive of its kind in the UK and one of the first worldwide. It provides online access to multi-media content (video, text, audio, image) as well as a comprehensive collection of materials that document the creative dance making process. The archive is designed to invite new ways to explore the content and provides tools to create new kinds of digital objects. The idea for the project first emerged in 2005 when there were a handful of online catalogues of dance but very few collections that included actual dance content, and no freely available digital dance archives, so it began its development with few external reference points or models to consult. Work on the archive began in 2007 and it was launched in June 2009 after 30 months of development.

Siobhan Davies is widely regarded as one of Britain's most cherished and respected choreographers. Her career began in the early 1970s at the very beginnings of contemporary dance in Britain. Providing access to her output would not only enable users to see the development of an individual artist's choreographic oeuvre, but would offer a valuable gateway to the broader history of contemporary dance in Britain, and the role Davies has played in shaping that history. As a researcher with a history of closely observing Davies' work[1] I became increasingly aware of the difficulties of accessing records of dance in performance. Having a relationship with Davies prior to the archive project meant I was able to borrow VHS copies of dances from the company for my own research and teaching needs, but I was keenly aware that these were not widely available and there were virtually no ways to easily locate, identify, or retrieve any documentation of her work. Records of her work in the public domain were limited to a handful of commercially available videos and published commentaries, critiques, and reviews of her live (performance) events. Because of this absence of records I suggested to Davies that we might join forces to build her archive; to collect and organize the many videos, photographs, and many other traces of her work that she held herself.

A series of planning meetings confirmed for us that the principal aim should be to archive in order to make the work itself more accessible rather than to collect purely for the purpose of preservation, so we questioned what "archive" would mean in this context. Consequently, the decision was made to construct a digital archive that would be available to all. A successful bid to the Arts and Humanities Research Council in the UK[2] enabled us to begin work at the start of 2007, coinciding with Davies opening her new building in south London, Siobhan Davies Studios. The archive project provided Davies with the opportunity to reflect back on her work whilst the building prompted Davies to consider how going forward her practice might be influenced by her new physical environment. The parallel projects drew attention to the relationship between the physical and the virtual and provided fertile ground for a series of questions that motivated the development of the project, guiding the early stages of the archive's development. What does it mean for an artist to create, and be the subject of, a digital archive of their work? Does distributing the work online change how the work is "read" and might new meanings emerge because of having easy access to what were previously "lost" dances? And what wider impact will digital archives have on dance makers, performers, viewers; and on students, researchers, and our cultural institutions?

Building *Replay*

The first task was to assemble the research team at Coventry University. I recruited two co-researchers[3]; one to provide technical expertise and one to manage the process of gathering, organizing and gaining permissions to include content. Because there was no physical, hard copy archive to digitize, the archive was going to be "born digital," so one of the initial tasks was to decide on the content management structure. With no one on the team with prior experience of archiving, or of cataloguing, we proceeded somewhat naively, confident that the task was straightforward. In short, we needed to digitize the content, and build a back-end architecture and a front-end website. Whilst we actively sought advice from experienced archivists during the project development, our naivety meant that we were not deterred by the ambition of the project, or by warnings by several that the task was probably unachievable within the timeframe.

The project was supported by a very active steering group[4] and Scott deLahunta was our special advisor to the project; a relationship which led to some very productive links with other projects that were similarly developing online dance resources. deLahunta brought the *Replay* team together with the researchers involved in making these other resources for a parallel AHRC-funded workshop program: *Choreographic Objects; Traces and Artifacts of Physical Intelligence.*[5] Three intensive workshops over the course of a year allowed a valuable "retreat" from the hard work of making our "objects." We all welcomed the opportunity to learn from each other and think about the broader implications for our digital dance objects as they were emerging and taking hold in the dance practitioner and scholarly community. Sharing our experiences of working in the digital environment reinforced for us that each of the projects was doing something very particular, reflecting the "signature practices" of each dance artist. It confirmed that there were some common challenges but there was no repeatable model.

The project proceeded by working on the practical aspects, including the selection and organization of content, data management, digitization, interface design, and managing the collaborative aspects of the work. From the beginning there needed to be pragmatic decisions. With limited time and resources we decided to purchase a proprietary system for asset management because the "open source" alternatives at that time would have needed considerable specialist work, which was beyond the team's capacity.

Deciding on the metadata schema was another early decision we needed to make. We based the metadata on an expanded version of Dublin Core, adapting it to acknowledge the particularity of dance content, whilst trying to retain an economical structure. This was in itself challenging, reconciling the need for simplicity and searchability with Davies' desire to categorize content in relation to how content and contributors are specifically described as part of the production process. We realized that whilst there was a lot of expert knowledge in the team, some of the vital information we needed to collect resided with those artists directly involved in the work. Fortunately, we were able to recruit Deborah Saxon to the archive team. Saxon is a dancer who has worked with Davies for many years. She brought with her invaluable knowledge about the video content and was entrusted by Davies to select and edit where necessary, particularly when it concerned the more sensitive material that was being made public for the first time. The aim was always to include everything possible, but some decisions had to be made when there were several versions of the "same" content. Additionally, Davies was involved herself throughout the project and although much of the day-to-day work was delegated to her company manager,[6] she was active in all key decisions and provided a critical role in determining its overall design as a reflection on and further manifestation of her artistic vision. Consequently, the design of the front-end website needed consideration of the visual impact, functionality, and accessibility, as well as linkage with Davies' other web presence. We were concerned that the web interface should illuminate and not diminish the dance content. Agreeing that it should be an "open" resource also influenced the design. We were clear that whilst it could educate it should not be didactic in its form, so users coming with widely different interests and needs could find their own route through the archive. This meant working hard to find a balance between creating a highly designed, aesthetic object, and a user-friendly, easily searchable source of information.

Considerable time was spent solving issues of copyright and ownership. Dance is frequently co-created and brings together many contributing artists so we quickly realized that assumed ownership of content is often not the reality. Efforts were made to trace everyone who would be included in *Replay*, agreeing permissions with individual artists and content contributors, and negotiating licences with music publishers. In our discussions with dancers in particular we discovered that this unavoidable legal process can be unsettling and creates anxiety about what might happen to content once placed online. Audiences do not have ready access to much of dance's history, something which *Replay* was aiming to address. The digital archive was going to bring the past together with the present, collapsing time, which can be disturbing for those who feature in the archive and who have to re-engage with work that they thought was "lost" to the past. Experiences and memories resurface, sometimes in less than comfortable ways.

Engaging our users

As the principal aim of the project was to increase access to dance, and particularly to bring new viewers to dance who might discover it by searching for other artists, compositions, literary sources, and so on, testing the site was important as we neared the launch. The responses we received helped us to make modifications and to consider the range of "tools" we could add to assist users in navigating through the site, finding content and doing more with it. *Replay* includes a simple-to-use virtual scrapbook, which allows users to collect and reflect on their searches. A series of "guest scrapbooks" offer ready-made examples of how others have found and collected content, supported by personal narratives.

Our thinking about how we could draw users into the archive and provide a richer user experience, and at the same time expose something of the dance making process, led to the development of two microsites we call "kitchens," which "drill down" into two works, *Bird Song* (2004) and *In Plain Clothes* (2006). These kitchens provide materials from each member of the creative team to offer a unique insight to how a dance is formed; and how the "ingredients" of a dance are "cooked" and become the final dance. They are playful prototypes, offering a rare opportunity to see a visual representation of the creative process as it develops and becomes shaped into a final work.

Replay provides access to more than 5,500 core assets (which generate nearly 80,000 individual digital objects). The principal content is video to address the scarcity of readily available dance video content. Photographs, audio, and text (including journal articles, scholarly papers, and some Labanotation scores), as well as publicity and marketing materials are also available. Video extends back to the early 1970s and many of those early records are captured during theater performances, filmed front-on, so film quality is variable. *Replay* also provides an important collection of materials never before seen in the public domain, including a good number of "scratch tapes," made by the dancers themselves whilst making dance material in the studio. These "memory objects" offer users a valuable insight to the dancers' thinking process, showing the journey from studio to public event; documenting what is discarded and what remains. There are also draft designs, artist notes, and other material which tends to be lost or buried in the art making process, providing access to the contributions of all those who create the work; something which Davies has always been keen to acknowledge. Together they also reveal the precision of Davies' making process and the thinking that guides and shapes her choreographic method.

The whole site is publically available and free to access, although registration is required to access the scrapbook tool and as agreed with the dancers who are featured, the scratch tapes, to indicate that this content is principally for the "serious user." Much of the content was provided directly by Davies and her many collaborators. Additional content was sourced from other collections, including the Rambert Dance Company archive, the V&A Theatre Museum, and a few individuals who were happy to loan items for inclusion. We anticipated that more content would be sourced from private donors once the archive went "live" but relatively little has been found this way.

Throughout the archive's development there were frequent discussions about what to name it. Our ambition was always to make something living and interactive. Davies' view of what it is, how it looks, and how it represents the work is important; it reflects back on her work, changing what she does and how she makes new work as a result. Rather than existing simply as a static, "back catalogue" of her work, *Replay* would be more dynamic, growing and changing over time. As we neared the launch we wanted to make clear that it is much more than a website, and because there was increasing nervousness that "archive" would imply something dead and dusty, we decided to remove "archive" from the landing page and named the site *Replay*. Although it describes well the process of replaying work already made it has been confused with Davies' other web-presence, named *Relay*. Two years after the launch we have returned to the discussion and "archive" is now added as a strap-line to the landing page, acknowledging that it is a meaningful descriptor for the project, at the same time that *Relay* is disappearing as Davies' company website is redesigned.

Replay now and into the future

Replay continues to evolve so we can never describe it as finished. Putting aside the challenges of sustaining the archive beyond the period of funding, it was always our intention to add more content over time, to keep the archive fresh. Each new project is systematically added to the archive. But since launching the archive, Davies' work has shifted in new and quite radical directions. Moving out of the theater into galleries and other spaces that bring audience and performer closer together, Davies is now working with a broad range of arts practices and discipline experts. This means that her work is now quite different from that made for the theater, which provides interesting problems to solve for how this work is archived within the existing structure. As with any archive, the architecture needed to be decided early on in the process and this was determined by the nature and range of the content at that time. Davies is also now an enthusiastic collector of the documents that are generated through her making process so what began as a modest collection is expanding rapidly. Managing larger volumes of content and different kinds of content is testing the structure that was devised and unavoidably fixed at the start of the project. There are also real costs to this updating. Ensuring that there are sufficient resources to maintain the site is a task shared by the University and

Siobhan Davies Dance. All our agreements with content providers are based on the principle of a free-to-access site so there is no opportunity to generate revenue through the archive without renegotiating all the agreements, so future work is always dependent on securing funding.

A clutch of related funded projects have enabled us to enhance aspects of the archive further. Firstly, the recently completed *D-TRACES*[7] project enabled us to explore how to embed the archive within the dance curriculum at Coventry University. Students have used the archive as a model for self-archiving in the form of reflective blogs, using the Jerwood Bank blog as a model to support their development as dance artists as part of their personal development planning portfolios. The project also enabled students to work directly with Davies' dancers and hear about their experiences of blogging. Importantly, it also provided us with time and resource to find out much more about our users; not only the numbers of users but also where they come from and what they are doing with the archive. Davies' performance work tends to be predominantly seen within the UK. The archive has enabled audiences from around the world to view her work, generating interest from students, teachers, and researchers in and beyond dance, as well as galleries, archives, and cultural institutions worldwide; it has been a valuable tool for "exporting" Davies' work. Between September 2009 and August 2010, we had nearly 45,000 visits from c10,000 unique visitors, from more than ninety countries worldwide.[8] The majority of the users are students and those working in education, but interest is growing amongst gallery curators, archivists, and cultural heritage experts.

The archive is also one of the collections included in the *Digital Dance Archives* (DDA) project (see also Chapter 7 in this volume).[9] DDA provides access to a broad range of visual content related to dance spanning the last 100 years. It also provides users with some novel interactive tools, including a virtual "scrapbook" that offers more functionality than that on *Replay* and a prototype tool for searching by visual similarity (by colour, shape, gesture, and sequence). Our work on DDA enabled us to develop our user community for *Replay* by paying attention to how dance artists use and engage with digital dance archives. We offered a choreographic commission to two UK-based dance artists, inviting them to construct two choreographic responses to the archival collections, resulting in performances and the production of accompanying virtual scrapbooks, which are now included on DDA.[10] The aim of these commissions was to involve artists directly in "dancing the archive" by exploring archives as source material for new performances and novel methods of artist documentation rather than for faithful re-enactment or reconstruction, leading to interesting questions about reusing digital content for new art/dance projects. As a result of these two projects, *Replay* now includes a new microsite named *Learning Space*, which is a repository of teaching and learning materials to support engagement with *Replay*.

In summary

Davies now has a very rich digital presence having established what might be described as a "digital venue" to support and complement the physical building.

Her company website broadcasts digital exchanges of ideas about dance and choreography, and features talks, videos, and images from exhibitions and events; there continues to be a dynamic relationship between the physical and the virtual. The archive provides a critical and longitudinal context for this more transient digital presence.

The project to build *Replay* was characterized by its valuable knowledge exchange between a major dance company and a university research team, but it also meant confronting challenges in terms of different working methods, expectations, and organizational structures. Through the archive we have established a very positive and enduring partnership.[11] We are all wiser about what is involved. For example, having obtained all the necessary agreements to archive work made in the past, Davies now secures permissions before beginning work rather than trying to do so retrospectively.

Replay is a valuable source for viewing, analyzing, and reconstructing dance—and seeing the evolution of an artist's work over time. It is simultaneously a product of Davies' past work and a new form of creative output. But a digital archive is not only a resource but also a new kind of representation of dance. It is not a simple conversion from the analogue to the digital; it is a translation, and that means that the work does change, or has the potential to change because of the different environment in which it is situated. It is not a facsimile of the live. It also does more than merely describe; it probes, questions, and provokes. Importantly, by providing users with access to at least some aspects of the dance making process the archive can reveal, but not explain, the knowledge that is particular to dance and embodied by the dancers. Perhaps this is the most exciting potential of the archive and has had the greatest affect on Davies, who is increasingly interested in how she can leave evidence of the making of the work in the moment; what she once described as the "isness" of the moment.[12] At the same time, new kinds of digital objects can be created because of the juxtaposition of content, and because users have ready access to different kinds of content and tools. So it is not simply a distribution of "old art" but it can be used generatively to create new forms of art; this is perhaps the best way of keeping it fresh and living, and with it, new and better informed audiences for dance.

Replay has influenced the development of other archival projects by providing a model of how to select, organize, and design dance documentation online, and how to work collaboratively with artists.[13] This is something that feeds back into the ongoing development and enhancement of the archive. Most of all, *Replay* not only seeks to honour and celebrate Davies' work, but helps us connect with artist histories, providing us with more knowledge about our dance lineage to increase appreciation for the dance of today and into the future.

***

Siobhan Davies Replay can be accessed via www.siobhandaviesreplay.com.

Notes

1 My PhD provided a detailed analysis of Davies' movement vocabulary, and several papers published since, and prior to the archive project, have developed this work. See Whatley, S., *Beneath the Surface: The Movement Vocabulary in Siobhan Davies' Choreography since 1988* (unpublished PhD thesis, University of Surrey Roehampton, 2002).
2 The archive was funded as part of the AHRC's Resource Enhancement Scheme.
3 The researchers on the project were Ross Varney and David Bennett, who replaced Paul Allender who left the project in the second year for personal reasons.
4 Members of the steering group were representatives of both Coventry University and Siobhan Davies Dance, together with Gill Clarke MBE (Independent Dance) and Ann Ogidi (Online Services Projects Manager at Department for Culture, Media, and Sport).
5 Funding was awarded from the AHRC Beyond Text program. The workshop series was led by social scientist James Leach and brought together the teams involved in four artist-led projects. In addition to *Replay* these projects were William Forsythe's *Synchronous Objects*, Emio Greco and Pieter Scholten's *Capturing Intention*, and Wayne McGregor's *Choreographic Language Agent* (all of them also represented in this volume. See also James Leach's chapter "Making Knowledge from Movement" in this volume). See http://projects.beyondtext.ac.uk/choreographicobjects/index.php, accessed May 26, 2016.
6 Sanjivan Kohli was Company Manager at the start of the project until he left the company. He was succeeded by Franck Bordese.
7 D-TRACES is the acronym for the project Dance Teaching Resources and Collaborative Engagement Spaces. See http://dancetraces.wordpress.com/ to find out more about the project (funded by JISC; Joint Information Systems Committee).
8 Further information about our users during this period is available via the D-TRACES user impact analysis, available from http://dancetraces.wordpress.com/, accessed May 26, 2016.
9 The DDA project is a collaboration between the University of Surrey, the National Resource Centre for Dance and Coventry University; see http://www.dance-archives.ac.uk/, accessed May 26, 2016.
10 Oliver Scott and Efrosini Protopapa were the two commissioned artists; see http://www.dance-archives.ac.uk/scrapbook/DDA/1 and http://www.dance-archives.ac.uk/scrapbook/DDA/10, both accessed May 26, 2016.
11 The *Library of Processes* is another AHRC-funded project focusing on a digital library, documenting the making processes of artists working in Siobhan Davies Studios and directly commissioned by Davies. It is another partnership between Siobhan Davies Dance and Coventry University.
12 In conversation with Michael Stanley (director of Modern Art Oxford) and Mark Rowan-Hull (Creative Fellow), Wolfson College, University of Oxford, October 21, 2011.
13 For example, the Walker Art Centre's "living" collection catalogue (Minneapolis, USA) and the Routledge digital archive for the Theatre and Performance Series; both under development.

7

SEARCHING MOVEMENT'S HISTORY

Digital Dance Archives

Rachel Fensham

When the screen opens, one frame starts to move—circles of dancers, men and women, wearing rainbow-colored unitards are dancing outside in a field. After Rudolf Laban's death in 1954, Lise Ullman, his protégé, continued teaching at Dartington College and we know much of his methods through her publication of his books *The Mastery of Movement* (2011) and *Choreutics* (2011). This rare footage of Laban Movement Choirs filmed in the 1970s evocatively reveals the balance between kinesthetic impulses, orchestrated groupings, and dynamic pathways that characterized this form of modern dance training. Bending and sweeping their arms overhead, the dancers rotate and combine into starbursts, and perform slow rocking gestures that lift each dancer to the sky. Slightly comic, or childlike, the syncopated movement lines traverse the open ground like small battalions. Completely different to the velocity of contemporary ballet, or the body isolations of conceptual choreography, the rhythmic energy in this filmic representation of Laban movement seems anachronistic but fascinating.

In this example from the *Digital Dance Archives* web platform (DDA), the complex relationship between embodied knowledge, mediated reproduction, performance aesthetics, and cultural history is simultaneously visible and problematized. Such digital collections, now proliferating, invite critical questioning about what objects of dance's past dynamics or living present should be archived, and thus preserved or disseminated. Since all digital archives face the tension of emphasizing storage and reproduction over access and communication, or of fixing provenance and citation but neglecting movement and interaction, these were sharply in focus in the *Digital Dance Archives* project. Initially inspired by GAMA—Gateway, a project for gathering Media Art from across Europe (http://www.gama-gateway.eu/), the aim was to create a platform for multiple dance resources and collections located in the National Resource Centre for Dance (NRCD), at the University of Surrey, in partnership with the online artist archive *Siobhan Davies Replay* (see Chapter

6 in this volume).¹ By linking different information media from diverse dance sites—both historical and contemporary, of companies and of individuals—via one portal, we also wanted to investigate ways of enhancing user interaction through searching and creation of content. Conceived in the digital humanities, notions of interoperability, copyright, and interactivity were also tested through a series of interdisciplinary research questions and a collaborative methodology.

Tara McPherson (2009) makes a useful distinction between the "computing humanities," which establish infrastructure, platforms, and collections, and the "blogging humanities," which produce peer-to-peer communication methods and writing, and in fact, the multi-modality of the *Digital Dance Archives* was designed to deliver a bit of both for dance research. The project team, including Sarah Whatley, Helen Roberts, John Collomosse, and myself, wanted to bridge the apparent divide between the use of historical dance materials and objects within the material archive of the NRCD and the recent development of choreographic technologies for artistic practice and documentation. Our investigations were thus both pragmatic and conceptual—how to select a metadata scheme in order to build a digital infrastructure from the existing catalogues? What website design would function across different search engines?—as well as more analytical, such as how might a non-linear cultural history arise if visual materials from different dance styles and historical periods could be retrieved? How would a transversal temporality of dance images modify understandings of continuity or adaptation within choreography? By privileging the user experience in relation to the field of human computer interaction, we wanted to acknowledge that the user drives the mode of discovery and enquiry in an online environment in order to make knowledge an interaction that might be both personalized and self-reflexive. Finally, the project team was interested in identifying ways in which an online archival resource might reflect and respond to the visuality of dance and the viewer's speculation with movement in an online environment.

In its current form, the *Digital Dance Archives* includes eight different collections spanning the early twentieth and early twenty-first centuries, and searchable by names, keywords, and more informal tags: *Revived Greek Dance* (1914–1954), *Natural Movement* (1917–1950), *Rudolf Laban* (1938–1958), *Ludmila Mlada* (1950–1960), *Extemporary Dance Theatre* (1975–1991), *V-TOL Dance Company* (1991–2001), *Yolande Snaith* (1987–2005), *Kokuma Dance Theatre* (1979–2000), and *Siobhan Davies Replay* (1988–present). Each collection contains visual content (primarily photos, some videos, drawings, and costume photos) with background information on the collections as well as basic metadata such as creators, music, venues, dates, and a brief description for each item; it also provides the URL for future citation.² One of the issues for constructing platforms that access diverse source websites or digital content is the different systems of metadata, and one ambition of this project was to identify how more standardized models of archival design in the performing arts might enhance interactivity and longevity. The NRCD catalogue was based on the standardized UK archival database, called CALM, that functions at a "lower resolution" or coarser level of granularity, with maybe ten fields, while the bespoke digital design of the *Siobhan Davies Replay* website had up to thirty to forty fields, such as "choreographer" and "lighting designer," and used high resolution image functions to display content. The web interface for *Digital Dance Archives* therefore had to reconcile the different databases and draw down content from different servers in a way that could unify their display. The format is a rudimentary tile structure with a landing page that displays a random selection from the collections, with a navigation bar for more advanced searching. The default of ALL collections at the opening page aimed to enhance interaction with the range of materials, although narrowing results by collection, also identified by initial letters, quickly leads to filtered content and contextual information. The "collection" dropdown leads to the static page that includes a profile of the company or artist with a further link showing all the series records for each production. The content for a unique work appears in thumb-nail tiles which can be stretched to full screen while the full length videos can be automatically played. One of the delights of the *Digital Dance Archives* is this opportunity to watch otherwise inaccessible dance videos and locate them with related photographic material. Missing from the *Digital Dance Archives* is the supplementary textual content such as programs, reviews, or other notes that might enrich analysis of a production, although much of this material can be identified via the *Siobhan Davies Replay* site, or in the NRCD catalogue. As a dance archive then, the *Digital Dance Archives* is primarily a visual storage and retrieval system for digital content whose analogue storage and organization is maintained elsewhere.

Itinerant searching and choreographic 2.0

On a tag beside the Laban film sequence described earlier, five words appear—geometry, groups, color, solidarity, outdoors. I choose "geometry." It takes me to *Slow Arc Inside a Cube III*, a work created as a commission for Thtion (a collaboration between Siobhan Davies and Victoria Miro Gallery) in 2010 by Conrad Shawcross. The still image is rather dim, but shows interlocking grid boxes refracted by a beam of light and shadow across the floor and walls. Another click on the More Info text, and I am displaced into another milieu—a sculptural installation in a gallery-like setting. This is the website of the Victoria Miro Gallery, East London, and the formal dynamics of lines, circles, triangles, spirals, and cubes in Shawcross's work can be seen in numerous wood, steel, and string structures. It seems unlikely that Shawcross will know of the mathematical drawings and choreography of mid-century dance artist and theorist Rudolf Laban, however there seems to be some inexplicable resonance between these two representations—the colored dancers moving outdoors and the modular quasi-organic, interlocking geometric forms. With their dual interest in seriality and shapes that fold, multiply, and magnify, both artists investigate concepts about topographical replication and concentrated energy.

In the digital landscape, this itinerant methodology of searching is ubiquitous and we are habituated to its randomness and peripatetic modalities. While offering an organized framing of materials, searching on the *Digital Dance Archives* also disrupts, and supplements the location of moving dance images. Do sequences that combine information from modern dance and contemporary visual art constitute a different system of potential movement analysis? I return to the *Digital Dance Archives* site and type into the general search the word "grid"; two images appear, one marked SD (Siobhan Davies) and the other L (Laban). The Davies still is from *Rushes* made in 1982 for Second Stride, a postmodern company active in Britain during the 1980s and the graphic composition of the scorched orange and black costumes resemble a Russian constructivist painting. Notes from Whatley (2002) under "More Info" explain the compositional process: "phrases are made, remade, and shared between and amongst different dancers, but Rushes marked a move away from the more gentle work that preceded it to work that had a harsher, sharper quality and higher energy." By way of contrast, the Laban image, *50 Link Dodecahedral Space Grid*, is a pink and green line drawing like an amoebic plant with five heads of star-like petals. A blue line threads through the shape as a continuous movement path. Although there is no further description of the drawing, its organic form replicates tree and petal-like images that also appear in Shawcross's work. Each of these visual resemblances between Laban, Davies, and Shawcross highlight the reworking of machinic abstraction and organicist movement that have been critical in modernist aesthetics. The act of searching conceives of these discontinuous historical moments as a latent formal organization of ideas about design linked by the digital archive.

Even though YouTube has generated many fantastic conjunctions, its search modality is a text-based descriptor; both there and in other online environments, a dynamic interaction between still and moving images, of different dance genres and histories, is limited. In most dance archives, collections have been created by the dancer or dance company as author and thus serve a legitimating or propagandist function. Specialist dance collections in major museums or cultural institutions, on the other hand, are often fragmented archives limited to more official documents of an historical or archaeological period. By linking Davies' work with the historical dance images, the *Digital Dance Archives* facilitates annotation of diverse, born digital materials, and this marking of particular objects represents a new form of archival memory or social choreography of movement history.

To promote user interactivity, especially for those individuals who sign up as (free) members, *Digital Dance Archives* wanted to exploit some of the Web 2.0 functionalities that have been the "promise, perils and predictions" of the digital humanities (Davidson 2008). Meta-data tags in the form of text keywords and tag clouds were added as elementary devices, while annotation buttons make it possible to write and store personalized comments on an image or video. It is also possible to select and "like" video segments that can then be replayed by adding a marker to the timeline. The scrapbook function also allows an individual user to collect and organize a selection of materials within the *Digital Dance Archives*. Following a search, the drop and drag function can relocate an image in an album, arrange their display and add notes.[3] This tool could be used by teachers wanting students to research particular topics, for instance about a form, an individual work, or artist. In my scrapbook on expressionist dance, for instance, I sequenced a series of black and white photographs from Ludmilla Mlada, a student of Mary Wigman, that showed grotesque and gothic characters such as Lucifer and Lady Macbeth. Beside them, I placed a short film sequence from a Laban studio class that shows caped figures who loom at each other like terrifying bats. This clip and the photos provide rich content for investigating the dark forces of the German dance tradition and my annotations to these images add verbal description. Together they show how the concept of the shadow, in mid-twentieth-century psychology and aesthetics, could be interrogated as the metamorphosis of the figure into the shape of fear.

Is it also possible to use the scrapbook to construct a dance sequence? Another phase of the *Digital Dance Archives* project was designed to encourage students and artists to create their own "scrapbooks" of images as a research repository arranged into folders, displayed, tagged, annotated, stored, and shared. We conceived of this aspect of the *Digital Dance Archives* as akin to a choreographic process, whereby images, notes, and drawings instigate a studio activity. To stimulate this concept, we invited two choreographers to create scrapbooks for the Guest Artists section of the site.

Oliver Scott chose a selection of Siobhan Davies' rehearsal videos to investigate studio improvisation. In his scrapbook he quotes Andy Pink's analysis of Davies's *Birdsong*: "So it is with a vibrating object . . . the dancers are the center with the audience experiencing the ripples. . . . Flashes of light. A flock of birds flying seen through a series of apertures." In his demonstration performance during the research, Scott projected these archival tapes onto opposing studio walls, and improvised between the scale and intensity of different phrases in Davies' repertoire. His incarnation of her aesthetics of continuous flow and detailed absorption became a revitalized space of information exchange that belonged to neither the dancer nor the choreographer. According to Scott: "an endangered species feels very evocative to me now," although this intelligence existed only through his reworking of kinesthetic practices visually and digitally transmitted by the archive.

Choreographer Efrosini Protopapa in her collaboration with dancer Susanna Recchia, by way of contrast, sampled images that traversed all the Collections of the *Digital Dance Archive*. Her citation and re-assemblage established a chronological ordering marked out spatially on the floor of the studio. Performed mostly in silence as if watching a silent film or posed photographs, Recchia stepped from frame to frame through time and space. In her scrapbook Protopapa writes instructions: "closed eyes . . . space full of figures . . . sensitivity of hands-feet . . . the feminine . . . the atmosphere of lighting in the photograph . . ." Often wry, her observations include a critical distantiation of the past as a corporeal event, while in performance, the held or expressive moments of Recchia's dancing were interspersed with present day commentary from Recchia's diary. Eventually, Recchia's voice becomes more intrusive, from the taped score of a noisy postmodern studio to the difficulty of remembering what was done yesterday. As such this performing of the archive became another palimpsest, doubling the trace images, both objective and subjective, in a new score or mediation of cultural memory. There is potential then to add to these Guest Scrapbooks, as well as student portfolios, by sharing videos and artistic collaborations on the *Digital Dance Archives*.

Speculating on content-based image retrieval

Having constructed a basic interface and added sets of unique content to the *Digital Dance Archives*, one of the bigger questions in the project lay in our speculation about visual searching for the identification of dance objects in the archive. As Johanna Drucker and Bethany Nowviskie (2004) write: "Speculative approaches to digital humanities engage subjective and intuitive tools, including visual interfaces, as primary means of interpretation in computational environments. Most importantly, the speculative approach is premised on the idea that a *work* is constituted in an *interpretation* enacted by an *interpreter*" (431). While standard text forms of delivering content work for many archival databases, it seemed restrictive if dance literate researchers could not use their knowledge of distinctive dance poses and choreographic form. Media archaeologist, Wolfgang Ernst (2012), acknowledges this possibility as one of the distinctive features in our shift to a digital memory of cultural practices: "The next step might be the development of an interactive and visual agent capable of 'intelligent' retrieval of images by graphical sketches" (134).

An increasingly standardized visual detection system is that of color searching. Looking at how dancers and visual artists were utilizing organic tones as part of their sensory stimulation of the gaze, I return to the image of *Rushes*. I "like" the rich red textures in the light projections and select the color search function which enables the user to isolate a small section while the software identifies other works with a similar palette.[4] A clutch of images with red t-shirts, red lighting, red backdrops appear on the screen. I am attracted to some soft folding drapery and silky loose cloth that shivers. As I scroll across each frame, the names appear—I click on one called *The Doll* (1980) to find out more. Several photos show dancer Robb Fleming manipulating Avigail Ben Ari in a duet choreographed by Tom Jobe for Extemporary Dance Theatre. During a period in British dance history known for its austere postmodernism, this highly theatrical work with its distorted female figure—thrown limbs flailing around the dark-suited male dancer—looks more like a Pina Bausch piece. With this shift in perspective, visual searching by way of a chosen color aesthetic elaborates and attaches other layers of significance to certain typical categories in choreographic history.

In a real life context, however, user searching for movement content depends on visual recognition of complex patterns of movement however digital search engines have to be trained to replicate these more intuitive practices. The growing potential of pattern recognition in computing means that the moving shapes of choreography might be linked visually rather than by choosing a text or word search, such as "duet" or "back-bend."

The *Digital Dance Archives* became therefore the first project to research the applicability of Visual Content Based Information Retrieval systems in the specialized domain of dance archives.

The partner investigator, Collomosse was an expert in exploring novel forms of visual retrieval, having previously completed research on line drawings. In this project, he adopted an iterative development strategy that was based on identifying poses, constructed as a bag of visual words (BOVW), that could be scrambled and then applied as a coherent "sentence" or unit of visual meaning across the diverse media and images. In order to identify physical gestures and patterns to train the shape recognition software, we used a formal shape-design, in part motivated by Laban's drawings and his concept of the kinesphere, and translated these concepts into bodily zones around the figure of a dancer in a still image or sequence. Notably, this post-movement patterning differs from motion capture software; in this instance, the images of the human figure of previously filmed or photographed content exist only as screen surfaces. The discrete data sets of each BOVW associated with a discrete pose and identified by algorithms could search millions of image frames for poses that resemble each other within a photograph, movie, or video collection (see Reede, Collomosse and Jose). The system required hours of "training" on various videos to acquire sufficient mathematical accuracy across the diverse digital content of this archive. In one sample search, the pose of a single dancer with two arms raised above the head in the shape of an arabesque led to a series of movement images with varying degrees of affinity with the original, including two bodies conjoined, or someone doing a hand-stand! Paradoxically, the lack of fit between the human cognition of movement and visual computing technologies became a problem that was difficult to surmount, and highlighted the complex perceptual and somatic knowledge of the human agent in relation to dance.

FIGURE 7.1 Sample of the 65 pose search queries tested in the *Digital Dance Archives*. Screenshot by John Collomosse.

While we could identify dance gestures across the collections, the *Digital Dance Archives* video set represented significant variations in object appearance (human figures) in terms of pose, illumination and scale variations. From the perspective of the engineers: "Our core technical contribution is therefore a novel framework for pose retrieval on low fidelity dance footage, that does not require explicit pose estimation (Reede and Collomosse 1653)."[5] Assumptions of computer vision research that have relied on a "monolithic classifier" were not suited to the less predictable human bodily interactions of choreographic style, such as rolling on a floor or rapidly shifting alignments. Matching of the visual search data across the different types of choreographic content represented a key challenge, so a subsequent decision was made to utilize two existing pedestrian detection systems in order to align them with the pose identification calculations. In this instance, we had "to establish sufficient criterion to denote success" when the dance poses were tested against larger non-dance data-sets.[6] For the dance researchers, sufficient algorithmic performance as proof in the laboratory context did not translate into a sufficiently performing system on the *Digital Dance Archives* website.[7]

In this phase of the work we were attempting to retrofit identification of the human body to video content marked up and identified by pose-based searching as gestures to moving action in the choreography. Via the digital search engine, the digital object of the pose becomes dislocated from its provenance within a particular style or form and, to a lesser extent, from the dancer's corporeality (see Fensham "Choreographic Archives" for more on the ontology of choreographic archives). This syntactical mobility led to some confusion between what was an optimum recognition of pattern, although it also began to stimulate new relationships between researchers and systems, sometimes producing unexpected conjunctions and new sets of problems. Paradoxically the training of computing visual recognition lacked much of the complex perceptual and somatic knowledge of the dancer or spectator, even though other functions in the *Digital Dance Archives* were linking movement images asynchronously and spatially through the grid-like random selection of images. While we saw the evidence of the unpredictable and archival logics of pose-detection, its application across the existing archive has not yet proved possible.

Conclusion

The *Digital Dance Archives* remains an experimental Beta site, constructed during a period of rapid change in digital archive technologies, and its complex ownership and maintenance requirement raise questions about digital sustainability. The aim of the *Digital Dance Archives* project to provide cross-collection searching has been realized and this potential grows with the addition of new and more recent content from the *British Black Dance Archives* Project (http://blackdancearchives.co.uk) and from the extensive artist collections owned by the NRCD. With more content, it is possible to view a wide range of dance content and this unusual range of materials enables comparative study of modern and contemporary British dance practices.

Given the historical breadth of the collections, the multimodal and interoperable digital computing of the *Digital Dance Archives* also makes it possible to identify changes in bodily shapes and techniques over time, thus returning the researcher to the objective question of how corporeality is produced by history and by aesthetic paradigms. There is still the potential that a pedestrian detector will be developed with sufficient accuracy to showcase the pose-based visual search system and even the initial experiments on the moving pose have led to further recognition of how complex movement analysis becomes in relation to dance. The interpretation of histories of gesture and movement expression still seems to far exceed the spectrum of technologies that have attempted to capture, record, and analyze it. Nonetheless the speculative computing of the *Digital Dance Archives* provides enticing challenges for computer engineers, archivists, and dancer/choreographers to generate novel understandings and interactions with dance in the archive.

***

The *Digital Dance Archives* can be accessed via http://www.dance-archives.ac.uk.

Notes

1 Funded by the Arts and Humanities Research Council, UK and established as a resource enhancement project with an interdisciplinary team of researchers from the University of Surrey and the University of Coventry in 2010. I would particularly like to thank Helen Roberts and Sharon Maxwell from the NRCD, Professor Sarah Whatley from Coventry and Dr John Collomosse from Surrey for their insights in shaping this project.
2 Bullet Creative were responsible for the website design (front-end) although the back-end work linking to the archival content was managed by Dr Collomosse. Each Series includes brief descriptive text about the artist or the works, but it does not include supplementary textual materials, such as handbooks, scores, diaries, or news clippings that can be found in the NRCD catalogue or the SDR website. A unique feature is the provision of an automatic reference for each item that supports copyright principles for citation. The uploaded images and film content are only a selection of the full collections of the NRCD.
3 It is not possible to import content from other sites, such as YouTube, or company websites to the scrapbooks, but "post-it notes" can be added to support textual analysis.
4 The color search function has at the time of writing been de-activated.
5 The person detection and pose based search systems were demonstrated as viable algorithms and have been published using a rigorous scientific evaluation process in the review articles listed.
6 Testing of two bespoke pedestrian detection shelf approaches, Viola-Jones and Dalal-Triggs, required hours of training with the dance poses in order to identify human beings on manually marked videos in the *Digital Dance Archives*.
7 The overall system view is very simple and can be thought of as: Input Data → Pedestrian Detection System → Classifier Fusion → Annotated XML.

References

Davidson, Cathy N. "Humanities 2.0: Promise, Perils, Predictions." *Publications of the Modern Language Association of America (PMLA)* 123.3 (2008): 707–717.

Drucker, Johanna, and Bethany Nowviskie. "Speculative Computing: Aesthetic Provocations in Computing Humanities." *A Companion to the Digital Humanities*. Oxford: Blackwell, 2004. 431–447.

Ernst, Wolfgang. *Digital Memory and the Archive*. Minnesota: University of Minnesota Press, 2012.

Fensham, Rachel. "Choreographic Archives: Towards an Ontology of Movement Images." *Performing the Archive/Archiving Performance*. Ed. Gunhild Borggreen and Rune Gade, Copenhagen: Museum Tusculanum Press, 2013. 146–162.

Laban, Rudolf. *Choreutics*. Ed. Lisa Ullman. Alton, Hampshire: Dance Books, 2011.

—— *The Mastery of Movement*. Ed. Lisa Ullman. Alton, Hampshire: Dance Books, 2011.

McPherson, Tara. "Introduction: Media Studies and the Digital Humanities." *Cinema Journal* 48.2 (2009): 119–123.

Reede, Ren, and John P. Collomosse. "Visual Sentences for Pose Retrieval Over Low-Resolution Cross-Media Dance Collections." *IEEE Transactions on Multimedia*, 14.6 (2012), 1,652–1,661.

Reede, Ren, John P. Collomosse, and Joemon M. Jose. "A BOVW Based Query Generative Model." Lecture Notes in Computer Science (LNCS) 6,523, *17th ACM conference on Multimedia Modelling* (2011), 118–128.

8

THE *DANCE-TECH* PROJECT

How like a network

*Marlon Barrios Solano in collaboration
with Rachel Boggia*

Since October 2007, the *Dance-tech* project has explored the affordances of the bottom-up architectures of the internet and Web 2.0 technologies for collaborative knowledge production and creative expression by body-based artistic practitioners working at the intersection of dance, performance, new media, architecture, philosophy, cultural studies, anthropology, and science.[1] It is challenging to write about a project that is changing as I write, a project that is dependent on the dynamics of internet architecture, and driven both by my own research interests and those of more than 5,000 users. The knowledge producing interactions of these users are enabled by the relational and open potential of databases and aggregation architectures provided by the internet, with its continuously emergent constellations of tags and classifications, and flexible interactions between layers and overlays through time. This is the "nature of the beast": *Dance-tech* dynamically dwells within the networked condition of privileged sections of humanity where motion IS transmission and transmission begets motion.

Social flows

To talk about *Dance-tech* is to tell a story about storytelling: it is a tale about several online experiments articulating, reflecting and publishing stories about dance making, about moving bodies, and about many other socio-technological entanglements utilizing networked environments. I like to think of *Dance-tech* as a tactical media project—an intervention in the knowledge distribution systems of contemporary performance and their contexts. It is available for interdisciplinary explorers of the performance of movement and those makers sensitive to emergent performance forms within digital and networked spaces. *Dance-tech*'s interventions consist of a series of open and free of cost online and mobile platforms, curated series, and on-site research spaces. *Dance-tech* is a polyphonic knowing enacted by the "crowd" in the "cloud." Unfinished by design, it is an open-ended deployment of process, a relational space of digital instances moved by us and with us in a space of social flows. Yes, I said social.

Fast, cheap, and out of control

Like Rodney Brooks' insect robots in the 1997 Errol Morris documentary, internet digital networked architecture is "fast, cheap and out of control."[2] *Dance-tech* seeks to creatively, flexibly, and sometimes recklessly, explore the changing communicational potentials afforded by the bottom-up architectures of the web, specifically, its opportunities for creative collaboration and knowledge co-creation between interdisciplinary body-based art practitioners. The new internet, instantiating knowledge streams as data flows, besides easing processes of producing, publishing, and accessing content, may also allow us to amplify and re-inscribe stories about ourselves. As Web 2.0 platforms increasingly allow us to capture and make visible migrations and linkages of people, interactions, concepts, practices, and discourses, it becomes feasible to analyze and dynamically visualize connections, beliefs, influences, and encounters as a changing cultural ecosystem. In this way, new writeable web architecture and platforms afford a dynamic deployment of interfaceable knowledge instances: moving parts and wholes configuring a re-organizable, "narrative space" (O'Reilly). Like in a collaborative improvisational performance, dance-tech projects abandon linear, fixed, single-author narrative as a primary mode of explanation and re-conceive storytelling as a "more complex interaction among and between networks located in space and time" (Hayles 15).

Embodied, situated, and distributed

Varela, Thompson, and Rosch write that cognition should be understood as a fully embodied dynamic process, grounded in the acquired affordances in co-evolution with our environment, making cognition both situated and distributed. This position is echoed by Lucy Suchman writing from the field of socio-cognitive studies about human-machine interaction. Networked environments (including digital social networks) are socio-technological spaces that afford situated, distributed and embodied collective knowledge creation. Our embodiment affords us to be embedded in networked environments which are characterized by multi-mediality, multiple interfacing possibilities, dynamic instantiation, and mapping of data flows. It seems that our embodied embedded condition, understood as ontologically distributed, is multidimensional: it changes over time and it is participatory and collaborative.

Performing knowing . . . together

Dance-tech in its various manifestations has been my way to independently articulate, produce, and publish my research along two intersecting lines of inquiry: on the one hand, the interdisciplinary practices and ideas circulating in the dance and technology field and, on the other, the emergent modes of articulations circulation, expression, and affiliation afforded by digital networks. Through this practice-based research, I try to facilitate and understand the complex and constantly changing couplings of human cognition with computational networked systems. This dynamic coupling is made apparent by the layering of different temporalities of interactions in online spaces (for example, a chat alongside a live video stream being shown at a conference). In these hybrid configurations "inequalities and inefficiencies in their operations drive them towards breakdown, disruption, innovation and change" (Hayles 13). We are dancing bodies interfacing with computers enmeshed in networks of dynamic and multi-directional social, economic, and technological relations.

Dance-tech is basically a "cloud" that is layered and re-articulated by the "crowd" that are its users. It is a networked environment, a horizontal performative landscape that is open for enactments, re-enactments, for telling and retelling, generating potential linkages and derivative content. I am interested in how this networked environment can facilitate and augment the generation of distributed and collective knowledges and reflections. *Dance-tech* aims to do so through a combination of strategies and tactics, including:

- encouraging open participation and community development;
- emphasizing user generated content platforms for text, image, and video sharing;
- developing media production collaborations with emphasis on online interview video production and mobile technology;
- aligning curatorial, production, education, communication, and collaborative strategies;
- exploring mobile technologies as crucial element of production and interfacing element of networked environments;
- using open access culture and technologies;
- developing and facilitating process-oriented, decentralized, and collaborative knowledge production methods.

I will now introduce *Dance-tech*'s various instances and relevant interconnections in (more or less) chronological order.

Dance-tech.net

Dance-tech.net started in October 2007 when I was living in NYC. I was performing dance improvisation within interactive systems mainly designed in MaxMSP-Jitter. I was also working as a web developer of collaborative platforms, teaching some courses as an adjunct professor, and I was employed as a sales person at the MoMa Design Store. I was very excited about the improvisational character of the writable web. It seemed to me that both developing an online collaborative platform and my own dance practice could be considered as means to create spaces for improvisational knowledge jams.

The *Dance-tech* project 83

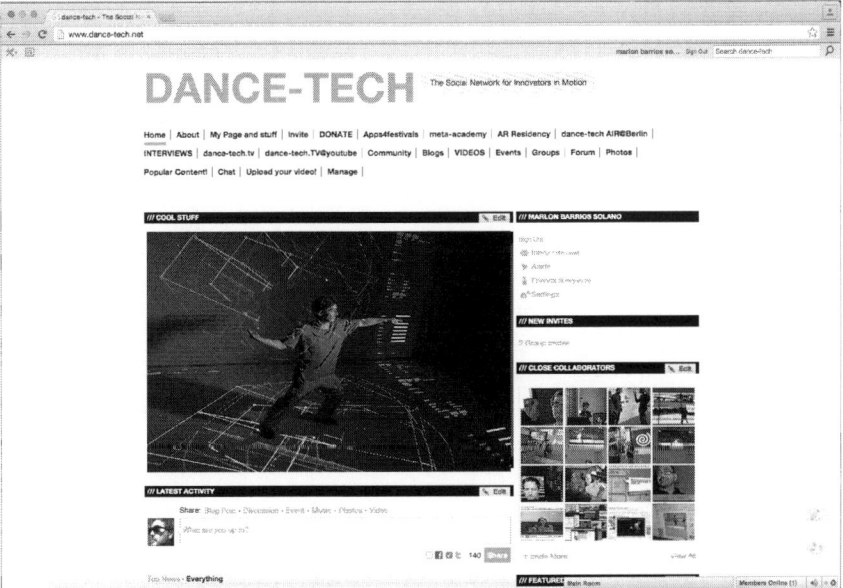

FIGURE 8.1 The dance-tech.net home page featuring the video *Pathfinder* by and with Mio Loclair. Photo by Ragnar Schmuck. Image by Marlon Barrios Solano, 2015.

One evening at 2am, feeling isolated and alienated, I launched dance-tech.net, a social networking site. This seemed to me a necessary upgrade, taking a new step beyond the dance and technology listserv that the community had been using to communicate for the past ten years. At that time, social networks and blogs were not much appreciated by some of the academic members of the *Dance-tech* community. The web allowed me "do it myself" and to involve others. The technology was available, so why not?

I launched dance-tech.net as an independent art research project, a space open to my community. This community was undergoing changes as it expanded beyond the few dance and technology university educational programs and the small cluster of independent pioneering artists. The community was ready: dance-tech.net attracted more than 600 international members during the first six months of its existence. Seven years later, with now more than 5,000 members, dance-tech.net is a robust and diverse online community and the gateway to most of the other *Dance-tech* projects.

From the very beginning, I realized that dance-tech.net needed to be open to all actors in the knowledge production and distribution ecosystems of contemporary performance and the digital arts related to this field. It was also obvious that it needed to be international. Dance-tech.net, therefore, is curated (membership, content production, and partnerships) with a broad and inclusive perspective on life, art, and movement practices, and offers a participatory space for a wide range of creative practices, from hip-hop dancers, to well-known choreographers, curators, musicians, creative technologists, makers, theorists, arts administrators, bloggers, educators, international interdisciplinary collaborative projects, and interdisciplinary belly dancers. I have also consulted for, and helped to create, other international dance related digital networks such as Movimiento.org created by the South American Network of Dance in Spanish and Portuguese, Urdimbre.org in Colombia, and gvadancetraining.org in Switzerland.

One of the challenges that I face as the main administrator is to find the funding necessary to offer dance-tech.net as free resource. Although the costs are low, web hosting is not free. And the international nature of the project comes with some additional challenges. Because the project is "housed" in my own research, which takes shape through international collaborations and residencies, the project moves with my internationally mobile body. This means it lacks a permanent address or legal affiliation required for certain large-scale grants. Dance-tech.net has been associated with organizations from three continents who have supported the project through their generous support of me as educator, embedded vlogger, online producer, digital journalist, and social media specialist. I have sought support from individuals, institutions, and users at various points and have not as yet found a sustainable way for the social network (and other projects) to pay for itself.

Interviews and views

One year after founding dance-tech.net, I started to produce video interviews, using portable mobile devices and online collaborative editing platforms. All content is produced and published for free access under a Creative Commons license. Since 2008, I have produced and published more than four hundred video interviews with international artists, curators, cultural managers, scientist, theorists, and creative technologists. The interviews, in combination with the development of the platforms, became the core of my curatorial practice and my way to simultaneously formalize a research methodology, a knowledge production tactic, and a publishing strategy. I started to combine mobile video production with collaborative online editing, mashable video content, networked clips, and nonlinear presentation. Organizing this collection with tags became my way of "writing" in the cloud, a way of creating a space for connections and juxtapositions between the artists, works, and ideas.

Dance-tech.tv

In 2010, I created dance-tech.tv, an online video-on-demand and video streaming platform for contemporary experimental choreography and more. Online video offers an unprecedented opportunity for the distribution of contemporary performances as well as knowledge about them: of dancing bodies and talking heads. Videos with stories told in first person ("talking heads") offer what I have come to call instances of mediated orality that stand next to the unprecedented proliferation of videos of humans performing dances.

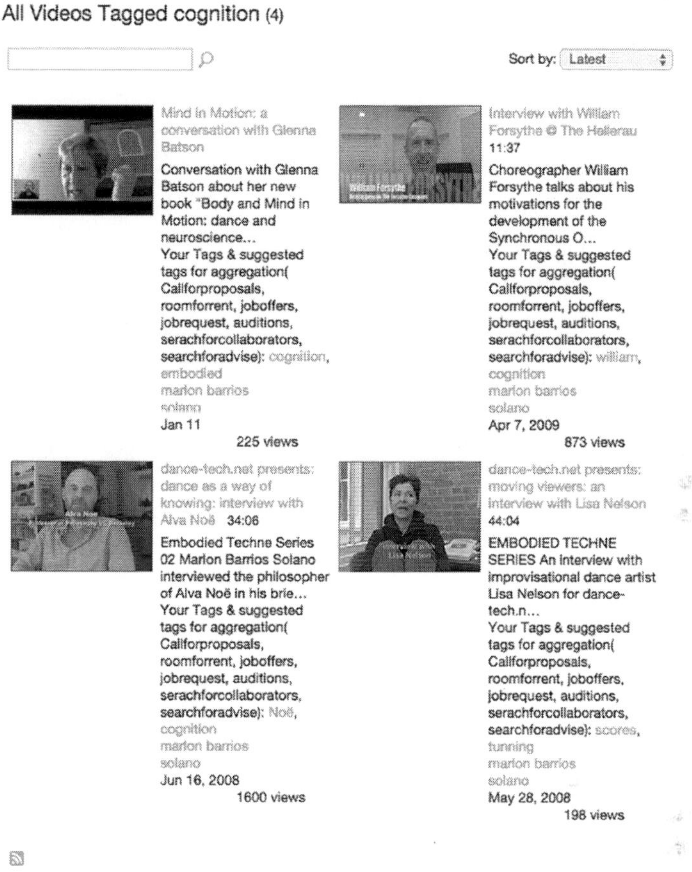

FIGURE 8.2 A page of dance-tech.net with videos tagged with "cognition" featuring conversations with Lisa Nelson, Alva Noë, William Forsythe and Glenna Batson. Image by Marlon Barrios Solano, 2015.

Collaborations with choreographers and institutions started to emerge. Thanks to a sustainable partnership with Livestream from 2010 to 2015, I was able to offer live streaming channels to the community for experimental performances, lecture series, and conferences. Live video broadcasts from more than fifteen countries have been done to date, including broadcasts from Brunel University (UK), Festival Panorama (Brazil), Joyce Soho (USA), HZT-Berlin (Germany), ImPulsTanz (Austria), Trans-Media-Akademie Hellerau (Germany), L'Arsenic (Switzerland), Bipod-Beirut (Lebanon), Uferstudios (Germany), GAM (Chile), and a broadcast on the occasion of the fortieth anniversary of the journal *Contact Quarterly* (USA). More than seventy lectures on contemporary performance have been broadcast and archived in collaboration with Brunel University and Giessen University.

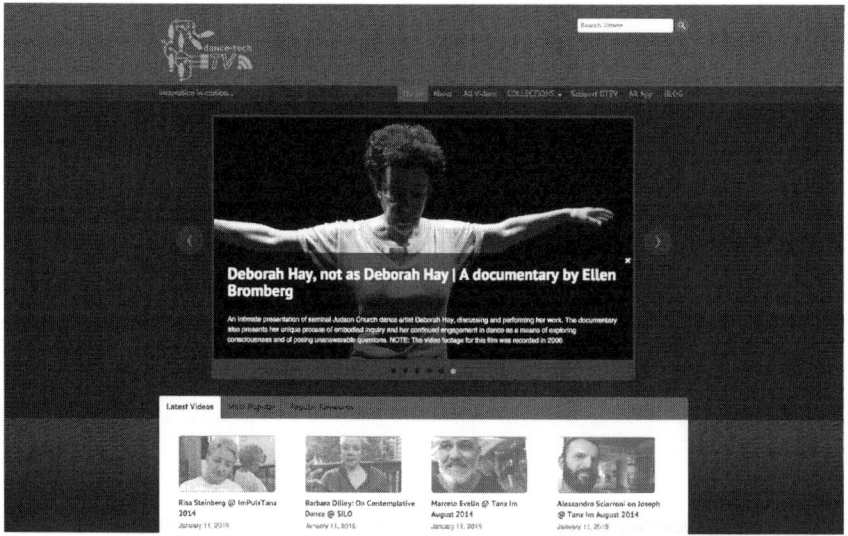

FIGURE 8.3   The home page of dance-tech.tv. Image by Marlon Barrios Solano, 2015.

Pop-up media labs

In 2009, during a research residency with the Gilles Jobin Company in Geneva, I developed the first dance-tech pop-up media lab. It was hosted by the Extra Festival, produced by the Bonlieu Scène Nationale in Annecy, France. These labs started as a collaborative research format to produce the *Dance-tech* interviews and views within the context of dance and new media festivals. The labs invite festival participants and members of the local communities to become the social media documentation team and encourage them to investigate communication systems as performative spaces.

As the labs expanded beyond the production of video content, they began to resonate with new curatorial approaches, operations, and formats already happening at some venues. At the 2011 Festival Panorama, I added more performative aspects to production and communication. Taping sessions for interviews became open to the public, and we installed public interactive video installations that displayed word clouds, data flows, and media mashups of festival content. Augmented reality was added to the installations in 2012. In 2014 at ImPulsTanz, the focus of the lab turned firmly to knowledge production. Lab participants produced fourteen interviews with young choreographers about their pieces, creative processes, and intentions. Each interview was juxtaposed with a word cloud visualization of keywords surveyed from the audience and describing the experience of watching the respective piece. Word Clouds about the collective experience of watching were given to the artists.

The labs facilitate local explorations of the generative potential of producing, interfacing, re-sampling, combining, and juxtaposing online content. They align what I call "knowledge based marketing" with experiments in video documentation, peer2peer ethnography, information visualization, and creative project-based pedagogies. Labs have been deployed in more than fifteen international festivals and they also started to be requested for universities and other instructional settings.

Choreography or ELSE

In January 2012, I launched on dance-tech.tv the collaboratively curated collection called *Choreography or ELSE*. This project consists of an online collection of recordings of complete creations together with supporting materials such as interviews, programs notes, reviews, artist notes, and essays. *Choreography or ELSE* presents works by artists who question traditional notions of choreography, theater, narrative, space, authorship, memory, and labor. To date, the collection includes over thirty works by contemporary choreographers such as William Forsythe, Ivana Müller, Mette Ingvartsen, La Ribot, and Tere O'Connor, and offers an online annotated space of reflection about experimental contemporary movement based performance practices. Most of the artists donated their full works to the collection. For many of them, it was the first time they had published these complete works online. Several of them began to publish more of their works online soon after joining the *Choreography or ELSE* collection. Ivana Müller even published full videos of works that were still on tour. In this way, the collection is both a repository and a dialogical testament to the quickly shifting landscape of choreographic knowledge.

Meta-academy

In 2013, with the support of a research fellowship from ICK Amsterdam, I conceived meta-academy, a research framework for online education about movement based performing arts and creativity. The first meta-academy was launched in collaboration with Rachel Boggia and Josephine Dorado at the Bates Dance Festival 2013 in Maine, USA. In this pilot, we collaborated with the improvisation artist Nancy Stark Smith and explored and co-created online tactics and strategies tailored to her pedagogy for teaching her seminal improvisational score, the Underscore. More than sixty international participants collaborated in this free online workshop. In the summer of 2014, we created a series of live conversations between dance professionals at three festivals: ImPulsTanz (Vienna), Bates Dance Festival (Maine, USA), and Taking Place (Ohio, USA). An online education module about choreographic thinking and conceptual dramaturgies supported by HZT-Berlin and Bates College was deployed in September 2015.

88 Marlon Barrios Solano

FIGURE 8.4 Collage of screenshots taken during work sessions and creative projects during Meta-Academy@Bates 2013. Images by Marlon Barrios Solano, collage by Rachel Boggia.

Augmented reality app and Apps4festivals

Augmented reality uses a smartphone or other devices to access visual content from the cloud using printed materials or spaces as triggers. The dance-tech.tv augmented reality app premiered at Festival Panorama, in Rio de Janeiro in 2012 and has been used at several international festivals, museums, and workshops since. A mobile app was developed for ImPulsTanz 2014. This app included an event guide and other features specially geared to increase audience engagement and community interaction around the festival activities. The app was updated for ImPulsTanz 2015 and Tanz Im August 2014 and 2015.

Augmented AIR

In the summer of 2013, *Dance-tech* invited several artists to explore the potential of mobile augmented reality technology as a creative space. Conceptual and technical support was provided and the artists were given access to their own AR channel and virtual studio. During his AR residency, choreographer Adam Weinert created *The Reaccession of Ted Shawn* as a digital installation in The Museum of Modern Art in New York. The MOMA had invited Weinert to reconstruct and reperform solos of Ted Shawn as part of the exhibit *20 Dancers of the XXth Century* (2012–2013) curated by Boris Charmatz. Using augmented reality and without asking for the museum's consent, he "placed" a permanent installation of his recent performances in the MoMA. Visitors of the museum are able to view footage of his performances simply by pointing their smartphones or tablet to the museum galleries where he performed or use the illustrations from the printed programs as triggers.[3] New media artist and educator Bruno Vianna used the AR residency to provide training in graphic and digital arts to urban underserved youth, students. or graduates at the OI Kabum! School of Art and Technology in Rio de Janeiro, Brazil.

Relations in flux

The *Dance-tech* projects provide space for the movement of knowledge within a shifting networked cultural landscape. They have afforded me to continue rethinking what Gabrielle Brandstetter describes as "strategies of curating in terms of composing space, objects and bodies, in opening paths and structures of participation and placement through movement" (in Malzacher et al. 25). The online platforms, the interviews, the collections, and the labs are externalizations of my engagement with the practice of online relational spaces as well as with developing reflection on contemporary choreographic practices. They belong to a curatorial condition in the sense described by Beatrice Von Bismarck, who argues that "the curatorial" sets the archive in motion through creating relationships between the acts of collecting, assembling, ordering, presenting, and mediating with objects, information, sites, persons, and contexts. She adds that those relations are multiple and constantly open to redefinition and presents the curatorial activation as an ongoing, never to be finalized process. The *Dance-tech* projects offer such a landscape of constantly changing materials, processes and activities, of knowledge in FLUX.

***

The various manifestations of the Dance-tech project can be accessed via

- http://www.dance-tech.net/
- http://dance-tech.tv/
- http://dance-tech.tv/2011/12/18/choreography-or-else/
- http://www.dance-tech.net/group/meta-academy-bates-2013
- http://www.dance-tech.net/page/dance-tech-augmented-reality-creative-residency
- http://www.dance-tech.net/profiles/blogs/app4festivals-sustainable-mobile-apps-for-art-festivals-imspulsta.

Much gratitude for your trust and support: Thomas Dumke, Jaki Levi, William Forsythe, Deirdre Towers, Gilles Jobin, Eduardo Bonito, Isabel Ferreira, Nayse Lopez, Bertha Bermúdez Pascual, Tamara Ashley, Deufert & Plischke, Nik Haffner, Jeannette Ginslov, Rio Rutzinger, Virve Sutinen, Maaike Bleeker, and Rachel Boggia.

Notes

1 The term Web 2.0, popularized by Tim O'Reilly, is generally used to describe the second stage of the development of the worldwide web, particularly sites "that emphasize user-generated content, usability, and interoperability" (http://en.wikipedia.org/wiki/Web_2.0, accessed May 26, 2016).
  Web 2.0 is discussed in detail by O'Reilly here: http://www.oreilly.com/pub/a/web2/archive/what-is-web-20.html, accessed May 26, 2016.
2 *Fast, Cheap and Out of Control* (1997) is a documentary by Errol Morris, produced by American Playhouse and Fourth Floor Pictures.
3 http://www.thereaccessionoftedshawn.com/, accessed October 24, 2015.

References

Hayles, N. Katherine. *How We Think: Digital Media and Contemporary Technogenesis*. Chicago: University of Chicago Press, 2012.
Malzacher, Florian, Tea Tupajić, and Petra Zanki. "This Curator-producer-dramaturge-Whatever Figure. A Conversation with Gabriele Brandstetter. Hannah Hurtzig, Virve Sutinen and Hilde Teuchies." *Frakcija Performing Arts Journal* 55 (2010): 22–27.
O'Reilly, Tim. "Remaking the Peer to Peer Meme." *Peer-to-Peer: Harnessing the Benefits of a Disruptive Technology*. Ed. Andy Oram. Sebastopol, Calif.: O'Reilly Media, Inc., 2001. 29–40.
Suchman, Lucille Alice. *Human-Machine Reconfigurations: Plans and Situated Actions*. 2nd ed. Cambridge: Cambridge University Press, 2007.
Varela, Francisco J., Evan Thompson, and Eleanor Rosch. *The Embodied Mind: Cognitive Science and Human Experience*. Cambridge, Mass.: MIT Press, 1991.
Von Bismarck, Beatrice. "Relations in Motion: The Curatorial Condition in Visual Arts and Its Possibilities for the Neighbouring Disciplines," *Frakcija Performing Arts Journal* 55 (2010): 50–57.

9

DOUBLE SKIN/DOUBLE MIND

Emio Greco | PC's interactive installation

Bertha Bermúdez Pascual

The *Double Skin/Double Mind* interactive installation offers participants the possibility to take part in a virtual version of a workshop by Emio Greco and Pieter C. Scholten. This workshop was developed to transmit the artistic ideas and practices developed within the company Emio Greco | PC. Focusing on qualities and intentions related to the form and execution of movements, the *Double Skin/Double Mind* workshop has throughout the years built a structured mode of transmission specific to the work and to the company. This involves not only the movements and concrete development and selection of the exercises and their order, but also the words that are used to transmit how to understand and execute the movements.

The interactive installation *Double Skin/Double Mind* is not only a virtual version of the workshop, allowing both dancers and non-dancers to participate in the exploration of Greco's movement language, but also a proposal for new modes of notating and documenting dance. Defined by the research team during its development phase as an adaptation of the *Double Skin/Double Mind* workshop, where participants can receive verbal instructions, and visual and sonic feedback, the development of the interactive installation brought up additional research questions like: What is it exactly that we do in our attempts at capturing dance? How do we deal with its ephemeral nature? Which are the existing systems for its documentation? How do these systems deal with qualities and intentions? How may motion capture and new media developments allow not only for a quantitative capturing of movement but also for an analysis of its qualities? And how may this help us to develop further understanding of the specificities of the knowledge that is dance?

From workshop to interactive installation

Double Skin/Double Mind is an interactive environment designed by Chris Ziegler. The installation consists of an aluminum frame construction with one projection screen, four sound speakers, and one camera tracking the movements of the participant.

FIGURE 9.1 *Double Skin/Double Mind*, the installation. Photo by Thomas Lenden, 2009.

When participants are inside the installation, a life size figure of Emio Greco asks them to follow his guidance, just as would happen in a live workshop. Oral directions and explanations are mixed with movement demonstrations, inviting the participant to execute movements. Other cues and elements have been added to inform and enhance the experience of the participant, such as sound, iconic visualizations signaling the main features of each chapter of the *Double Skin/Double Mind* workshop, and visual representations of the participant. These visual representations are abstractions graphically representing the participant's silhouette.

Gesture Follower, a movement-tracking program developed by Frédéric Bevilacqua, IRCAM (with contributions from Bruno Zamborlin, Remy Muller, Riccardo Borghesi, and Norbert Schnell), captures the movements executed by the participant and translates it into mathematical formulae that the software can interpret and connect to various sound environments. Additional visualization software also translates the analysis into a graphic display that responds to different qualities of the movements performed (the display was developed by Sarah Fdili Alaoui, Christian Jacquemin, and Frederic Bevilacqua). Different types of feedback (through sonification and visualization) and music accompany the experience of participants as they mentally and physically travel through the *Double Skin/Double Mind* workshop and learn about different aspects of Greco's movement language.

In Emio Greco | PC's movement, Pieter C. Scholten observes, it "is the body's own logic that serves as a starting point for dance. Dance is not used as a means to convey a message, neither is it intended to shape the theatrical space."[1]

In Emio Greco | PC's choreographies, the brain and the body are in constant dialogue, and concept and movement are expressed as a single unit that can be called "dance." Over the course of many years they have created many productions together and also invested in long-term research on dance dramaturgy and the position and potential of dance within the arts and society. Communication of their artistic findings has always been of importance for both artists.

Throughout the years, the *Double Skin/Double Mind* workshop served as a basis for transmission within the company, merging daily practice with the artistic and ideological urge of both artists to discover new means for physical transformation. As a result, the workshop has developed a structured mode of transmission that is specific to the company and its work. This specificity applies not only to the actions and concrete development, selection, and sequencing of the exercises, but also to the words, sounds, and movement directions that are used throughout the workshop structure. The workshop develops specific types of bodily awareness through breathing exercises (aiming for the extreme expansion of the body), long lasting reboundings and jumps, changes of rhythm and freezing moments, and extreme expansion and reduction. To describe and define the specificities of these movement qualities I developed, in collaboration with Emio Greco and Pieter Scholten, a glossary in which most relevant movement concepts are defined. This glossary provides basic information about the main movement principles and qualities that needed to be transmitted though the installation.

GLOSSARY: BREATHING
VERTICAL INCREASE IN BODY LENGTH AND EXTENSION THROUGH BREATH EMBODIMENT

Growing: gradual vertical increase in length of the body distancing the joints while installing the mechanism of breathing (breathe in extended; breathe out release length).

Ramification: development of growing by reaching with the arms into different directions, extending the boundaries of the body and splitting the previously established vertical path.

Exploring: articulation of ramification by an endless shift of weight initiated by the feet, dislocating the body centre into different positions in space.

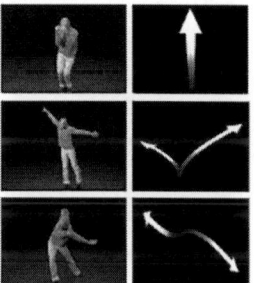

Other terms used in this section
Body: matter; object that can be shaped and become. *Boundaries*: limit; edge of the body. *Breathing*: relationship between inner and outer body. *Lines*: relationship with the space. *Shifting of weight*: change in the relation of body mass and feet, normally generating a change in movement. *Space*: internal and external environments in which the body is positioned and that it can interact with. *Splitting*: different use of the inner space of the body by dividing it. *Thin line*: selected path that can be created within the body. *Internal path*: possible imaginary points that can be connected within the body. *Input*: initiation of movement, starts to be generated/transmitted to the other body parts. *Lengthening*: distance between the different edges of the inner body.

FIGURE 9.2 The *Double Skin/Double Mind* glossary as it appears as part of the installation manual. Courtesy of the artists.

The installation modes

The *Double Skin/Double Mind* installation exists in two modes: basic mode and workshop mode. They differ with regard to structure, length, the performance of the gesture follower, and the types of sonic and visual feedback that are provided.

The basic mode is a short version of *Double Skin/Double Mind* for non-dance practitioners. The experience of this basic version is augmented through contextual explanations of what the action and purpose are of each chapter's use of sound feedback and different visualizations of the body (bounding box and silhouette). Participants can explore the installation for a period of a minimum of seven to a maximum of eighteen minutes. In this mode, the installation follows the actions of participants and responds to the way in which they execute the proposed actions. The main aim of this mode is to provide non-dance practitioners with an interactive physical experience as well as insight into principles of Emio Greco | PC's work.

The workshop mode is directed towards dance professionals and has a four- to five-day format. There are four levels: *workshop, learn, customize,* and *play*. The workshop level introduces participants to the space and content of the workshop through a 45-minute video of Emio Greco teaching as if in a real life situation. Emotive icons are projected on his body providing the participant with immediate information on the essential quality of each workshop section. No interaction with the tracking and analysis system is active during this section.

FIGURE 9.3 *Double Skin/Double Mind* showing choreographer Emio Greco giving instructions. Photo by Thomas Lenden, 2009.

FIGURE 9.4 *Double Skin/Double Mind* showing Bertha Bermúdez Pascual in the installation. On screen choreographer Emio Greco giving instructions. Photo by Thomas Lenden, 2009.

The *learn* level is a selection of the main chapters: breathing, jumping, expanding, and reducing. Here the information is segmented into explanations, demonstrations, and close up details. Participants are now introduced to visual responses and sonic feedback related to their actions. Explanations are given by means of a small monitor referred to as "talking head," where Greco's head occupies the full screen while explaining essential information regarding each section of the workshop. On the main screen in front of the participant, demonstrations of the movements are projected. Close ups show details of main body parts relevant to each chapter. As a reminder of the essential movement quality of each chapter previously presented, emotive icons are displayed on the talking head. Each chapter lasts 20 to 25 minutes, allowing participants to access detailed information of each chapter while taking in the different feedback.

The *customize* level's main concern is the possibility of choosing (customizing) the chapters and mode of interaction of the installation. In order to enhance the mode of learning of each participant, the system can be modified: participants can select chapters they wish to experience as well as the mode in which they want information to be displayed, that is, with or without introduction videos, sound feedback, bounding box, and silhouette visualization. A minimum of four chapters can be chosen through a system allowing for different combinations to be made. An important feature of this mode is that the participant is no longer guided by the full body image of Greco, demonstrating the movements and movement qualities.

The image of his body is replaced with written instructions that summarize relevant information from each chapter, thus activating memories of the previous level. The custom level aims to instigate self-reflection and self-evaluation, and to direct the attention of participants to their own actions.

The *play* level changes the rules of the game. Participants cease receiving information and are now the ones delivering information to the system. They improvise while the gesture follower "reads" their movements and movement qualities through pre-established parameters (breathing, jumping, expanding, and reducing). The installation then provides the participant with sonic, textual, and visual feedback. On the side monitors, words linked with the main qualities of movements appear as inspirational sources from which the participant can improvise. On the main screen, an abstract object "behaves" (i.e., moves and transforms) in relation to the movements of the participant and in response to four main qualities: breathing, jumping, expanding, and reducing. Each quality is also linked with a sound activated through the same process of recognition. The sounds vary in pitch depending on the intensity of the movements of the participant. This level aims to test previous acquired experiences (by the participant) while testing the possibilities of the system to recognize different movement qualities. The final goal is to give a life of its own to the learned material so that the dancer can feel free to develop new movements and movement qualities.

The *workshop* mode was developed in collaboration with an expert team of dance teachers as well as interdisciplinary researchers. Together, they helped develop an educational frame wherein the participant can have an enhanced learning experience through the use of emotive icons, text instructions, video explanations, and demonstrations as well as sonic and visual feedback produced through video.

The learning experience

Since 2010, the installation has been presented for both professionals and non-professional dancers in a variety of contexts, among them as part of the curriculum of the Amsterdam School for the Arts (Modern Dance Department). Developing new modes of learning (visual, kinetic, cognitive, and sonic) as well as discovering how these can be used to transmit the structure and main principles of the workshop is what motivated its development. Its design aims at providing new possibilities of relationship between digital data and physical experiences. Its mode of operating demands physical action: one needs to move, be active, and follow directions to navigate through its structure and content.

Inside the *Double Skin/Double Mind* installation, information is constantly being transformed into sensory experiences. The user enters the installation's framed space and can immediately process the information provided by the screens, but he or she needs to be physically active to experience and understand what is going on. This experiential aspect of the *Double Skin/Double Mind* installation is essential for all users, whether dancers or non-dancers, and whether participating or observing. The installation allows participants inside and outside to watch, listen and take action, while its multimedia format triggers various information sources that activate a wide range of learning modes. The *Double Skin/Double Mind* interactive installation was never conceived of as a replacement for the oral tradition of dance teaching. Rather, it is a proposal for a new way of documenting, archiving, transmitting, and learning dance.

Intended uses and beyond

The initial goal of the *Double Skin/Double Mind* installation was to support professional dancers in developing understanding of the specificities of Emio Greco's movement language. First steps were taken in 2004 with the making of a documentary film based on EG | PC's live workshop *Double Skin/Double Mind* and research conducted during a period as artists-in-residence at the Amsterdam School of the Arts (AHK).

This collaboration continued in 2006 with a follow up project titled *Capturing Intention* that evolved around the question of what notation system can capture inner intention as well as the outer shape of gestures and phrases. This second phase culminated in October 2007 in the publication of a book plus interactive DVD and a first version of the installation. The first version of the installation—a pilot full of possibilities and expectations—was tested by numerous visitors during the Dutch Dance Days festival in 2008 in Maastricht. The two-year collaborative, interdisciplinary research project *Inside Movement Knowledge* provided a context for the further development and testing of the installation.

Throughout the research that developed and finally created the installation, many questions were raised around the use and potential of this object for different kinds of users. While originally the main aim had been to transmit Emio Greco's movement principles to professional dancers, it became clear that the installation might serve different purposes. The development team was intrigued by the idea of making dance audiences, who love to watch dance, actually move before watching a performance. What influence might an installation such as this have as a pre-performance experience tool? While for the professionals the main focus was on learning and creating, what kind of surplus experience might such an object provide to the learning process of dancers? And, might this be a creative environment where new movements could be generated? The recognition that this installation could also enhance and enrich the experience of dance audiences resulted in the development of the basic mode, a kind of light version of the installation that can provide non-dance practitioners with an interactive physical experience as well as an insight into some principles of the work of Emio Greco | PC. Used by professionals, the interactive environment appeared to be useful not only to gain experience with Greco's movement principles but also for more creative uses and as a means to generate new movements. Furthermore, the experiential nature of the installation has inspired researchers to use this object as research tool to develop experiments around human perception and human computer interaction, e-learning, experiential knowledge, and generally the role and function of movement in processes of learning, understanding, and thinking. This was the subject of the interdisciplinary research project *Inside Movement Knowledge*. This project took the outcomes (book, interactive DVD, and installation) of *Capturing Intention* as its starting point for further explorations in the frame of a new consortium consisting of the Emio Greco | PC dance company, the Netherlands Media Institute, The Dance Department of the AHK, and Theatre and Dance Studies at Utrecht University, and coordinated by the Art Practice and Development Research Group of the AHK. This expanded research project was supported by the Dutch Ministry of Education, Culture, and Science through its Foundation for Innovative Alliance funding scheme, a scheme that funds new inter-institutional consortia focusing on improving the exchange of knowledge between non-for-profit institutes in the public sector, small and medium sized enterprises and the universities of applied sciences.

***

More information and documentation of the *Double Skin/Double Mind* installation, the research projects *Capturing Intention* and *Inside Movement Knowledge* as well as other research projects can be found at http://www.ickamsterdam.com under "research" and "education." See also http://www.insidemovementknowledge.net.

Note

1 See Pieter C. Scholten's text "About', Emio Greco | PC," http://www.emiogrecopc.nl, accessed May 26, 2016.

10

SYNCHRONOUS OBJECTS

What else might this dance look like?

Norah Zuniga Shaw

Originally published online in 2009 and updated in 2012, *Synchronous Objects* is a collaborative choreographic visualization project that flows from a dance to data to visual objects and back around again. In this work, we explore the question, "what else might physical thinking look like?" by delving deeply into the systems that organize one dance. We translate those systems into data and conceptual frameworks and then generate new manifestations of them in the form of interactive visual objects on a screen. The dance is William Forsythe's *One Flat Thing, reproduced*, a contrapuntal ensemble piece exhibiting an exquisite cacophony of thematic material that is tightly structured by its three interlocking systems of organization. It is our choreographic resource, the source from which everything else emanates. The objects are re-articulations of the dance via the data and our own research/ artistic interests. They are both creative and analytical. Some help reveal patterns and allow the eye to see or "read" the dance differently. Other objects use the patterns and ideas in the dance to generate new animated forms, and still others are tools that allow for a greater degree of user interaction.

In the making of *Synchronous Objects*, research was a creative interdisciplinary pursuit. I am one of the creative directors for the work along with the choreographer William Forsythe and animator Maria Palazzi. Many consultants and collaborators contributed to the work, including members of the Forsythe Company and a large interdisciplinary team of students, faculty, and staff researchers in the US and Europe. These architects, statisticians, cognitive psychologists, philosophers, visual artists, designers, animators, geographers, dancers, and computer scientists all brought unique perspectives to the choreographic ideas that Forsythe offered for examination and transformation.

We started our work from the vision that Forsythe brought to the project. He was interested in having an interdisciplinary team analyze the visual counterpoint that he creates in *One Flat Thing, reproduced* and then seeing what digital media offer

FIGURE 10.1 Opening interface online for *Synchronous Objects*. Courtesy of the artists William Forsythe, Maria Palazzi and Norah Zuniga Shaw.

as a way of scoring those ideas and sharing them with new audiences. I remember in an early 2005 meeting Forsythe explaining, "we are not trying to recreate the experience of the piece, nor the genesis of the piece, it's not etymological, it's not archeological. It's not historical; it's not any of that. It's simply about saying, watch space become occupied with complexity." We were not focusing on the live presence of the work, nor its restaging for performance but instead Forsythe invited us to imagine "what else might this dance look like?" So it was within this framework of discovery that we engaged with the difficult but also generative challenge of making dance knowledge explicit and sharing it not only on stage and in the studio (as dancers are accustomed) but also through digital media.

The resulting screen-based work offers up twenty interactive visualizations that we call objects. Some of the objects are videos with animations that can be turned on or off, others are standalone animations or slideshows of geographic, architectural, textual, and statistical interpretations, and still others are interactive applications (built with *processing*, an open source rapid application development software) that allow users to analyze, re-use, and extend ideas in the dance. Each one includes a textual description, links to key terminology or related data, audio or textual commentary, a process catalog (samples from the creative process), explanatory videos, and cross-links to related objects. The site also houses a blog with many outside contributors and three short introductory essays and videos. In short, they are synchronous objects to each other and to the dance itself. Our objects are perhaps most of all manifestations of the exuberant multidisciplinary exchange of ideas we experienced in their creation—an experience I highly recommend for any maker and a meaningful one for the too-often isolated practice of dance making.

FIGURE 10.2 The Data Fan object from *Synchronous Objects* created using choreographic cueing and alignment data from William Forsythe's *One Flat Thing, reproduced*. Courtesy of the artists William Forsythe, Maria Palazzi and Norah Zuniga Shaw.

The choreographic resource

The dance at the center of our research is *One Flat Thing, reproduced*, choreographed by William Forsythe and premiered by the Ballet Frankfurt in 2000. Of the hundreds of possibilities to focus on in this 15 minute and 30 second piece for seventeen dancers, our emphasis is on its choreographic structures or systems of organization. This emphasis came from Forsythe's interests and the instigating questions he asked throughout the collaborative creation of the project. Through our research and discussion with Forsythe and the Company, the systems of organization in the dance were distilled into three intersecting categories—Themes (movement material), Cueing, and Alignments—which work together to create the visual counterpoint of the work.

While the urgency and immediacy of the dance can make it appear to be improvised, *One Flat Thing, reproduced* is a carefully choreographed and tightly crafted work. Members of the company most often refer to the different segments of fixed movement as themes. The twenty-five main themes are repeated and recombined over the course of the dance in their full and partial forms. In addition to the themes and their interpretation, there are improvisation tasks in the piece that ask dancers to translate specific properties of other performers' motions into their own. The themes and structured improvisations are the building blocks of the work, and once the viewer becomes familiar with them they become a welcome visible pattern.

The timing of the dance is influenced by the choices made in the short instances of improvisation and in how the dancers perform the set movement materials. However, the true internal clock of the dance is the elaborate cueing system that

Forsythe and the dancers created over many years. The musical score by Thom Willems does not direct the timing of the dancers' motions. Instead they wait for and give cues in a constantly shifting network of attention. While cues are common in live performance, the volume in this piece, more than two hundred total cues in just over 15 minutes, is unusual. The cueing system also gives the feeling of cause and effect that audiences often note.

Last and perhaps most important is the system of alignments. Alignments are moments of synchronization between the dancers when their actions share some but not all attributes. On a spectrum from unison to difference, alignments are closer to difference. Within the field of complex action that is *One Flat Thing, reproduced*, alignments are those flickering moments of shared directional flows, similar timing, and analogous shapes that catch the eye. They occur in every moment of the dance and are constantly shifting throughout the group.

All three of these systems together—movement material, cueing, alignments—combine to create the tapestry of visual counterpoint that is *One Flat Thing, reproduced*. We define counterpoint in this dance as a field of action in which the irregular and intermittent coincidence of attributes produces an ordered interplay. This definition assumes as a starting point "a field of action" with a high degree of difference within which "irregular and intermittent" patterns can be recognized. Imagine the play of light on the water, the intersection of branches in a tree canopy, or the motions of pedestrians on city streets. Each of these phenomena presents the eye with complexity but also presents irregular patterns of interaction that can be discerned and highlighted. Those patterns are the ordered interplay.

From these three systems we generated data. Like any data set, these numbers are indications of what we (the research team and Forsythe) chose to prioritize. They are numeric translations of the choreographic structures in the piece. The process of decoding the dance was a profoundly collective endeavor conducted over several years in close collaboration with William Forsythe and dancers Jill Johnson, Christopher Roman, and Elizabeth Waterhouse. As we came to fully understand the counterpoint that unfolds in the dance we worked to devise methods for quantifying it in the data and expressing it in the objects. This effort produced two key sets of data: spatial data taken from our source video of the dance and attribute data gleaned from dancer accounts. As in many forms of inquiry, quantification requires a reductive process that necessarily obscures certain aspects of knowledge (the dancers' intentions, performance quality, and kinesthetic awareness) in order to reveal others (in this case, choreographic structure). Drawing from the methodologies of many disciplines—dance, design, computer graphics, geography, and statistics—we intentionally privileged the inside view of the dance and used this to drive our data gathering process.

From the data and our broader conceptual understanding of the dance, we were able to mobilize the choreographic ideas it holds beyond the body into other manifestations that we call objects and that relate to Forsythe's larger interest in "choreographic objects." As I have worked with this idea I have come to believe that the concept of a choreographic object is important in that it allows for the transformation of a dance from one manifestation (the performance on stage) into an array of other possibilities (such as information, animation, installation . . .). When discussing the subject, Forsythe often paraphrases René Magritte saying "an object is not so possessed by its own name that one could not find another or better," therefore suggesting the primacy of context and translation in his thinking. Like any good literary translation a choreographic object stays true to the original thinking space of the maker while allowing for new comprehension of the work. And as in all translation, where there are gains in communication there are losses as well. One can never fully comprehend German poetry in English and one can never fully comprehend dance without live performance. But we translate the poetry in order to give more people an experience of it; and we translate dances into choreographic objects in order to generate new expressions of the substance of the form. In the creation of a choreographic object, ideas are allowed to jump and swerve out of familiar territory and to become completely unrecognizable in their new forms. They are also made available for exchange. There is rigorous analysis and in-depth study of a source in order to bring forth its attributes, but then the outcome can become a new work in its own right.

Context

With the explosion of online video sharing, social networking sites, and significant improvements in image quality with the ubiquity of High Definition video, digital dance research has also been developing rapidly in recent years. This has led several established dance artists to re-consider the possibilities of digital tools for the re-articulation and transmission of bodily knowledge. A few examples that were developing around the same time as our project include Emio Greco's *Double Skin/Double Mind* project created with Bertha Bermúdez Pasqual, Chris Ziegler, and other collaborators (see Chapter 9 in this volume); Merce Cunningham Company's *Mondays with Merce* online streaming video of him in the studio; Steve Paxton's DVD-ROM *Material for the Spine* created with collaborators at Contredanse (see Chapter 3 of this volume); the book and DVD *Anarchic Dance* by and about Divas Dance Theatre; Nick Rothwell, Philip Barnard, and Scott deLahunta's work with Wayne McGregor on choreographic thinking (see Chapter 11 of this volume); and the generous online digital archive for Siobhan Davies' work created by Sara Whatley and her team in the UK (discussed by Whatley in Chapter 6 of this volume). With very different outcomes, each of these projects was concerned with the nature of choreographic knowledge and with discovering new digital possibilities for tracing, transmitting, and sharing ideas contained within dance.

Always interested in technology and interdisciplinary collaboration, William Forsythe has been at the leading edge of this evolving terrain. His 1996 CD-ROM, *Improvisation Technologies* (created with Chris Ziegler, ZKM, and Ballet Frankfurt dancers, see Chapter 4 in this volume) was an elegant example of the power of animation techniques to communicate ideas at work in the creation of a dance. At that time, Forsythe and his dancers were engaged in improvisation strategies that involved a lively geometric imagination and relationship to space. Ziegler's animations make these geometries explicit with ingeniously simple (although laborious to produce) white lines drawn on a video image of Forsythe demonstrating how points, lines, and architectural details can generate a vast range of movement. The CD-ROM (now a DVD-ROM and also a film installation) was taken up not only by dance students and professionals but also the MIT School of Architecture and others outside the field of dance interested in accessing dance knowledge and ideas. This experience was a meaningful precedent for Forsythe and laid the groundwork for his interest in creating *Synchronous Objects* and then *Motion Bank* (see Chapter 13 in this volume), the Forsythe Company's initiative focusing on digital scores for four other choreographers, Deborah Hay, Jonathan Burrows, Bebe Miller, and Thomas Hauert.

When we started *Synchronous Objects* in late 2005 YouTube was a new phenomenon (YouTube was founded in February of 2005), HD-DVD and Blu-Ray were in a format war with Blu-Ray yet to dominate the market, and the potential for sharing great quality video online was still emerging. The live stage version of Forsythe's *One Flat Thing, reproduced* had just finished a worldwide tour (because the piece is under 20 minutes, it was generally shown as the finale on a program with other works) with fourteen performers from the newly formed Forsythe Company (after the end of the Ballet Frankfurt in 2004). William Forsythe was preparing to shoot a dance film of *One Flat Thing, reproduced* for French television with director Thierry de Mey and he wanted to use that opportunity to gather quality video footage for a new project focusing on choreographic structure in the dance, counterpoint, and interdisciplinary exchange. I was newly relocated to Ohio for a position as faculty member in the dance department at The Ohio State University and director for dance and technology at the Advanced Computing Center for the Arts and Design (ACCAD), a research center that specializes in computer graphics, art and science collaborations, and artist-driven research. Forsythe and I met in New York, I shared samples of our work at ACCAD with him, he described what he was interested in exploring and the collaboration grew very naturally from there. Financing for the project was a mix of European support from Tanzplan Deutschland and educational partners, research grants from The Ohio State University, and personal investment and in-kind support.

Developments since 2009 and other outcomes

On April 1, 2009 we launched our project on the web and in a large museum exhibition at the Wexner Center for the Arts (including other sculptural and film works by Forsythe), and an accompanying symposium and webcast. The online presence of the work remains the primary way that our ideas are shared with hundreds of thousands of visitors each year from around the world. The interesting wrinkle now in the evolution of our project is the slow demise of Adobe Flash (the multimedia platform we used to develop the interface for *Synchronous Objects*) and what that means for the future accessibility of the work online. For now it continues to be available but some new browser and device compatibility issues are emerging and we are investigating possibilities for archiving the work or re-imagining it for the current world of mobile devices.

We designed the work to attract a diverse audience. We wanted to create accessible experiences but also to include rich content that would reward sustained engagement with the material and would hold value for experts. And we hoped to engage thinkers and makers from many different disciplines by offering an array of different perspectives on the work. The interface we decided on reflects this broad and multivariate audience that we had in mind. When you encounter the home page, all twenty visual objects are sliding by, providing multiple points of entry, and from any one of them you can get to all others. There are many threads that move through our work: interdisciplinary collaboration, creative research methods, knowledge transmission, participatory pedagogy, information visualization, art and technology, cognition and perception research, design, and of course, contemporary dance. This perhaps explains the broad range of domains in which it has been taken up.

Over the past years, we have received feedback (some of which is published on our blog) from educators using the site in university classrooms for choreography and dance history certainly, but also for design, architecture, art history, philosophy, engineering, and visual arts. The work has been referenced in publications by artists and theorists and we have presented it in lectures, workshops, and exhibitions for participants and audiences at arts, dance, and humanities festivals, design and computer graphics conferences, university symposia in dance, media arts, architecture, philosophy, and in the context of conversations about archiving, scoring, interdisciplinary research process, contemporary arts, and philosophies of the object, of gesture, of relationality, of human perception, and of memory.

Secondary to the site itself, I have had the opportunity to re-imagine the screen-based original as a series of site-specific video installations for venues in Europe, the US, and Asia. I made the first installation in 2010 with a commission from German curator Andreas Broeckmann to create a piece at PACT Zollverein during the RUHR 2010: European Capital of Culture events. At PACT, the installation included three spaces starting with large format projections of the full 15 minutes and 30 second dance in proscenium view. In the second space, visitors encountered a table from the performance of the piece (donated by the Company) and a top view of the dance appearing and disappearing on three HD screens with our analytical lines weaving them together. These lines visualize the cueing and alignments in the work. In the third and final space, visitors entered from the diagonal so that there was no clear sense of front. Twelve screens were hung at different heights and facings in what we called our "video forest." The videos on the screens were synchronized in the timeframe of the dance so that patterns between different objects could be discovered, something that is impossible in the online version.

The sound of the dancers performing the piece moved through the space jumping from speaker to speaker in a composition of multichannel sound. Forsythe's voice also moved throughout the speakers as he calls out the phrasing of the piece in what I call his "sing through." Also included in this installation was a "proliferation of paper process." Three paper rollers hung high in the back were programmed to drop thousands of papers onto the floor in contrapuntal timing for visitors to pick up, read, and take home. On the papers were snapshots from our creative process of making *Synchronous Objects*, including early sketches, samples of code, conversations between the makers that were transcribed from an internal website for our process, and images of early prototypes. After this installation, the Goethe Institute produced a tour of modules from it along with lectures and studio workshops to venues in Ankara, Bangalore, Beijing, Budapest, Khartoum, New York, Taipei, Tokyo, and Zagreb. In addition to the Goethe tour, I have had the opportunity to teach movement and interdisciplinary design workshops using *Synchronous Objects* to dancers in many of the Tanzplan Deutschland projects in Germany, artists at the ICK Amsterdam BEYOND workshops in the Netherlands, and to my own students in dance at The Ohio State University, among others. It has been a very meaningful time of exchange and development of the work, taking the ideas beyond where

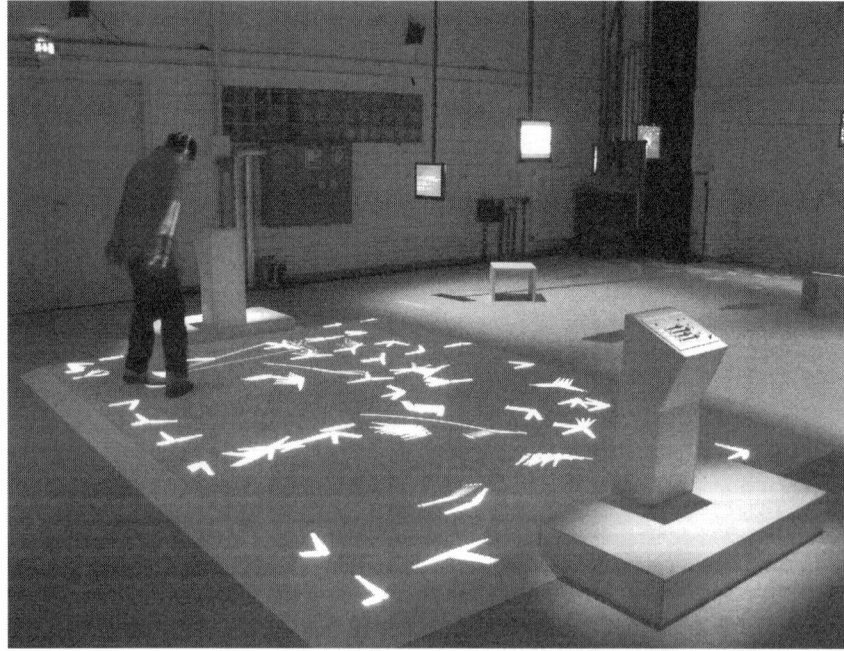

FIGURE 10.3   Image from *Synchronous Objects: Reproduced* video installation at PACT Zollverein Essen, Germany, August 2010. Curator Andreas Broeckmann. Courtesy of the artists William Forsythe, Maria Palazzi and Norah Zuniga Shaw.

they were in 2009. For this reason and because many have requested a hard copy resource, I published a book/catalog about the work, *Synchronous Objects: Degrees of Unison* (available via Blurb.com) with text and images from the site, an extensive catalog of process, several new essays on the dance, the data, and the objects, and complementary essays by scholars and artists who either collaborated on the project or have written about it in their own work. In this way, Forsythe's ideas that started in the body keep moving, from a dance, into ideas, data, and visualizations, and back around again into discourse, dialog, and exchange, and into the embodied experiences of visitors to gallery installations, students and writers at their computers, and artists and scientists in the studio and lab. This was always our hope.

In closing

Since the publication of *Synchronous Objects* in 2009, it has been the story of visual counterpoint as it is enacted in Forsythe's work that has surfaced as one of the most important aspects of the project. In counterpoint, difference and dissonance are the primary visual effects. It is at the layer of the deep structure that the relationships, alignments, and forms of agreement are at work. For contemporary society in which there is very little unity, counterpoint may be a valuable metaphor for living. What if we were to encounter those instances of disagreement or difference in our work lives, in our schools and on our streets with contrapuntal attention? What as yet unseen structures of agreement, fleeting instances of relationship and alignment of ideas might be percolating under the surfaces of our lives? And what implications does this have for the importance of dance knowledge as it unfolds in interdisciplinary contexts and in the world?

***

Synchronous Objects can be found at http://synchronousobjects.osu.edu.

11
WAYNE MCGREGOR'S *CHOREOGRAPHIC LANGUAGE AGENT*

Scott deLahunta

The paper notebook with its companion pencil or pen is a creative tool for many contemporary choreographers and their dancers. Using the notebook affords a relationship with a set of external objects inscribed "on the page" in the form of drawn sketches, notations, and diagrams combined with text (Blackwell et al.). This relationship can be described in cognitive terms, for example, where the page becomes a surrogate for working memory, or a way for seeing something new by modeling structures or processes. The notebook in this sense becomes a site for the encounter of cognition and creativity, providing a place for thinking generatively with external objects (sketches, notations, etc.), an idea this essay will revisit.

This concept that the choreographer's notebook affords a relationship with objects on the page underpins the development of the *Choreographic Language Agent* (CLA) as an extended interactive digital notebook.[1] The CLA evolved out of a vision London-based choreographer Wayne McGregor had for a suite of creative software tools that would use artificial intelligence algorithms to generate unique solutions to choreographic problems and augment McGregor's creative decision-making processes in the studio. The resulting software tool, developed conceptually and technically through many iterations over several years, provides McGregor and his dancers with an interactive system for assembling choreographic phrases from a set of named operations selected from drop-down menus. These assembled phrases contain simple 3D geometric transforms that can be combined and layered on top of each other to increase their overall complexity. These are all laid out against a time-line upon which they are "played" to animate a three-dimensional drawing built from minimalist point-line-plane geometry. This creates a wide variety of kinematic and dynamic 3D sketch-like configurations that the dancers use as inspiration for movement generation in the rehearsal studio (see Figure 11.2).

Background: concepts and interdisciplinary research

Artificial intelligence (AI), along with psychology, neuroscience, linguistics, and philosophy, is considered part of the broader study of the brain and mind that the cognitive science field has come to represent.[2] In early AI research, computers and the brain were thought to be performing similar processes, and modeling brain-like mechanisms in the computer was seen as a way of studying intelligence.[3] It seemed logical that the first step in a project to develop artificially intelligent software tools to use in dance creation was to acquire more information about the intelligence behind making dances. This inspired the collaborative interdisciplinary research project titled *Choreography and Cognition* (2003–2004), set up to draw on the field of cognitive science to enhance understanding of the choreographic process. Five scientists from diverse backgrounds were invited to work in residence with the McGregor dance company on various studies focused on topics such as movement control and perturbations, phrase segmentation, and the cognitive dimension of notations.[4] The project overall generated a rich landscape of concepts, vocabulary, descriptions, and models; a landscape that eventually evolved into separate research projects that would support the creation of the CLA software tool with practical and theoretical developments.[5]

The initial interdisciplinary engagement with cognitive scientists was followed by a period of research into the field of AI, its historical relation to the development of cognitive science, and its successes and failures. The particular class of AI problems and solutions known as "agent-based" appeared to offer a way forward for the project.[6] This laid the groundwork for conversations with specialists working in the field of AI and related areas.[7] Some specific writers and artists doing related work were considered. AARON, for example, is a computer program developed by Harold Cohen to autonomously produce aesthetically accomplished drawings. Starting out as a painter in 1971, Cohen became interested in AI and the possibility of building a "machine-based simulation of the cognitive processes underlying the human act of drawing" (Kurzweil). Cohen has written a succession of increasingly complex software programs, each a new version of AARON. Cohen's project features in Margaret Boden's 1990 book *The Creative Mind: Myths and Mechanisms*, in which Boden, founder of the School of Cognitive and Computing Sciences, Sussex University, explores how human intuition and creativity might be better understood with "the help of ideas from artificial intelligence" (15). Boden's useful book notwithstanding, the field of AI, with its communities of practice largely motivated by non-art engineering goals and computer science research questions, proved to be a difficult one within which to find a tractable approach for building creative choreographic tools.

Assembling the CLA creative team

In the artist and artificial intelligence researcher Marc Downie, the CLA project found a collaborator with the overall sensibility and specific know-how to help design and build an autonomous choreographic agent. Downie had developed award-winning digital artworks using the "agent-based" approach from AI before completing his 2005 PhD thesis entitled "Choreographing the Extended Agent" at MIT's Media Lab. Downie's thesis provides the background for his work as a member of the digital arts OpenEndedGroup where, working alongside other members Paul Kaiser and Shelley Eshkar, he has collaborated with choreographers Trisha Brown, Bill T. Jones, and Merce Cunningham (see also Kaiser's chapter about Cunningham's *Loops* in this volume, Chapter 2). He approaches making agent-based artworks as "a software engineering problem," but one requiring solutions that work for the art domain. This differentiates his process from computer science research where the algorithm itself is the locus of innovation. Downie credits the refinement of his "agent-based aesthetics" to the development of his series titled "The Music Creatures." Inspired by the acoustics abilities of birds, "The Music Creatures" utilize a "range of AI techniques to maintain a position of 'dynamic disequilibrium' with the gallery space and each other, conveying a sense of effort, intention and ultimately transience and instability" (Downie, "Choreographing the Extended Agent" ix).

An "agent" in software terms is part of an "overall intelligent system" in which the agent can perceive its environment and take autonomous action based on these perceptions. Downie's arts practice applies this concept using the algorithms of AI in the context of artistic creation. Software programming is a rigorously exacting process, and for his earlier agent-based artworks Downie wrote thousands of lines of custom code. When he began collaborating with non-programming artists, including the aforementioned choreographers, and needed to work more quickly in real-time, Downie developed *Field* as an authoring environment that would allow algorithmic systems to be rapidly created, revised, and reused as necessary. This enabled his "agent-based approach to meet the realities of collaboration, rehearsal and improvisatory choreographic practice" ("Choreographing the Extended Agent" xii). With this built-in sensitivity to working rhythms in the dance studio, *Field* became the environment of choice for the development of the CLA. It has since been released as open source software and is now in use by a growing community of artist programmers.[8]

Also working on the CLA since its inception was composer and programmer Nick Rothwell. Based in London, Rothwell has worked on other dance projects, exploring the computational relationship between software and choreographic structure.[9] For example, for *ChoreoGraph* (2002) he worked in collaboration with Austrian dance maker Michael Kliën to create software that re-arranges the order of a duet each time it was performed by dancers from Ballet Frankfurt (deLahunta, "Duplex/ ChoreoGraph"). Rothwell made a significant contribution to the early conceptualization of the CLA as a means for exploring variations in choreographic instruction based on McGregor's approach described in the next section. The other key members of the CLA project team were Alan Blackwell and Luke Church from the Computer Laboratory at Cambridge University, whose areas of research include the development of programming interfaces for non-programmers. Blackwell was one of the scientists participating in the *Choreography and Cognition* project, for which he conducted research into the cognitive dimensions of McGregor's use of notations, and he brought this experience to bear on the interface design of the CLA.

A choreographic context for tool use

As mentioned earlier, choreographers and dancers use notebooks as things to think with. They also use "bodies to think with," particularly at certain points in a creative, learning, or rehearsal process (see Kirsh, "Thinking with the Body," and Kirsh et al., "Choreographic Methods"). The CLA is envisioned to make its contribution to the choreographic process situated somewhere between these two different areas: between notebooks and bodies. Specifically, it is envisioned as an environment for exploring variations in choreographic instruction that are not possible with non-digital notebooks and bodies alone.

Choreographic instructions refer to the types of problems, tasks, games, and/or scores the dancers may be asked to solve or apply in the creation of movement material. As a method for generating movement material the choreographer may use or select from, the giving of instructions or formal tasks has been common practice for a range of contemporary choreographers, including Merce Cunningham, William Forsythe, and Trisha Brown.[10] For McGregor, instructions stimulate a certain interior landscape of thinking that should bring "intentionality" (artist's use of the term) to the dancers' performance, rendering visible what the dancer is paying attention to during execution of the instruction or task. Tasks also support the dancers in their exploration of novel non-habitual movement patterns and are often derived from a conceptual or thematic starting point, for example an image of the Vitruvian Man. They may feature geometric lines or planes drawn both inside and outside the body's own space and include procedures to be performed with these geometries and conditional statements governing the time or place in which actions may occur. Some instructions are extremely formal, based on numbers and coordinates; others are more narrative, involving different forms of imagery designed to trigger non-visual sensory experience, for example, acoustic (paying attention to sound) and kinesthetic (paying attention to the sensing of movement).

Notebooks are an important part of this process and contemporary choreographers who work this way use them to develop and record possible instructions or tasks. And notebooks are used by their dancers to record the instructions or tasks as they are given, used to work out features of possible movement solutions to be tried out, and if successful the result recorded in the notebook for future recall. As mentioned earlier, the notebook thusly affords a relationship with a set of objects "on the page" in the form of drawn sketches, notations, and diagrams combined with text. Notebooks are things McGregor and his dancers think with, they are part of the context of their "mental activity" (Robbins and Aydede 3). The CLA aims for a similar quality of situated-ness in the creation process, as an extended interactive digital notebook to support creative problem-solving. As such, the CLA "posits a new form of dance notation; one that aids the choreographer in generating dance movements rather than in recording existing movements" (Downie, *Choreographic Language Agent*). The CLA however, does not propose a general model of movement, choreography, and meaning, rather it "focuses on the individual and even idiosyncratic methods of a given language movement system" (Downie, *Choreographic Language Agent*), in this case as recorded in sets of choreographic instructions used by McGregor which have been converted into a machine-readable language.

The primary salient feature of the autonomous CLA is that it takes instructions, interprets them, and renders dynamic graphic imagery as a potential proxy for the dancer: another problem-solving movement generating "body" McGregor and his dancers can refer to in the studio. The graphic rendering model takes as its point of departure a minimalist point-line-plane vocabulary instead of a sophisticated, anatomically correct joint hierarchy. The idea is to rapidly sketch movement explorations in a 3D referent space—a "stage" within which abstract figures can be rendered and controlled by the language elements. This "stage" configuration serves only as a reference and is unconstrained in any real physical world sense. Given a sentence written in the converted language now known to the tool, the CLA can interpret this sentence to produce a short animation of this body. This means that the user performs "pseudo-linguistic operations on the language level, thus generating sequences, superpositions, and modulations" (Downie, *Choreographic Language Agent*). After studying and labelling sets of sentences and correspondences between them, one can begin to determine the conditions under which an agent (or multiple agents) can autonomously deploy this language to generate possible movements. McGregor and the dancers already know how to manipulate various types of visual imagery in the context of executing instructions or tasks to create novel movement material for a dance. The CLA both enhances and perturbs this process by offering a unique programming environment for the dancer to explore and work at harnessing dynamic visual structures and syntactic (language-like) relationships, which they build further understanding of by assimilating them into their movement generation in the studio. Additionally, with its digital memory, the CLA uniquely documents aspects of their decision making—making a part of the choreographic thinking process available for revisiting and examination.

Working with the CLA in the studio

The CLA was designed so that the McGregor and the dancers with relatively little training would find the "right balance of surprise, expectation and controllability" in working with it (Downie, personal communication, February 23, 2009). By October 2009, the creative team had developed a working prototype which included sentence (or phrase) construction, animation playback, and history visualization. The prototype was then tested and further developed in workshop contexts with McGregor and his company in residencies at EMPAC (Troy, NY, February 2010), the Jerwood Space (London, September 2010) and at a three-day training session with the company at Sadler's Wells, June 2011.

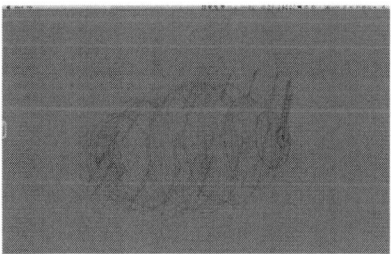 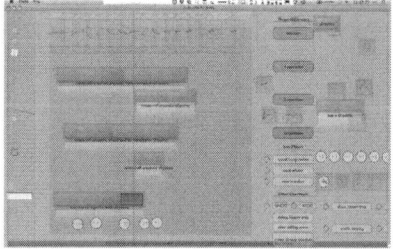

FIGURE 11.1 The left and right screens of the Choreographic Language Agent. Courtesy of the OpenEndedGroup & Wayne McGregor|Random Dance.

Here is how the CLA now works: the choreographer and/or dancers first construct a 3-D drawing comprised of points, lines and planes on the left screen in the visual space (Figure 11.1, left screen). They then use drop-down menus on the right screen to select some aspect of their drawing, for example all points on the left side (Figure 11.1, right screen). Then they select an instruction to apply to them, for example "rotate these points around their own axis." These two parts are assembled one after the other on the right screen, and dragging the playback bar across them animates the drawing in the visual space. This sounds simple, but these assembled phrases can be layered one on top of another to produce surprising and complex animated drawings. The dancers take these as inspiration for movement generation into the studio space, returning to the CLA sketching environment to try out new combinations.

FIGURE 11.2 Experimental sketching of a new movement sequence (left), followed by dance exploration of the geometry created (right). Dancer is Jessica Wright. Photos: Luke Church.

The CLA was used in the creative process of the work *UNDANCE*, a collaboration between McGregor and visual artist Mark Wallinger and composer Mark-Anthony Turnage, premiering November 2011. McGregor, Wallinger and Turnage drew inspiration for the creative process of *UNDANCE* in part from the "verb list" of Richard Serra.[11] A selection of these was given to the dancers (to wrap, to twist, to roll, to hang, to rotate) with the instructions to build a phrase (in Figure 11.1, right screen) and a 3D animation (in Figure, 11.1 left screen) in the CLA, then to translate this animation into movement.

Choreographic thinking tools

McGregor's original vision of a suite of creative software tools drawing on AI technologies spawned a series of collaborative exchanges with cognitive scientists, which in addition to the CLA creation gave rise to two research projects with overlapping but different objectives. The first, *Choreographic Thinking Tools* (CTT), has been in development under various headings since 2004 with Phil Barnard from the Cognition and Brain Studies Unit, MRC, Cambridge. The project seeks to uncover "the kinds of intelligences (choreographic thinking) that are involved in contemporary dance making" (Barnard and deLahunta) and make this information available to choreographers in a format that is useful. Methods used and results from the CTT project range from how to organize mutually valuable exchanges of ideas between dance and science (deLahunta, Barnard, and McGregor) to the development of empirical research and practical application in the dance studio of tools to support the choreographic process based on scientific theory (May et al.; deLahunta, Barnard, and Clarke).

The second project is a close collaboration with David Kirsh, who directs the Interactive Cognition Lab at the University of California San Diego. Kirsh specializes in the interaction between individuals in a working context, including how these individuals do things together to solve problems, develop and use tools, and adapt to changes in their environment.[12] His aim with McGregor and the company has been to record and analyze the coordination of choreographic thought and action between choreographer and dancers during the creation process. Under the heading *Distributed Choreographic Cognition*, Kirsh has documented and studied thousands of hours of the making of three of McGregor's company works, including *UNDANCE* when the CLA was used—resulting in not only providing McGregor with fresh insight into his own choreographic methods ("Choreographic Methods") but also in a rigorous new conception of physical thinking. ("Thinking with the Body").

Decisions taken when building the CLA were guided by insights gained in these collaborative exchanges, for example the use of creative imagery extensively studied for the development of the CTT with Phil Barnard, and the use of forms of multi-modal instruction explored by David Kirsh and earlier unpublished research by Alan Blackwell looking into the cognitive dimensions of McGregor's use of notations in his notebooks.[13] The CLA is also considered as a "novel" representation of computation, one that gives the dancers access to computational behaviors they are normally excluded from with traditional software tools (Church and Blackwell). This makes the CLA a significant research outcome for the designers involved in its development (Church et al.). A future development of the CLA is envisioned as an interactive audience installation aiming to involve users and viewers in those aspects of "choreographic thinking" that are embedded and embodied in the CLA, thus providing a deeper insight into how dances are made—through a direct engagement with its creative tools.[14]

***

More information on the *Choreographic Language Agent* can be found here: http://openendedgroup.com/artworks/cla.html and in two of the videos developed for the Wellcome Collection Exhibition *Thinking with the Body*: http://wellcomecollection.org/thinkingwiththebody.

Notes

1. CLA development was supported by Portland Green Cultural Projects. Luke Church's research was supported by Kodak. Nick Rothwell's work was supported in part by a Digital Futures in Dance residency at Dance Digital.
2. For a history of cognitive science including in-depth material on artificial intelligence see Margaret Boden (*Mind as Machine*). For a quick glance at a description of cognitive science including its history and methods see http://plato.stanford.edu/entries/cognitive-science/, accessed October 13, 2012.
3. One of the most influential books in the field of artificial intelligence from that time was titled *Design for a Brain* by W. Ross Ashby, first published in 1952.
4. For more details of these studies, see the documentation website *Choreography and Cognition* (2003–2004), available at http://www.choreocog.net, accessed October 13, 2012.
5. See http://www.randomdance.org/r_research/current_projects, accessed September 21, 2012.
6. An agent is seen as part of an overall intelligent system in which the agent can perceive its environment and take autonomous action based on these perceptions; real world examples include software agents that search the internet for goods and services, and data mining agents.
7. These conversations comprised key meetings with specialists in a range of fields including robotics, computer vision, artificial intelligence, and computational neuroscience, involving a visit to the University of San Diego, California in April 2007 followed by the ENTITY Think Tank in London in November 2007 where some of the UCSD scientists were invited to join several from the UK in an interdisciplinary "brain storming" session to envision autonomous choreographic agents.
8. See http://openendedgroup.com/field/, accessed October 12, 2012.
9. See http://www.cassiel.com/about/, accessed November 11, 2015.
10. For example: Cunningham's use of chance techniques dating back to the 1950s (see Vaughn); Brown's algorithmically determined dance structures include *Locus* 1975 (Livet 54). A CD-rom and booklet detailing William Forsythe's *Improvisation Technologies* methods, first published for a wider public in 1999, has been recently reprinted (Forsythe).
11. From: Richard Serra, "Verb List Compilation: Actions to Relate to Oneself" [1967–1968], available at http://www.ubu.com/concept/serra_verb.html, accessed September 20, 2012.
12. See http://adrenaline.ucsd.edu/kirsh/publications.html, accessed September 21, 2012.

13 A brief description of Alan Blackwell's research with McGregor's notebooks can be found at http://www.choreocog.net/exper.html, accessed November 11, 2015.
14 An earlier version of this paper was published as "The Choreographic Language Agent." *Dance Dialogues: Conversations Across Cultures, Artforms and Practices: Proceedings of the 2008 World Dance Alliance Global Summit, Brisbane, 13–18 July*. Ed. C. Stock. Canberra: QUT Creative Industries and Ausdance, 2009.

References

Barnard, Phil, Scott deLahunta, and Wayne McGregor. "A Summary: Principles of Choreographic Thinking." *The Embodied Mind*. December 12, 2008, Squire Bancroft Studio, Royal Academy of Dramatic Art, London. Ed. Siân Ede. London: Calouste Gulbenkian Foundation, 2008. 14–15, available at http://www.gulbenkian.org.uk/publications/publications/61-THE-EMBODIED-MIND.html, accessed May 18, 2016.

Boden, Margaret. *The Creative Mind: Myths and Mechanisms*. 2nd ed. London: Routledge, 2004.

—— *Mind as Machine: A History of Cognitive Science*, Vols. 1 and 2. Oxford: Oxford University Press, 2006.

Blackwell, Alan, Scott deLahunta, Wayne McGregor, and John Warwicker. "Transactables." *Performance Research, On The Page* 9.2 (2004): 67–72.

Church, Luke, and Alan Blackwell. "Computation, Visualization and Critical Reflection." *Visualisation in the Age of Computerisation*. Oxford, March 2011. Conference paper.

Church, Luke, Mark Downie, Scott deLahunta, and Alan Blackwell. "Sketching by Programming in the Choreographic Language Agent." *Psychology of Programming Interest Group Annual Conference*. November 21–23, 2012, London Metropolitan University. London: n.p. Ed. Yanguo Jing, 2012. 163–174.

deLahunta, Scott. "Duplex/ ChoreoGraph: in conversation with Barriedale Operahouse." *Software for Dancers* (2002), available at http://www.sdela.dds.nl/sfd/frankfin.html, accessed December 10, 2012.

deLahunta, Scott, Phil Barnard, and Gill Clarke. "A Conversation about Choreographic Thinking Tools." *The Journal of Dance & Somatic Practices* 3.1–2 (2012): 243–259.

deLahunta, Scott, Phil Barnard, and Wayne McGregor. "Augmenting Choreography: Using Insights from Cognitive Science." *Routledge Reader in Contemporary Choreography*. Ed. Jo Butterworth and Liesbeth Wildschut. London: Routledge, 2009. 431–448.

Downie, Marc. *Choreographing the Extended Agent: performance graphics for dance theater*. Diss. Boston: MIT, 2005, available at http://openendedgroup.com/writings/downieThesis.html, accessed October 12, 2012.

—— *Choreographic Language Agent* (2008), available at http://openendedgroup.com/index.php/in-progress/choreographic-language-agent/, accessed December 10, 2012.

Forsythe, William. *Improvisation Technologies: a Tool for the Analytical Dance Eye*. Karlsruhe: ZKM, Karlsruhe and Hatje Cantz Verlag, 2012.

Kirsh, David. "Thinking with the Body." *Proceedings of the 32nd Annual Conference of the Cognitive Science Society*. Ed. S. Ohlsson and R. Catrambone. Austin, TX: Cognitive Science Society, 2010. 2,864–2,869.

Kirsh, David, Dafne Muntanyola, R. Joanne Jao, Amy Lew, and Matt Sugihara. "Choreographic Methods for Creating Novel, High Quality Dance." *Design and Semantics of Form and Movement*. October 26–27, 2009, Taipei. Ed. Lin-Lin Chen, Loe Feijs, Marina Hessler, Steven Kyffin, Pei-Ling Liu, Kees Overbeeke, and Bob Young. Amsterdam: Koninklijke Philips Electronics N.V., 2009. 188–195.

Kurzweil, Raymond. "Biography of Harold Cohen: Creator of AARON." Kurzweil Cyberart Technologies (2001), available at http://www.kurzweilcyberart.com/aaron/hi_cohenbio.html, accessed October 14, 2012.

Livet, Anne. *Contemporary Dance*. New York: Abbeville Press, 1978.

May, Jon, Beatriz Calvo-Merino, Scott deLahunta, Wayne McGregor, Rhodri Cusack, Adrian Owen, Michele Veldsman, Cristina Ramponi, and Phil Barnard. "Points in Mental Space: an Interdisciplinary Study of Imagery and Tasks in Movement Innovation." *Dance Research* 29.2 (2011): 404–430.

Robbins, Philip, and Murat Aydede, eds. *Cambridge Handbook of Situated Cognition*. Cambridge: Cambridge University Press, 2009.

Vaughan, David. *Merce Cunningham: 65 Years*. New York: Aperture Foundation, 2012. iPad ebook.

12
BADco. AND DANIEL TURING
Whatever Dance Toolbox

Nikolina Pristaš, Goran Sergej Pristaš and Tomislav Medak

Whatever Dance Toolbox (WDT) is a product of the long-standing collaboration between the performance collective BADco. and German human-machine interface developer and artist Daniel Turing. *Whatever Dance Toolbox* reflects some of their mutual concerns regarding dancer-computer interaction and related choreographic thinking. A suite of software tools designed for analysis and development of dance and movement, it is a simple-to-use, technically non-demanding set of real-time video analyses which can work as an interactive mirror by displaying various transformations of a real-time video image and/or visualizations of the body/movements actually being performed. Daniel Turing explains it like this:

> My experiments involving real-time video analysis of human motion all circle around this question: What does the machine see? In my interactive setups, I am applying well-known computer vision techniques to a video signal recording human actors, trying to give a glimpse into the underlying processes, visualizing basic recognition methods and producing imagery that exemplifies the computer's "perception."[1]

The differences between human perception of movement and the way a machine represents that movement enables a shift in the way dancers and non-dancers alike relate to the creation of movement in terms of placement, quality, and spatial and temporal organization. By transforming the image of movement, the interactive mirror highlights previously unnoticed qualities in that movement, thus inviting new ways of relating to actions and how they are performed. Additionally, moving in front of an interactive mirror induces a split in the attention of the observer/dancer so that s/he needs to consciously process two images of her moving body, an internalized image and an on-screen, transformed one, almost simultaneously. This also has some far-reaching consequences for the decision-making process in dance.

How do the tools work and what can be done with them?

WDT contains six applications: *Matching Positions, Cage, Inertia, Delay/Reverse, Capture/Replay*, and *Appear/Disappear*. *Matching Positions, Cage*, and *Inertia* are all based on the same type of video analysis: a human body or any other object placed in front of the camera is represented onscreen as a white shape/silhouette against a dark background. The software either analyzes how that white shape extends across the screen area (*Matching Positions*), signals when the shape crosses the border of a previously defined onscreen area (*Cage*), or follows the mathematical center of the shape (centroid) with a red cross (*Inertia*). *Delay/Reverse* and *Capture/Replay* differ in that they display a video image as seen through the camera lens and perform various temporal transformations of the real-time video stream. Their names point to their functions. Lastly, *Appear/Disappear* is a live video stream that blurs parts of the image proportionally to the speed of the moving body, ranging from in-focus still object or body to out-of-focus moving body.

Matching Positions is a task-based tool. The task consists of seeking a body position that allows the individual's onscreen shape (or the collective onscreen silhouette if there are multiple people in front of the camera) to match the angle or point given as a task. Once each task is completed the software moves onto the next. Accomplishing a task means moving through space and shaping the body relative to information read from the screen. One also needs to, at least intuitively, understand the difference between the three-dimensional space in which s/he moves and its two-dimensional on-screen representation. When multiple people simultaneously solve a task, various other components of the dynamic organization of group choreography are immediately revealed, emphasizing the exchange between

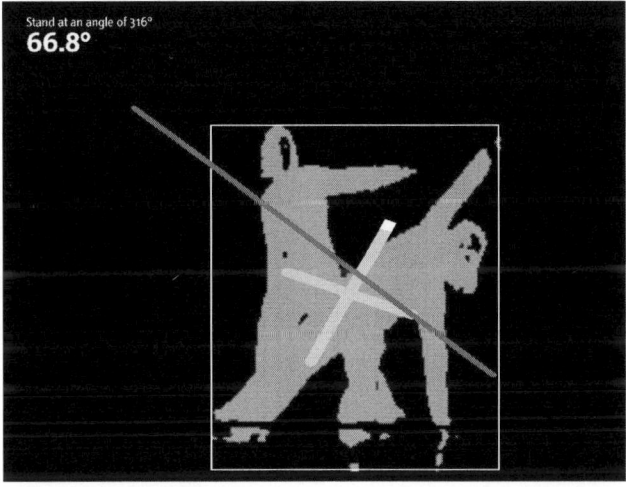

FIGURE 12.1 Screenshot of *Matching Positions*. Image courtesy of BADco.

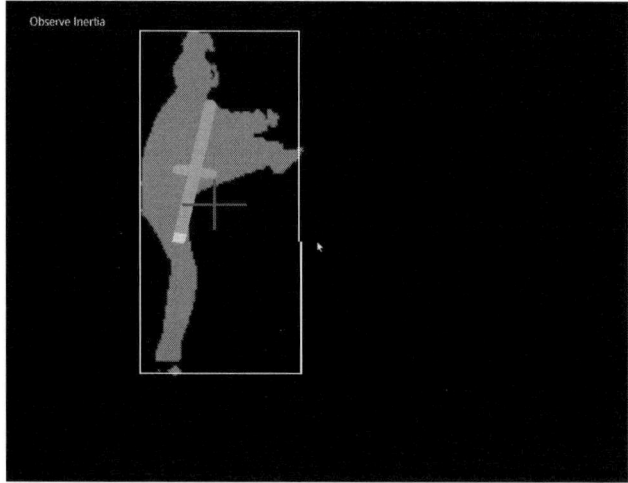

FIGURE 12.2 Screenshot of *Inertia*. Image courtesy of BADco.

bodies. Because all performers watch the screen as they are moving through space, they have to resort to other communication capacities than language (i.e., touch and gesture) in order to negotiate the space-taking and body shaping. This ad hoc composition rapidly becomes complex, producing specific social choreography that is otherwise not so easy to accomplish.

Cage is a resizable onscreen rectangle representing a perspectival pyramid that extends from the center of the camera lens into the space being filmed. This makes explicit the difference between the two spaces, onscreen 2D and real 3D space, as captured by the camera's perspectival projection. *Cage* allows non-dancers to play with precisely defined distances in space, boundaries, and spatial arrangement of movements.

Inertia is a variation of *Matching Positions* that is not task based. It tracks the individual's or the collective's onscreen silhouette and follows its geometrical center (centroid) with a small red cross indicator using a preset degree of inertia. Although it can easily be used as a fun, fast warm-up tool (because it makes one move fast to the right, left, up, and down to avoid overlapping the red cross with the centroid), it produces particularly interesting choreographic situations when applied to a fixed group choreography. *Inertia* analyzes all dancers as one silhouette, connecting them through one center. The dancers, if they want to avoid the red cross, need to constantly rearrange the choreography. But because their attention is divided they create additional, disorderly movements, making "wrong" moves while still retaining a degree of the organization that the initial choreography had.

Delay/Reverse has two functions, both of which perform simple temporal transformations of the captured interval of a video stream. The Delay-function continuously captures and reproduces the captured video stream delayed by a pre-set time interval. The Reverse-function continuously captures video stream, but creates discontinuities

FIGURE 12.3   Zrinka Užbinec using the *Capture/Replay* tool. Image courtesy of BADco.

by reproducing it in reverse, again delayed by a pre-set time interval. These two functions can be used in many different ways including as a technology of improvisation through montage (other functions will be described later in this text).

Capture/Replay can capture up to 30 seconds of live video stream that can be reproduced three ways: simple replay, replay backward, and in slow motion. It can be used to capture and reproduce movements from a distance by waving a hand across the trigger areas on the top of the screen. Its primary purpose is to be of help to dancers and choreographers who prefer working with fixed phrases of movement, repetitive structures, and precise timings.

Appear/Disappear can be thought of as a photographic plate constantly re-imprinted by the captured video stream as more static parts of the image remain in focus while all quick movements become blurred or disappear entirely. It serves to render the body as fragmented through working with different speeds of movement within one body or, on the other hand, to play with speeds of different dancers through space.

Why did we develop *Whatever Dance Toolbox?*

One of the key preoccupations of BADco.'s choreographic work is to make visible the process of compositional, improvisational, and dynamic decision making in the very act of performing. We have never had much interest in the conception of movement as self-expression of a dancer or movement as an auto-referential, choreographic object. We are more concerned with the question of how to make visible the relational conditions between the performance and its environment, both material and immaterial conditions. That is why the performers' decision-making process, in micro-situations and micro-events on stage, is firmly grounded in their capacity to analyze the environment around them, including, in some cases, audience behavior, the network of the distribution of attention in the performance space, and also the internalized effects of temporal and spatial organization of movement that come from working with various software. For each staging we developed specific, almost systemic procedures. For example, in *Deleted Messages* (2004) each performer begins the performance with a choreography based on five parameters, each of which falls under one of five categories: type of movement, space, quality, relation, and image—a system we adapted from Thomas Lehmen's toolbox *Funktionen*.² As the performance progresses the parameters/choreographic materials transform according to the processes of viral infection: mutation, recombination, re-assortment, deletion, and insertion. Particular choreographic materials associated with particular parameters "infect" bodies of different performers at various points in the performance. However, some parameters are also deleted in the exchange between performers. Movements of the audience, since the audience moves freely across the performance space, also get incorporated into the choreography. And lastly, the spatial organization of performers in space at any moment depends heavily on the overall spatial arrangement of the various members of the audience. To give another example, in the performances *Changes* (2007) and *Black and Forth* (2012) dancers spatially rearrange the choreography according to regimes of visibility by means of sensor lamps that turn on and off when triggered by movement, and by means of a light that moves stage right-stage left in varying rhythms, and so on.

With time, as specific poetic assumptions crystallized in our choreographic work, the procedures became more evident, albeit not always immediately comprehensible to the audience, since they were never demonstrated in a didactic manner. The complexity of assumptions that the performers operated with while performing often created the impression that the performance was governed by an alien, external logic. This exterior "artificial" logic is what interests us. It seems to us that this artificial logic is a key mode of correspondence between performance, theatre, performers, and the environment, whether environment be determined in the objectal, contextual, conditional, or social sense. Such alien logic, it seems, results from re-naturalization of the "artificial" environments mentioned above.

Our aim is not to delegate the operative and organizational agency to external mechanisms (algorithms, chance, or the like) but to domesticate the environment with all the resistances and benefits it offers. In such an approach to performance it is impossible to avoid one of the key aspects of expression of the objectification of thought and procedure in our environment: algorithmic-based forms of mediation and reflection. Furthermore, Daniel and we share an interest in using new computer technologies as a tool for learning. To quote Daniel:

> For the *Toolbox* specifically, I started from two premises. First was to see what "low-hanging fruits" I could reach—technically relatively simple things that might have big potential for your work. We went through a few things, some of which got sacked and some got refined. None of those required detailed planning but instead allowed me to just "hack along" and see what works.

It was of great help to me that we decided to move the computers "off stage" and into your rehearsal process—eliminating many constraints and requirements that "the show" would require, and focus on the dancer/computer relationship instead of the audience. Second was to explore some differences in perception of human and computer. Intuitively, we think computers are precise. Turns out, dancers have a different and in lots of ways much more precise understanding of "space" than the algorithms I use.[3]

Working analytically with these simple features opened up a whole range of important questions: What changes fundamentally at the level of dancer's attention when dancing in front of an interactive mirror? How does the way we think when we dance change in relation to the information we get from the screen? How is the qualitative difference of reproduced movement from habitual dance movement to be understood? How precise do we actually need to be? What do we practice indeed in such a technologically conditioned environment? How does our relation to other bodies in space modify due to the fact that we organize group movement by predominantly using information we get from the screen? What are the principles of algorithmic composition of this dis-continuous image and what is the shift in compositional choreographic thinking when applying them to ad hoc improvisational composition? In short, these simple tools helped us observe and analyze our dances more accurately. This helped to build up a shared vocabulary between dancers and non-dancers in the collective because we all saw the same things and were able to explain certain improvisational decisions much more clearly. Further, it helped us to develop our improvisational imagination starting from very simple movement inputs and, most importantly, to put the complex problem of split attention and the dancer's conscious decision-making process to the forefront of our thinking about improvisation and performing in general. But the problem of divided attention—the economy of the performer's attention—revealed itself as the most important problem, one calling for a methodological elaboration.

How was *Whatever Dance Toolbox* developed?

The process of work that produced what would become WDT was intuitive, research-oriented and not product driven. Initially, the tools were intended for our internal use only. There were five important moments, though, when the process condensed and was propelled to the next stage of development. In 2005, BADco. organized a six day open laboratory that hosted both finished and unfinished work by the collective together with the individual works of our collaborators. Daniel Turing made an installation with a "raw" piece of motion capture/motion analysis software he was occupied with at the time. The software captured whatever was there in front of the camera and reproduced it in real time by applying different types of visualization. Simple and effective, it made an immediate impact on people's motivation to move and on how they composed their own movements or changed established relations to the movements of other bodies or objects in space. It was clear then that there could be much more to this specific human/machine interaction than just playfulness, although playfulness proved to be a valuable path to follow.

In 2006, while we were making the choreography for *Memories Are Made of This . . . Performance Notes* (2006), our interest was in creating an image of a dancing body that looked as if it had "lost" its technical knowledge—a body in which forms become conflicting, dissonant geometric structures; a dance that seemed to lack flow, as though without any cause and effect between the impulse for movement and the executed movement. We understood that the way to achieve this was to try to change certain habits our bodies had acquired through years of training in contemporary dance. Primarily, this involved changing the way the body deals with inertia. Even though we knew what we were supposed to produce, our bodies appeared to be resistant. We kept falling into the same habitual movement logic: flow, succession of forms, inertia, predictable movement phrasing, and so on until one day, by mistake, we were recorded with a camera tilted by 90 degrees. In the recording, it looked as if we were dancing on the wall. Our contact with the floor looked as if there was some lateral force that kept pulling all our movements towards or away from themselves. Incorporating this lateral force into our dance was the first step towards our goal. The second was provided by Daniel suggesting that we try working with software that reproduced movement in delayed, backward, and jittery forms.

At that time, these three "functions" were not unbundled and the image would jump from one distortion to the next with no discernible pattern. But even in this unpolished and rather confusing form, specific image features did provide specific insights. The delayed image facilitated faster exchange of dynamic forms between dancers. It inspired us to use the time/space jump cuts between any two sequences of the reproduced video stream as a compositional tool. Additionally, it sped up the learning process, and increased the combinatorial aspect of our improvisations. The backward image, on the other hand, reversed the logic of movement impulse and this reversal had many implications. Small preparatory movements transformed into intensive movement endings. Articulation intensified at the body's extreme periphery. Movement of the head and the direction in which dancers were looking lost their apparently natural connection with the rest of the body. The mechanism of impetus reversed completely and the intentionality of movement as well as its gestuality became more visible. This inspired us to create a dance that looked as if the body was moving from present to the past but was actually never moving backward.

In spring 2007 Daniel installed the first working version of WDT on a BADco. laptop, thus making the tool accessible for ongoing experimentation. A couple of months later, we met in PAF[4] in order to communicate our experiences so far and present the tools to others present at PAF, mostly from the performing arts. This first version of WDT consisted of three simple applications divided into two groups: *What the Machine Sees 1-space* and *What the Machine Sees 2-time*. WTMS 1-space was a task-oriented visual analysis tool designed so that the user, by solving tasks, intuitively learns the essential differences between the three-dimensional, real space and its two-dimensional representation shaped by the camera lens. WTMS 2-time consisted of a delay and backward replay of continuous video stream with the capacity to capture up to 10 seconds of video stream and replay it endlessly either as it was captured, or backwards, or in a jittery manner (i.e., movements were reproduced at varying, messy speeds).

As was mentioned earlier, "experimentation" with the WDT was spread over a little more than four years, but the process itself was discontinuous, both because Daniel Turing is based in Hamburg and BADco. in Zagreb, and because WDT was something we did as the side-activity to our regular theatre work. It made headway as much due to our desire to extract as much practical knowledge as possible from our interactions with it and develop it further according to discoveries made in those interactions as it did through other users in our workshops. The insights we got from workshop encounters were inspiringly profuse since they came from very heterogeneous groups of potential users: dancers with different technical backgrounds, choreographers, dramaturges and theatre directors, dance and theatre critics, theorists, non-professional dancers, dance teachers, students of acting, regular audiences, architects, cultural workers, programmers, special educators, and older children. The majority of these workshops were dubbed Do It Yourself! They gave people a chance to first experience the tools intuitively and then, once they fully understood how it operates, we would further support their imagination by giving them time to teach other users themselves. The enthusiasm manifested by these people and their desire to use WDT for substantially different purposes and with radically different aesthetic concerns than ours actually brought about the idea to make it publicly accessible.

In 2008, BADco. conducted an internal, ten-day long research titled "Symmetries: Towards Object Oriented Theatre,"[5] the focus of which was to reflect on the status of objects in our performances, or more precisely, to find out what kind of objects are of artistic interest to us at all. No matter whether they were treated as instruments or symbols, whether they were animated or mobilized by choreography, objects remain persistently passive and subordinated to performers on stage. A far more intriguing creative problem was articulated when the inquiry went in the direction of objects possessing agency. When does an object attain agency? How to produce from the object's agency? How do we operate/perceive/react when we ourselves become a part of a complex machine created jointly by humans and machines? Learning about computational processes and scrutinizing different analyses of video stream revealed a lot about the creative potential that arises from an unavoidable dissimilarity between the precision of the machine compared with the opaqueness of dancer's decision-making processes. Soon after and related to conclusions reached in that inquiry, Daniel Turing upgraded the existing applications by adding new features. *Cage* and *Inertia* were added to the WTMS 1-space, the captured interval of *Capture/Replay* was prolonged significantly and Jitter replay was replaced by Slow Motion replay. *Whatever Dance Toolbox* started to resemble its final version.

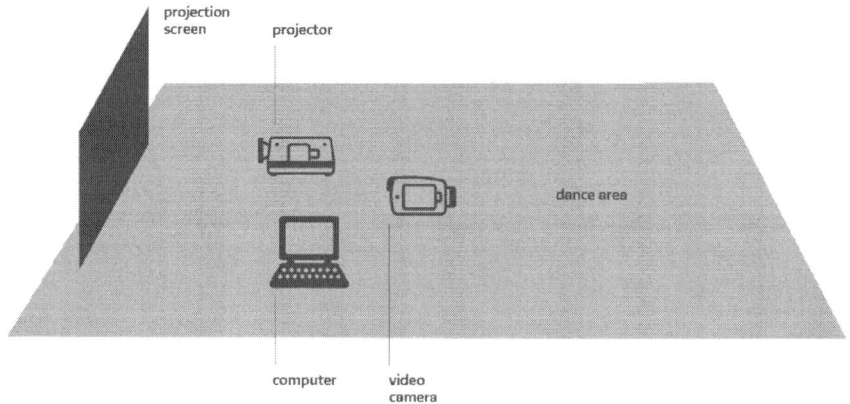

FIGURE 12.4 *Whatever Dance Toolbox* set-up. Image courtesy of BADco.

Finally, in 2010, WDT was released with an accompanying manual. The decision to publish a manual containing instructions for use along with examples of our methodology of working with WDT required that the whole BADco. collective work on translating the heterogeneous experience accumulated over the years into knowledge that could be useful to other potential users. It also placed a lot of responsibility and work solely on Daniel's shoulders since the software was supposed to be fully operative on a variety of computer configurations, a job usually done by a number of developers. The software was eventually packed on an Ubuntu GNU/Linux LiveCD containing a light version of Linux operating system that can be booted from the computer's CD/DVD drive without having to install it on the hard drive. If booted as instructed, WDT runs without interfering with the operating system installed on the computer.

Technical set-up

In terms of technical set-up WDT is simple, non-demanding and relatively easy to use. It needs no more than a well-lit room with a stable source of light, clear background surface (a wall, curtain, or the like), a computer with a CD/DVD drive, FireWire cable, digital video camera, and optionally, a video projector and projecting surface (clear wall, screen, or the like).

Availability

The software itself is available for free download from BADco.'s website as is an electronic version of the manual containing all the necessary information on how to operate the software. A printed manual contains exercises and choreographic commentaries not included in the electronic version. The *Whatever Dance Toolbox: Manual* by BADco. is licensed under a Creative Commons Attribution—ShareAlike 3.0. Croatia Unported License.

Other uses

Besides dance and choreography there were, as was mentioned, other interests articulated by experts from the fields of special education and child pedagogy. However the use of WDT for their specific purposes still remains unexplored. There is also a growing demand to make WDT available to students at several European universities by installing it on computers in their studios.

How it was financed

WDT was over the years occasionally financed by the Ministry of Culture of the Republic of Croatia, the City Office for Culture, Education and Sport, and the Zagreb and Croatian Academy of Science and Art. There was no financial support for software development, only for workshops and public laboratories BADco. organized using *Whatever Dance Toolbox*. It was not until 2010 that conditions allowed for the release of WDT, due to our participation in Labo21—European Platform for Interdisciplinary Research on Artistic Methodologies. Labo21 was a partner project of BUDA Arts Center (Kortrijk), Laboratorium (Antwerp), University of Circus and Dance (Stockholm), and BADco. (Zagreb), with the support of the Culture Programme of the European Union.

***

See also:

- http://badco.hr
- http://danielturing.com.

Notes

1 http://danielturing.com/wtms/0-prerequisites/, accessed July 21, 2015.
2 See http://www.thomaslehmen.de/funktionen-132.html, accessed May 26, 2016.
3 From an interview with Daniel Turing published in *Whatever Dance Toolbox: Manual* (April, 2011).
4 PAF (=Performing Arts Forum) is a user-created, user-innovative informal institution. It is a place initiated and run by artists, theoreticians, and practitioners themselves. Neither a production-house and venue, nor a research-center, it is a platform for everyone who wants to expand possibilities and interests in his/her own working practice. (Taken from http://www.pa-f.net/basics, accessed May 26, 2016.)
5 The conclusions of that research are published on *Whatever DVD* (2008) and can be found as a PowerPoint presentation under the tag Object Oriented Theatre.

13

MOTION BANK
A broad context for choreographic research

Scott deLahunta

Motion Bank, the four-year research project of The Forsythe Company that began in 2010, was a convergence of two key trajectories. One followed the interest William Forsythe had in providing access to his archive of rehearsal and production materials as part of The Forsythe Foundation initiative established in 2004 "dedicated to advancing the art of dance by promoting critical thinking in dance education and practice."[1] The plans drafted for the Foundation focused on accessing the "embodied knowledge" of the dancer and developing unique and accessible ways of "communicating choreographic ideas."

Nearly a decade earlier, Forsythe and his research collaborators had embarked on the creation of what would eventually become the multimedia CD-ROM titled *William Forsythe: Improvisation Technologies. A Tool for the Analytical Dance Eye* (see Chapter 4 in this volume). This project has been conceived in 1994 as the "first interactive documentation of the new 'dance school' of Bill Forsythe" based on ten years of movement research with the Frankfurt Ballet.[2] One of the core ideas of the Foundation was to build on the success of this project to "develop a large portion of The William Forsythe Archive as an interactive multimedia database."[3] Under the direction of Rebecca Groves, a former dramaturg with the Frankfurt Ballet, the Foundation set out to raise the funds required to digitize over 3,000 hours of video recordings, which would form the main corpus of this multimedia database. At the same time, Groves set a number of multimedia education projects in motion, including one focused on Forsythe's ensemble choreographic work, *One Flat Thing, reproduced* (premiered in 2000), which would eventually become the web-based publication *Synchronous Objects* created in collaboration with The Ohio State University and launched in 2009 (see Chapter 10 in this volume).

During this time in the early 2000s, similar initiatives involving renowned choreographers were gaining recognition. A selection of these was acknowledged in a short article in *Performance Research* subtitled "Creation of the Choreographic

Resource" (deLahunta and Zuniga Shaw). This article drew attention to the concerns and motivations of four choreographers, including Forsythe, whose body of work had achieved the status of "resource" for researchers in a wide variety of fields. This and other questions from the artists, some of whom expressed the desire to "step back" from their body of work, had given rise to distinctive research projects aiming at sharing choreographic process and ideas with both general audiences and other specialist knowledge areas. While the projects had a variety of ways of doing this, there were many similar features, and bringing the four initiatives together in a single article would lend support to the idea of an emergent "dance literature—or set of core visual references—to stimulate the exchange of ideas and innovation in the discipline" (deLahunta, Groves, and Zuniga Shaw 91).

In early 2007, Forsythe announced the name *Motion Bank*,[4] and in March 2007 *Motion Bank* was announced in the annual report of the German Dance Plan as an "an online interdisciplinary research environment for dance, including the first interactive score of his exceptional choreography, *One Flat Thing, reproduced*" (Groves and Forsythe 67). During this time, The Forsythe Foundation ceased to be the driving organization behind the project, and *Motion Bank* was conceived to be a separate project, envisioned by Forsythe as the place for "peer to peer" exchange between choreographers. He did not want the site to become "exclusively focused" on his own work, but that it should become a "medium for knowledge transmission" rather then a "personal platform".[5] At that time, Forsythe was referring to artists such as Trisha Brown, Anne Teresa de Keersmaeker, and Jonathan Burrows as peers he would like to see involved; he was also envisioning on-line exchanges with scientists and mathematicians who could offer insights into dance-related phenomenon.

During the two years to follow, while Norah Zuniga Shaw and Maria Palazzi lead the research team at The Ohio State University working closely with Forsythe toward the publication of *Synchronous Objects for One Flat Thing, reproduced* in April 2009, Forsythe and his company continued to plan ahead for the larger more inclusive *Motion Bank* project. This involved milestones, such as achieving the full support of The Forsythe Company board, for which several drafts were prepared describing the goals of *Motion Bank*. These drafts emphasized the idea of "digital dance scores" and a "universal library of visual references" which would contribute to a "new type of dance literature" that would also connect dance to other fields.[6] After the approval of the board in May 2008, more detailed project proposals went into development and the search for more institutional partnerships and financial support got underway.

Around the same time, the Arts and Humanities Research Board in the UK approved funding for a network project entitled *Choreographic Objects: Traces and Artifacts of Physical Intelligence* (Leach et al. 2009). This project brought together four research teams working in collaboration with William Forsythe, Siobhan Davies, Wayne McGregor and Emio Greco | PC to create the choreographic resources, renamed in this project as "choreographic objects," described in the *Performance Research* article published in 2006. These included interactive scores (Forsythe's *Synchronous Objects*) and installations (Emio Greco | PC's *Double Skin/Double Mind* installation), choreographic software agents (McGregor's *Choreographic Language Agent*) and digital dance archives (*Siobhan Davies Replay*), all of which are also represented in this volume. The AHRC funded project brought these initiatives together in the same investigative context for the first time to "engage theories of knowledge production and knowledge transfer" with established social science researchers lead by James Leach (see also James Leach's chapter in this volume, Chapter 14). One of the results of this study was to draw attention to an "emergent international 'community of practice'" involved in the making of choreographic objects (Leach, Whatley, and deLahunta; Leach). By this time, the philosopher Alva Noë had joined the small team thinking about and drafting plans for *Motion Bank*. Both Leach and Noë would continue working alongside scholars such as Maaike Bleeker and scientists David Kirsh and Kate Stevens: all important collaborators in exploring the impact of making choreographic ideas and processes available for study by other research domains.[7]

In Autumn 2008, Forsythe produced a comprehensive diagram showing the relationships he envisioned for the development of *Motion Bank* as the world's "first library of digital dance scores." Citing "computer-aided design" that could enable the "ideas incumbent in choreography to be graphically displayed as the work itself plays before the viewer" and referring to *Synchronous Objects* as the "first publication of *Motion Bank*," the diagram summarized the important motivations for developing the project, including interdisciplinary research seeking to identify correspondences between choreography and "other fields of organizational practice." The diagram also referred clearly to the filming of the work of guest choreographers to "ensure the content diversity of *Motion Bank*."[8] In early 2009, the various draft plans for *Motion Bank* were brought together for a presentation to the director of the German Federal Cultural Foundation, Hortensia Völckers, as the Foundation had shown an interest in supporting the Motion Bank project.[9] One of the challenges was to find a way of expressing the complex ideas in the diagram in simpler more direct terms, in ways that could be compelling to a jury, for example the invention of a new system of dance notation. Additionally, if the Foundation would support the project they would expect 50 per cent of the overall budget to come from local partnerships. Around that time a new rehearsal and work venue called The Frankfurt Lab shared by several key Frankfurt-based performing arts institutions including The Forsythe Company opened west of the city center at Schmidtstrasse 12.[10] By providing a dedicated studio and office space for The Forsythe Company and having additional studio space that could be reserved for recordings and workshops, The Frankfurt Lab helped to establish the local conditions for a possible *Motion Bank* project.

In August 2009, Stefan Mumme, a lawyer for The Forsythe Company, submitted a final detailed plan and budget for a four year *Motion Bank* project (2010–2013) for €2.7 million to the German Federal Cultural Foundation. In mid-December 2009, the Jury for the Foundation approved the project to begin in 2010 with financing from the Foundation of €1.2 million with the expectation that the partners on the project would match these funds. By April 2010, the four key necessary institutional partnerships were finally in place so the project could definitely continue. These partners, referred to as the Score Partners responsible for the creation of the digital dance scores with the guest choreographers, were the Advanced Computing Center for the Arts and Design and Department of Dance at The Ohio State University, Fraunhofer Institute for Computer Graphics Research, Hochschule Darmstadt—University of Applied Sciences, and the Hochschule für Gestaltung Offenbach. The local matching funding came from Hessian Ministry for Science and the Arts, Kulturfonds Frankfurt Rheinmain, and the Altana Kultur Foundation. Joining the two named education partners, Frankfurt University of Music and Performing Arts and Palucca Hochschule für Tanz Dresden, an International Education Workgroup was formed to research ways to integrate the new on-line digital scores and related choreographic resources produced by other artists into their academic programs. Additional separate funding of approximately €90,000 was secured from the Volkswagen Foundation for a series of interdisciplinary research meetings under the title Dance Engaging Science aiming to stimulate new forms of collaborative research in which dance plays a greater constitutive role.

Getting underway . . .

One of the first tasks for the *Motion Bank* team was to write a short description of the project for The Forsythe Company's 2010–2011 Season Brochure. The result was as follows:

> *Motion Bank* is a new four-year project of The Forsythe Company providing a broad context for research into choreographic practice. The main focus is on the creation of new on-line digital scores in collaboration with selected guest choreographers to be made publicly available via the *Motion Bank* website. Both these unique score productions and development of related teaching curriculum will be undertaken with and rely on the expertise and experience of key collaborative partners. Public educational activities and events reflecting the diverse issues related to score creation will be offered at The Frankfurt Lab, and will include performances and presentations of the guest choreographers as well as lectures. Workshops and residencies organized with senior scientists and scholars aim to stimulate interdisciplinary research based on questions coming from dance practice. Exchange of information with and support for related projects is facilitated through working groups and associate networks.

The core *Motion Bank* team working out of the office at Schmidtstrasse 12 had to administer and manage the large financial grant, an international network of institutional partners and an internal research pool of more than seventy individual artists, researchers, and support staff. The makeup of this core team varied, but consistently over the four year period comprised a project leader (Scott deLahunta), production management and administration (Marion Rossi), a workshop coordinator, dramaturg

(Célestine Hennermann), and collaborative workspace and scores coordinator (Florian Jenett). Important additional legal, financial, technical, and administrative assistance came from The Forsythe Company staff. There is extensive documentation on the *Motion Bank* website where the names of all individual researchers, choreographers, performers, score team members on both sides of the Atlantic, associate researchers, workgroup members, and workshop leaders can be found. The documentation website contains descriptions of more than thirty discrete events that took place throughout the four years. These include detailed chronological process reports on each of the individual on-line "digital dance score" projects with the guest artists: Deborah Hay, Jonathan Burrows and Matteo Fargion, Bebe Miller, and Thomas Hauert. These artists were invited on the basis of their distinctive choreographic work and commitment to ongoing research in relation to their methods of practice. One of the main *Motion Bank* goals was to use these diverse approaches to further explore how "computer aided design" could be applied successfully to the documentation, analysis, and transmission of choreographic ideas, following the example of the two previous projects undertaken by Forsythe and his collaborators, *Improvisation Technologies* and *Synchronous Objects*.

Under the heading SCORES on the website, these process reports for each guest artist include details from the initial concept development, such as three meetings over a one-year period with Burrows and Fargion used to prepare for their test filming session, with detailed notes available for download for anyone interested to study that aspect of the *Motion Bank* score creation process. For the Frankfurt-based score team, these sessions were followed by guest performances at The Frankfurt Lab then a final filming. After this the digital score material went into production sessions, with additional meetings with the artists to finalize the content for their on-line scores. For each guest artist, the length of project time varied from one-and-a-half to two-and-a-half years between first meetings and initial online release of their *Motion Bank* scores publication. The filming set up at the Frankfurt Lab relied on 2D video cameras and used computer vision algorithms to extract 3D pathways, a technique applied to the Deborah Hay recordings. A different choice took place at The Ohio State University where the score team under the direction of Norah Zuniga Shaw and Maria Palazzi recorded the material for the *Motion Bank* scores for Thomas Hauert and Bebe Miller using high-resolution 3D Motion Capture. The thinking behind and results of these varying choices can be studied on the *Motion Bank* documentation pages and on the published Scores website.[11]

While the creation of the on-line digital scores in collaboration with the guest artists was a main focus of the *Motion Bank* project, this work was embedded in a wide field of other activities, as the description written for the 2010–2011 brochure states, a "broad context for research into choreographic practice." A series of practical workshops that took the theme of scores as an inspiration for inviting a particular workshop leader or speaker were open to all disciplines and created opportunities to meet and exchange. But it was the choreographic resources, the "on-line digital scores" *Motion Bank* was creating, and the methods and approaches for developing and publishing similar resources with artists, for example, Anne Teresa de Keersmaeker (2012) and Steve Paxton (2008), that were points of departure for much of the important research of the project. This involved the "community of practice"—acknowledged by the 2009 *Choreographic Objects* research project—and recognition of a growing collection of published materials adding to and expanding on the existing "intrinsic discourse coming from dance practice" (deLahunta, "Publishing Choreographic Ideas" 171). Acknowledging these other publications on the documentation website (those existing as of December 2013), exploring the use of these publications in dance education, and inviting other teams of artists, editors, and designers to share and exchange inside the *Motion Bank* framework helped to create in part the "peer to peer" exchange environment envisioned by Forsythe in 2007.

Everything is data: software systems and artistic responses

In an essay titled "Dance, Data, Objects," the creators of *Synchronous Objects* explain how the dance *One Flat Thing, reproduced* was analyzed, decoded, and quantified into the data to be used as material to generate the visual interpretations or what they refer to as "Objects" that exist on their website (Zuniga Shaw, Forsythe, and Palazzi). Building on this approach, the *Motion Bank* score team in Frankfurt emphasized digitization as an "integral part of *Motion Bank* from the start" (deLahunta, Jenett, and Cramer) and designed recording setups to ensure that everything captured could be available to computation. All recording situations were installed and calibrated to allow for as little "noise" as possible so software algorithms might help extract features and recognize relevant patterns in the data. This was combined with the use of an annotation tool called Piecemaker, a software that assists in scoring video recordings of dance and sharing this information with others. Piecemaker was initiated as a research project by The Forsythe Company member David Kern to support the organization and recall of materials created by Forsythe and his performers in the rehearsal studio. In the context of *Motion Bank*, this software was reprogrammed for use in the development of the on-line digital scores and as a standalone tool for use in the studio. Using this software, renamed Piecemaker2 (PM2), annotation sets or markers could easily be related and provide access to multiple versions of the same event (e.g., video, audio, motion capture, scores, etc.). This enabled the building of connections that could generate useful visualizations or other representations both during and post-annotation. As with the *Synchronous Objects* project, the quantification of the dances of the *Motion Bank* guest artists into data involved a combination of computational and manual work. This often meant many hours of computer-based video processing, for example to subtract the background of the image leaving only the silhouettes of the performers, alongside watching the same video for nearly as many hours in order to annotate and describe time-based events the computer would not be able to recognize on its own.

Motion Bank had as one of its goals the development of software that might be used by others to create their own on-line scores to add to the *Motion Bank* collection. This was achieved through the development of two systems. One of these is the reprogrammed version of Piecemaker, PM2, based on the original research of David Kern. PM2 is currently in use by the Pina Bausch Foundation and the MA Contemporary Dance Education, Frankfurt University of Music and Performing Arts. The other software is MoSys, the publishing system developed for the publication of the on-line scores. MoSys consists of a private editor to browse collections of recorded, analyzed, and annotated material and arrange it into "views" as sets and a frontend to view them. Each set comprises a grid-like system of cells that can interact with each other using a unique messaging system. Since the end of the *Motion Bank* in 2013, an additional system, Piecemeta (PMa), has been in development. PMa is a platform for sharing and collaborating on dance-related data. It enables simplified data storage through a variety of import formats and recording tools and offers the possibility to play back, remix, and extend the stored data sets through the services' programming interface. These data sets can be made public to be further analyzed, transformed, and enhanced by other researchers and artists.

PMa is used in the context of the Choreographic Coding Labs, one of the outcomes of the first phase of *Motion Bank* offering an exchange and collaboration format for digital media "code savvy" artists who have an interest in translating aspects of choreography and dance into digital form and applying choreographic thinking to their own practice.[12] The possibility that access to dance-related databases might serve as an artistic source for digital media artists was inspired by the *Motion Bank* score project with Deborah Hay and the creation of a new digital adaptation based on Deborah Hay's choreography by Amin Weber, a member of the Frankfurt-based score team. Having extensive access to all digitized recordings and his own insights into Hay's work coming from working intensely with her on her score project, Weber was invited to create an artistic response using his own digital tools, the 3D computer animation software with which he has a deep expertise. Viewing the results of Weber's artistic work on the website and listening to him interviewed by Jeanine Durning, one of Deborah Hay's performers, the possibility emerges of an artistic response revealing the rich choreographic thinking of the invited guest choreographer.[13] This development resonates with and extends on the work of the *Synchronous Objects* project in developing both analytic and aesthetic responses to the collected dance-related datasets.

Summarizing and the future

Importantly and with due respect, with his archive no longer included in the project, the *Motion Bank* project achieved a unique autonomy inside the enabling framework of Forsythe's vision for the sharing of dance knowledge. Both the work of the score teams with the guest artists and the practical workshops have been mentioned. In addition, twice yearly meetings of the International Education Workgroup were instrumental in supporting the research and development of teaching applications with the two main Education Partners in Dresden and Frankfurt. The Dance Engaging Science workgroup brought dancers together in a series of meetings with researchers from a range of disciplines including

FIGURE 13.1 Video still from digitally rendered overlay of twenty-one versions of the solo adaptations of *No Time To Fly* (dancers/choreographers: Jeanine Durning, Juliette Mapp and Ros Warby). Deborah Hay took this video as an inspiration for a new work commissioned by the Cullberg Ballet, *Figure a Sea*, which premiered in September 2015. Video still credit: Motion Bank.

cognitive science, architecture, and philosophy. These meetings triggered a number of outcomes, including various experiments, new successful funding proposals, publications, and public events. Motion Bank also published a 41-page printed brochure and a 130-page book focused on "Starting Points and Aspirations" (deLahunta et al 2011, deLahunta and Hennermann 2013) and produced two short films explaining the project, its results, and future plans. *Motion Bank* has also seen results integrated back into the practice of the Guest Artists. Figure 13.1 is a still from digital video material (twenty-one versions of the solo adaptations of *No Time To Fly*) Deborah Hay is using as inspiration for a new commissioned work.

The future plan is to establish a small Motion Bank Institute (MBI) to continue the work of digitizing the training, rehearsal, and production practices of key choreographers and dancers for non-commercial education, research, preservation, and creative purposes. Having gained, through the experience of the first phase, a profound understanding of the significant potential and challenges associated with translating dance into digital form, the Institute intends to maintain a core focus on the development of its open software systems for recording and data management, annotation and online publication. These systems will be made available for use and further development with artists, educators, and researchers worldwide. The MBI will continue to organize and participate in interdisciplinary projects with the aim of fostering productive relations and forms of transfer between dance and other fields and practices.

***

For more documentation about the first phase of the *Motion Bank* project see http://motionbank.org/. For direct access to the on-line digital scores created with and for Deborah Hay, Jonathan Burrows and Matteo Fargion, Bebe Miller, and Thomas Hauert see http://scores.motionbank.org/. See also http://choreographiccoding.org.

Notes

1 Groves, Rebecca. The Forsythe Foundation and William Forsythe Archive Mission Statement and Description of Activities (2004). Working draft as of December 21, 2004. Personal copy.
2 Kuchelmeister, Volker, and Christian Ziegler. Improvisation Technologies/Self meant to Govern (2004). Internal company proposal. Personal copy.
3 See Footnote 1.
4 Rebecca Groves, email to: Scott deLahunta. Subject: Re: tanzplan meet. Date: Fri, 16 Feb 2007 03:13:18. Personal email.
5 William Forsythe email to Ingo Diehl. Subject: Re: Biennale. Date: Fri, 18 May 2007 20:16:58. Forwarded to me. Personal email.
6 deLahunta, Scott, and Forsythe, William. "Motion Bank: Dance Knowledge Resources for the 21st Century" (2008). Draft version for the board not for distribution. Personal copy.
7 During Motion Bank, all of these individuals participated in the Dance Engaging Science project aimed at setting up interdisciplinary collaborative research in which dance plays a greater constitutive role.
8 Forsythe, William. The Forsythe Company Motion Bank Diagram (2008). Personal copy.
9 The German Federal Cultural Foundation was responsible for establishing Tanzplan Deutschland (http://www.tanzplan-deutschland.de/) from 2005–2010, running with a budget of €12.5 million to provide dance in Germany with more recognition and establish it as an art form of equal value to opera and theater.
10 Frankfurt LAB is intended as a "laboratory of contemporary artistic expression," a place for experiments that can scarcely been realized within the organizational and spatial constraints of theaters. See http://www.frankfurt-lab.de/.
11 See http://scores.motionbank.org/.
12 Choreographic Coding Labs; see http://choreographiccoding.org/, accessed November 13, 2015.
13 http://scores.motionbank.org/dh/#/set/digital-adaptation-of-no-time-to-fly, accessed October 5, 2015.

References

deLahunta, Scott, Florian Jenett, and Franz Anton Cramer. "A Conversation on Motion Bank." *MAP* 6 (2015), available at http://www.perfomap.de/map6/medien-und-verfahren-des-aufzeichnens/a-conversation-on-motion-bank, accessed November 11, 2015.
deLahunta, Scott. "Publishing Choreographic Ideas: Discourse coming from Practice." *SHARE: Handbook for Artistic Research Education*. Ed. Mick Wilson and Schelte van Ruiten. ELIA: Amsterdam, 2013. 170–177.
deLahunta, Scott, Rebecca Groves, and Norah Zuniga Shaw. "Talking About Scores: William Forsythe's Vision for a New Form of Dance 'Literature'." *Knowledge in Motion: Perspectives of Artistic and Scientific Research in Dance*. Ed. Sabine Gehm, Pirkko Husemann, and Katharina von Wilcke. Bielefeld: Transcript, 2007. 91–100.
deLahunta, Scott, and Celestine Hennermann. *Motion Bank: Starting Points and Aspirations*. Frankfurt: Motion Bank/The Forsythe Company, 2013.
deLahunta, Scott, Saskia Martinez, and Célestine Hennermann. Motion Bank Brochure. Frankfurt: Motion Bank/The Forsythe Company (2011), available at http://motionbank.org/en/event/motion-bank-brochure, accessed November 11, 2015.
deLahunta, Scott, and Norah Zuniga Shaw. "Constructing Memories. Creation of the Choreographic Resource." *Performance Research* 11.4 (2006): 53–62.

Groves, Rebecca, and William Forsythe. "William Forsythe Motion Bank." *Tanzplan Deutschland Jahresheft 2006/07.* Ed. Christiane Kühl and Barbara Schindler. Berlin: Tanzplan Deutschland, 2007. 66–67.

Keersmaeker, Anne Teresa de, and Bojana Cvejić. *A Choreographer's Score: Fase, Rosas Danst Rosas, Elena's Aria, Bartók.* Brussels: Rosas and Mercatorfonds, 2012.

Leach, James. "Choreographic Objects: Contemporary Dance, Digital Creations and Prototyping Social Visibility." *Journal of Cultural Economy* 7.4 (2014): 458–475.

Leach, James, Sarah Whatley, and Scott deLahunta. "Choreographic Objects: Traces and Artifacts of Physical Intelligence." *Beyond Text Network Project* (2009), available at http://projects.beyondtext.ac.uk/choreographicobjects/, accessed October 4, 2015.

Paxton, Steve. *Material for the Spine: A Movement Study.* Brussels: Contredanse, 2008.

Zuniga Shaw, Norah, William Forsythe, and Maria Palazzi (2009) "The Dance The Data The Objects." *Synchronous Objects for One Flat Thing, reproduced,* available at http://synchronousobjects.osu.edu/assets/objects/introduction/danceDataObjectEssays.pdf, accessed November 11, 2015.

PART II

14

MAKING KNOWLEDGE FROM MOVEMENT

Some notes on the contextual impetus to transmit knowledge from dance

James Leach

It is often observed that knowledge is crucial to contemporary developed economies (see, e.g., OECD). "Knowledge" now denotes something people strive to produce, strive to have recognized, and to evaluate, rank, and transact (Strathern; Ong and Collier; Camic, Gross, and Lamont). Indeed it might be fair to say that "knowledge" has become a value term in its own right. As Klein writes, commenting on the recognition of contemporary dance as a form of knowledge, "[i]n the globalised world of the 21st century, knowledge is considered the key to prosperity, influence and power" (26). In political, business, and media rhetoric, innovation, creativity, and knowledge are often directly connected with economic dynamism, both in labor and in product innovation. In short, knowledge is a product of specific currency in a "knowledge based society" (Klein 27), the societies described by sociologists as operating a "knowledge economy" (Drucker; Powel and Snelman 200). This context is one in which an openness to new sources of knowledge (see Fensham in this volume, Chapter 7), and to new possibilities to extract and make useable knowledge from hitherto overlooked domains (see Zuniga Shaw in this volume, Chapter 10), is quite palpable (Strathern). Knowledge itself is one thing. Identifying new and alternative means of producing knowledge that might have economic or societal benefits is another. It opens up the possibility for innovating on knowledge production itself. The rise of funding schemes targeted to art and science collaborations in the first decade of this century is just one instance of this drive (see Leach and Davis), one that looks for knowledge production potential in arenas and domains hitherto considered "beyond" (Brandstetter 42) the rational and discursive production of knowledge in science (Klein 28).

A determined emphasis upon the value of knowledge is built in to a political economy reliant upon progress, novelty, product innovation, and technology. Digital technologies make issues of access to knowledge, and of its packaging, significant. This emphasis on value and on packaging or making knowledge available is not only evident in external pressure to make academic knowledge have "impact" for example (as in contemporary UK and Australian Universities) or to make academic knowledge production more directly profit oriented; it is evident in some subtle reshaping from the inside, as it were, of practices that have not necessarily thought to emphasize a knowledge component until now.

One contention in this chapter is that the desire to be recognized as knowledge producers compels people to make what they know and how they know it appear in a certain form. That is, as something that is detachable from its source, transactable across disciplines or domains, and thereby demonstrating, internally to its form, "usefulness" or applicability (Strathern; Leach "Self of the Scientist"). In this regard, while there is a powerful institutionalized and politicized drive towards innovation and knowledge production in the contemporary world, the kind of thing that "knowledge" is, is often actually quite narrowly specified. That narrowness comes from an emphasis on demonstrating the utility of knowledge, and on its potential economic exploitation. Within the search for new methods of knowledge production and new sources of knowledge then is a hierarchy of knowledge that places utility as paramount.

In pointing out some specifics about this context, there is no implication (on my part) of a lack of agency on the part of dance makers engaged in finding forms for dance knowledge transmission, nor indeed, that the aspects I focus on are the only factor at work. It is quite obvious from reading the contributions to this volume (for example) that the desire to make knowledge and prove the value of dance as a knowledge-making enterprise sits alongside other motivations and desires. Nevertheless, I suggest we look at how these motivations run parallel to, feed into, or are fed by, the opportunities and obstacles generated by contemporary tropes around the social and economic value of knowledge, transmission, and utility.

Repositioning contemporary dance

Contemporary dance is a vital and fast moving genre of artistic practice, one in which emerging technologies, and multiple collaborations have figured prominently in the creative process of leading makers (Birringer; Dixon; Salter). As part of the extension of practice through collaboration with other disciplines, and utilizing new technologies as reported in this volume, a significant development in the genre has been the recent emergence of forms in which choreographic thinking (Stevens and McKetchnie) and making are re-presented through technologically mediated artifacts (deLahunta and Zuniga Shaw "Constructing Memories"). As Forsythe and deLahunta describe,[1]

> [i]n 1994, a prototype training instrument for dancers of the Ballet Frankfurt was produced in collaboration with ZKM. A commercially available version of this prototype, which constituted the first use of computer augmented representation of choreographic structuring, was released in 1999. *Improvisation Technologies: A Tool for the Analytic Dance Eye* has since been utilized in a wide variety of academic and professional settings, revealing the potential for such interactive platforms to *establish knowledge relations between dance and other fields.*
> (Forsythe and deLahunta 10, my emphasis)

Following from this pioneering project, people in and around contemporary dance have taken up the possibilities and potentialities of digital technology and new media to document and disseminate aspects of the process of making dances. It is worth noting that the use of digital technology was initially for the transmission of technique within a company. Once it was demonstrated that knowledge of technique could be abstracted from process, teaching tools became potential archives of technique, and then possible vehicles for the transmission of a technique to investigate and understand space and structure to those outside the domain. There are now a growing number of these initiatives; to the extent it seems accurate to note both an emerging genre, and an emerging community of practice (Leach, Whatley, and deLahunta).[2]

In this chapter I draw upon research undertaken with four projects in particular, projects that were studied under an UK Arts and Humanities Research Council *Beyond Text* Network Grant in 2009.[3] They are also represented in this volume. These are: the *Choreographic Language Agent*; *Double Skin/Double Mind*; *Siobhan Davies Replay*, a digital archive of the work of the renowned UK Choreographer Siobhan Davies (http://www.siobhandaviesreplay.com/); and *Synchronous Objects for One Flat Thing, reproduced*, a suite of tools and entry points ("an online information base") for understanding and viewing the William Forsythe piece *One Flat Thing, reproduced* (http://www.synchronousobjects.osu.edu/). The latter was "intended to serve as a prototype for sharable principles of visualizing information and facilitating understanding of time-based arts" (Forsythe and deLahunta 10) as well as more specifically of "making dance knowledge explicit . . . through digital media" (Zuniga Shaw, this volume, Chapter 10). I will also refer to the project for which *Synchronous Objects* was the "pilot," *Motion Bank*, based at The Forsythe Company in Frankfurt. *Motion Bank* is an extension of initiatives aimed at capturing and transmitting aspects of the choreographic practice of four leading choreographers. These projects, and the "objects" they have produced, are different enough to provide a range across the emerging genre, but linked not only by the use of new media, but in their aspirations, motivations, and concerns.

The quotation by Forsythe and deLahunta above points to one initial impetus. This was to make available techniques for generating dance material in teaching environments to inform more general audiences. Consistent with current developments, it also refers to the possibility that once in this form, choreographic practice offers knowledge that may be used outside contemporary dance itself. "The data and animations reveal deep structure and make possible a new level of generative relations with other disciplines such as philosophy, architecture and geography" (deLahunta and Zuniga Shaw "Choreographic Resources" 132). A rapid move from how to educate dancers within companies in the specific making techniques of these companies segued into a way to educate others about what dance is and how dance is made. This has its current apotheosis as an opportunity for contemporary dance to offer *knowledge* to other fields.

As a leader in the genre, Forsythe (with his *Improvisation Technologies* CD-ROM referred to above) is one of the international stars of contemporary dance itself. It is worthwhile quoting from his published statements at some length to address the complex question of motivation and its intersection with the possibilities of digital technology on the one hand, and the knowledge economy on the other. He writes: "[dance]'s transient nature does not allow for sustained examination or even the possibility of objective, distinct readings from the position that language offers the sciences and other branches of arts that leave up synchronic artefacts for detailed inspection" (7). It is in this context that he asks the question,

> is it possible for choreography to generate autonomous expressions of its principles, a choreographic object, without the body? The force of this question arises from the real experience of physical practices, specifically dance, in western culture. Denigrated by centuries of ideological assault, the body in motion, the obvious miracle of existence, is still subtly relegated to the domain of raw sense: precognitive, illiterate. Fortunately, choreographic thinking being what it is, proves useful in mobilizing language to dismantle the constraints of this degraded station by imagining other physical models of thought that circumvent this misconception. What else, besides the body, could physical thinking look like?
>
> *(6)*

Forsythe points to the marginal status of contemporary dance as an art form, and links this to the ephemeral status of its time-based realization. In this and other texts, he makes a direct comparison to a musical score and other inscriptions that render ephemeral practice into enduring artifacts. He writes,

> The current convergence of dance with digital technologies, disciplinary perspectives and emerging global audiences seeking to learn offers an unprecedented opportunity to illuminate the movement arts as systems of embodied knowledge. Motion Bank stands as a pioneering project at this critical juncture.
>
> *(Forsythe and deLahunta 11)*

Unlike other classical arts then, contemporary dance has no widely accepted (or perhaps better, widely practiced and understood) mode of lasting inscription.[4] The artists and the research teams involved in these projects see themselves as developing forms in which to make such inscriptions. In doing so they are taking charge of demonstrating the possibilities for sustained engagement with and critique of dance making. The challenge is in finding forms of inscription that are true to choreography's form of creativity.

A brief example from one of the other contributions to this volume is illustrative. Florence Corin reports on the conversation with Steve Paxton during planning

Material for the Spine. Paxton describes two aspects to "sensation" (the focus of his research practice). Firstly, it can not be anything other than experienced, and secondly, the idea of "product" seems antithetical to lengthy, open ended, research which is core to the "knowledge" achieved. What "was at stake" in making the DVD was "how to express by text or by image your knowledge of the sensations of the body?" (page 36 in this volume).

Note the emphasis on thinking, research, and knowledge in the above quotations. It is a vital counterpart to the desire to find appropriate inscriptive methods to preserve contemporary dance pieces: that is, there is knowledge and intelligence inherent in choreographic practice, and appropriate modes of recording, inscribing, and teaching dance will make this apparent. Ephemerality, which performance scholar Peggy Phelan has argued is a uniquely political and essential element of performance, is not a problem for dance as dance, but it does have two consequences that are an issue: a lack of visibility in wider cultural and social milieu (Klein says "dance has a communication problem," 26), and that any form of inscription must show process and making, the temporal unfolding of choreographic thinking, not just a finished artifact.

Internal and external motivations

A version of this concern motivated the producers of all the objects that we investigated in the Choreographic Objects Network research. In discussion with them, it was very clear that there is the *internal motivation* for their endeavor elaborated above: they wish to show the value and interest of dance to a wider audience than it currently has (to demonstrate the "manifold possibility of our practice," Forsythe 7). There was a strong assertion that the practice has huge value and possibilities, but it is restricted to a small audience. Part of that is to do with its usual form of presentation: the performance that is live, ephemeral, and small scale. The internal motivation to see contemporary dance more widely recognized draws it into line with an *external motivation* as well.

The Forsythe Company, Siobhan Davies, and others represented in the genre receive significant public funding. We have seen above an explicit assertion in their statements that the value of dance is not just an aesthetic value. Dance and dance thinking has something to offer to the public, and to other disciplines and fields, they assert. The governments of the countries in which these contemporary dance companies are situated promote the knowledge economy. Governments justify funding the arts to themselves and the taxpayer through a notion, closely allied to the knowledge economy, of "creative industries." Linking "creative" to "industry" was a particular British example, coined by the Blair government, but it is characteristic. The arts are acknowledged as economically valuable to the nation. However, that value is of an "industrial" kind. They *produce* things that can be commodified. Indeed, "the function of art in contemporary society as a particular form of knowledge production" is so visible to art makers that some actively resist exactly this colonization (Cvejić 57). Yet against such resistance, the internal motivation of dance companies for recognition in contemporary terms runs up against an agenda around promoting an economically focused, and knowledge-centric aspect of art's value to society. As the state minister for the German region of Hess (where Frankfurt and the Forsythe Company are located) wrote:

> Motion Bank is demonstrating in its own unique way how dance can move the field of information technology forward, taking it in unexplored directions . . . Today it is generally agreed that culture and art—all creative endeavours, in fact—can be seem as drivers of innovation and technological progress . . . As a state government, we therefore promote diverse projects that allow the "creative economy" to unfold and realise its full potential.
> *(Kühne-Hörmann 8)*

Promoting the value of dance in terms of knowledge is characteristic for an economy that places value in knowledge (internal motivation), while at the same time dance must appear as knowledge in order to be perceived and acknowledged as valuable (external motivation).

At this juncture then, contemporary dance has found itself, through internal and external motivations, justifying its practice as a form of knowledge production. As an outcome, contemporary dance requires something other than the performance. It needs to show the knowledge aspect. Choreographers have found a new medium in which to present and make dance making available to others, and in this, the genre is aligning itself with the wider political and policy interest in stimulating innovation and creativity in a knowledge economy.

I link this to the desire to show aspects of the *process of making*. This is, after all, what digital media are so apt at facilitating. Knowledge *in* or *of* a performance seems less significant in this context than the knowledge-making process of creating material for a performance. It could be that is because the creation process is a series of explorations and experiments that generate knowledge, and thus is more similar to the investigations of science. It is often termed "research." It could also be that, as stated above, it is not a single product that is of interest in the knowledge economy, but the capacity to create knowledge. "Creative industries" are surely key to "creative economies" because the very essence of dynamism and innovation lies in the creative capacity.[5]

What needs to be demonstrated is that choreography and dance involves practice and intelligence of a particular kind. That each piece realizes a long process of stimulating, testing, generating, and organizing material. And that this process is one of intellectual activity that relies on multi-sensory and multi-modal skill. In its spatial awareness, its emotional intelligence, its integrated and syncretic character, there is something called "choreographic intelligence." It can offer something other knowledge practices cannot. And that is valuable.

For the value to be realized, there needs to be a form for its presentation and circulation that demonstrates the various aspects of its realization: the process of coming to, rather than the finished product. One could almost say that these "choreographic objects" are reverse engineering the final product—the dance piece—to show its component parts. The site *Synchronous Objects* provides multiple visualizations and descriptions of the structure of the dance, the cueing systems that dancers use and attend to in order to keep the structure and timing, and demonstrates the complex interplay of counterpoint and alignment in the piece. *Siobhan Davies Replay* is an archive not just of work, but of the scratch drawings of dancers in making pieces, of rehearsals, writings, and inspiration. *Double Skin/Double Mind* offers experience of "coming to know" the body through particular forms of attention and the *Choreographic Language Agent* abstracts a part of the choreographic thinking process, making the operation of thinking with the body legible. Both *Replay* and *Synchronous Objects* are a "resource" for those who want to understand more. Resource in itself is an interesting term, directly connected to exploitation and use. In their form therefore, they anticipate the needs of others. That is, while each is an object that demonstrates and makes available the process of choreographic problem solving, by pointing to choreography as a site of knowledge production, they reposition dance. As Forsythe put it, "Ideally, choreographic ideas in this form would draw an attentive, diverse readership that would eventually understand and hopefully, champion the innumerable manifestations, old and new, of choreographic thinking" (7).

The constitution and circulation of choreographic objects

Now we have a sense of the context in which the objects are formed, it becomes obvious that contemporary dance practitioners are experimenting with forms of self-presentation that on the one hand are impelled by a desire to extend choreographic thinking as a rigorous and specific artistic form, and on the other respond to value propositions arising from wider social and political interests. The idea of take-up, or use, is crucial here, and marks the endeavor out as very much of its time (where knowledge transfer metrics were being developed by the national arts funding body of the UK during 2011 and 2012, for example). In short, the objects are a means to several ends. The possibility for making this transition appears in the way dance practice and knowledge can inform and collaborate with other scientific and technological innovations and developments.

Given this particular impetus, the issue for those involved in *Replay* and *Synchronous Objects* for example became what to show of contemporary dance, and how best to do so. Digital technologies make issues of access to information/knowledge or its packaging significant (Brinkley 5). I turn now to some more fine-grained ethnographic material, and report on things said in and around the processes of making the two sites. I will intersperse this material with the development of a simple analytic approach to attend to the further question of *why* certain aspects appear in the objects in relation to the notions of transmission, circulation, and the knowledge economy.

The research team behind the online archive *Siobhan Davies Replay* described their work as "a way of generating a larger audience for dance."[6] This meant for them that "it needs to be attractive." It was also a "way of showing its [dance's] value beyond its original domain" through giving access to a body of work. Meant as much for humanities and dance researchers as the general public, the archive was structured around a series of layers or levels of engagement. For Siobhan Davies, enthusiastically collaborating on *Replay*, there were moments of discomfort in allowing such access. As she said, "things that are there on video is one perspective or aspect of the work and that is uncomfortable." Whatley (65 in this volume) reports that seeing things in the archive "can be disturbing for those who feature," and "memories resurface, sometimes in less than comfortable ways." The researchers creating the archive elaborated: "in practice, [Davies] always remakes a work. She never repeats it and that does pose questions about why post 'this' [version] when if it was remade, it wouldn't look like that." The choreographer "wanted something that allows her to have a dialogue with others." But on whose terms, and how can these terms be enforced? What rules and norms are to govern the circulation and use? A certain authenticity was important to them for the inter-twined reasons of producing something the choreographer could stand by, and thus allowing an ongoing formation of relations to others through that material that could be sustained from her side. Access to information might allow further interest and engagement, but what "knowledge" would be transmitted in doing so? Decontextualization of things and information is facilitated by information and communication technologies. The presentation of process-based, personal artistic knowledge as transactable or usable knowledge involves a form of translation, and a decontextualization. And thus there are inevitably changes in both the "knowledge" available, and the purposes and uses to which it might be put, in giving access to material as "knowledge." One interesting aspect of this is to consider the kind of knowledge that the choreographer has about her pieces as something very personal, as existing in a context of relationships and a temporality, and the kind of knowledge that can exist in an archive as a "resource" for others. Perhaps the former is not in fact transmissible?

Behind *Synchronous Objects* for *One Flat Thing, reproduced* was the driving motivation of Forsythe who, as we have seen already, was concerned that the thought/intelligence in choreographic practice is not given enough legitimation. Exchange with other domains of knowledge is a way of legitimating dance and choreography as *thinking* that shows utility. Thus *Synchronous Objects* renders the structural complexity of coordinated movement in space into mathematical formula ("choreographic data") that are then presented through different techniques of data visualization. I have suggested some reasons why showing "knowledge" means having to show aspects of process, that is, where "knowledge is coming into being." With *Synchronous Objects*, the makers chose specifically to highlight the structure of the piece, to make clear the intricacy of the movement and how it has its effect, through tools that make its conceptual underpinning apparent. Something is abstracted from these processes as an object that can circulate, an object that becomes the basis for relations with other disciplines.

Underlying my choice of language here (abstraction, circulation, exchange) is a simple anthropological device: the description of exchange systems and the objects that circulate within them as following the logic of gift or commodity forms of exchange.

The location of choreographic objects at a point somewhere in between these two ideal forms is illuminating (cf. Humphrey and Hugh-Jones) and perhaps highlights elements of turning the transmission of dance into the transmission of knowledge.

The gift in classical anthropological theory is a form of transaction that creates and maintains ongoing relationships between the transactors. At the other end of the (simplified and highly abstracted) continuum lies the commodity form, a transactional form that implies no future relation between the transacting parties but an overarching set of laws that govern such decontextualized transactions (see Mauss; Gregory). To make this concrete, the conventional form for the transaction of contemporary dance is the performance. Performances are a kind of "commodity form." An audience member buys a ticket, watches a performance, and leaves. Transaction complete. No ongoing obligation or connection, other than individual (subjective) memories. There are conventional ways of further engaging in a relationship with a dance performance through criticism, discussion, and so on. And the genre is self-referential, with new works building on or having allusions to previous work. But such engagement is again both subjective, and with the *performance* as a finished entity; something presented as a complete and un-encumbered moment of experience.

In the formation of the performance as the "object" of transaction there is a high degree of control exercised by the choreographer over what is released to others. The making process is out of picture, as it were. Thus what is made available is closed in certain ways. It is presented as something that reveals what the choreographer wants to reveal, and not other things. The possibilities for an ongoing relation are circumscribed *in the object itself* to an important degree by the process of making it, a process in which it comes to take the form of an object appropriate for transaction at a singular moment. Perhaps we can think of the ticket purchase as giving access to *what* is made. Not to *how* it is made. One could gain knowledge *of* an artist, a piece, an oeuvre, but not knowledge of a productive process itself.

Now choreographic objects such as those discussed here, with a different intention, and containing different elements, occupy a different kind of transactional space. They are intended to carry the intentions of their makers in different ways, and with different consequences. In a revealing process, specified in part by two needs (that of demonstrating and presenting choreographic making processes as knowledge producing, and that of making longer term and ongoing relations to audiences, users and so forth) choreographers are "releasing" previously unreleased material. I think we might argue that in terms of the knowledge economy, this is because it is the *process* of creation that is associated with "knowledge."

The object that circulates is what brings people together. It is the reason for the relationship between people, serving as a "boundary object" (Star and Greisemer) around which people gather and realize different interests and value. It specifically enables knowledge to "travel" (Strathern *Commons and Borderlands*). This forms a different relationship than that between the ticket-buying public and the performers/performance in conventional practice. This is evidenced by many aspects, one being that all those involved in making these objects repeatedly used phrases such as how "brave" the choreographers were in revealing private process, about how they were making themselves "vulnerable," and being "generous" in what they were doing. The language is important for this analysis.

An "issue" for *Replay* was that of "[w]hen does one make the transition between process and performance?" That is, the excerpts of dance were chosen by a dancer who had worked for a long time with Davies, as "someone [Davies] trusts" to know when this transition occurred. Trust was continually the basis for inclusion, yet commodity transactions imply no personal relation of trust, only trust in the overall system of law governing property and alienability. The new forms of relationship to others made possible through *Replay* were just not institutionalized in the same way. They do not have the same set of rules.

Performances, or highly produced videos of performances, are made specifically for circulation as a commodity. They give access to *what* is made. In these forms, the self is removed, the vulnerability not apparent, and the problems, tensions, and negotiations that are bound to be part of a creative and complex generative process are taken out. This makes them suitable for transaction as a kind of commodity where the recipients are anonymous. But what is the outcome of the relationships formed through viewing the archive? The choreographers could not know what others would make of the material (in both senses of "make," i.e., comprehend and fabricate). In fact, they are invited *to* make something of it, as this is a demonstration of its value. But making has to involve *using*. There was a negotiation, in other words, in a complex space in which public and private, use and reuse, ownership and control, were real issues. The website was located as something between performance and relationship.

In the making of *Replay*, Davies exercised a degree of control over its content and form. It does not just contain everything that the research team could collect, but only things judged appropriate to be included. There are no costumes (described by Davies as "dead and limp" without their animating bodies). There is no video of her working in the studio. I have already noted that she was uncomfortable with showing videos of past performances. To remain true to her vision and realization of contemporary dance, it was important to be clear that "dance works evolve." Were the archived pieces to be staged now, "these pieces would be re-made," would reflect where she is at now in her practice, not where she was then, and so on.

Now we could say that this level of control makes the archive look rather like a performance. What guided decisions about the material to include was not a desire for comprehensive documentation, a desire to make anything and everything to do with a work available (this is not just knowledge about), but to find an appropriate form for knowledge that might be taken up, made use of, released. The form of object, what it is constituted as, was in part determined by the demands of a new context for exchange in which conceptions of "knowledge" played a significant role. But the artistic form and the personal nature of the creative process, we might say, complicated the presentation of the archive as knowledge with utility.

Choreographic objects not only demonstrate something about dance making itself, they simultaneously show it as a knowledge-making enterprise. What choreographers and dancers "know" and do in movement has the potential then to become valuable for other disciplines, ranging from those interested in spatial organization (such as architecture), through psychology interested in the coordination of movement and thought (with possible medical and therapeutic application) to modes of visualizing and problem solving in the presentation of information through ICTs in other epistemic practices (such as geography or physics). By finding modes to capture and make available the knowing and the knowledge-making practice of dance, they demonstrate the worth of contemporary dance as a knowledge practice in its own right, and to thus reposition the practice and its cultural recognition and valuation. This route to recognition, absolutely responsive to contemporary political economy, to the needs and strictures of a "knowledge economy" (where the uses of arts is continually questioned), is also a route to remaking contemporary dance itself.

Conclusion

Choreographic objects achieve a transformation of contemporary dance's relationship to other parts of society. Dance knowledge is not alienated but extended through them. The fact that these objects expose issues of trust, temporality, and reciprocity in digitally mediated relations draws us towards asking how people try to enforce a form of relationship through the form of the knowledge they present. These concerns are driven by the need to exchange "knowledge" rather than something else.

In a context where value is seen not just in ability, but in the articulation of ability (as knowledge), there is an understandable desire to represent skilled action as more than just technique or control (Marchand et al.). That dance is not just intuitive or primitive. That is, to re-present skill and creativity in contemporary dance as a specific process of "thinking," and the outcome, a form of knowledge. While nothing new (see Baxmann 209) the impetus to see movement as containing knowledge now manifests in contemporary dance as an emphasis on choreographic practice as a particular kind of intelligence (deLahunta "Publishing Choreographic Ideas")[7]—one that, once rendered in other forms (amenable to transmission and transaction) will be both visible, and communicable, as a contribution to wider cultural and economic development (see contributions by Bermúdez Pascual, and Zuniga Shaw, this volume).

Underlying this is a stated perception among some highly successful dance makers that dance is a marginalized art form. More public understanding of it would increase its visibility and enlarge its cultural footprint. Then there is the requirement for dance companies to demonstrate the value of public investment through what is called "reach" (in the UK at least). They need to show work to a certain number of people each year to justify public funding. (And therefore undertake to engage the public in other ways than dance performances, including education projects.[8]) There is also a strong desire to convey the depth and quality of the work.

Several dance companies are achieving these ends through "a growing collection of materials that is starting to define this new space for knowledge." "These publications are not artworks, but are developed with the aim of furthering understanding of choreographic ideas and processes and bringing these into newly productive relations with both general audiences and other specialist practices" (deLahunta "Publishing Choreographic Ideas" 174). Contemporary dance practitioners seek "self determined" (Cramer) ways to demonstrate the intelligence and thinking involved in movement. Terms such as "choreographic intelligence," "the thinking body," and "physical thinking" are used. And there has been at first an incipient, and now a much more consciously articulated desire to see this kind of thinking, the knowledge made in dance, *transfer into other domains of practice*.

In the current political economy of knowledge, to achieve such uptake is in itself a political marker of value. Transfer, travel, take-up, and recognition, are all key to demonstrating relevance and worth (Strathern *Commons and Borderlands*, "Useful Knowledge"). This contemporary political economy of knowledge then offers an opportunity for actors to show the value of their practices, if they demonstrate those are practices of knowledge production. In parallel, recent anthropological attention to practice and skill focuses on rendering skilled action as a mode of knowing, a way of thinking in action, thus emphasizing the cultural contribution of skill and its validity as knowledge (Harris; Ingold). While the validation of choreographic practice as knowledge producing may be a liberating recognition of a value in contemporary dance, the re-rendering of practice as a knowledge-producing enterprise also establishes certain parameters (given in the context) and interlocutors. It carries with it a series of challenges to the genre about how to make appropriate modes for the transmission of the art form. The projects referred to in the volume meet these challenges in various ways, and in some senses, consciously resist utility or appropriation. Yet the seduction of "knowledge," rendered by the knowledge economy as something alienable from its source, and the political pressure to achieve such a form for dance knowledge, surely remains.

Acknowledgements

Maaike Bleeker's comments were very helpful in focusing this chapter on knowledge transmission in the knowledge economy. This makes it rather different from a previous paper called "Choreographic Objects" published in the *Journal of Cultural Economy*. I am nevertheless grateful to the editors of JCE for permission to reproduce parts of that text. I also thank the other participants in the "Choreographic Objects Network" research project: Matt Ratto, Sarah Whatley, Bertha Bermúdez Pascual, Norah Zuniga Shaw, Siobhan Davies, William Forsythe, Peter C. Sholten and Emio Greco, Wayne McGregor, Tim Ingold, Gill Clark, Jessica Wright, and Nick Rothwell.

Notes

1 And Ziegler elaborates in chapter 4 of this book.
2 See also http://motionbank.org/en/resources-2/.
3 http://projects.beyondtext.ac.uk/choreographicobjects/index.php; http://insidemovement knowledge.net/context/background/double-skindouble-mind; http://openendedgroup.com/ index.php/in-progress/choreographic-language-agent/.
4 The dance notation systems Laban and Benesh are the traditional modes of inscription in dance often compared to music notation, but without the same widespread usage.
5 One might render the logic as something like: "How crazy that this has been locked up in mere aesthetic stimulation for a tiny population of elite consumers for so many centuries!"
6 Unattributed quotations are taken directly from fieldnotes and reference people working on the teams that were making or had made these sites.
7 Rather than of dance as a store of sociological and psychological patterns, for example (Baxmann 208–9).
8 http://www.randomdance.org/creative_learning.

References

Baxmann, Inge. "The Body as Archive. On the Difficult Relationship between Movement and History." *Knowledge in Motion: Perspectives of Artistic and Scientific Research in Dance.* Ed. Sabine Gehm, Pirkko Husemann, and Katharina von Wilcke. Bielefeld: Transcript Verlag, 2007. 207–216.

Birringer, Johannes. *Performance, Technology and Science.* New York: PAJ Books, 2008.

Brandstetter, Gabriele. "Dance as a Culture of Knowledge." *Knowledge in Motion: Perspectives of Artistic and Scientific Research in Dance.* Ed. Sabine Gehm, Pirkko Husemann, and Katharina von Wilcke. Bielefeld: Transcript Verlag, 2007. 37–48.

Bundes Kultur Stiftung. "Introduction." *Motion Bank.* Frankfurt a.m.: The Forsythe Company, 2011.

Camic, Charles, Neill Gross, and Michele Lamont, eds. *Social Knowledge in the Making.* Chicago: University of Chicago Press, 2011.

Cramer, Franz Anton. "Dance Archives and Digital Culture: The Current Situation in Germany." *Goethe-Institut e. V., Online-Redaktion* May 2010 (2010), available at http://www.goethe.de/ins/nz/en/wel/kul/mag/tanz/6087441.html, accessed November 25, 2015.

Cvejić, Bojana. "Trickstering, Hallucinating, and Exhausting Production. The Blackmarket for Useful and Non Useful Knowledge." *Knowledge in Motion: Perspectives of Artistic and Scientific Research in Dance.* Ed. Sabine Gehm, Pirkko Husemann, and Katharina von Wilcke. Bielfeld: Transcript Verlag, 2007. 49–58.

deLahunta, Scott. "The Choreographic Language Agent." *Dance Dialogues: Conversations Across Cultures, Artforms and Practices, Proceedings of the 2008 World Dance Alliance Global Summit, Brisbane, 2008, 13–18 July.* Ed. C. Stock. Canberra: QUT Creative Industries and Ausdance, 2009.

—— "Publishing Choreographic Ideas." *SHARE: Handbook for Artistic Research Education.* Ed. Mick Wilson and Schelte van Ruiten. ELIA: Amsterdam, 2013. 170 177.

deLahunta, Scott, and Frédéric Bevilacqua. "Sharing Descriptions of Movement." *International Journal of Performance and Digital Media* 3.1 (2007): 3–16.

deLahunta, Scott, and Norah Zuniga Shaw. "Constructing Memories: Creation of the Choreographic Resource. *Performance Research* 11.4 (2006): 53–62.

—— "Choreographic Resources: Agents, Archives, Scores and Installations." *Performance Research*, 13.1 (2008): 131–133.

Dixon, Steve. *Digital Performance. A History of New Media in Theater, Dance, Performance Art and Installation*. Cambridge, Mass.: The MIT Press, 2007.
Drucker, Peter. *The Age of Discontinuity: Guidelines to Our Changing Society*. New York: Harper and Row, 1969.
Forsythe, William. "Choreographic Objects," *William Forsythe: Suspense*. Catalogue from the exhibition at Ursula Blickle Stiftung, Kraichtal May 17–June 29, 2008. Zurich: JRP/Ringier, 2008. 5–7.
Forsythe, William, and Scott deLahunta. "Motion Bank." *Motion Bank*. Frankfurt a.m.: The Forsythe Company, 2011.
Gregory, Chris. *Gifts and Commodities*. London: Academic Press, 1982.
Harris, Mark, ed. *Ways of Knowing*. Oxford: Berghahn Books, 2007.
Humphrey, Caroline, and Stephen Hugh-Jones. *Barter, Exchange and Value*. Cambridge: Cambridge University Press, 1992.
Ingold, Tim. *Making: Anthropology, Archaeology, Art, and Architecture*. London: Routledge, 2014.
Klein, Gabriele. "Dance in a Knowledge Society." *Knowledge in Motion: Perspectives of Artistic and Scientific Research in Dance*. Ed. Sabine Gehm, Pirkko Husemann, and Katharina von Wilcke. Bielefeld: Transcript, 2007. 25–36.
Kühne-Hörmann, Eva. "Hessisches Ministerium für Wissenschaft und Kunst," *Motion Bank*. Frankfurt a.m.: The Forsythe Company, 2011.
Leach, James. "The Self of the Scientist: Material for the Artist. Emergent Distinctions in Interdisciplinary Collaborations." *Social Analysis* 55.3 (2011): 143–163.
Leach, James, and Richard Davis. "Recognizing and Translating Knowledge: Navigating the Political, Epistemological, Legal and Ontological." *Anthropological Forum: A Journal of Social Anthropology and Comparative Sociology* 22.3 (2012): 209–223.
Leach, James, Sarah Whatley, and Scott deLahunta. *Choreographic Objects: Traces and Artefacts of Physical Intelligence*. Final Report (2009), available at http://projects.beyondtext.ac.uk/choreographicobjects/, accessed May 26, 2016.
Marchand. Trevor, ed. *Making Knowledge*. Special issue, *Journal of the Royal Anthropological Institute* 16 (2010), suppl. S1.
Mauss, Marcel. *The Gift: The Form and Reason for Exchange in Archaic Societies*. Trans. W.D. Halls. London: Routledge, 1990 [1923–1924].
OECD. *The Knowledge Based Economy*. Paris: Organisation for Economic Co Operation and Development (1996), available at http://www.oecd.org/sti/sci-tech/1913021.pdf, accessed November 21, 2015.
Ong, Aihwa, and Stephen Collier, S., eds. *Global Assemblages: Technology, Politics, and Ethics as Anthropological Problems*. New York: Blackwell, 2005.
Phelan, Peggy. "The Ontology of Performance: Representation without Reproduction." *Unmarked: The Politics of Performance*. London: Routledge, 1993. 146–166.
Powell, Walter, and Kaisa Snellman. "The Knowledge Economy." *Annual Review of Sociology* 30 (2004): 199–220.
Starr, Susan Leigh, and James Griesemer. "Institutional Ecology, 'Translations' and Boundary Objects: Amateurs and Professionals in Berkeley's Museum of Vertebrate Zoology 1907–39." *Social Studies of Science* 19.3 (1989): 387–420.
Stevens, Catherine, and Shirley McKetchnie. "Thinking in Action: Thought Made Visible in Contemporary Dance." *Cognitive Processing* 6.4 (2005): 243–252.
Strathern, Marylin. *Commons and Borderlands: Working Papers on Interdisciplinarity, Accountability and the Flow of Knowledge*. Wantage: Sean Kingston Publishing, 2004.
—— "A Community of Critics? Thoughts on New Knowledge." *Journal of the Royal Anthropological Institute* 12.1 (2006): 191–209.
—— 2007. Useful Knowledge. 2005 Lectures. *Proceedings of the British Academy* 139.

15

DANCING IN DIGITAL ARCHIVES

Circulation, pedagogy, performance

Harmony Bench

In his 1995 text *Archive Fever*, Jacques Derrida interrupts his discussion of Freudian psychoanalysis and the archive to briefly imagine the effects, or shocks, late-twentieth-century communications technologies would have introduced into the young discipline. Enjoying a speculative detour into the electronic terrain of email and word processing, Derrida concludes that a different set of writing technologies would have reformatted the explanatory frameworks of psychoanalysis, which were predicated on analog models of inscription and archival memory, and therefore would have rewritten the history of the field. He notes that the archive does not neutrally conserve archivable materials, "No, the technological structure of the *archiving* archive also determines the structure of the *archivable* content." He continues, "The archivization produces as much as it records the event" (Derrida 16–17, original emphasis). Archival technologies have a profound, even deterministic effect on what can be preserved, and therefore on the possibilities of documentation, memory, and transmission. Derrida stresses the impact the structure of the archive has on what can be archived or what is considered archivable content, and further suggests that the process of archivization not only serves a recording function, but perhaps in a more significant way, produces the events it is charged with memorializing.

One could interpret Derrida's comments to mean that archives shape historical narratives by preserving some materials as evidence of events while ignoring others. The process of preservation, in other words, articulates (past) events along the conceptual or ideological lines embedded within archives themselves. Archivization produces events by making them visible and their artifacts legible; unrecognizable formats are made invisible to the historical record. If, however, we insist that Derrida's rumination upon digital communications technologies is integral to his understanding of the productivity of the archive as such, his assessment of the archive opens alternate avenues for analysis. What, for example, are the consequences of the technological structures of digital archives for "archivable content" in the early twenty-first century?

With the advent of digital archives such as YouTube and Facebook, Derrida's *mal d'archive* has transformed from the feverish collection, categorization, and preservation of a relatively small number of artifacts and documents into a frenzied creation of digitized content to fill our bottomless caches of information. While some digital archives, particularly collections sponsored by libraries, museums, and other institutions of memory, maintain the conservationist impulse behind traditional analog archives (reworking the model only to provide greater access to the materials), in the hands of others, particularly youths, archives no longer preserve the past for the future, but serve as generative repositories of the present and recent past for contemporary audiences. Reading Derrida's *Archive Fever* in light of digital writing practices such as blogging, Kate Eichhorn offers, "To write in a digital age is to write *in* the archive, but do we also write *for* and even *like* the archive?" (Eichhorn 1, original emphasis). To reorient Eichhorn's query for the purposes of this chapter, to what extent have dance practices operating in digital culture also taken on a likeness to the archive, mimetically reproducing its effects such that dancing in the archive, dancing for the archive, and dancing like the archive are visible, if not always distinguishable, strategies of dance production?[1]

If archivization both produces and records events as Derrida suggests, in this chapter I argue that digital archives have the capacity to produce, that is, to generate the performances they are also employed to document and store, and that this is tied to how digitality redirects or reconceives dance pedagogies. In making this argument, I refer to examples of music and dance videos on the web-based video archive YouTube, dance videogames, and works by dance-media artists. My intent is not to conduct close readings of individual pieces, but to show how they collectively participate in a reconfiguration of the archive and archival modes of knowledge production. I argue that digital technologies have redirected the archive's social, political, and historical purposes and achievements, prioritizing circulation over preservation. Digital archives ask us to reconsider the role of print and televisual media in spreading dance practices, and to reexamine the pedagogical ideal of body-to-body transmission. Furthermore, digital archives offer an occasion for performance, indeed, they provide a crucial (perhaps *the* crucial) meeting place of dance pedagogy and dance performance for a generation of amateur as well as professional dancers participating in a neoliberal information economy.

In his reading of the archive, Derrida suggests that an archive requires a "gathering together" of coordinated materials, a "stable substrate" and a place for the preservation of these materials, and a "legitimate hermeneutic authority" for their interpretation (3). The movement archives I explore in this chapter conform to, yet challenge each of these parameters insofar as the logic of gathering together is unpredictable, the stability of digital media as a substrate is questionable, and every participating media user and consumer takes on the mantle of interpreter and respondent as regards the contents of digital archives. Scholars of performance have already suggested ways in which performance confounds archivization; digital media, which initially seem to make performance more available to the archive as such, overcome the "ephemerality" of performance only to succumb to the "obsolescence" of digital technologies. I thus begin with theorizations of the archive by performance scholars, which must be reconsidered for archives of a digital nature, and especially for digital archives that remain tied to the ephemeral tense of performance[2] as are the movement archives I describe below.

Reconsidering the archive

For centuries, dance practitioners have summoned a range of documentary technologies to compensate for what dance and performance theorist André Lepecki describes as "dance's somewhat embarrassing predicament of always losing itself as it performs itself" (126). Anxieties around preserving dance in a European context arose as early as the sixteenth century when dance master Thoinot Arbeau (Jehan Tabourot) discussed the importance of writing down dances with his interlocutor Capriol: "I foresee then that posterity will remain ignorant of all these new dances . . . Do not allow this to happen, Monsieur Arbeau, as it is within your power to prevent it. Set these things down in writing" (quoted in Lepecki 125). Never fully assuaged by the promises of dance notation and documentation,[3] these archival anxieties returned to the fore in the 1990s and early 2000s as the effects of Derridean deconstruction reverberated in dance and performance studies. This was at the same time that the primary functions of the archive as such were on the cusp of a significant reconfiguration in response to digital technologies. In other words, just as digital technologies were preparing to engulf and redefine processes of preservation and dissemination, an incredible anxiety arose in relation to, in Peggy Phelan's words, the "ontology of performance."

This disquietude, filtered through the language of performance's ontology, ephemerality, and presence and/or absence, obscured the profound changes that the archive was rapidly undergoing. Even Philip Auslander, who championed digital art for its fluidity and similarity to performance as it was then understood and differentiated from other media and arts practices, could not have anticipated that by 2010, the questions of the digital archive would be around access rather than absence/presence, circulation rather than preservation. Nor could performance scholars have foreseen that the most pronounced tensions would not concern a philosophical contention between performance and documentation, but a legal debate between access and circulation on the one hand and monetization and copyright/intellectual property on the other.

Performance—whatever its manner of being, appearing, or disappearing—was never what was at stake. What was at stake was the shift from the archive as a state-sponsored repository for and producer of histories to the archive as a market-authorized site of circulation for cultural memories. What was at stake was nothing less than the (neo)liberalization of the archive.

Before delving into the effects of circulating—some might say emancipating—archival materials, I find it useful to first understand how storage and transmission media were strategically positioned as performance's negative ontology. In attempting to define the parameters of performance as an analytical tool or set of aesthetic practices, to identify what "performance" is as compared to but inclusive of dance, music, theater, or other recognized performing arts disciplines, performance studies scholars cleared away those elements that signaled something performance "was not." This position is most clearly articulated in the opening lines of Peggy Phelan's 1993 seminal essay "The Ontology of Performance: Representation without Reproduction." Phelan argues,

> Performance's only life is in the present. Performance cannot be saved, recorded, documented, or otherwise participate in the circulation of representations *of* representations: once it does so, it becomes something other than performance. To the degree that performance attempts to enter the economy of reproduction it betrays and lessens the promise of its own ontology. Performance's being . . . becomes itself through disappearance.
> *("Ontology" 146, original emphasis)*

Phelan argues that performance is characterized by its radical temporality, by the co-presence of performers and audience, and the non-reproducibility of the experience. Recognizing the proliferation of digital media and transmission technologies in the early 2000s, Phelan reaffirmed her position in a 2004 essay, reframed in terms of liveness: "Now we have streaming video, webcasts, digital video, and other media able to record and circulate live events. These technologies can give us something that closely resembles the live event, but they remain something other than live performance" (Phelan, "Marina Abramović" 575). Liveness and disappearance, in Phelan's view, make performance resistant to commodification, which she deems an inherently radical position in an era of global capitalism ("Marina Abramović" 571), and allow for spectators' and performers' mutual transformation.

In his work on media and performance, Philip Auslander has challenged Phelan's insistence upon the ontological difference between performance and reproducible media. He argues that the theatrical apparatus mediates so-called "live" performance, and further, the integration of audio recordings, projected images, and other media elements in theatrical settings renders Phelan's distinction untenable. Auslander also argues that the notion of live performance is a historical function of mediation. Theater, dance, music, or other performances could only be perceived as "live" when there was a means of recording them ("Live" 16). The opposition since erected between media and performance is a little too convenient, and appears even more problematic when set alongside arguments familiar in dance and performance studies that suggest both language and the human body are themselves archives—of social practices, of technical training, of cultural patterning, of contractual arrangements—the evidence of which is manifested through ritual enactments, everyday performances, and everything in between.

Performance theorist Diana Taylor has tried to capture performance and performers' capacity for historical memory in her book *The Archive and the Repertoire: Performing Cultural Memory in the Americas*. Taylor suggests that the "archive" as such is associated with objects "supposedly resistant to change," from archaeological remains to written documents, films, videos, and even CDs (19).[4] The "repertoire," Taylor argues, is constituted by bodily practices such as dancing and singing that are "usually thought of as ephemeral, nonreproducible knowledge" (20). The archive and the repertoire operate in tandem and also appear alongside other mechanisms of transmission, namely, Taylor notes, digital modes. Reciting the same ontological concepts attributed to performance, Taylor offers that digital technologies invite a reconsideration of presence, ephemerality, and embodiment (4–5). I argue, however, that digitality implies modalities of performance that cannot be sufficiently thought through utilizing the same criteria for defining performance.

Like Taylor, Rebecca Schneider has attempted to pull performance back from the brink of disappearance. In *Performing Remains: Art and War in Times of Theatrical Reenactment*, she asks, "If we consider performance as 'of' disappearance, if we think of the ephemeral as that which 'vanishes,' and if we think of performance as the antithesis of preservation, do we limit ourselves to an understanding of performance predetermined by . . . a logic of the archive?" (97). Where Taylor turns to the repertoire as a way to disrupt the archive's hegemonic hold on both performance and memory, Schneider offers reenactment as an example of the persistence rather than disappearance of performance, calling the distinction between the live and the recorded, the performed and the archived "bogus" (102).

When looking at dance in the contexts of digital and social media, dances become a part of the cultural repertoire through their reenactment, restaging, or reperformance—just think of the phenomenon of flash mobs performing Michael Jackson's "Thriller" or internet users posting their renditions of the choreography for Beyoncé Knowles' hit song "Single Ladies (Put a Ring on It)." But the logic of these reperformances is not that of "living history" or of maintaining cultural memory through repetition as seems to be the case for both Taylor's repertoire and Schneider's reenactment. Nor is the primary value one of performers' physical co-presence with audience members, as is usually understood to be of central importance to performance as a concept and as an event. Instead, the logic is one of circulation, a logic enabled and fueled by a specifically asynchronous relationship between performer and viewer.

Performances intended for circulation in social media channels raise similar questions to what Auslander calls "performed photography"—instances in which performances occur only within the space of documentation, having been "staged solely to be photographed or filmed and [having] no meaningful prior existence as autonomous events presented to audiences" ("Performativity" 2). Such works are not documentations of performances, but are instead the performances they document. In the case of dance circulating in digital archives, however, any individual performance may not have a "meaningful prior existence" outside its documentation, but the choreographies they cite absolutely do—hence their appeal for restaging or reperforming. Performances proliferate because they circulate. Take, for example, the popularity of "planking" and "owling" internet memes—photographs of individuals in flat (plank-like) or perched (owl-like) positions in natural and man-made environments. It is not simply the case that the documentation is the performance, it is that the circulation of the photographs produces more photographs, or, in the case of dance, the online circulation of a performance of a choreography produces more performances of that choreography.

Digital performance and digital archives thus require operating assumptions that may continue to revolve around the ephemeral tense of performance, but which necessarily distance themselves from other foundational notions such as presence, embodiment, nonreproducibility, and liveness. Furthermore, digital archives of dance, especially social media archives, offer an opportunity to place performance in a larger context that includes training and rehearsal alongside performance and documentation. Toward that end, I turn my attention to digital dance pedagogies below.

Dance as gift

Twentieth-century communications technologies made themselves invaluable to envisioning and practicing dance in a social context, from the elegant ballroom dances in Hollywood musicals, to television programs such as *American Bandstand* and *Soul Train* that broadcasted new styles of movement to teenage viewers, to the exchange of VHS tapes capturing local club and street dance scenes for export to another city. Lepecki has argued that in the Western theatrical tradition, "dance cannot be imagined . . . outside writing's space" (124), and I would similarly contend that since the advent of YouTube and similar technologies of sharing, dance in social and popular contexts can no longer be imagined independently of mediatization. Popular dance and popular media have become inextricable as digital media have exponentially increased the reach of choreographies' circulations.

Dancers extend their movement repertoires as they learn new dance styles or routines from videos and videogames, and the internet then offers a place where those individuals can upload footage of newly acquired skills, thereby contributing to a collective digital dance archive. Though new media have not radically altered the modes of dance's transmission (despite the mythology, written and visual records have long been central to maintaining a repertory), they have intensified transmission to prioritize the archival record over the dancing body; digital archives keep dances in circulation through media and across dancing bodies. In other words, dancers keep movements circulating through their images more than through their co-presence with audiences, students, or fellow dancers. Whether learning choreography from music videos or playing dance videogames, dancers interface with the archive itself. How might we therefore think through the relation between dancers and the media that permeate dance pedagogy at the beginning of the twenty-first century, and how might we think through the economics of movement's circulation through or as media? I propose that the anthropological concept of the "gift," as redeployed by dance theorist Mark Franko, provides a provocative framework for considering digital dance pedagogies, one that complements and complicates the circulation of choreographies in digital culture.

Although circulation does not require viewers to embody a choreography—they can simply "like," share, or comment for similar effect—this section focuses on those viewers who do choose to engage digital archives by embodying their gestures.

In his essay "Given Movement: Dance and the Event," Franko reflects on the possibility and dilemma of artistic response to disasters on the order of September 11, 2001. Of particular concern for Franko is what he sees as the appropriation of theatrical means for terrorist ends—violence as spectacular televisual event. "Because the performative event has been turned against itself as the disaster," Franko asks, "has not its instrumentality for performative positioning been indefinitely suspended?" (114). If acts of terrorism have co-opted the structure of the event and thereby "disarmed" performance (116), on what ground and with what set of tools can performance respond? Franko suggests that the gift can provide a space in between performance and event that will eventually lead performance back to event, where it can regain its footing for critical response. Indeed, according to Franko's reading of anthropologist Marcel Mauss, who famously theorized the functions of gift-giving, the gift-giver's desire to render response impossible demonstrates the aspirational quality of the gift: "Every gift aspires to the structure of the event" (117). In the realm of social media, this desire is fulfilled with the likes of internet memes and viral videos, but I do not wish to follow this trajectory. Instead, I wish to linger in the intellectual space Franko carves out for dance as gift, which provides a useful model for thinking through the transmissions of gesture that mark participation in digital dance archives and paves the way for considering how dance functions as both immaterial labor and intangible commodity in the high-tech gift economy.[5]

In approaching dance as gift, Franko analyzes a scene from Gregory Bateson and Margaret Mead's 1936–1939 film *Learning to Dance in Bali* at some length. Though Franko recognizes the contrived nature of this erstwhile documentary, he focuses on a particular moment of transmitting dance from master to student that more or less adequately illustrates the Balinese approach to dance pedagogy. In this scene, a master teacher guides a novice student through the motions of a dance by standing directly behind the dancer, pressing his own body into his pupil's and moving the student's limbs. The teacher provides a physical support for the dancer as he manipulates him, moving him through the motions of the dance. Animating the student, the teacher brings the dance to life through the student in this moment of body-to-body transmission.

As this example demonstrates, as gift, movement becomes what Franko calls an "incorporative donation" (113). The teacher "gives" the movement to the student, but as gift, it is a "donation" that cannot be met with a response; the student incorporating the movement "gives" nothing to the teacher in return. Movement can only be circulated or paid forward, not exchanged. Thus it is crucial that in Franko's description of *Learning to Dance in Bali*, a second important scene shows an advanced student "giving" movement to a younger student while the teacher looks on. Franko describes this scenario of gifting or giving movement as a "posteconomic" form of circulation that requires one to give (of) oneself (120). This is a pedagogical mandate with an ethical orientation. Dance cannot be transmitted without the performer or teacher giving of him/herself in the process, and to give of oneself is to offer one's labor (or one's very being) as voluntary contribution rather than in exchange for monetary compensation. Performance is thus a mode of "self-donation" (121) in Franko's terms, in which the giving of movement (or music, or drama, etc.) as performance or as pedagogy does not diminish one's own supply of the same. A similar principle is at work in social and popular media contexts. Dancers who have mastered a choreography, and sometimes the choreographers themselves, "share" dances without the expectation of response or return.

Optimistically, dancers and choreographers who mine familiar (or unfamiliar) extant choreographies for public performance ("Thriller" flash mobs, for example) do not plunder the archive so much as offer a means of perpetuating the circulation of dance as gift by giving of themselves. Pessimistically, such re-use can be described as appropriation, plagiarism, or outright theft (of which Beyoncé Knowles has been repeatedly accused regarding the content of her music videos)—which begs the questions, "To whom is (a) dance given?" and "Who benefits, the giver or the receiver, and under what conditions?" With corporate capital's sponsorship of internet gift economies, such questions are pressing, but also difficult to parse. Thus, when we see dance pedagogies in the 2000s and 2010s that demonstrate dance-as-gift in relation to digital archives rather than archives of a corporeal nature as Franko describes, we should not let ourselves think that these circulations somehow position themselves outside the market as a set of "posteconomic" relations. Indeed, they mirror neoliberal market structures exactly. It is precisely the inexhaustibility of performance as a resource that drives the consumer market, which is always in search of something new. It is simply the case that, unlike music or film—industries that have been financially hard-hit by the unauthorized distribution of recordings—dance is rarely economically harmed by circulation because the market has yet to capture dance and movement effectively. To put it colloquially, there's no money in it.

Certainly the designers of videogames and television competitions have found effective ways to monetize movement, but dances, choreographies, and routines continue to circulate unfettered on YouTube and other social media sites. Online videos are routinely taken down for violating music and motion picture copyright protections, but rarely choreographic ones.[6] Learning and performing choreographies from music videos, television shows, Hollywood or Bollywood films, dance videogames, or other media that collectively form dance's popular and cultural archive is not prohibited, and is often encouraged through the many online tutorials demonstrating choreographed routines or teaching popular steps to online viewers. Online videos have become a significant mode of teaching and transmitting movement. Unlike Balinese dance pedagogy, however, which returns again and again to body-to-body contact, learning from a game or video maintains bodily separation, replacing physical intimacy between teacher and learner in a shared space with dancers' anonymity and instructors' distance.

Circulation, pedagogy, performance   **163**

This changes the ethical undercurrent of dance and other apprentice models of education: students and teachers are not accountable to each other, nor are they accountable to the dance that they perform or the communities of dancers that have invested time, energy, and money in the form. Choreographic commodities circulate within the same terrain of disavowal regarding their conditions of production as do other commodities. Circulation facilitates this disavowal; monetization requires it.

The archive as pedagogue

There is, therefore, a politics to transmitting movement outside of body-to-body contact, one that has a long history in dance but which has been obscured by the rhetoric of co-presence and ephemerality: circulating mediatized gestures maintains a separation between bodies not likely to share a physical space—whether due to geographical or historical distance, or to socio-cultural differences such as those of race or class. In this way, dances that incorporate racially/ethnically coded movements drawn from urban settings can circulate as intangible commodities in domestic suburban spaces without the discomfort or perceived threat of racialized bodies, and without the recognition of their creative labor or movement history. The choreographers employed to create routines for dance videogames, for example, are largely drawing from dance in social and popular contexts, engaging in a form of movement-aggregation rather than "innovating" movement for the games. This is in keeping with the popular forms referenced, with the exception that originators' and innovators' creative labor as well as the histories of movement practices are obscured in this form of transmission.

Take, for example, the "Apache Dance," a short comedic choreography from the "Viva Lost Wages" episode of 1990s sitcom *The Fresh Prince of Bel-Air*. Or Matt Harding's series of *Where the Hell is Matt?* videos, which offer a humorous (if neo-colonial) image of a dancer whose popping-stomping feet, swinging elbows, and swaying upper body grant him access to the furthest reaches of the globe. There is no shortage of parodies of and responses to these videos circulating online. After a clip of the "Apache Dance," featuring Will (Will Smith) and Carlton (Alfonso Ribeiro), was posted to YouTube, the choreography became a staple for (mostly white suburban) male youths competing in talent contests or goofing off at home. Given the racial and age demographics of those who perform the choreography and post it online, they have most likely learned it from watching *Fresh Prince* in television reruns or from clips of the scene circulating online—not because they recognize the "Apache" song by the Sugarhill Gang as a hip-hop anthem, and not because they frequented the clubs where the dance Smith and Ribeiro cite would have been popularized. Similarly, online viewers recreate Harding's dance in all possible venues, accompanied by the signature global new age soundtrack—but their enjoyment borne of mockery should not be mistaken for dismissal. Internet audiences respond favorably to the brand of global community Harding creates, complimenting him on his ability to create a utopian world united through silly dancing, transcending politics with his giddily prancing feet, oblivious to the implications of his arrivals and departures and unaware of the movement forms practiced locally (except as exotic color).

Viewers keep both the "Apache Dance" and *Where the Hell is . . .* videos in circulation not only by forwarding them or "liking" them; they keep the choreographies in circulation by learning and restaging them, adding their own performances to the mix. Social media support a mode of learning and performing choreography that resembles Franko's gift. There is no expectation of return or response, only of circulation, and because movement is not afforded the protections of intellectual property,[7] when people perform these choreographies for their own purposes, whatever creative ownership might have been asserted over certain moves becomes reframed in terms of a collective cultural literacy.

Home console dance videogames proliferate choreographies in a slightly different fashion. Rather than learn a choreography by watching an online video or tutorial, gamers learn sequences of movement set to specific songs, and their performances are evaluated to a greater or lesser degree by the videogame platform. Watching an animated character dancing onscreen, they match their bodies to the dancing image, creating the same shapes at the same time as the animation.[8] Just as one might learn a routine in a dance studio, gamers practice by mimicking movement, though gamers follow an onscreen dancing image rather than a co-present instructor. Gamers accumulate points for their accuracy in performing the choreographies, though how accurate one needs to be varies from platform to platform. The Nintendo Wii, for example, only tracks the movement of the hand-held Wii Remote, so players of *Just Dance* and spin-offs from the series, including the highly choreographed *Michael Jackson: The Experience*, need only duplicate the motion of one arm to fulfill the game's requirements. Xbox 360 Kinect, in contrast, features full-body tracking and the *Dance Central* series of games measures a gamer's physical displacements against motion capture data from the game's choreographers, which animate the onscreen dancers. The choreographically challenging *Dance Central* and even the party-pleasing *Just Dance* manifest a pedagogical imperative more strictly than videos of the "Apache Dance" or Matt Harding's dance, both of which were recreated by viewers and fans without the express encouragement of the creators. In contrast, the premise of dance videogames is for gamers to successfully reproduce the choreography, and many gamers circulate videos of themselves playing/dancing to show off their high scores and new moves.

Because videogames are directly purchased in a way that online videos and experimental dance-media are not, they complicate the dance-as-gift model, but not more than other instances of dance pedagogy. After all, teachers and performers generally receive some type of compensation for their offerings. Though the choreographers for *Just Dance* and *Dance Central* do not physically manipulate players the way a Balinese dance teacher physically moves a novice through a choreography, they do animate the onscreen images that players mimic. Dance videogame choreographers move novice dancers at a remove through a technologized embrace—the motion capture data and tracking software standing in for the instructors provide an asynchronous tether to them. The games "plant" the dances in the gamers who incorporate the dances' and the choreographers' gestures, but do so without implying an ethics of mutual responsibility for co-creating the dance. The gift is not returnable.

Two additional examples are *Move-Me* (launched in 2006), a hybrid on-ground and online work by dance-media artists Katrina McPherson and Simon Fildes,[9] and *If/Then Installed* (2008), an interactive museum installation created by Richard Siegal with many collaborating artists. Both works actively challenge the tensions and boundaries between performance and archivization. McPherson and Fildes have created something like a large photo booth in which on-ground participants perform a dance in response to the verbal prompts of one of eight contemporary choreographers, including American postmodern choreographer Deborah Hay, British hip-hop choreographer Jonzi D, and the London-based Spanish cross-over choreographer Raphael Bonachela. Solo, in pairs, or in groups, the on-ground participants reconstruct the dances or abandon the dictated choreography in pursuit of their own aesthetic visions. A camera in the booth records the performances, which are uploaded to the website Move-Me.com where they contribute to a growing online archive of dances performed in the booth. In *If/Then Installed*, Richard Siegal performs movements from Yvonne Rainer's choreography *Trio A*. His video image is shown in an upper corner of the screen demonstrating the movement, and, like the videogames mentioned above, participants are asked to match their gestures to his. The majority of the screen is taken up by another image of Siegal, which moves through a sequence of gestures in response to the participant's movements. When a tracking system determines that the participant has performed a gesture adequately, the participant's video image is added to a database of gestures, which forms an archive showing the uniqueness with which diverse performers interpret (Siegal's performance of) Rainer's gestural vocabulary.

Just as in the videogame and online video examples, the performances of *Move-Me* and *If/Then Installed* participants are no less a form of "incorporative donation" for the physical absence of the choreographers or other performers. In *Move-Me*, the choreographers' words rather than their movements are incorporated, gesticulated, and performed for an archive—which is to say, with the intention (or at least awareness) of being documented. *If/Then Installed* complicates Franko's pedagogical model, however, in that mimicking one of Siegal's images causes another of his images to move. The novice/participant gives movement to the instructor's image, but this is not a form of "giving back" such that it could be described as a relationship of exchange. Unlike the other examples I have cited, wherein gestures continue to circulate online or in popular venues, these gestures have nowhere to go but back into the system. *If/Then Installed* forms a closed-circuit in which gestures circulate between images and participants, but not beyond. To complicate matters further, however, the piece as a whole contributes to the rather broad circulation of *Trio A*, which has been restaged innumerable times outside digital venues.

In the examples above, drawn from instances of dance in social media, videogames, and experimental media art, archivization is not secondary to performance. Rather, dancers interface with the archive, they perform the archive, and their performances return to the archive. Social media and digital modes of sharing have deeply influenced each of these examples and the ways they trouble the relation of performance to the archive. Indeed, one could argue that the increased accessibility of choreography as digital commodity is inextricably tied to the circulation and transmission of gestures in social media.

A final example emphasizes this point. In July 2012, while I was writing this chapter, an online video starring a young man, Ton Do-Nguyen, went viral in the United States. Facing the camera, he flutters his eyes, strokes his face, and proceeds to reproduce Beyoncé Knowles's 2011 music video *Countdown* in its entirety shot-for-shot while lip-synching and dancing for most of the video in a Snuggie (a wearable blanket). As with so many of her other music videos, Beyoncé borrowed heavily from extant choreography for *Countdown*, incorporating choreographic and cinematographic material taken without acknowledgement from Thierry De Mey's dancefilms of Belgian choreographer Anne Theresa De Keersmaeker's pieces *Rosas danst Rosas* and *Achterland*. Of course De Keersmaeker's choreography in turn samples everyday gestures, familiar club dance movements, even tap dance, which are held together with the glue called a postmodern choreographic aesthetic. When De Keersmaeker and De Mey created these films, did they foresee the possibility of their choreography and cinematography circulating through video sharing websites or reappearing in new commercial and amateur enterprises? When Do-Nguyen put on his Snuggie and set about recreating *Countdown* for a YouTube audience, did he recognize that he was performing a choreographic archive (a video of a video of a choreography) and that his performance for the archive (YouTube) was keeping the choreography in circulation? My guess is no, yet this is precisely the situation contemporary dance makers and dance audiences face: the archive no longer secures the authenticity of a dance event by documenting its occurrence (if, in fact, it ever did); in an era of digital archives and social media, the archive surpasses the danced event to produce and proliferate performances, and does so in a movement economy in which dance-as-gift and dance-as-commodity intersect with digital dance pedagogies.

Many thanks to the participants of the 2012 Mellon Dance Studies Summer Seminar for their many insights and comments. Special thanks also to Rebecca Schneider, Clare Croft, and Kate Elswit.

Notes

1 To be sure, these strategies are already apparent in reconstructions of historical dances.
2 By ephemeral tense, I mean to suggest that performance corresponds to the "aspect" or temporal shape grammatically identified as imperfective—denoting processual, habitual, and/or progressive activities without clear beginning or end, but which, in the case of performance and spectatorship, are generally characterized as fleeting and are assigned to the past. I intend to foreground impermanence without suggesting either disappearance or liveness.
3 Including Feuillet notation, kinetography/Labanotation, Benesh notation, Eshkol-Wachman notation, as well as more recent developments in motion capture.

4 Taylor is quick to add, however, that the archive's contents are subject to the manipulations of the state.
5 See Richard Barbrook, "The Hi-Tech Gift Economy," *First Monday* 3.12 (7 Dec 1998).
6 YouTube's 2009 shutting down of the Ketinoa channel, which contained some copyrighted material covered by the Balanchine Trust among its 1,300 videos, is one of few examples of digital content being removed on the basis of its choreographic content. Many thanks to Olivia Sabee for bringing this to my attention.
7 See in particular Anthea Kraut's work on dance, choreographic copyright, and the complications race and gender have posed to assertions of dance as intellectual property.
8 *Dance Dance Revolution* is a notable exception to this characterization, as are dance games for handheld devices.
9 http://www.move-me.com.

References

Auslander, Philip. "Live from Cyberspace: or, I Was Sitting at My Computer, This Guy Appeared He Thought I Was a Bot." *PAJ* 24.1 (2002): 16–21.
—— "The Performativity of Performance Documentation." *PAJ* 28.3 (2006): 1–10.
Derrida, Jacques. *Archive Fever: A Freudian Impression*. Chicago: University of Chicago Press, 1995.
Eichhorn, Kate. "Archival Genres: Gathering Texts and Reading Spaces." *Invisible Culture* 12 (2008): 1-10.
Franko, Mark. "Given Movement: Dance and the Event." *Of the Presence of the Body: Essays on Dance and Performance Theory*. Ed. André Lepecki. Middleton: Wesleyan University Press, 2004. 113–123.
Lepecki, André. "Inscribing Dance." *Of the Presence of the Body: Essays on Dance and Performance Theory*. Ed. André Lepecki. Middletown: Wesleyan University Press, 2004. 124–139.
Phelan, Peggy. "The Ontology of Performance: Representation without Reproduction," *Unmarked: The Politics of Performance*. New York: Routledge, 2003. 146–166.
—— "Marina Abramović: Witnessing Shadows." *Theatre Journal* 56.4 (2004): 569–577.
Schneider, Rebecca. *Performing Remains: Art and War in Times of Theatrical Reenactment*. New York: Routledge, 2011.
Taylor, Diana. *The Archive and the Repertoire: Performing Cultural Memory in the Americas*. Durham: Duke University Press, 2003.

16
DIGITAL DANCE
The challenges for traditional copyright law

Charlotte Waelde and Sarah Whatley

As an embodied practice, dance comprises a fusion of cultures and practices, but its fluidity has been characterized by a dispersed and fractured documented history. Perhaps because it is a heterogeneous practice and the body is the most complex instrument to "write down," dance has produced few hard copy records of itself. Certainly there are many records of "the body": from medicine to the visual arts, the body, and its documentation, has played a central role in enriching our understanding and appreciation of the sciences and arts. But none seem yet to have adequately addressed the challenges of capturing the dancing body in ways that fulfil the intention of the choreographers and dancers with respect to the dance. This may be changing. There have been rapid developments in recent years in terms of the intersection between dance and computational processes. Digital dance projects have experimented with new ways to create and remediate dance, to capture the processual aspects of dance making, and to devise new modes of choreography and dance inscriptions.

This confluence of dance and technology within projects that have created innovative tools for capturing, analyzing and visualizing dance has generated new dance inscriptions and raises the possibility for dance to take its place as part of our cultural heritage. Being recognized as a "formal" part of our cultural heritage has important consequences. Not only do states have certain safeguarding obligations under international law with respect to the dance, but in addition, the legal framework has implications for dance's authorship, ownership, and development, which lead into the domain of intellectual property in general and of copyright in particular. Whilst many dance projects that engage with digital technologies seek to embed open systems of authorship and ownership, the overarching system of law entrenched within international, regional, and domestic treaties, agreements and legislative measures (many of which were drafted with the analog era in mind) insist upon ascribing ownership to individuals, or to narrow, and legally defined, small groups. On development of works of dance, there seems to be a void between the law's notion of what is acceptable to take from pre-existing works when creating afresh, and what happens in practice. This leads to uncertainty and tension not only for the participants, but also for their peers and promoters. In the digital domain these questions become increasingly acute as dance practices are recorded, analyzed and re-interpreted.

To understand how the legal frameworks might support digital dance projects, we must understand what we mean by cultural heritage and what makes something part of this store of knowledge. We thus begin with an examination of what is meant by cultural heritage through a legal lens. What are the international legal frameworks that determine what is and is not cultural heritage, who are the stakeholders and what are their interests? How does that relate to or support digital dance projects? The second part of this contribution will consider the mediation and selection of cultural heritage and consider how that is changing most particularly with the advent of digital technologies.

Cultural heritage and the dancing body

There is no legal definition of cultural heritage. Rather, the term is used in a number of international and regional legal instruments that carry their own particular meanings. Many emanate from the United Nations Educational, Scientific, and Cultural Organization (UNESCO), the United Nations body charged with safeguarding our cultural heritage. Within the UNESCO tradition, cultural heritage and its ilk are firmly based in human rights norms themselves deriving from general International Human Rights treaties which include the protection of culture mostly grounded in notions of cultural diversity and integrity. While the idea of human rights goes back to mediaeval times, natural law, and the Enlightenment, and was developed by philosophers such as John Locke and Francis Hutcheson, it was the horrors of the Second World War that gave the impetus to formalize the human rights system under the auspices of the United Nations (UN). While the UN system of human rights is directed towards crimes perpetrated on individuals, UNESCO initiatives were initially driven by the desire to deal with sources of cultural conflict between states, a reaction partly to the activities of the conqueror taking cultural artifacts from the conquered.[1]

The meaning and content of the term cultural heritage, along with the related terms cultural property and common heritage of mankind, is highly contested and driven by a mostly politicized process within which its sense is debated and shaped.[2] From the destruction and looting that took place in the aftermath of the Second World War[3]; to the demolition of the Buddhas of Bamiyan[4]; to the treatment of indigenous peoples and their cultural identities[5]; to the increasing commodification of cultural works under the TRIPs agreement and bilateral treaties[6]; and to the recognition that valuable and diverse art forms will disappear if not actively supported, the discourse is driven by state interests, by the rhetoric and reality of notions of property, and by multifaceted alliances between shifting political and economic interests. These alliances constantly slide as between East/ West, West/West, developed/developing, developed/developed and developing/ developing nations' interests, depending on the issue on the agenda. The discourse is at once broad, focusing on cultural diversity and integrity, and narrow, focusing on specific cultural rights. It is intimately bound up in ideas of cultural and political identity, in individual and community norms, and in individual and collective rights. These characteristics have led one commentator to opine: "Too much is asked of heritage. In the same breath we commend national patrimony, regional and ethnic legacies and a global heritage shared and sheltered in common. We forget that these aims are usually incompatible" (Lowenthal 227).

Culture-specific conventions

Since the earliest UNESCO Conventions, different descriptions have been used for the subject matter in this area: cultural heritage, cultural property, and the common heritage of mankind are the three main ones.[7] These are not interchangeable as such and each brings its own connotations. Allied to this is the need to bear in mind the different types of cultural heritage and their classification in the rhetoric of property. These range from the intangible (the dance, the folklore, the know-how, the musical tradition); the tangible (the monument, the statue, the picture, the book); the heritable (the museums, libraries, and archives; the trees in the rainforest); and the moveable (the painting, the sculpture, the photograph, the film).

The UNESCO Cultural Conventions cover these types of property in different ways. Prior to 2000 the focus was on tangible objects and how policy could respond to the challenges faced in wartime,[8] the tendency of states to remove cultural artifacts from countries,[9] the growing need to protect world cultural and natural heritage,[10] and the need to protect underwater cultural heritage.[11] Each of these Conventions has its own definition of cultural property or heritage. The 1954 Convention dealing with the protection of cultural property in the event of armed conflict, for example, refers to "cultural property" and to both movable and immovable property "of great importance" such as monuments and works of art and to the buildings designed to preserve and exhibit cultural property such as museums and libraries. The 1970 Convention, which aims to prevent the illicit import, export, and transfer of ownership of cultural property, also refers to the term "cultural property," this time as property designated by each state as being of importance for inter alia literature or art and which belongs to defined categories including paintings, sculptures, and rare manuscripts and archives including cinematographic archives. Both the 1972 Convention on the protection of world cultural and natural heritage and the 2001 Convention on underwater cultural heritage refer to cultural heritage rather than cultural property.[12] The former defines cultural heritage as certain monuments, groups of buildings, and sites, while natural heritage is natural features and sites and geological and physiographical—all of which must be considered to be of outstanding universal value (articles 1 and 2). The latter defines cultural heritage as "all traces of human existence having a cultural, historical or archaeological character which have been partially or totally under water, periodically or continuously, for at least 100 years" and goes on to include such things as buildings, vessels, and objects of prehistoric character.

By contrast to these efforts to protect largely tangible culture, the two main UNESCO Conventions negotiated in the 2000s deal with intangible cultural heritage. The 2003 Convention for the Safeguarding of the Intangible Cultural Heritage defines intangible cultural heritage as "the practices, representations, expressions, knowledge, skills—as well as the instruments, objects, artefacts and cultural spaces associated therewith—that communities, groups and, in some cases, individuals recognize as part of their cultural heritage." The Convention goes on to state that this intangible cultural heritage is:

> transmitted from generation to generation, is constantly recreated by communities and groups in response to their environment, their inter action with nature and their history, and provides them with a sense of identity and continuity, thus promote respect for cultural diversity and human creativity.[13]

Key points arising from this definition are that heritage is transmitted from generation to generation, thus situating heritage for these purposes as something more than transitory or created for the moment; the recognition that cultural heritage is recreated—so not static or fixed; the idea of cultural heritage being important for identity; and the human rights language in referring to cultural diversity and human creativity. This has clear relevance for dance as it is relevant to inter alia the performing arts. However, the criteria that it be passed from generation to generation and constantly recreated in response to the environment means that it is not necessarily a sufficient criteria for dance. Whilst many dance practices might be passed from generation to generation through the bodies of the dancers, depending on the link from person to person, by "human chains of dancers, choreographers, and others involved in its creation and performance"[14] the labeling of dance as "contemporary" can suggest it exists only in the present, negating its presence in the past and tending to disappear into oblivion.

The Convention for the protection and promotion of the diversity of cultural expressions 2005[15] refers not to cultural heritage but to the "cultural heritage of humanity," which it seeks to protect through recognizing cultural diversity "expressed, augmented and transmitted through the variety of cultural expressions, but also through diverse modes of artistic creation, production, dissemination, distribution and enjoyment, whatever the means and technologies used." As with the 2003 Convention, there is strong use of human rights language in reference to cultural values, and stress is laid on the importance of cultural identities. By contrast with the 2003 Convention, the 2005 Convention protects current artistic creativity and values, partly encompassed within definitions of cultural expressions,[16] cultural content,[17] and cultural activities.[18] This, then, is the Convention that has the most relevance for the art form under discussion in this chapter, namely, dance.

The relationship between cultural heritage and intellectual property rights

There is a complex relationship between cultural heritage and intellectual property (IP) rights of which copyright is a part. The UNESCO Conventions implicitly if not explicitly recognize copyright and its importance in and to cultural heritage. For those Conventions dealing with tangible heritage, much of the very subject matter protected by the Conventions can be thought of in terms of copyright. In international copyright conventions, copyright protects literary and artistic works, works of architecture, and cinematographic works among others—all of which are explicitly mentioned in the UNESCO Conventions as protected subject matter.[19] Both the 2003 and 2005 Conventions dealing with intangible cultural heritage refer to IP rights. In the 2003 Convention it is stated that nothing should interfere with state obligations in respect of intellectual property rights;[20] and in the 2005 Convention IP is noted in the Recitals as being important to "those involved in cultural creativity." It is also notable that as part of the process of safeguarding cultural heritage, the 2003 Convention exhorts national states to establish documentation centers[21] and at international level to draw up and publish a list of intangible cultural heritage;[22] and in the 2005 Convention States are directed to ensure the *preservation, protection, promotion and dissemination of cultural expressions and diversity*. Each of these acts forces the intangible to become tangible through fixation. While fixation is not a necessary precursor in all jurisdictions to the existence of copyright,[23] making the intangible tangible immediately raises questions over copyright authorship and ownership and rights to exploitation.[24] The act of recording fixes property rights (copyright) in dances and determines authorship and ownership of the works. What might have been considered part of the cultural heritage of humanity as a process and performance through fixation in law becomes an item of cultural property. This raises interesting questions as to how something can both be owned in common by "humanity" and as private property in the hands of individuals at one and the same time.

As noted above, it has become clear that the international legal framework does not support one definition; rather there are multiple meanings depending on the context. It has been said that this lack of an agreed definition means that "international cultural heritage law has developed with an uncertainty at its center over the exact nature of its subject-matter and based on a set of principles which are not always coherent" (Blake 85), which echoes Lowenthal's lament that too much is asked of cultural heritage (see note 7). There are, however, elements pertaining to cultural heritage that are found repeatedly in international law. These have been summarized as follows:

> Cultural heritage is some form of inheritance that a community or people considers worth safekeeping and handing down to future generations.[25] Cultural heritage is linked with group identity and is both a symbol of the cultural identity of a self-identified group (a nation or people) and an essential element in the construction of that group's identity.
>
> *(Blake 84)*

In this next part, the focus is first on the process of selection and mediation of cultural heritage; and second, on digitally mediated/produced dance. Both of these are relevant to the two components of cultural heritage outlined above.

Selection and mediation of cultural heritage

There is a continuous mediation and selection process that determines what cultural heritage is, and by virtue of which decisions are made over what is worth preserving for the future.[26] This occurs not only within the politicized process that governs the meaning of cultural heritage within the international conventions discussed above,[27] but also in the processes through which something is chosen to become a part of our cultural heritage, and in the allocation of resources that makes that selection happen. Museums, galleries, libraries, and archives have traditionally played the role of intermediary within the international and state mandated definitions of cultural heritage.

It is from these mediated repositories with their carefully crafted selection and curation processes that dance plays only a small part, primarily because it has evaded ways to capture it in any form that adequately provides access to the practice itself. Dance might produce text and objects as a byproduct of the art form (costumes, designs, photographs, performance ephemera, etc.) but the dance itself is almost entirely absent. However, relationships in this role seem now to be changing and becoming more decentralized—at least in some quarters—as digital technologies present increasing opportunities to individuals and communities to choose what should be preserved.[28] This brings with it challenging questions over the process of making and securing cultural heritage. As has been said in relation to the capture of dance, and dance-like performances, the process of "making, performing, documenting and archiving" is collapsing, and "who decides what is to be preserved and how such varied events might generate new taxonomies to secure their own future is not yet clear" (Whatley "The Challenges of the *Inter*" 225). Even in this decentralized system resources are often needed for the act of preservation, a process that then involves mediation and selection in deciding what should be funded as, for instance, when an artistic work is sponsored through an organization supported by the state.[29] It also raises questions over the fact of decentralization and what this then means for what is included in or excluded from our cultural heritage.

Dance and the digital

The integration of digital technologies in the creation and documentation of dance works presents a further challenge to the question of what is included in our records of cultural heritage. Whilst digital technologies may enable greater imagination in the making process, more access to dance as well and new ways to engage with dance, the continual changing nature of digital technologies may actually render the work more vulnerable to long-term conservation and preservation. Technologies that were adopted as recently as the 1990s by artists wanting to innovate new ways of creating and experiencing dance are now effectively obsolete. For example, dance artists making multimedia web-based work were creating projects that utilized technology that was of poor quality due to limitations in hardware, online signal, and pixel resolution. As technology advanced and new means became available, dance works depending on earlier systems disappeared and often with little record. Moreover, by producing "new forms of hybrid human and machine subjectivities" (Salter 29) digital dance projects are not easily archived in a form that offers any real sense/access to the "work" as it was intended to be experienced. Many projects are dependent on interactivity whereby the audience instigates or even becomes the content. Consequently, many of these projects are effectively co-created involving audiences and technologists as equal collaborators with the artists. Coupled with so much more of the artist's work freely available online and many more tools to share and distribute dance content, questions about authorship and copyright arise.

Dancers have traditionally been somewhat reluctant to engage with copyright in relation to their work, partly perhaps due to the collaborative nature of dance practice, but copyright might be a useful tool for ensuring financial survival when public funding for the arts is shrinking. The UK's Arts Council of England is promoting a strong message to the creative sector: commercialize to survive.[30] Alternative modes of financial survival have to be developed and one of these may be through greater commercial exploitation of creative outputs. Commercial exploitation of dance would depend on the exclusive rights granted under the copyright framework. Fundamental to developing an exploitation strategy would be to identify the author and owner of the copyright in the dance. This is an area that has been underexplored in law: there is little case law or literature on dance and copyright, but there are certain assumptions within the dance community as to authorship and ownership.

Dance and copyright

Historically dance has been almost entirely absent from our legal discourse concerning copyright, particularly in the UK. One is hard pushed to find case law on copyright and dance. What there has been has included questions of ownership of copyright by a choreographer under the 1911 Copyright Act; questions of infringement of the copyright in an Oscar Wilde story when adapted in the form of a ballet;[31] and a finding that a dramatic work must be capable of being performed to be protected by copyright.[32] Neither has there been much focus on dance in our law literature, although there was some excitement recently over a dance performed by Beyoncé that seemed to draw heavily on earlier work by the choreographer De Keersmaeker.[33] Other jurisdictions have paid more attention to this art form and the place of copyright in its exploitation. In the US for instance dance was put on the legal map as a result of a court case concerning the ownership of dances by the choreographer Martha Graham. This spawned much literature and seemed to result in a greater appreciation of intellectual property rights in dance, at least in the US.[34]

The dance community, unlike the music industry, has seemed hesitant about asserting rights. That is not because they do not know about copyright but because it seems rarely to be of concern within their artistic endeavor. What is rather more important, particularly to those who work alone or in small groups, is the process of creation of the dance and all that brings with it (Waelde and Schlesinger 257). From a legal perspective the key point is identifying *who* has expressed the correct authorial input into the work. Here it is important to emphasize that it is the *work* in which copyright resides once fixed that is under investigation, and not the performance of the work.

So we are concerned with "what is the work," and who makes the right sort of authorial contribution to that work. There seems a clear assumption in the dance community that the choreographer is the author of the dance and the owner of the copyright in it.[35] The one British case to have considered the question, Massine v de Basil,[36] was decided under the 1911 Copyright Act, which in turn included a reference to "choreographic work," as did the 1956 Copyright Act. The Copyright Designs and Patents Act 1988 (CDPA), however, says nothing about choreography or choreographic work but does provide that a dramatic work includes a work of dance (CDPA s 3) and the author is the person who creates that work (CDPA s 9 (1)). UK case law on identification of a dramatic work is sparse. It seems that a dramatic work cannot be purely static and should have movement, story, or action,[37] and should be capable of being performed,[38] but we know little beyond that.

What is the dance?

While the UK case law on identifying a dramatic work or work of dance for the purposes of copyright is sparse, as noted above, the position is currently complicated by the development of jurisprudence from the Court of Justice (CoJ) around both the categorization of works and in relation to the level of originality needed for the subsistence of copyright. Under the CDPA, a work has to fall into a particular category in order to be protected by copyright: for our purposes, a dance must fall into the category of dramatic work (CDPA s 3(1)). In terms of the level of originality required, this has historically been very low in the UK, requiring only "skill labor and effort" and that a work should not be copied.[39] This in turn has meant that few works have been denied protection. The CoJ case law seems to challenge these criteria in a way that appears to conflate the concept of the work and the requirement of originality (see Eechoud; Handig "Sweat of the Brow" and "Infopacq"; Pila; Rahmatian; Rosati "Towards an EU-wide Copyright?"). The CoJ has stressed that the European scheme of protection for copyright protects works where the subject matter is original in the sense of being the author's intellectual creation.[40] What the work is called, in other words for our purposes whether it is a work of dance being a subset of the category of dramatic works, is irrelevant, although it seems that a work would need to fall under the Berne Convention categories of a literary or artistic work.[41] The standard of originality for all types of work is the same: it is one of intellectual creation.[42] To reach this level the author should express her creative ability in an original manner by making free and creative choices,[43] and stamp her "personal touch" on the work.[44] Where choices are dictated by technical considerations, rules, or constraints which leave no room for creative freedom, then these criteria are not met.[45]

What is fixation?

Although there is no requirement of fixation in the international framework for copyright to subsist,[46] the law in the UK does require that the work be fixed in some material form[47]: copyright only arises on fixation. What form fixation takes is left open and needs only to be "in writing or otherwise" (CDPA s 3(2)). Traditionally fixation has been thought of as being in writing, reflecting the historical text-based roots of copyright law. For dance, one of the notation systems such as Laban or Benesh might be deployed, both of which have relatively modern origins, having been invented in the mid-twentieth century. More modern examples of dance fixation include film and video, computer animation, motion capture, and holography.[48]

For dance, however, meeting the requirement of fixation is perhaps too easily assumed. These methods might fix the work but may not capture the essence of the dance. Choreographers voice different opinions as to what amounts to fixation as well as challenging the requirement itself. As to the dance, some view its fugitive nature as presenting particular problems for capture; others point to the technicalities of the art form occupying both space and time as being too challenging for fixation (see Cook). Yet others assert that the dance is fixed or "set" in the "memories and bodies of the dancers" where the bodies are considered material objects (Taylor 227). For others the idea of any form of record is an anathema: the dance is meant only to be ephemeral, that is, to exist at the time of performance, where fixation ossifies the work (see for instance Théberge 139, 140). But this raises challenges in law for dance: the paradox is that fixation is the key to copyright protection for works of dance, but at the same time presents a high hurdle. To gain the protection of copyright what has to be captured is *a* version of the work, whatever the participants and the community might think about the quality of the work and its ossification, or however challenging notation systems might be for a true representation of a dance. If there is no fixation, there is no protection at all.

What is the authorial input?

The much more difficult questions lie at the interface between the authorial input necessary to be considered an author for the purposes of copyright, and the input that instead interprets a work and is thus in the nature of performance.

The more that the creation of the dance is an iterative, collaborative process, the more such input must be recognized as being of the right sort to be considered authorial whoever has made that input. While it is fully accepted that dance moves as such could not, and should not be the subject of protection by copyright—it is rather how they are combined in the dance that is important and relevant—it seems difficult to equate these as they feed into the creation of the work. With the new case law from the CoJ mentioned above, it seems that the concept of "work" as we have understood it in the law of copyright may not be relevant. If so, then this may leave space for hitherto unprotected elements, or combinations of elements, to be considered as suitable for protection by copyright. There could perhaps be challenges for some dances in relation to the "dictated by technical considerations" proviso. Some works which have historically been protected may no longer receive copyright status because they are limited by their technical function. An example from music is the skill, labor, and effort exerted in updating musical scores to recreate the music of a Baroque composer: the input may be considered to be dictated by technical requirements and therefore may not be capable of protection by copyright.[49] By analogy, would the recreation of an historic dance to conform to an original production now earn its own copyright protection? Arguably not if its re-creation was dictated by the technical requirements of the original choreographer.

How much, however, of the dance should be considered personal to the dancer as opposed to fixed on the body by the choreographer or an interpretation of the choreographers' intent, needs further examination. Moreover, when a dance work that was first performed "live" is re-presented within the digital environment (for example within a digital archive) it can call into question the nature of the collaborative process that gave rise to the work in the first place. In some digital dance projects authorship is less clear and may be distributed amongst many involved in the production and among many different works that themselves attract copyright protection. Digital technologies may completely re-configure the creative process to the extent that there is no longer the traditional role of choreographer. Characterized by convergence, hybridity, and the blurring of disciplinary boundaries, digital dance projects frequently involve a range of creatives who may have equal claim on the works, including programmers, designers, coders, engineers, and new media artists. Alternatively, choreographers may employ digital tools to create choreographic objects that reveal more about their own making process that make their authorship of their work more transparent and tangible.

Rethinking copyright law: foundations for the future

Copyright can be a protection and support for all those involved in dance. We might argue that where a dancer interprets the choreographer's intent through making choices as to how the dance will be expressed on her body, then she is the author of the copyright in her arrangement of that dance. Where dancers collaborate in the creation of a dance through an iterative process, and during which they all make choices as to how the dance will be embodied, then they are joint authors of the resultant work so long as they have expended the "right sort" of authorial originality. Digital dance projects may complicate the traditional relationship between choreographer and performer but the principle that all co-authors have a stake in the work is the same. In the absence of agreement to the contrary or an employment relationship, each author is then an owner of the copyright, and each is entitled to have a say in how that work is exploited. Some have argued that this is unworkable because of the challenges that would be raised by having to seek consent from numerous copyright owners. Two comments spring to mind. The first is that complexity in exploitation is not a reason for denying an author her (intangible) property right. The second is that ownership can be streamlined by way of licensing. Much as the various layers of copyright in a musical work tend to be consolidated in the hands of the record company, so the layers of copyright in a dance could be consolidated in the hands of the choreographer—if it was her hands that could best exploit the work. In addition, it should be remembered that social media in particular offer many diverse ways in which exploitation can occur. No longer are we tied to, say, royalty streams from licensing recorded forms of the dance.

The act of recording of the dance for its preservation will also provide its own challenges within the dance community where it is widely acknowledged that the ephemerality of the art form makes it difficult to capture.[50] Add to that the spectre of intellectual property rights in the dance combined with tortuous questions over who owns and who can control what in respect of the recording—questions that almost inevitably arise in the cultural sector once a cultural production starts to gain traction (and may generate money)[51]—and so the scene may be set within the dance sector for major changes that could, properly managed, serve to heighten awareness of the dance for the benefit of all. Few would argue with the sentiment that "our contemporary/present-day artists are a precious resource" (Whatley "The Challenges of the *Inter*" 225). From a legal perspective, it is when dance enters our cultural heritage that important consequences flow concerning the safeguarding of this resource. So it is not *whether* we should turn our attention to these pressing matters, it is rather *what* we should do and how we should go about it.

Notes

1 Convention on the Means of Prohibiting and Preventing the Illicit Import, Export and Transfer of World Cultural Property November 14, 1970; Convention Concerning the Protection of the World Cultural and Natural Heritage November 17, 1972. Before this, the discourse developed after the Napoleonic Wars and the insistence of the British in the Vienna Treaty of 1815 to the return of moveable artefacts of cultural heritage thus linking territories, peoples, and cultural objects (Macmillan 356).
2 Article 4 of the UNESCO Convention Concerning the Protection of the World Cultural and Natural Heritage 1972 places the following duty on a contracting state: "ensuring the identification, protection, conversation; presentation and transmission to future generations of the cultural and natural heritage."

The challenges for traditional copyright law 179

3 This led to the UNESCO Convention for the Protection of Cultural Property in the Event of Armed Conflict 1954 249 U.N.T.S. 24.
4 For comment see Macmillan (35).
5 UN Declaration on the Rights of Indigenous Peoples 2007.
6 Trade Related Agreement on Intellectual Property Rights 1994 and its spread of IP norms and standards.
7 In discussions on UNESCO routes the term "cultural" is used to mean anything produced by man and not limited to cultural manifestations in the narrow sense exemplified by art, literature, and architecture. Report on the Expert Meeting on Routes as a Part of our Cultural Heritage (Madrid, Spain, November 1994) WHC-94/CONF.003/INF.1.
8 The Convention for the Protection of Cultural Property in the Event of Armed Conflict 1954.
9 Convention on the Means of Prohibiting and Preventing the Illicit Import, Export and Transfer of Ownership of Cultural Property 1970.
10 Convention Concerning the Protection of the World Cultural and Natural Heritage 1972.
11 Convention on the Protection of the Underwater Cultural Heritage 2001.
12 See Brown (41): "The shift from the expression cultural property to cultural heritage signals growing doubt about the Universality of Western notions of property and widespread recognition that culture cannot be reduced to an inventory of objects without marginalizing its most important features."
13 The types of works that would be protected under the convention can be seen in the representative list of intangible cultural heritage maintained by UNESCO. See http://www.unesco.org/culture/ich/index.php?lg=en&pg=11&type=2, accessed September 1, 2015.
14 "From toe to toe, from hand to hand, from eye to eye, dance, more than any other of the performing arts, has been transmitted through time by human chains of dancers, choreographers, and others involved in its creation and performance" (Brooks and Meglin 1).
15 The UNESCO Convention on Cultural Diversity of Cultural Expressions was drafted in October 2005 and came into force March 2007. For further information see Burri.
16 Article 4(3) of the Convention on the Protection and Promotion of the Diversity of Cultural Expressions 2005 "Cultural expressions" are those expressions that result from the creativity of individuals, groups, and societies, and that have cultural content.
17 Article 4(2) of the Convention on the Protection and Promotion of the Diversity of Cultural Expressions 2005 "Cultural content" refers to the symbolic meaning, artistic dimension and cultural values that originate from or express cultural identities.
18 Article 4(4) Convention on the Protection and Promotion of the Diversity of Cultural Expressions 2005 "Cultural activities, goods and services" refers to those activities, goods, and services, which at the time they are considered as a specific attribute, use, or purpose, embody or convey cultural expressions, irrespective of the commercial value they may have. Cultural activities may be an end in themselves, or they may contribute to the production of cultural goods and services.
19 Article 1 of the Berne Convention for the Protection of Literary and Artistic Works 1886.
20 Article 3B of the UNESCO Convention for the Safeguarding of Intangible Cultural Heritage 2003.
21 Article 13 d iii of the UNESCO Convention for the Safeguarding of Intangible Cultural Heritage 2003.
22 Article 16 of the UNESCO Convention for the Safeguarding of Intangible Cultural Heritage 2003.
23 The Berne Convention leaves it open to States to decide whether fixation is needed for the existence of copyright protection for a work.
24 Whether this ought to be the case or whether there should be space within cultural heritage for works to which private property rights are ascribed is another matter. See

Macmillan (355). See also for example sites for preserving endangered dance, http://www.coreofculture.org/, accessed September 1, 2015.
25 Macmillan sums this up as cultural heritage "being those things (moveable and immoveable, tangible and intangible) that a community or people considers worth handing on to the future" in "Arts Festivals: Property, Heritage or More?" in Kathy Bowrey and Michael Handler, *Law and Creativity in the Age of the Entertainment Franchise*. Cambridge: Cambridge University Press, 2014.
26 ". . . for tradition (our cultural heritage) is self-evidently a process of deliberate continuity, yet any tradition can be shown, by analysis, to be a selection and reselection of those significant revived and recovered elements of the past which represent not a necessary but a desired continuity" (Williams 187).
27 ". . . the identification of cultural heritage is in itself a political act given its symbolic relationship to culture and society in general" (Blake 68).
28 Fisher 193: "An attractive society is one rich in 'communities of memory.' Persons' capacity to construct rewarding lives will be enhanced if they have access to a variety of 'constitutive' groups—in 'real' space and in 'virtual' space."; Sunder "IP3," 257. "At the same time that identity politics has turned its attention to questions of development through the capacity to produce and participate in culture, the new technologies of the Internet Protocol make such cultural democracy more possible. In the Participation Age, people with access to a computer and relatively cheap but powerful digital hardware challenge the hegemony of traditional cultural authorities and create new cultural meanings from the bottom up."
29 See, for example, Girl Jonah by Caroline Bowditch, http://www.girljonah.org/, accessed September 1, 2015. Here there is an intermediary in the form of bodies that fund artistic projects who make the funds available for the work to be made, captured, and preserved.
30 Waelde, Whatley, and Pavis. Note that this article forms the basis of the comments in this next part. See also Arts Council England have welcomed applications for grants which have a commercial motive: http://www.artscouncil.org.uk/media/uploads/pdf/gfta_information_sheets_june_2013/Creative_media_and_digital_activity_June_2013.pdf, accessed September 1, 2015.
31 Holland v Vivian Van Damn Productions Ltd., [1936–45] MacG. Cop. Cas. 69 (Ch. D.).
32 Norowzian v Arks Limited, [2000] F.S.R. 363 (C.A.). See Rivers 389, Arnold 10.
33 Yeoh "The Copyright Implications of Beyoncé's "borrowings" 95; Yeoh "Choreographers' Moral Right of Integrity" 43-58; Yeoh "Choreographer's Copyright Dilemma" 201; Yeoh "The Choreographic Trust" 224; Jennings; Mackrell.
34 Martha Graham School and Dance Foundation Inc. v Martha Graham Center of Contemporary Dance, Inc., 43 Fed. Appx. 408 (2nd Cir. 2002); Martha Graham School and Dance Foundation Inc. v Martha Graham Center of Contemporary Dance, Inc., 374 F.Supp.2d 355, 363 (S.D.N.Y. 2005); Martha Graham School and Dance Foundation Inc. v Martha Graham Center of Contemporary Dance, Inc., 466 F.3d 97 (2006); Braveman, 471; Connelly 837.
35 Waelde and Schlesinger. See also De Mille 256. "[T]he choreographer is glued immobile as a fly in a web and must watch his own pupils and assistants, suborned to steal his ideas and livelihood. Several dancers made paying careers out of doing just this."
36 Massine v De Basil, (1937), 81 Sol. Jo. 670 (Ch. D.); aff'd (1938), 82 Sol. Jo. 173 (C.A.).
37 Creation Records v News Group [1997] EMLR 444.
38 Norowzian v Arks Limited, [2000] F.S.R. 363 (C.A.).
39 University of London Press v University Tutorial Press [1916] 2 Ch 601.
40 Case C-5/08 Infopaq International A/S v Danske Dagblades Forening (Infopaq) paras 33, 38. See also Case C -393/09 Bezpečnostní softwarová asociace para 45 What is not protected is expression which is limited by its technical function. Case C- 406/10 SAS Institute Inc. v World Programming Ltd paras 38–40. Case C-145/10, Painer v Standard VerlagsGmbH et al In the UK see SAS Institute Inc. v World Programming Ltd [2013] EWHC 69 (Ch) para 27.

41 Berne Convention Article 2(1). SAS Institute Inc v World Programming Limited [2013] EWHC 69 (Ch) para 27.
42 Case C-5/08 Infopaq International A/S v Danske Dagblades Forening, Case C-393/09 Bezpečnostní softwarová asociace paragraph 45; Joined Cases C-403/08 and C-429/08 Football Association Premier League and Others; see also Rosati "Originality In a Work"; and Derclaye.
43 Infopaq, para 45; Bezpečnostní softwarová asociace, para 50; Painer, para 89, Football Dataco para 38.
44 Painer, para 92; Football Dataco para 38.
45 Bezpečnostní softwarová asociace, paras 48 and 49; Football Association Premier League and Others, para 98; Football Dataco para 39.
46 Berne Convention Article 2.2 leaves fixation to members of the Union.
47 This is so the extent of the monopoly claimed may be known to others. Tate v Fulbrook 1908 1 KB 821 at 832.
48 Each of which may have separate protection in their own right.
49 Sawkins v Hyperion Records Ltd, [2005] EWCA 565.
50 "The ephemerality of dance means that it is the most difficult of the performing arts to substitute with a hard copy recording" (Whatley "Dance Identity" 89). "Video and film recordings of dance performances, however, do not allow us access to those dance performances. We do not see dance performances when we look at video or film; we see representations of them. The video and film media are not transparent since they do not present us with the first-person spatial information that is essential to vision. With dance this means that important spatial information, and spatial experience (for example, the experience of having the dancers move towards you) . . . is missing?" (Meskin 46).
51 See Sunder "Intellectual Property" 69. Sunder warns that characterizing cultural identity in intellectual property terms would lead to static and homogeneous identity and culture.

References

Arnold, Richard. "Joy: A Reply." *Intellectual Property Quarterly* 1 (2010): 10.
Blake, Janet. "On Defining Cultural Heritage." *International and Comparative Law Quarterly* 49 (2000): 61–85.
Bowrey, Kathy, and Michael Handler. *Law and Creativity in the Age of the Entertainment Franchise* Cambridge: Cambridge University Press, 2014.
Braveman, Ann. "Duet of Discord: Martha Graham and her Non-Profit Ballet over Work for Hire." *Loyola of Los Angeles Entertainment Law Review* 25 (2005): 471.
Brooks, Lynn, and Joellen Meglin. *Preserving Dance Across Time and Space*. Oxford: Routledge, 2013.
Brown, Michael. "Heritage Trouble: Recent Work on the Protection of Intangible Cultural Property." *International Journal of Cultural Property* 12 (2005): 40–61.
Burri, Mira. "The UNESCO Convention on Cultural Diversity: An Appraisal Five Years after its Entry into Force" NCCR Trade Regulation Working Paper No. 2013/1, *International Journal of Cultural Property*. 20 (2014): 357–380, available at http://papers.ssrn.com/sol3/papers.cfm?abstract_id=2223922, accessed September 1, 2015.
Chatzichristodoulou, Maria, Janice Jefferies, and Rachel Zerihan. *Interfaces of Performance*. Farnham: Ashgate, 2009.
Connelly, Sharon. "Authorship, Ownership and Control: Balancing the Economic and Artistic Issues Raised by the Martha Graham Copyright Case." *Fordham Intellectual Property, Media & Entertainment Law Journal* 15 (2006): 837.

Cook, Melanie. "Moving To a New Beat: Copyright Protection for Choreographic Works." *UCLA Law Review* 24 (1977): 1,287.
de Mille, Agnes. *And Promenade Home*. Boston, Toronto: Little, Brown and Company, 1956.
Derclaye, Estelle. "Wonderful or Worrisome? The Impact of the ECJ Ruling in Infopaq on UK Copyright Law." *European Intellectual Property Law Review* 32.5 (2010): 248.
Eechoud, Estelle van. "Along The Road to Uniformity: Diverse Readings of the Court of Justice Judgments on Copyright Work." *Journal of Intellectual Property Information Technology and E-Commerce Law* 3.1 (2012) para 60.
Fisher, William. "Theories of Intellectual Property." *New Essays in the Legal and Political Theory of Property*. Cambridge: Cambridge University Press, 2001.
Handig, Christian. "The 'Sweat of the Brow' is Not Enough!—More Than a Blueprint of the European Copyright Term 'Work'." *European Intellectual Property Law Review* 35.6 (2013): 334.
Handig, Christian. "Infopaq International A/S v Danske Dagblades Forening (C-5/08): Is the Term 'Work' in the CDPA 1988 in Line with the European Directives?" *European Intelllectual Property Law Review* 32.2 (2010): 53.
Jennings, Luke. "Beyonce vs De Keersmaeker: Can You Copyright a Dance Move?" *The Guardian*, October 11, 2011, available at http://www.theguardian.com/stage/theatre blog/2011/oct/11/beyonce-de-keersmaeker-dance-move, accessed Sepember 1, 2015.
Lowenthal, David. *The Heritage Crusade and the Spoils of History*. London: Viking, 1977.
McFee, Graham, ed. *Dance, Education, and Philosophy*. Oxford: Meyer and Meyer, 1999.
Mackrell, Judith. "Beyonce, De Keersmaeker—and a Dance Recreated by Everyone." *The Guardian*, October 9, 2013, available at http://www.theguardian.com/stage/2013/oct/09/beyonce-de-keersmaeker-technology-dance, accessed September 1, 2015.
Macmillan, Fiona. "The Protection of Cultural Heritage." *Northern Ireland Legal Quarterly* 64.3 (2013): 356.
Meskin, Aaron. "Productions, Performances, and Their Evaluations." *Dance, Education, and Philosophy*. Ed. Graham McFee. Oxford: Meyer and Meyer, 1999.
Nesti, Paolo, and Raffaela Santucci, eds. *Information Technology for Performing Arts, Media Access and Entertainment*. April 8–10, 2013, Porto. Berlin, Heidelberg: Springer, 2013.
Pila, Justine. "An Intentional View of the Copyright Work." *Modern Law Review* 71:4 (2008): 535.
Rahmatian, Andreas. "Originality in UK Copyright Law: The Old 'Skill and Labour' Doctrine Under Pressure." *International Review of Intellectual Property and Competition Law* 44.1 (2013): 4–34.
Rivers, Tom. "Norowzian Revisited." *European Intellectual Property Law Review* 389 (2000): 389.
Rosati, Eleonora. "Towards an EU-wide Copyright? (Judicial) Pride and (Legislative) Prejudice." *Intellectual Property Quarterly* 1 (2013): 47–68.
Rosati, Eleonora. "Originality in a Work, or a Work of Originality: The Effects of the Infopaq Decision." *European Intellectual Property Law Review* 33.12 (2011): 746.
Sunder, Madhavi. "IP3." *Stanford Law Review* 59 (2006): 280–82.
Sunder, Madhavi. "Intellectual Property and Identity Politics: Playing with Fire." *Journal of Gender, Race and Justice* 4:1 (2000): 69.
Théberge, Paul. "Technology, Creative Practice and Copyright." *Music and Copyright*. Ed. Simon Frith and Lee Marshall. Edinburgh: Edinburgh University Press, 2004. 21–53.
Traylor, Martha. "Choreography, Pantomime and the Copyright Revision Act of 1976." *New England Law Review* 16 (1981): 227.

Van Eechoud, Mireille. "Along the Road to Uniformity: Diverse Readings of the Court of Justice Judgments on Copyright Work." *Journal of Intellectual Property Information Technology and E-Commerce Law* 3.1 (2012): 60–80.

Waelde, Charlotte, and Schlesinger, Philip. "Music and Dance: Beyond Copyright Text?" *SCRIPTed* 8.3 (2011): 257.

Waelde, Charlotte, Sarah Whatley, and Mathilde Pavis, "Let's Dance! But Who Owns It?" *European Intellectual Property Law Review* 36 (2014): 217–228.

Whatley, Sarah. "Dance Identity, Authenticity and Issues of Interpretation with Specific Reference to the Choreography of Siobhan Davies." *Dance Research: The Journal of the Society for Dance Research* 23.2 (2005): 87–105.

—— "The Challenges of the *Inter* in the Preservation of Cultural Heritage; The Intangibility of the Material and Immaterial Dancing Body in Performance." *Information Technology for Performing Arts, Media Access and Entertainment*. April 8–10, 2013, Porto. Ed. Paolo Nesti and Raffaella Santucci. Berlin-Heidelberg: Springer, 2013. 218–226.

Williams, Raymond. *Culture*. Fontana: Glasgow, 1982.

Yeoh, Francis. "The Copyright Implications of Beyoncé's 'borrowings'." *Choreographic Practices* 4.1 (2013): 95.

Yeoh, Francis. "Choreographers' Moral Right of Integrity." *Journal of Intellectual Property and Practice* 8.1 (2013): 43–58.

Yeoh, Francis. "Choreographer's Copyright Dilemma." *Entertainment Law Review* 7 (2012): 201.

Yeoh, Francis. "The Choreographic Trust: Preserving Dance Legacies." *Dance Chronicle*, 35.2 (2012): 224.

International instruments

Berne Convention for the Protection of Literary and Artistic Works 1886.

Convention on the Means of Prohibiting and Preventing the Illicit Import, Export and Transfer of World Cultural Property November 14, 1970.

Convention Concerning the Protection of the World Cultural and Natural Heritage November 17, 1972.

Convention for the Protection of Cultural Property in the Event of Armed Conflict 1954.

Convention on the Means of Prohibiting and Preventing the Illicit Import, Export and Transfer of Ownership of Cultural Property 1970.

Convention on the Protection of the Underwater Cultural Heritage 2001.

Convention on the Protection and Promotion of the Diversity of Cultural Expressions 2005.

Report on the Expert Meeting on Routes as a Part of Our Cultural Heritage (Madrid, Spain, November 1994) WHC-94/CONF.003/INF.1

Trade Related Agreement on Intellectual Property Rights 1994.

UNESCO Convention for the Safeguarding of Intangible Cultural Heritage 2003.

Case list

C-393/09 Bezpečnostní softwarová asociace.

C-403/08 and C-429/08 Football Association Premier League and Others.

Case C-5/08 Infopaq International A/S v Danske Dagblades Forening (Infopaq).

Case C-145/10, Painer v Standard VerlagsGmbH et al.

Case C- 406/10 SAS Institute Inc. v World Programming Ltd.

Creation Records v News Group [1997] EMLR 444.

Holland v Vivian Van Damn Productions Ltd., [1936–45] MacG. Cop. Cas. 69 (Ch. D.).

Martha Graham School and Dance Foundation Inc. v Martha Graham Center of Contemporary Dance, Inc., 43 Fed. Appx. 408 (2nd Cir. 2002).

Martha Graham School and Dance Foundation Inc. v Martha Graham Center of Contemporary Dance, Inc., 374 F.Supp.2d 355, 363 (S.D.N.Y. 2005).

Martha Graham School and Dance Foundation Inc. v Martha Graham Center of Contemporary Dance, Inc., 466 F.3d 97 (2006).

Massine v De Basil, (1937), 81 Sol. Jo. 670 (Ch. D.); aff'd (1938), 82 Sol. Jo. 173 (C.A.).

Norowzian v Arks Limited, [2000] F.S.R. 363 (C.A.).

SAS Institute Inc. v World Programming Ltd [2013] EWHC 69 (Ch).

Sawkins v Hyperion Records Ltd [2005] EWCA 565.

Tate v Fulbrook 1908 1 KB 821.

University of London Press v University Tutorial Press [1916] 2 Ch 601.

17
BETWEEN GRAMMATIZATION AND LIVE MOVEMENT SAMPLING

Sally Jane Norman

Documentary and archival traces of dance, encountered in media spanning several millennia, form an abundant, ambivalent set of records. Meanings derived from such traces are remediated by multiple, possibly contradictory cultural forces due to the often unpredictable resurgence of layers of history, and to the specific slant of our own readings. These are further confounded by the ways digital technologies record and restore compelling projections of live phenomena: computational models whose nested scales, patterns, and textures of events characterize complex dynamic systems (the dancing body being one such system) yield holistic, evolving visions that can belie their discrete digital underpinnings. Yet however sophisticated their outputs, our means of engaging with digital recording and archiving technologies are marked by prior cultural traffic with indices and symbols, souvenirs and mementos, and other such echoes of movements. Past practices elucidate our approaches to traces as witnesses of passed time, revealing the diverse epistemic sediments on which they are founded, and to which they appeal. These revelations in turn shed light on the idiosyncratic, contingent nature of our own quests.

Four-thousand-year-old Egyptian tombstone reliefs feature sequential inscriptions testifying to choreographic practices that honour the deceased through the rejoicings of the living. Depictions of Hathoric rites from the Sixth Dynasty tomb of Mereruka show dancers holding a mirror in one hand and a wand topped with a sculpted hand in the other: use of the mirrors supposedly to capture reflections of the dancers' hands or of their wands suggests a giddy choreography of physical and virtual images, with whirling movements accentuated by weights tied to the ends of the dancers' long hair. Ostensibly sparse etchings offer environmental and lifestyle clues: depictions of dancers executing steps that evoke the movements of the crane have been interpreted as auspiciously linking this migrant bird's Nile fishing halt to the grape harvest. Black- and red-figure paintings on Athenian ceramics (600–400 BC) provide information on human movements and gestures per se, and intriguing insights into how we might be physically moved to read them: intricate scenes or serial images on amphoras or circular dishes, which must be rotated in order to be fully perused, demand (and reward) their beholder's gestural engagement in keeping with notions of embodied interaction that seem remarkably contemporary.

Dance records like these are pictorial constructs created by human hand for specific cultural contexts. By virtue of their chiropoietic status (*cheiro*: hand, *poieo*: to make), such traces belong to the broader domain of writing practices. Their modes of transmission are analogous to and part of the wider history of dissemination of written (chirographic), printed (typographic), then digital documents. This opens up comparison between the status of dance records with respect to live motion, and that of writing with respect to spoken language. Questions as to how "live" speech and "dead" writing have been addressed by analog then computer recording and archiving technologies have spawned original scholarship and concepts, including reflection on technological "grammatization" (Auroux[1]) and digital "discretisation" (Stiegler[2]). In keeping with the spirit of Renaissance, Enlightenment, and later positivist traditions, systematic and analytical rather than more synthetic, systemic approaches to movement have tended to dominate the history of dance since its sketchy beginnings as a theoretically transmissible art form. Its positioning as a legitimate domain of study has inevitably brought dance in line with prevailing scientific methods and discourse.

Digital tools that today record and transmit human movement in keeping with principles of direct capture and sampling, instead of indirect inscriptional and notational conventions, seem to offer a more flexible and fitting modus operandi than the drawn-and-quartered analyses of earlier computational systems. Rotman's reflection on the corporeally grounded nature of our most rarefied concepts and practices, and his differentiation between the notation and capture of movement, inspire new ways of apprehending and transmitting human motion.[3] The following thematic sections attempt to trace a range of approaches to the recording, capturing, and archiving of dance, in order to set contemporary developments in a wider historical and conceptual context.

Records and readership

To make a truistic if often overlooked observation, the establishment of records concerning dance in European history has been subject to broader ideological factors that have shaped dance history in general, including waves of bans and dispensations, licenses, and exemptions: Gregory I had to give missionaries permission to allow neophytes to dance in early German churches, and Odon of Cluny had to authorize ill-tolerated rounds—Greek-inherited *choreas*—to farewell departing Crusaders. Community forms like the chorea and chain dance were transformed in late Mediaeval and early Renaissance aristocratic halls into *danses à figures*, where actions of undifferentiated throngs gave way to increasingly virtuoso displays by couples and individuals (including *basses-danses, pavanes, galliards*). Discourse on and codification of choreographic practices accompanied the enthusiasm of wealthy social groupings for new kinds of documented learning. Such discourse may have been precipitated by the need to secure enjoyment of cultural privileges, while marking a safe distance from popular energies that regularly welled up in reaction to prohibitions and repression.

Consequently, and as often remains the case, documents designed for the transmission of dance revolved tightly around predefined audiences, that is, the comfortably resourced commissioners and practitioners of noble and learned traditions. Rudimentary notation systems feature in treatises including Antonio Cornazzano's *Il libro dell'arte del danzar* (1455), which describes the qualities one must develop for dancing (Memory, Measure, Manner, Spirit, Variety, and Use of Space). Renaissance dance and emerging court ballet were influenced by well sponsored Italians: Quattrocento authors Cornazzano, Dominico da Piazenca, and Guglielmo Ebreo de Pesaro paved the way for work by Fabritio Caroso (published in Venice in 1581, Caroso's *Il Ballarino* combines text, tablatures, and illustrations of attitudes), and Cesare Negri (*Nuove Inventioni di Balli*, published in Milan in 1604). Catherine de Medicis's engagement in 1571 of the acrobat Archange Tuccaro as dancing master for the French princes sparked his collaboration with Baldassarino di Belgiojoso (known as Balthazar de Beaujoyeux) on the production of spectacular court ballets. Tuccaro's *Trois dialogues de l'exercice de sauter, et voltiger en l'air. Avec les figures qui servent à la parfaite démonstration & intelligence dudict art* (1599), a pioneering gymnastics manual which frequently refers to dance, features woodcut illustrations showing physical and mental preparation for virile *tours de force*.

Except for a few texts exempt of music notation (Ebreo, Tuccaro, de Lauze's *Apologie de la danse et la parfaicte methode de l'enseigner tant aux Cavaliers qu'aux Dames* (1623)), early dance publications tend to be related to or represented by compilations of music bearing the same names as the choreographic forms they accompanied. Value of the score as a system allowing the symbolic representation and regulation of time continues to mark notation methods to this day. Early musical scores posed a challenge for authors of both manuscript and print forms because of the number and intricacy of symbols to be reproduced. The process launched by Venetian Ottaviano Petrucci in the early sixteenth century required three successive pressings to produce staff lines, words, then notes. Subsequent single-impression methods long vied for quality with woodcut and engraving systems (Breitkopf, the oldest European music publisher founded in Leipzig in 1719, prepared manuscripts manually for over a century). Works referencing dance with visual symbols were still more complex to publish because they needed additional lines and signs for choreographic parameters. Notwithstanding such constraints, archiving of music and dance treatises amongst theological and scientific compendia made these areas of scholarship integral to a flourishing body of knowledge: writing and annotation practices enabled the recording, thence validation, of carefully reproduced observations on which all kinds of scientific axioms could be built.[4]

Alongside the Biblioteca Apostolica Vaticana, created in 1475, European universities and patrician houses commissioned and collected books (sometimes censoriously destroying them, as in Reformist Protestant England), and set up or granted titles to professional printing presses. Printed works proliferated with the invention of typography: archives, readership, and prestige were boosted by publishers' obligations to deposit copies in royal and academic libraries. While books were generally dedicated to and sponsored by monarchs and aristocrats, documents on dance began to permeate and reflect specific professional groups, as evidenced by the six "Old Measures" which form the *London Inns of Court Manuscripts* (*c*1570), describing dances that English gentlemen of the robe were expected to master. Early European dance theory bore the blazons of sovereigns, patrician and wealthy patrons, and powerful professional corporations. Its history nonetheless remained strongly subject to individual and topical factors, and might have taken a very different turn if, for example, the Medicis family had not appreciated the exploits of a Tuccaro, or if Louis XIV had been as keen on *sauts périlleux* as he was on *entrechats*.

Interest in dance as a field of knowledge transmissible through scholarly media as well as through physical apprenticeship prompted Louis XIV's creation of the Royal Academy of Dance in 1661 under the direction of Pierre Beauchamp, who codified the five foot positions and *ports de bras* of classical ballet. Beauchamp also oversaw Raoul-Auger Feuillet's *Chorégraphie, ou l'art de décrire la danse par caractères, figures et signes démonstratifs* (1700), which remained the key notation system throughout Europe for 150 years (each line of music printed at the top of a page indicates timing, with symbols below showing the steps and patterns that form a choreographic phrase). An expanding range of dance practices drew learned attention: John Playford's *The English Dancing Master: OR, Plaine and easie Rules for the Dancing of Country Dances, with the Tune to each Dance* (London, 1651), where musical scores and simple symbols bore witness to popular British traditions, perhaps inspired Academician André Lorin's *Livre de Contredance présenté au Roy* presented to Louis XIV in 1697, which described country dances observed at the English court. Whereas early dance treatises exalted noble forms, later enthusiasts were apparently eager to reinvigorate their art with previously disdained techniques from vernacular repertories, in keeping with an age-old, sometimes cyclical movement between "low" and "high" culture.

Gestural tablatures and pitfalls

Orchésographie ou Traicté en forme de dialogue par lequel toutes personnes peuvent facilement apprendre & practiquer l'honneste exercice des dances (1589) was published by French cleric Jehan Tabourot, known by the anagram Thoinot Arbeau. The dialogue explains a series of tablatures featuring a vertical stave on the left, showing pitch and duration of the musical notes, and a list of dance steps on the right. This layout facilitates conjoined reading of melodic and corporeal movements associated with various dance forms (e.g., *basse-dance, pavane, gaillarde, volte, branle*). Arbeau's attempts to apprehend movement by means of segmented representation announce methods that persist across later sequential techniques like chronophotography and keyframe animation. *Orchésographie* also presents the same mechanistic drawbacks that beset these later techniques, insofar as such analyses can accommodate neither intuitive, comprehensive movement qualities nor irreducible microgestures, and require the strict simplification if not suppression of determinant contextual factors.[5]

Reliance on notation systems like Arbeau's risks limiting our ability to recognize movement, leading us to overlook that which cannot be grasped by analysis and to perceive only that which is legible from an abstract theoretical perspective: "because our system seems to account for all movement, we end up thinking that all movement derives from our system, mistaking the word for the thing it denotes. This unconscious imperialism of discursive thinking expresses itself through language, at the cost of muscular intelligence" (Guilcher 27). Forgoing muscular intelligence to follow the succinct instructions of a treatise is moreover likely to produce uninspiringly deadly performance. But *Orchésographie* nonetheless marks a major step in dance history towards grammatization (http://arsindustrialis.org/grammatisation), defined by Stiegler as "the transformation of a temporal continuum into a discrete spatial unit: it is a process of description, formalisation, and discretisation of human behaviours (calculations, languages and gestures), that allows their reproducibility; it is an abstraction of forms by the exteriorisation of flows in 'tertiary retentions' that are exported into our machines and apparatus" (no page).[6]

A key question here is the meaning of "reproducibility": to what extent can tablatures, hieroglyphs, or any media devoid of explicit reference to *ergon*, to physical work, be said to "reproduce" gestures or languages, rather than simply models thereof? How, if at all, might grammatization account for what Gil describes as the body's tenuous unity as translator of codes and anchor of floating signifiers, as an infralinguistic nexus for information that is necessarily and profusely polysemic? (Gil 107–152). The development of gesturology aligns with the goals of grammatization, making "gestemes" or gestural units comparable to "phonemes," and proposing division of the dynamic continuum into discrete, objective, measurable units, then apprehension of syntagmatic units formed by combinations of these elementary units. Gil counters claims by authors such as semiotician Paul Bouissac that any dynamic sequence can be studied as an ordered series of volumes, independently of the body which has described them. Difficulties merely isolating gestural units, with their inevitably overlapping segments and multiple levels of imbrication (phalanges, fingers, forearms, etc.), and their constantly divisible microgestures, limit the applicability of approaches like Bouissac's to consensually predefined and precodified domains where artificial divisions are readily recognized. As Gil points out, "one cannot, in the case of the signs of the body, separate the signifier from the signified except, precisely, at the price of gathering up and ordering these signs in a determined language, a corporeal language like that of dance or mime" (112).

Because a "determined language" allowing discretization of movements is necessarily prescriptive, we are stuck with the wider issue of how unambiguously context-independent yet meaningful the descriptors of reproducible corporeal movement can be made. In Kirsh's terms, "What information is encoded explicitly? Is any ? Must explicit encodings be non-ambiguous ?" (341). Like flat-footed performances that strictly obey tablatures, readings of historic inscriptions and transcriptions are subject to contextual drift and loss of cues obvious to their original publics. Although we spontaneously flesh out these lossy, time-compressed legacies, contemporary interpolations may significantly alter their initial interpretive scaffolds and domains of use. On the other hand, attempts at restoring potentially limitless contexts to enhance legibility and accessibility of information are as labor-intensive as they are ultimately futile. The imperative to weigh up hermeneutic freedom against clearly articulated anchorage points is an old one that has resurged vigorously with the advent of search-and-query languages and web-based ontologies. What we once assumed to be readily separable explicit versus implicit types of information in fact form knotty areas where contexts represented by metadata, annotations, and mark-up languages are ever more entangled with the contents they are destined to carry and serve.[7]

From one-off and serial images to live motion capture

Dance notation systems that tend towards grammatization, describing and transcribing motion by means of sequential and syntagmatic approaches, weave a parallel historical option to that adopted by single, unitary images, like the floor plans underpinning the intricate rose design in Caroso's *Nobiltà di Dame* (Venice, 1600). Diagrams where cumulative movement traces are made to converge in a unique image (or dense, consecutive images, combining serial and non-serial representational modes) arise from sometimes obvious contexts and constraints: for example, upper gallery viewing of court ballet justified elaborate choreographies which spelled out royal crests or monograms (e.g., Beaujoyeux's *Ballet comique de la Reine*, Paris, 1581); complex floor plans were required by Luigi Manzotti's spectacles to specify movements of massive cohorts of dancers (e.g., *Amor*, Milan, 1880). Oskar Schlemmer's color-coded *Triadische Ballett* drawings (1936 reconstitution), and Merce Cunningham's pencilled *Space Patterns from Summerspace* (1958) are hybrids that mix sketched floor trajectories with numerical and alphabetical signs. Notation history seems to be punctuated by vacillations between or combinations of sequentially deployed inscriptions requiring bookish literacy, and condensed, unitary images demanding expert visual decryption.

The eighteenth-century atlas and encyclopedia drew together textual and graphic expertise to promote masterfully classified, newly democratized visions of science,[8] where artist-illustrators supplied "true-to-nature" observations of the "pure phenomenon" (Goethe): "To depict it, the human mind must fix the empirically variable, exclude the accidental, eliminate the impure, unravel the tangled, discover the unknown" (quoted in Daston and Galison 59). The move towards selectively and scrupulously "true-to-nature" representation is illustrated by Kellom Tomlinson's *The Art of Dancing* (1735), which associates Feuillet's notation with fine engravings of performers: successive plates of a minuet wed choreographic floor patterns to elegantly clad dancers whose suggested, gently sweeping moves are ruled by an overarching line of music.

Salon and popular science visualizations of living bodies were at this same period revealing hitherto unknown yet real, coherent movements by means of spectacular changes in scale. The solar microscope, a modified magic lantern, projected magnified agitations of live specimens deposited on its lens. This early motion capture system presented dramatically amplified screenings of bugs or blood circulating in a frog mesentery or tadpole's tail, as documented by experimental scientist Abbé Nollet (trapped in burning light, the frantic writhing of these tiny creatures added to their sensational impact as projected monsters). While such real-time capture has as much in common with a zoo as with motion transmission systems, the solar microscope (or its lucernal successor, connected to an oil lamp for more flexible use) significantly made more widely shareable spectacles that were previously limited to scientific laboratory and salon audiences. Ways of witnessing live motion imputable to otherwise imperceptible agents brought fresh insights to the apprehension and analysis of human movement.

Ergometric instruments starting with Edmé Régnier's dynamometer (1798) were explicitly geared towards recording human exertion (Windgätter[9]). These were typical inventions for a dawning century that championed mechanical objectivity, that is, "the insistent drive to repress the wilful intervention of the artist-author (champion of 'truth-to-nature') putting in its stead procedures that would, as it were, move nature to the page through a strict protocol, if not automatically" (Daston and Galison 121). Régnier's apparatus, which provides comparative readings of pressure exerted by organisms or machines, led to Karl Ludwig's wave recorder or kymograph (1847), whose mercury manometer and revolving drum graphically record variations in vital signs, then to Helmholtz's myograph (1876), which uses a similar self-registering technique. Angelo Musso's ergograph (1884) also affords direct inscription of effort: a positioning apparatus with arm support and tubes to keep the index and ring finger straight is connected to a recording device with a pin and goose quill, moved via a tension wire with leather band, weight, and pulley. By connecting the ergograph to a flame-blackened kymograph one can compare successive recordings and identify fatigue (the char layer of a completed recording is fixed with shellac). The ergograph thus becomes a chronograph, temporal input being diagrammatically homogenized and standardized by a coordinate system.[10]

Devices for recording human movement in terms of mechanical effort, rather than visual or kinematic parameters, offer a means of "asymbolic mediation," that is, a sampling or capture, in contrast to the symbolic representational means offered by alphanumerical systems (Rotman 426). This opens up new ways of thinking about the signifying relations whereby notations can be categorized as icons, indices, or symbols, as in Peircean semiosis. Though the trace of the flame-blackened kymograph is an indicial sign-vehicle in semiotic terms (i.e., it attests to direct physical action), its technically mediated form as geometric spikes precludes homologous, readily legible links to authorial gesture, giving it, rather, status akin to the iconic or symbolic. Messy polyvalence of data testifying to corporeal energies pertains to what Peirce calls the interpretant, that is, the grounds upon which the sign is seen to be related to something else as signified. It pertains to our understanding of the sign/object relation, and this understanding is subject to cultures of literacy, to notions of what possibly constitute and can be read as traces of embodied movement. But in keeping with an endlessly recursive process, our ability to read and decipher is inextricably bound up with the instruments and prostheses we develop to convey and render information: "In other words, science is not merely a question of the interpretation of a preexisting reality, in terms, for example, of mechanism or of vitalism, of forces or of isolatable particulars. Rather, 'reality' is actually created in and reflected by the chosen approach" (Miller 48). Systems for the notation and transmission of dance integrate complex variables: "in any culture, what counts as a natural object and its spatial relations, rather than being an invariant characteristic of the world, may instead form part of that culture's world view, episteme, cognitive schema, ontology, call it what you will" (Turnbull, 2).

Mapping motions back in place[11]

We experience corporeal motion physiologically and physically in space and time, yet our systems to record and review it remain largely predicated on abstract, clean room type environments. Distortions caused by culling and simplifying experimental data for analysis are consequently aggravated by wrenching movement information from the phenomenological context that usually makes it meaningful. Dance notation systems produced in manuscripts or printed publications like those mentioned earlier make scant reference to physical surroundings—though perhaps their original readers were edified by lines hinting at the ground plan for Tuccaro's acrobatics or Tomlinson's gavottes. Discretization of the dancing body, amputated from its environment, is part of a wider cognitive shift brought about by inscriptive practices, which heralded what Ong describes as a new noetic world with its own modalities of spatial organization, "making the book less like an utterance, and more like a thing" (123). In this noetic world where knowledge could be reified in durably transmissible form, and detached from the reality of the flesh, print encouraged "the mind to sense that its possessions were held in some sort of inert mental space" (Ong 129).

Separation of living organisms from their surroundings evokes the positivism of laboratory type control, long believed to guarantee accurate and robustly true-to-life experimental findings. Artefacts designed to frame live human action (apart from the laboratory) include theatres, arenas, circuses, zoos, broadcast, and networked spaces whose purportedly neutral settings are eclipsed by the performers on whom attention is all the more readily focused. Whether it is embodied by athletes sprinting round the stadium,[12] trapezists traversing the big top, or ballerinas pirouetting across the stage, physical virtuosity may be more easily recognized and esteemed if staged in conventionally formatted sites. Like the living pine at Kasuga Shrine replaced by the painted pine of Noh theatre, many of our cultural spaces have gradually become derealized and codified together with the human movement they contain. The race to master time, space, and mass has worn down the hedges and rocks that once dramatized sports events, eroding environments considered as more-or-less natural reality in favour of artificial conditions that facilitate comparisons of prowess. Normalized synthetics and alloys (surfacing materials, sports equipment and gear) supposedly put performers on an equal footing[13]; atmospheric standardization was broached at the 1968 Olympics (souvenir tins of Mexican air were labeled "Especial para batir récords").[14] As part of our increasingly globalized cultural apprehension of human motion, rarefaction of the spaces in which we collectively encounter it has tended to favor formal, measured, and ultimately somewhat static modes of transmission. How, then, can we maintain frameworks to enhance the appreciation of movement, without stultifying it in over-standardized containment vessels?

Perhaps the answer lies partly in the technologies with which we are today multiplying and diversifying our "motion spaces": locative media and distributed networks literally bring home the diverse and singular dynamics of all kinds of places, from the familiar to the unlikely, invested by moving if not dancing humans (Norman "Locative Media"). Networked, mobile-device borne and digitally extended environments, symptomatic of an "epoch of juxtaposition . . . of the near and far, of the side-by-side, of the dispersed," are Foucauldian heterotopias "capable of juxtaposing in a single real space several spaces, several sites that are themselves incompatible" (cf. Foucault). Creative experiments with digitally augmented realities and locative media have engaged real and virtual agents in heterotopic spaces for many years, inspiring original approaches to movement notation and archiving practices.

Location sensing in Teri Rueb's *Choreography of Everyday Movement* (2001) used GPS traces of dancers moving through a city to print real-time outputs on acetate sheets. These were sandwiched between stacked glass plates in an installation that grew taller as journeys were added to the recordings. Rueb's work relates to diverse notation systems with its combined qualities of serial and uniquely, cumulatively instantiated movement. *Choreography*'s archiving and mapping cannot be construed as passive recording activity, but form an active, emergent, inherently creative process: "Mapping builds the site in a very special way . . . [it] literally constructs and *produces it* incrementally by the iterative conjugation of diverse registers and layers interleaved and relieved within the map: compounding them, aligning them so they begin to cohere, conjugating them to form patterns of interlacing and association" (Tawa 119). In *Choreography*, individual dance trajectories are fused and sublimated by a transparent, potentially monumental contour map that reflects and is replete with their collated, latent energies.

The *Motion in Place Platform* (MiPP) research consortium led by Woolford in close collaboration with archaeologist Stuart Dunn proposed a radical alternative to the locationally abstracted motion capture generally undertaken in laboratories or studios. Combining artistic experience (in still and moving images, interactive and immersive installations, and motion capture) and expertise in programming and interface development, Woolford sought to establish a platform usable in outdoor settings that are not amenable to high levels of technical control, making captured motion subject to and revelatory of "real" environmental influences.[15] An inertial Animazoo motion capture suit, consisting of networked gyroscopes, magnetometers, and accelerometers, provides a fairly unencumbered, portable means for obtaining individual gestural data from a freely moving wearer; this data is then mapped to a virtual skeleton using Animazoo software. MiPP sought to connect the resultant un- or dislocated moving figures to their environment, testing ultrasonic, GPS, and video systems with varying success. Studies of human movement (of field workers, dancers) commenced at the Roman archaeological site in Silchester, which offered a spectacularly spatially and temporally loaded starting point for the research.[16] Subsequent experiments were designed to explore the impact of the environment on movement by comparing the same activities in virtual and physical locations: task-bound motion sequences were successively executed in controlled studio conditions, and in a reconstructed Iron Age roundhouse at Butser Ancient Farm in Hampshire. Interpretations of domestic Iron Age chores (e.g., querning grain, sweeping, fetching water, making bread) showed thick description to yield vastly more useful information for archaeologists and movement specialists alike. For example, sweeping activities were executed very differently in a clean room type studio and a dusty round-house setting, revealing as much about affordances of the artefacts, as about their actual impact on human motion (Dunn, Woolford et al.). Intriguingly, whereas much motion capture activity exploits the possibility to detach movement from its ostensible carrier and its surroundings, de- and re-territorializing its derivative kinetic patterns to animate all manner of forms (Rotman 430), MiPP is focused on the relocation and siting of live movement through the parallel capture of environmental data.

Movement databases and eido-kinetic intuitions

Carter calls "eido-kinetic" the inherent sense "mobile subjects have of their relationship with their surroundings. . . . It is the capacity to intuit directly the nearness of things and to have the measure of them. It seems to stem from our capacity to see the components of our world under the aegis of movement" (268). This intuition tends to be suppressed by conventional modes of knowledge: "Even those who believe that rational thought advances step by step cannot deny that thinking begins in an orientation to one's human surroundings. But nothing of this provenance survives in what is counted as knowledge. We think as we draw, creating self-enclosed figures, cut off from one another and from the history of their coming into being" (Carter 5). We thus ignore "dark writing," whose meaning "resides in the footstep, the leap and the instant between two strides. It is the dappled history of those marks; its blotches are the signature of time, its litter the resistance of slovenly nature to every attempt to clean it up" (Carter 1).

This contrasts with what might be called "light writing," based on discretization and grammatization, which tames—or stifles—"slovenly nature," instead of embracing it as richly, inextricably polysemic.

Yet blotches of dark writing, those stains of uncontainable vibrancy, have prompted massive developments in computational and notational systems as part of the drive to bridge ever yawning gaps between abstract models and their living subjects. Aspirations to integrate multiple, complexly interacting agencies and emergent processes, and to achieve modeling means that can traverse diverse spatial and temporal scales, underlie ontologies, markup languages, and data hierarchization principles. The growing importance of annotation and metadata—that is, notes, commentaries, or other such resources previously considered secondary or superfluous to core data—translates heightened recognition of contexts as an essential if not determinant part of usefully transmissible information (as per the explicit/implicit tangle mentioned earlier). Where contextually embedded approaches show computational systems to bear ultimately embodied forms of knowledge and understanding (Rotman), discretization and grammatization can perhaps be lured onto the shady terrain of dark writing, opening up novel expressive and cognitive possibilities.

Capture media, operating under the regimes of metonymy and synechdoche to produce direct, iterable traces of actual occurrences in space and time, offer alternatives to notational media regulated by metaphor and similitude and described in terms of figures of speech (Rotman 427–428). The temporally pregnant "kinematic writing" of motion capture goes beyond frozen residues of movement produced, for example, by Musso's ergo-kymograph, or by arts including painting, carving, calligraphy, pottery, weaving. And unlike solar microscopy or live performance, mediation implemented by motion capture techniques puts us at one remove from the visceral liveness they portray and convey. Additionally, the not-quite-raw digital material they use makes their products infinitely de- and recomposable, taking on configurations and patterns that may substantially diverge from those borne by their prime movers. Consequently, these achiropoietic creations need not be obediently isomorphic traces of their makers, like Veronica's Veil, but can haunt us with uncanny autonomy. When programmed to move or hover between states of mirroring and independence, capture-generated forms can impart compelling dramaturgic energies.[17] Digitally sampled legacies of dancers or other moving beings constitute malleable datasets which are open to re-scaling, re-shaping, fragmentation, sampling, and mashups—in short, to all manner of miraculous transsubstantiations.

"Gesturo-haptics" and "eido-kinetics" announce means of transmission that bring together opposing conceptions of human movement, considered indivisible and elusive on the one hand, and infinitely divisible and manipulable on the other. Fixed qualities of a *skhema*, a form realized and viewed as an object, might thus be folded into the flow of *rhythmos*, a form assumed by what is moving, mobile, and fluid.[18] Perhaps this synthesis is in fact an ideal. If so, perhaps precisely such an ideal is needed to fire our quest for ontologies that can lodge discretized motion in databases, without lessening our sense of enthrallment before the unfathomable dancing body.

September 2012

Notes

1 In his analysis of the advent of dictionaries, grammars, and comparative linguistics, Auroux considers grammar as a cognitive tool that modifies our modes of communication, rather than as a mere describer of natural language, in arguments extending to the mechanized and automated language processing required by computational expert systems.
2 Drawing on Leroi-Gourhan's account of the influence of cognitive and pragmatic tools in shaping human behavior, Stiegler defines discretization as the constitution and organization of literal, analog, and digital units of information, which have distinctive social and epistemic effects as technical mnemonic supports. He specifically addresses the impact of discretized, industrially automated gesture in *For a New Critique of Political Economy*.
3 Rotman defines gesturo-haptic writing as digitally sampled or captured human movement that goes beyond existing written and spoken language systems, giving gestures conceptual and pragmatic mobility similar to that which writing gave to speech.
4 "One consequence of the new exactly repeatable visual statement was modern science.... What is distinctive of modern science is the conjuncture of exact observation and exact verbalization: exactly worded descriptions of carefully observed complex objects and processes" (Ong 123).
5 "... each step away from total movability—total context independence—is a step which increases the complexity of the processes which recognize a symbol and its meaning. At some point these recognition costs become too high and a language becomes unable to encode information explicitly" (Kirsh 356). Questions of discretization of early notation and computational movement representation systems are addressed in Norman, "Generic versus Idiosyncratic Expression in Live Performance Using Digital Tools."
6 Tertiary retention designates "objects as supports of memory and mnemo-techniques, which enable traces to be spatially, materially and technically recorded" (Stiegler, "Desire and Knowledge: The Dead Seize the Living" n.p.).
7 "Because implicit is defined largely negatively as information that is present but not explicitly encoded, any inquiry into implicit information must presuppose a theory of explicit information" (Kirsh 349).
8 Diderot and D'Alembert's *Système figuré des Connaissances humaines* omits dance from its genealogical tree (inspired by English philosopher Francis Bacon's classification of the sciences). Their *Encyclopedia* nonetheless acknowledges dance, notably with the inclusion of texts by Jean-Jacques Rousseau.
9 Cf. Windgätter for a documented and illustrated account of the dynamometer and related historical apparatus described hereafter.
10 The AMUC prototype sets related methods in the current context. Spatial and temporal parameters gleaned from input to a graphics tablet are used to create a text-free database query mechanism: a string-matching algorithm retrieves image sequences from a motion capture base by comparing sketch coordinates with stored data. For all its crudeness, implementation of this sketch-based retrieval system obliged a highly interdisciplinary team to address key questions about descriptors of motion. Cf. Norman et al., "AMUC: Associated Motion capture User Communities."
11 This title draws on Kirk Woolford's *Motion in Place Platform* (2010–2011), dedicated to spatially located and enriched motion capture experiments. Cf. http://www.motioninplace.org.
12 Stadion is a measure of length. For discussion of the imbrications of standardized sites and optimized performance of "the impossible body" (sports, circus, dance), cf. Norman, "Le Spectacle vivant, arène de modélisation du corps."
13 Growing control of athlete equality including at the pharmacokinetic level makes it hard to imagine how marathonian Thomas Hicks, winner of the 1904 St. Louis Olympic Games, boosted his performance with a cocktail of strychnine sulfate and cognac.
14 Temperature, hygrometry, and oxygen controlled chambers are used regularly for physical training, and motion scenarios tested under water and in microgravity are mapped to Martian conditions in preparation for future manned missions.

15 Woolford and Dunn point out that much emerging technologies experimentation purportedly carried out "in the wild" in fact boils down to expedient injections of heavily controlled laboratory research into more or less exotic settings.
16 Archaeological approaches to archives and embodied knowledge have substantially contributed to performing arts research: see referenced works by Michael Shanks and Mike Pearson; and Gabriella Giannachi, Nick Kaye, Michael Shanks, eds.
17 Mappings between performers and their motion capture avatars were dramatically modulated at the 1998 *Real Gestures, Virtual Environments* workshop led by the author at the International Institute of Puppetry (Charleville-Mézières) and Zentrum für Kunst und Medientechnologie (Karlsruhe). Cf. referenced paper by Hirsh et al.
18 *Skhema* is "a fixed 'form,' realized and viewed in the same way as an object. On the other hand, *rhythmos* ... designates the form in the instant that it is assumed by what is moving, mobile and fluid, the form of that which does not have organic consistency; it fits the pattern of a fluid element, of a letter arbitrarily shaped, of a robe which one arranges at one's will, of a particular state of character or mood. It is the form as improvised, momentary, changeable" (Benveniste 285–286).

References

Auroux, Sylvain. *La Révolution technologique de la grammatisation*. Liège: Pierre Mardaga, 1994.
Benveniste, Etienne. *Problems in General Linguistics*. Trans. Mary Elizabeth Meek (original French publication 1966). Florida: University of Miami Press, 1971.
Carter, Paul. *Dark Writing: Geography, Performance, Design*. Honolulu: University of Hawai'i Press, 2009.
Daston, Lorraine, and Peter Galison. *Objectivity*. New York: Zone Books, 2007.
Dunn, Stuart, Mark Hedges, Kirk Woolford, Leon Barker, Sally-Jane Norman, Milo Taylar, Martin White, Michael Fulford, Amanda Clarke, and Helen Bailey "Motion in Place: a Case Study of Archaeological Reconstruction Using Motion Capture". *Revive the Past: Proceedings of the 39th Conference in Computer Applications and Quantitative Methods in Archaeology*, ed. Philip Verhagen. Amsterdam: Amsterdam University Press, 2012, 98–106.
Foucault, Michel. *Of Other Spaces, Heterotopias*. Trans. Jay Miskowiec (original French publication 1967), available at http://foucault.info/documents/heteroTopia/foucault.heteroTopia.en.html, accessed July 22, 2015.
Giannachi, Gabriella, Nick Kaye, and Michael Shanks, eds. *Archaeologies of Presence*. London: Routledge, 2012.
Gil, José. *Metamorphoses of the Body*. Trans. Stephen Muecke (original French publication 1985). Minneapolis: University of Minnesota Press, 1998.
Guilcher, Yves. "L'orchésographie." *La Recherche en Danse* 3.27 (1984): 25–28.
Hirsch, Sabine, Michael Koch, Berndt Lintermann and Sally Jane Norman. *Production Tools for Electronic Arenas* (1999), available at http://www.nada.kth.se/erena/doc/aD4_3-D4_4.html, accessed July 22, 2015.
Kirsh, David. "When is Information Explicitly Represented?" *Information, Language and Cognition*. Ed. Philip Hanson. Vancouver: University of British Columbia Press, 1990. 340–365.
Miller, Elaine P. *The Vegetative Soul: From Philosophy of Nature to Subjectivity in the Feminine*. Albany: State University of New York Press, 2002.
Norman, Sally Jane. "Generic versus Idiosyncratic Expression in Live Performance Using Digital Tools." *Performance Research: A Journal of the Performing Arts* 11.4 (2006), 23–29.
Norman, Sally Jane. "Locative Media and Instantiations of Theatrical Boundaries." *Leonardo Electronic Almanac* 14.3 (2006), available at http://leoalmanac.org/journal/vol_14/lea_v14_n03-04/essays.asp, accessed July 22, 2015.

Norman, Sally Jane. "Le Spectacle vivant, arène de modélisation du corps." *Les Actes du corps au corpus technologique*. Bordeaux: Odyssud-Blagnac, 1996.

Norman, Sally Jane, Sian E.M. Lawson, Patrick Olivier, Paul Watson, Anita M.-A. Chan, Martyn Dade-Robertson, Paul Dunphy, Dave Green, Hugo Hiden, Jonathan Hook, and Daniel G. Jackson. "AMUC: Associated Motion Capture User Communities," *Philosophical Transactions, Royal Society A*. 367.1,898 (2009): 2,771–2,780, available at http://rsta.royalsocietypublishing.org/content/367/1898/2771, accessed July 22, 2015.

Ong, Walter. *Orality and Literacy. The Technologizing of the Word*. London and New York: Routledge, 1988.

Rotman, Brian. "Corporeal or Gesturo-haptic Writing," *Configurations* 10.3 (2002): 423–438.

Rueb, Terri. "The Choreography of Everyday Movement" (2001), available at http://www.terirueb.net/choreography/index.html, accessed July 22, 2015.

Shanks, Michael, and Pearson, Mike. *Theatre Archaeology*. London: Routledge, 2001.

Stiegler, Bernard. *For a New Critique of Political Economy*. Trans. Daniel Ross (original French publication 2009). Cambridge: Polity Press, 2010.

Stiegler, Bernard. "Grammatisation (techniques de reproduction)," *Ars Industrialis* (n.d.), available at http:arsindustrialis.org/grammatisation, accessed July 22, 2015.

Stiegler, Bernard. "Desire and Knowledge: The Dead Seize the Living," *Ars Industrialis* (n.d.), available at arsindustrialis.org/desire-and-knowledge-dead-seize-living, accessed July 22, 2015.

Tawa, Michael. *Theorising the Project. A Thematic Approach to Architectural Design*. Newcastle upon Tyne: Cambridge Scholars Publishing, 2011.

Turnbull, David. *Maps are Territories: Science is an Atlas*. Chicago: University of Chicago Press, 1993.

Windgätter, Christof. "'. . . with mathematic precision': On the Historiography of the Dynamometer." *The Virtual Laboratory* (2005), available at http://vlp.mpiwg-berlin.mpg.de/, accessed July 22, 2015.

18
WHAT IF THIS WERE AN ARCHIVE?
Abstraction, enactment and human implicatedness

Maaike Bleeker

Archives have been (and often still are) associated with places where things come to rest, where they are stored and kept, and where they can be found again. In the archive, documents and other traces from the past are placed in a clearly organized manner, each fixed in the right place by classification systems and fixed in time by practices of preservation. Digitalization is bringing about transformations in this archival logic with far reaching implications. These transformations involve a shift from what might be called "archival order" to "archival dynamics" (Wolfgang Ernst *Digital Memory*). This is a shift from the archive as place that keeps and orders documents of events that took place at one time and in one place towards the archive as a "dynarchive" (Ernst): a place of (re)generation (co)produced by users. These transformations can be seen reflected in projects from the field of dance that engage with new possibilities of digital technology to store and transmit dance knowledge while at the same time, dance and these projects appear most useful to think through implications and potentials of the new archival logic brought about by digitalization.

Dance has a history of dissatisfaction and discomfort with the traditional archive. Steve Paxton's initial resistance to the archive and to his work being archived, as described by Florence Corin in her account of the making of the DVD-ROM *Material for the Spine* (Chapter 3 in this volume) is symptomatic for this discomfort. He is "not keen" on a historical overview of his work and does not want to focus on the past. He does not want to become a model for imitation. Key to both his distrust of more traditional forms of documentation as well as to his interest in the potential of DVD-ROM as alternative, is the difficulty of transmitting of what to him is essential to his work, which he describes as "the sensations of the body." Eventually, he agrees with the inclusion of some historical materials insofar as they reinforce his thinking in "present tense." Sarah Whatley, in her description of the making of *Siobhan Davies Replay* (Chapter 6) describes a certain "nervousness that 'archive' would imply something dead and dusty" and how this informed the decision to remove "archive" from the landing page and name it *Replay* instead, thus shifting focus from capturing and storing something towards re-doing it in the present. *Replay*, so the name suggests, is not a place of storage of things (choreographies) from the past but allows these choreographies to be brought to life again, in the present. This shift touches a fundamental characteristic of the transformation of the archive as a result of digitalization. Whereas the traditional function of the archive is to collect, store, and categorize documents of events that took place at one time and one place, digitalization shifts the emphasis to (re)generation in the present.

Dance, it might be argued, is itself a practice of constant (re)generation. Dance exists only in the doing. Movement is there only while it is being performed and even then it is never there in its entirety. When a dancer performs, say, a plié, the beginning of the plié is no longer there when she is performing the end of the movement. In order to perceive the plié as movement, the plié has to be abstracted out of a succession of impressions. Movement is the phenomenon *par excellence* of what Brian Massumi (*Semblance and Event*) calls "lived abstraction." Abstraction here does not mean disembodiment but draws attention to what Maurice Merleau-Ponty (*Phenomenology and Perception*) describes as the double sense of embodiment: embodiment as encompassing both the body as lived, experiential structure, and as the milieu of cognitive mechanisms. Movement exemplifies how these two are thoroughly intertwined in how humans make sense of what they encounter. Experience with self-movement is fundamental to how we grasp the logic of contingency in sensory impressions as a result of which we perceive, for example, a movement rather than a blur of diverse sensory impressions. Abstraction, Massumi explains, is "a technique of extracting the relational-qualitative arc of one occasion of experience—its subjective form—and systematically depositing it in the world for the next occasion to find, and to potentially take up into its own formation" (15). From this perspective, movement as well as what we call objects are actually lived relations.

The idea that abstraction is fundamental to how humans perceive and make sense of what they encounter is confirmed by enactive approaches to perception. Alva Noë (in *Action in Perception*) gives the example of a rectangular box that we feel in the dark. Touching the surface of the sides of the box itself does not inform us about its rectangularity. Grasping the rectangularity requires grasping the relationship between various sensations. The same for seeing objects and space around us: we do not only perceive the surfaces of objects directed towards us. We perceive three-dimensional objects. We do so because of our experience with how sensations co-vary, or would co-vary, with actual or possible movements. As a result of such experience we are capable of grasping relations between sensations and this way we live, or enact, our perception of objects, movements, and space. Perception is a matter of enacting our understanding of the logic of sensory impression as a result of which we can make sense of them in terms of objects, space, and movement. Enacting perception, perceivers abstract the shape of, for example, the rectangular box mentioned by Noë, out of the multitude of sensory impressions. The box thus emerges, one might say, as a complex of lived relations.

Massumi's elaborations on lived abstraction and Noë's enactive approach to perception both imply a radical relational approach to what objects are. Radical relational because relationality is not only a matter of relations between object, perceiver and environment, and how these are constitutive of how the object appears the way it appears to a perceiver. More than that, lived abstraction and enactive approaches to perception illuminate how objects exists in how they can be grasped as sets of relationships. This understanding of objects becomes highly relevant in relation to the rise of media culture, and particularly in relation to the transformations brought about by digital and networked media. In a traditional archive, objects and texts are filed by means of systems that define relationships and differences between them. In a digital archive, the objects and documents filed themselves exist only in terms of sets of relationships and differences. This allows new modes of searching. It also means that the objects emerging from the search are not so much found in the archive as (re)generated as a result of how algorithms grasp relationships and differences between sets of data stored in the archive. How algorithms do so differs from how humans do so. Their ways of abstracting objects are not lived, not grounded in lived experiences, as it is the case with humans. As a result, digital archives afford new ways of searching and interpreting, and new objects of knowledge to emerge. I will come back to this.

Digitalization opens new possibilities while also raising important questions for the archive. "The testimonial function of archival records was once firmly rooted in their material authenticity" Ernst observes (88). Digitalization, however, involves the resolving of texts, images, and other objects into numbers and resynthesizing them upon request. The objects found in the dynarchive are mechanically (re)generated and lack grounding in material authenticity. The transformations brought about by digitalization, therefore, are not in the first place a matter of expansion of what can be archived, like the expansions of the archive made possible by the emergence of media like photography, film, sound recording, and video. More fundamental are the transformations in the archival logic of knowledge transmission and the relationship between the logic of the archive and conceptions of knowledge. If (re)generation replaces material authenticity, how then to conceive of that what is "in" the archive as something that can be transmitted across distance, over time? How to conceive of its permanence, its continuity and authenticity? In this context, I argue, dance's resistance to the more traditional archival logics, as well as explorations of new modes of knowledge transmission afforded by digital technology undertaken from the field of dance, are most relevant for rethinking the implications and potentials of the archive as dynarchive. Dance's resistance to being fixed as stable archivable object (see also Waelde and Whatley's Chapter 16 in this volume) is not resolved by digitalization. Rather, dance's resistance to fixation and how this inspires alternative approaches to knowledge transmission draws attention to mediality and performativity as fundamental aspects of how knowledge is transmitted, and also to how transformations brought about by digitalization highlight the intimate connection between conceptions of what it means to know and the media we use to store and transmit knowledge.

The ephemeral character of dance—the fact that dance is continuously disappearing in the doing—has been reason to argue that dance therefore cannot be adequately archived. At the same time, one might argue, movements like the plié mentioned above, do not really disappear but persist in the embodied knowledge of both performer and perceiver. The plié is part of the repertoire (Diane Taylor *The Archive and the Repertoire*) that persists in and through embodied practice and exists in the embodied knowledge to generate this and other movements. In dance, the repertoire of a company consists of the choreographies they are capable of performing. These performances exist, one might say, in the embodied knowledge of the companies' dancers and their knowledge to regenerate these dances. Knowing the repertoire is given in the practice of knowing how to execute the performances. This is also reflected in practices of transmitting this knowledge: in how dancers learn the repertoire from one another, sometimes mediated through designated persons who know the dances from the inside and act as guardians of the legacy of a choreographer. What is thus transmitted is not dances as fixed objects but the know-how to (re)generate these dances in performance.

Taylor distinguishes between the archive and the repertoire as two different practices of knowledge transmission. The archive separates the source of knowledge from the knower, in time and/or space, and works across distance, over time and space. The archive describes a "a public building," "a place where records are kept," like "documents, maps, literary texts, letters, archaeological remains, bones, videos, films, CDs, all those items supposedly. resistant to change" (19). The repertoire, on the other hand, requires presence, participation in the production and reproduction of knowledge by being part of the transmission and enacting that what is transmitted. The repertoire:

> both keeps and transforms choreographies of meaning. Sports enthusiasts might claim that soccer has remained unchanged for the past hundred years, even though players and fans from different countries have appropriated the event in diverse ways. Dances change over time, even though generations of dancers (and even individual dancers) swear they're always the same. But even though the embodiment changes, the meaning might very well remain the same.
>
> *(20)*

Although they stand for different practices of knowledge transmission, the archive and the repertoire are not mutually exclusive. They usually work in tandem. The relationship between them, Tayler observes, is not sequential. "Nor is it true versus false, mediated versus unmediated, primordial versus modern. Nor is it a binary. Other systems of transmission—like the digital—complicate any simple binary formulation." This complication brought about by digitalization is my subject here.

The archive as agent

"Our sense of history—of facticity in relation to the past—is inextricable from our experience of inscription, or writing, print, photography, sound recording, cinema, and now (one must wonder) digital media that save text, image, and sound," Lisa Gitelman observes (in *Always Already New: Media, History and the Data of Culture*). This is not only a matter of how media represent history, or capture and transmit traces of historical events, but also of how they afford different ways of engaging with what is captured and stored: different ways of searching, investigating and interpreting. Exploring the implications of Gitelman's observations for our understanding of performance history, Sarah Bay-Cheng ("Theatre in Media") points out that "[d]igital access to documentation via computers (searching library databases, viewing digitized documents, scanning photographs, and most significant, sharing these within digital networks) affects the ways in which we approach and organize performance history" (32). Bay-Cheng observes that "[a]s archives and libraries digitize their historical documents, the traditional paths and processes of scholarship inevitably shift from discovery to creation—the reperformance of documentation" (32). The transformations brought about by digitalization and pervasive mediatization bring to the fore how our engagement with information is itself a performance while at the same time understanding what is performed here requires to think of performance less as a discrete event and more as a mode of proceeding. Bay-Cheng refers to the *OED* definition of performance as "[a] way or manner in which something is done or takes place; a method of proceeding on any activity, business, etc." (35). This means "[r]ather than framing a phenomenon *as* performance, it proposes to adopt performance *as the mode* through which we assess phenomena, including digital documentation" (35). Thus understood, "performance itself functions . . . as a network of interrelated components, both on- and offline, both overtly mediated and immediate to various and dispersed recipients. What we encounter in performance (and what we may seek to historicize later) is a network of constitutive parts" (35).

Many of the projects discussed in the first part of this volume explicitly facilitate such becoming performance of ways of engaging with digital documentation. They afford new modes of active engagement and creative use. *Siobhan Davies Replay* and the *Digital Dance Archives*, for example, explicitly state the aim to afford more active and creative engagement of users. They invest in developing tools to support this and invite choreographers to explore the potential of their creative use. The *Dance-tech* project invites users to "investigate communication systems as performative spaces" (86). *Double Skin/Double Mind* explicitly requires physical performance as mode of interaction. These interactions result in new materials that can be included in the archive, like the scrap-books created by the guest choreographers and other users of the *Digital Dance Archives* and *Replay*, or the video documentation and peer-to-peer ethnography of the *Dance-tech* project. Many of the projects discussed also aim to contribute to new artistic creations and to make the materials stored and transmitted available as source for new work that then in its turn can be documented and included.

Digitalization of archives thus brings to the fore aspects of archival research that although not unique to the digital, become more prominent as a result of new technological affordances. The fact that archival research is performative, in the sense that it is itself constitutive of new objects of knowledge, is not something that only happens with digitalization. The same might be said about analog archives. They contain documents and other traces from the past, books and other resources, all of which can be accessed through the archive in which they are placed. Both analog and digital archive provide access to materials on the basis of which interpretations can be made and things can come to be known one way or another, and this can then result in new materials that can be included in the archive. Important difference, however, is *how* they mediate; how they afford access to materials, what kind of materials can be accessed, and how interpretation and knowledge production can be performed. Different as well is the role of the archive itself as an agent in knowledge production.

In analog archives, interpretations are produced by humans: they do the searching, make the connections, selections, relations, and so on. The archive is co-constitutive of how interpretations and knowledge can emerge from interactions with it as a result of how materials to be archived have been selected and catalogued and how this affords modes of searching and finding (a point also made by Harmony Bench in her chapter in this volume). Yet this way of being co-constitutive of interpretations and knowledge differs from how digital archives are themselves participants in the production of new objects of knowledge. Digital technologies like computers, databases, and digital archives continue many of the information storage and transmission functions of books and analog archives. Books and analog archives, however, do not process what is stored in them. Computers do. Computers are not merely means to retrieve objects of knowledge somewhere stored in the archive but actively co-constitute them. The sample search in the *Digital Dance Archives* described by Fensham (on page 76) presents an example that demonstrates how:

> [o]nce digitized, the electronic sound or image is open to real-time access and new search options such as similarity-based image retrieval. The traditional architecture of the archive has been based on classifying records by inventories; this is now being supplemented or even replaced by order and variation and fluctuation, that is, dynamic access. This "archive" is no longer a passive storage space but becomes generative itself in algorithmically ruled processuality. Sound and images at the borderline of digital addressability can be navigated through large amounts of data unfiltered by linguistic words. Images and sounds thus become calculable by pattern recognition algorithms.
> *(Parikka 29)*

Computers are capable of performing searches in ways different from human modes of searching and interpreting. Fensham's reflections on the sample search draw attention to these differences. The computer operates at scales and speeds impossible for humans and are capable of searching huge amounts of documents in virtually no time. Furthermore, the computer does not look at images the way humans do but compares data sets. As a result, computer searches produce different objects of knowledge than humans would do. When a human researcher would go to the archive to investigate, say, the development of Siobhan Davies' choreographies between 1980 and 1990, she would probably look for recordings of work from this period, descriptions and responses in reviews, perhaps also other documents like interviews with and artistic statements of Davies, texts in program leaflets, and so on. On the basis of this she would probably construct a narrative describing how the work developed. A computer cannot perform these kind of searches, and the kind of interpretations and answers it can come up with are quite different. Computer algorithms look for patterns in data. This results in answers in terms of numbers and patterns of relationships and differences, like the search in the *Digital Dance Archives* described by Fensham. This difference draws attention to the intimate connection between objects of knowledge and ways of knowing: how ways of interpreting, of grasping connections and relations are constitutive of objects of knowledge. And also how new digital technologies afford new objects of knowledge to emerge, and of dance to be known in new ways. This is explored in a radical way in *Synchronous Objects* (see also Chapter 10 of this volume).

Patterns and randomness

The website *Synchronous Objects* offers 22 different visualizations of ways of knowing (aspects of) William Forsythe's choreography *One Flat Thing, reproduced*. These visualizations are based upon two sets of data: spatial data taken from a video recording of a performance of the choreography and attribute data gleaned from dancers' accounts. Each visualization deals with a different aspect of the organizational structures of *One Flat Thing, reproduced* as it can be derived from these data. These visualizations show how structural principles develop over time. What is visualized, therefore, is not bodies, nor the movement of the individual dancers, but aspects of the structural relationships that are part of the choreography as it unfolds over time. For example, the *Cue Score* is a graph showing the cues given and received between dancers over time. The *Motion Volume Visualization* shows a visualization of the outer edge of the dancers' motions transformed into volumes that emerge and disappear over time. The *Movement Density Map* shows how much time dancers spent in any location during the execution of the choreography and how this develops during the performance.

The way *Synchronous Objects* shows that the choreography can be known reminds us of Katherine Hayles ("Virtual Bodies") observations on how the development of information society and the theories reflecting this development make us aware that information is conceptually distinct from the markers that embody it:

that information is a pattern rather than a presence, and how this requires a different way of thinking about information:

> Questions about presence and absence do not yield much leverage in this situation . . . Instead, the focus shifts to questions about pattern and randomness . . . What parameters control the construction of the screen world? What patterns can the user discover through interaction with the system? Where do these patterns fade into randomness? What stimuli cannot be encoded within the system and therefore exist only as extraneous noise? When and how does this noise coalesce into pattern?
>
> *(72–73)*

In information society, information appears as synchronous objects emerging from technologically mediated ways of knowing that consist in the grasping of patterns as a result of which objects of knowledge are "cut out." This situation alerts us to the fact that information is not something that is somewhere. Instead, information has to be understood in terms of patterns and randomness, whereby it is important not to confuse the pattern with presence and randomness with absence (which would bring us back to the old opposition). Rather, information emerges from how the distinction is being made between pattern and randomness. This is what the creators of *Synchronous Objects* also found themselves confronted with. With *Synchronous Objects,* they demonstrate how this distinction is a matter of ways of knowing. *Synchronous Objects* shows *One Flat Thing, reproduced* as different objects of knowledge: each object is a visualization of how the choreography can be known under a different aspect. One way of knowing is how the dance is structured by means of cues: who is giving what cue at what moment, what happens in response, and how does this provide new cues for new movements. Another way of knowing the object is through counterpoint, another one is through patterns of alignment. From each of these ways of knowing different distinctions between pattern and randomness can be made.

Synchronous Objects thus shows *One Flat Thing, reproduced* to be not one object of knowledge, but a multiplicity of objects existing synchronously. These differences are not a matter of different subjective perspectives on what *One Flat Thing, reproduced* is. Claiming one of these to represent what *One Flat Thing, reproduced* is would mean to bring in a subjective perspective. As *Synchronous Objects*, however, they merely demonstrate different ways of knowing *One Flat Thing, reproduced* and demonstrate how *One Flat Thing, reproduced* appears as different objects in relation to different ways of knowing. *Synchronous Objects* shows how something is known to be always partial and that this is not a matter of the limitations of a subjective perspective, but of knowing being, as Alfred North Whitehead (*Process and Reality*) describes it, a selective, ordering, and structuring force. Showing different objects side by side, the *Synchronous Objects* website illustrates Tara McPherson's observation (discussed in Hayles, *How we Think* 38) that the same repository of data elements can serve different purposes and how this draws attention to the constitutive role of interfaces and data visualization, that is, mediatization, in how things can be known.

From storage to regeneration

Historically there is a close connection between the archive and the medium of writing and print. The invention of writing and print as means to capture, store, and transmit information was constitutive to the development of the traditional archive as place where documents and other objects are stored and classified. In his seminal *Orality and Literacy: Technologizing the Word* (1989), Walter Ong traces how the invention of writing and print inaugurated what he calls the *mind-set* of literacy: modes of knowing and thinking made possible by the new modes of handling language. Part and parcel of this logic is the emergence of the archive as place where records can be kept, where knowledge can be transmitted across distance, over time, and where knowledge is separated from knowers. The emergence of newer media like photography, film, sound recording, and video meant an expansion of the kind of objects and materials that can be archived. Yet these expansions do not fundamentally change the logic of the archive as place of storage of documents and other material traces from the past. This logic does change with digitalization.

Part and parcel of digitalization is a rigorous remediation that results in the disappearance of the material records in which the testimonial function of the archive used to be grounded. Digitalization involves the resolving of texts, images, and other objects into data sets and resynthesizing them upon request. The new modes of searching afforded by the digital archive are made possible by this dissolution of the material authenticity of archival records. To return to Fensham's sample search in the *Digital Dance Archives* once more: the archive does not contain the pictures visualized in the search outcome. In the digital archive they exist only as data sets. The visualization illustrating her article shows a regeneration of the pictures for human users. As Parikka observes, "[w]hat is being digitally 'excavated' by the computer' is a genuinely code-mediated look at a well-defined number of information patterns that human perception calls 'sound' or 'image'" (29). In fact, digital data processing is undermining the separation into the visual, auditory, textual, and graphical. Ernst explains: "What looks like an image on the computer monitor is nothing but a specific actualization of data (imaging)" (132). These actualizations are only part of how the interface translate data into something that corresponds to human modes of perceiving. The term multimedia, therefore, is as Ernst puts it, actually "an interfacial betrayal on the computer screen" created for human eyes only. For:

> in digital space, the difference between the aesthetic regimes exist only for the human user, simulating the audiovisual human senses under one surface. A close reading of the computer as medium, though, reveals that there is no multimedia in virtual space but just one medium, which calculates images, words and sounds basically indifferently because it is able to emulate all other media.
>
> *(118–119)*

In this respect, digital archives are characteristic for what Mark Hansen (*Feed Forward*) describes as the transition from nineteenth- and twentieth-century media to twenty-first-century media. With twenty-first-century media Hansen does not refer so much to a particular new type of technical equipment as to what he calls a particular tendency in how media function that becomes especially prominent with the rise of digital and networked media. Whereas nineteenth- and twentieth-century media offer us things that can be perceived as captured perceptions, like cinema or sound recording do, twenty-first-century media function in ways that to a large extend have nothing to do with human modes of perceiving. This difference is illustrated by the difference between a cinematic recording of a moving body and this same movement captured by motion capture. Unlike a cinematic recording, motion capture does not record and store something that looks like a record of a perception of a moving body, but captures and stores data sets that describe the relations between points in space as they develop over time. Humans cannot perceive these. In order to be perceptible for humans an additional layer of mediation is required. Here again *Synchronous Objects* can serve as example.

The data visualizations present ways of knowing the choreography *One Flat Thing, reproduced* that are quite different from human ways of looking at and understanding the choreography. These visualizations mediate between the computer generated interpretation of the data and human perceivers. These visualizations are means to make the computer interpretations accessible to humans. They do not show (aspects of) the choreography as it is usually perceived by humans (as a film or video recording would do) nor do they describe aspects of the choreography in written language or by means of other symbolic notation. Rather, they visualize relationships between aspects of the choreography as these develop over time. *Synchronous Objects* proposes ways of knowing the choreography *One Flat Thing, reproduced* that are not based on human perception of a performance of the choreography but on machine readings of data. Furthermore, *Synchronous Objects* suggests that a performance of *One Flat Thing, reproduced* is actually also one specific manifestation or mediation, a manifestation in which choreographic ideas are made manifest by means of dancers moving in space. This is an understanding of choreography that is also suggested by William Forsythe in his essay "Choreographic Objects" (also available on the *Synchronous Objects* website).

Choreographic objects

Historically, choreographic ideas materialize in bodily action, Forsythe observes. Yet, he wonders, "are we perhaps at the point in the evolution of choreography where a distinction between the establishment of its ideas and its traditional forms of enactment must be made? . . . Could it be conceivable that the ideas now seen as bound to a sentient expression are indeed able to exist in another durable, intelligible state?" (2). Choreography, Forsythe argues, describes a class of ideas, and these choreographic ideas are traditionally expressed in dance, yet they may also be expressed in other choreographic objects. This possibility becomes most interesting and relevant in the context of questions about mediality and the transmission of ideas in and through different media.

Forsythe's reflections about choreographic objects shift attention away from questions of representation of dance in other media and towards questions of enactment and the role of media in how ideas can be enacted and accessed. Choreographic objects are enactments of choreographic ideas and these enactments mediate in the transmission of ideas. From this perspective, trying to notate, capture, and transmit a dance performance in all its fullness is actually to attempt a kind of double mediation of the choreographic ideas. A different approach to the transmission of these ideas would be to provide access to the ideas expressed in the choreography in a different, more permanent, medium. The fact that Forsythe's essay is made available on the website of *Synchronous Objects* suggests that we might understand the synchronous objects on the site as such attempts to create choreographic objects that mediate in the transmission of choreographic ideas by other means than dancing bodies. *Synchronous Objects* is not presented as an archive. Yet if we look at *Synchronous Objects* as if it were an archive, it suggests an approach to archiving dance that consists in providing access to *One Flat Thing, reproduced* in a way that is not a matter of representations of a performance of the choreography, stored somehow in the archive, but by mediating the (re)generation of the ideas also enacted in a performance of *One Flat Thing, reproduced* by different means. If *Synchronous Objects* were an archive, it would thus suggest an approach to archiving as mediating in the (re)generation of lived abstractions. This is an approach to archiving dance radically different from attempts at capturing the dancing body and the fixation of performances, which as Waelde and Whatley (in Chapter 16) observe are at odds with how many choreographers conceive of their creations. Although choreographies are actualized in performances, individual performances cannot be equated with the choreographies actualized in them. *Synchronous Objects* suggests an alternative approach to archiving that moves away from storing representations of performances and towards developing interfaces that afford users to enact ways of engaging that will regenerate the choreographic ideas. We might say that this is also what is explored and experimented with in the projects of the *Motion Bank* as well as the *Double Skin/Double Mind* interactive installation.

Enacting the archive

The aim of the *Double Skin/Double Mind* installation (see Chapter 9 in this volume) is to transmit an embodied understanding of dance company Emio Greco | PC's work. The installation consists of a space with a projection screen at one end. In this space, the user is made to enact movement triggered by cues, some of which are downright instructions of what to do while others function in a more associative way: for example, metaphorical descriptions of what to imagine, how to feel and what to think, or sounds coming from different directions, or a schematic outline of a human figure that transforms in response to the movements of the user. The installation invites a corporeal interpretation of the signs and cues given, an interpretation in movement. It thus aims at generating understanding of Emio Greco | PC's work by means of an address that invites an enactment of one's corporeal interpretation of the address. *Double Skin/Double Mind* is not an archive. Yet the question whether this technology could also be used to transmit Emio Greco | PC's choreographies was explicitly part of reflection around the development of the installation, in particular in the *Inside Movement Knowledge* research project. If this installation can be used to transfer an understanding of the logic of Emio Greco | PC's modes of moving, can it then also be used to transfer their choreographies? What would this entail? What if this were an archive?

In Chapter 9, Bermúdez Pasqual describes the two modes and four levels in which the installation can be used, and how at the so-called custom level the image of Emio Greco—guiding users through the workshop and demonstrating movement—is removed in order to "instigate self-reflection and self-evaluation, and to direct the attention of the participants to their own actions" (. . .). This level in particular is interesting with regard to questions of archiving since its mode of operating involves the furthest remove from transmission of choreographic ideas by means of a demonstration of an actualization of these ideas in the image of a moving body captured and fixed in the archive. Instead, the installation aims to generate movements that result from how users enact their interpretation of the cues given. Movement thus does not result from copying or mimicking movements of the image of a body seen but result from how users makes sense of cues given. The challenge of using this technology for transmission of Emio Greco | PC's choreographies then would be to find ways of addressing users in such a way that their bodily response regenerates Emio Greco | PC's choreographies. Whether this can actually be achieved and how exactly is not known at the time of writing.

What is clear, however, is that these explorations of the potential of *Double Skin/Double Mind* as an archive confront us with the intimate connection between the archival logic of the analog archive and representational thinking, and how the modes of operating of *Double Skin/Double Mind* subvert this logic. The archival logic of the analog archive assumes the transmission of knowledge to happen via documents that represent (aspects of) that what is known through them. Through these representations users of the archive gain access to realities existing independent from these representations and that are (more or less adequately) represented by what can be found in the archive. If *Double Skin/Double Mind* were an archive, it would be one in which transmission does not happen via representations of the choreographies but via enactment of the address presented by the installation. *Double Skin/Double Mind* does not communicate choreographic ideas by means of representations of performances of these ideas but aims to generate the (re)performance of them. This is a mode of operating closer to that of the repertoire.

However, there are also important differences between the modes of operating of *Double Skin/Double Mind* and the logic of the repertoire. In *Double Skin/Double Mind*, transmission does not happen from body to body but is mediated by technology that affords a separation of ideas from bodies and transmission across time and space. Furthermore, digitalization turns the archive itself into something that has to be regenerated time and again. "Archiving with analog storage media (for instance, photographed texts on microfilm)," Ernst observes, "has distinct advantages over digitization in terms of quality and shelf life. The strength of digitized archivalia lies not in their (highly vulnerable) migrability into the technological future but in their substantially potentized present online accessibility—discourse in their immaterial circulation as information" (87–88). The increased accessibility provided by digitalization and the new possibilities for searching the archive goes at the cost of disconnection from (and even disappearance of) grounding in the permanence of material documents and even of the archival infrastructure. The life-span of technology providing access to digitized materials is limited. Interesting in this respect are Paul Kaiser's observations as part of his reflections about creating *Loops* (Chapter 2): "One way to make a thing that lasts through the ages is to make it out of nearly indestructible materials . . . A different approach is to make a thing whose form is permanent but whose materials are perishable—perishable but replaceable" (30). Kaiser gives the example of Japanese sacred structures made out of wood. As the wood decays, it is replaced. This results in structures that even though their materials have not been in place for more than a few decades, are rightly claimed as being thirteen hundred years old. Like a choreography, the permanence of these structures is that of continuous regeneration. Kaiser and his collaborators attempt a similar approach to *Loops*, and Kaiser's reflections point to how this involves acknowledging a double complexity: on the one hand it involves acknowledging that *Loops* as choreographic object exists separately from specific actualizations in which it is regenerated, but can be known (and captured) only through specific actualizations. On the other hand it involves acknowledging that the life-span of the media that permit capturing *Loops* and making it accessible is limited, and that therefore permanence requires strategies of permanent replacement of the media through which that which has been captured of *Loops* is made accessible. Kaiser's observations thus point to how choreography as object to be archived draws attention to how digitalization further complicates the distinction between the archive (as materially grounded storage) and the repertoire (as practice of continuous regeneration in doing) because although constant regeneration replaces storage, this regeneration involves a disconnection from the knower (characteristic of the archive) in modes of archiving in which perpetuation is not a matter of material permanence nor resulting from human to human transmission but a matter of constant regeneration in which humans and technology interact as agents in networks. This is a situation in which knowledge is not grounded in the materiality of documents, nor in the know-how embodied in practice, but in practices of constant regeneration in which humans, objects and technologies participate, and in which, as Ernst observes, the archive itself becomes a function of transfer processes (98).

Likewise in *Double Skin/Double Mind* transmission of dance knowledge is not a matter of users controlling the technology but of users interacting with the technology. Unlike the logic of the repertoire, in which the know-how to move is transmitted from person to person, here it is technology that generates this know-how in a user as a result of how she is made to enact her response to the address presented. The construction of *Double Skin/Double Mind* puts the user in a situation in with her modes of perceiving and sense making are, to speak with Hansen, implicated within the address presented to them by the installation. The rise of twenty-first-century media, Hansen observes, requires that humans develop increased awareness of how their modes of perceiving, making sense, and thinking are implicated within the way they are addressed by media: how they are implicated within what media afford them to do and how media afford them to interact, navigate, grasp, make sense, and understand.

Twenty-first-century archival logics

As tentative explorations of future modes of archiving, *Synchronous Objects*, *Loops*, and *Double Skin/Double Mind* confirm Taylor's observation that digitalization complicates how the logic of the archive and the repertoire function in tandem. They also point to how these complications are not merely a matter of the ways in which ideas and knowledge are transmitted but beyond that, of the intimate relationship between modes of transmission and conceptions of what knowledge is, what ideas are, and how they can be shared. In this context, Forsythe's proposal to conceive of choreography in terms of choreographic ideas and choreographic objects is interesting for how it suggests an understanding of choreography as expressing and embodying choreographic ideas without representing these, and of the transmission of ideas as not a matter of representations but of enactment. Choreographic ideas are thus conceived as kinds of abstractions that cannot be equated with their concrete manifestations in dance or other media, yet can only be communicated via dance or other media in which they are enacted and which afford perceivers to grasp ideas in enacting their perception of what they encounter. Ideas, although being abstractions, thus do not exist independent from materiality but are entangled with materiality and take shape in and through materiality, and vice versa. Since the only way of conceiving, communicating, and transmitting ideas is in and through one medium or another, the media used to transmit and communicate will unavoidably impact how communicating, knowing, and thinking takes shape, and even what counts as knowledge and our understanding of what ideas are.

Furthermore, *Synchronous Objects*, *Loops*, and *Double Skin/Double Mind* show how the shift in archival logics from storage to regeneration draws attention to the address presented by the archive, and how the affordances for enactment offered by this address are co-constitutive of the (re)generation of that what is transmitted. With regard to this address, Hansen's observations about the double mediation characteristic for the functioning of twenty-first-century media are helpful for how they alert us to the difference between mediation as it is required to store and search data by technological means and mediation as interface with human users.

In *Synchronous Objects* this interface visualizes readings of the data in ways that make computer readings of the data perceptible for humans. This opens the possibility of new ways of knowing the choreography while at the same time raising questions about what it means to know. The new ways of knowing proposed by the visualizations may alert us to the centrality of human perception in more common conceptions of what it means to know the choreography. Furthermore, *Synchronous Objects* shows how the data stored afford the choreography to emerge as object of knowledge in different ways. These ways of knowing do not exist as fixed objects within the archive but are generated from the data by means of different interfaces. *Double Skin/Double Mind* presents the user with an interface that aims to (re)generate embodied understanding of Emio Greco's movement language. This understanding is not stored within the computer system behind the installation in the form of fixated representations of such knowledge but results from how the interface affords enactment and how the system is programmed to respond to the ways in which users enact their responses. This is an approach in which knowledge is not understood as something stored somewhere but exists as lived abstraction, and where transmission involves creating the affordances for such abstraction to take place.

Double Skin/Double Mind allows abstraction by means of an interface that literally implicates the response of a user and offers a demonstration of Hansen's point that the rise of twenty-first-century media alerts us to how modes of perceiving, making sense, and thinking are implicated within the way users are addressed by media and what these media allow users to do. In this respect we might add another additional purpose of the installation to the ones already observed by Bermúdez-Pascual in Chapter 9 in this volume. Bermúdez-Pascual describes how originally the main aim of the installation had been to transmit Emio Greco's movement principles to professional dancers. While working towards this aim, however, it became clear that the installation might serve other purposes as well, like engaging dance audiences in new ways of watching dance. Looking at the installation from the perspective of Hansen's observations on twenty-first-century media we might add to this the possibility of using the installation as a tool to demonstrate and investigate human implicatedness as a twenty-first-century condition.

Acknowledgements

A very short text also titled "What if this Were and Archive?" appeared in 2010 in the journal *RTRSRCH* published by the Artistic Research, Theory and Innovation research group at the Amsterdam School of the Arts (*RTRSRCH* 2.2: 2–5). This issue of *RTRSRCH* brought together materials from the Inside Movement Research project, including my brief and preliminary reflections on the potential of the *Double Skin/Double Mind* installation as an archive. I would also like to thank Sarah Bay-Cheng for the inspiring discussions during our joint session of the *Performing History in the Age of Digital Technology* seminar (November 2015, Utrecht University), which were most helpful in further developing the ideas presented in this chapter.

References

Bay-Cheng, Sarah. "Theater is Media: Some Principles for a Digital History of Performance." *Theater* 42.2 (2012): 27–41.

Ernst, Wolfgang. *Digital Memory and the Archive*. Ed. and with an introduction by Jussi Parikka. Minneapolis: University of Minnesota Press, 2013.

Forsythe, William. "Choreographic Objects," available at http://synchronousobjects.osu.edu/media/inside.php?p=essay, accessed January 25, 2016.

Gitelman, Lisa. *Always Already New: Media, History and the Data of Culture*. Cambridge, Mass.: The MIT Press, 2008.

Hansen, Mark. *Feed Forward: On the Future of Twenty-First Century Media*. Chicago and London: University of Chicago Press, 2015.

Hayles, N. Katherine. "Virtual Bodies and Flickering Signifiers," *October* 66 (1993): 69–91.

—— *How We Think: Digital Media and Contemporary Technogenesis*. Chicago and London: University of Chicago Press, 2012.

Massumi, Brian. *Semblance and Event: Activist Philosophy and the Occurrent Arts*. Cambridge, Mass.: The MIT Press, 2011.

Merleau-Ponty, Maurice. *Phenomenology of Perception*. Trans. Donald A. Landes. New York: Routledge, 2012.

Noë, Alva. *Action in Perception*. Cambridge, Mass.: The MIT Press, 2004.

Ong, Walter. *Orality and Literacy: The Technologizing of the Word*. London and New York: Routledge, 1989.

Parikka, Jussi. "Media Archaeology as Transatlantic Bridge," Wolfgang Ernst: *Digital Memory and the Archive*. Ed. and with an introduction by Jussi Parikka. Minneapolis: University of Minnesota Press, 2013. 23–36.

Taylor, Diane. *The Archive and the Repertoire: Performing Cultural Memory in the Americas*. Duke University Press, 2003.

Whitehead, Alfred North. *Process and Reality*. Corrected Edition. Ed. David Ray Griffin and Donald W. Sherburne. New York: The Free Press, 1978.

19
INDETERMINATE ACTS

Technology, choreography and bodily affects in *Displace*

Chris Salter

Scene 1. A slightly middle aged woman in bare feet, clad in loose red and white patterned pants and a long sleeve white top directly faces the camera. With intense eyes and the tiniest of a smile, she stretches her arms forwards and begins an intricate series of motions starting with the rotation of her fist with the thumb extended. Repeat. The next movement comes, a slight variation of the first. Suddenly, a new movement: extension of the right hand out and away from her chest. The movement seems different but emerges from the previous one. Another new movement: a slight bending of the right foot, which causes the entire body to shift in its vertical position. As new movements continually arise over the breathtakingly short minutes in which this "dance" occurs, they continually return to the initial starting point—the rotation of the fist with the extended thumb. To watch this almost mathematically executed series of actions demands a combination of extreme concentration coupled with a heightened perception of how the slightest change and variation on a theme can produce stunning effects.

Scene 2. Unlike the Zen-like austerity of the previous scene, the second is one of extreme, almost penetrating chaos. Clad in socks, colorful sweatpants and tank tops and spread across a mostly empty stage diagonally bisected with a massive wire cable, groups of dancers produce an ever-shifting web of intricate motions that challenge the eye's temporal lag as it confronts the body's kinesthetic potential. Performed in alternating moments of silence and within a cacophonous dread produced by digitally signal processed trombones, solos, duets, and triplets, indeed, all of the formal ploys of ballet, appear in lightning fast tempo only to dissolve again into a group mind. In contrast to the elegant simplicity of the woman performing her mathematically based actions described above, here the dancers' bodies undergo transformation: twists, spatial distortions, falling limbs hitting the floor that subsequently trace out magnanimous architectures in the air. When watching this ballet, one cannot figure out the steering mechanism—who is responsible for this locomotive complexity that defies the eye? Who has decided these accelerating motions that, at times, appear to displace the moving body, sending it into an atavistic frenzy? Who yells stop in order to advance the flux of this world? How do these bodies *know* what to do and what it is they are doing?

If you are somewhat informed about choreographic practice in North America and Europe over the past thirty years, you may immediately recognize these works or, at the very least, the "authors" of them. Both are choreographies rooted in different time periods, the first dating from 1971 and the second from 1995. But this time gap is small compared to what at first appears to be wild differences of intensity between the two. If the first (at least as I have attempted to describe it) is astonishing in its simplicity and elegance, the second overwhelms the act of human perception by blurring the already fragile borders between bodies in control of themselves and bodies possessed; ones that, as filmmaker Maya Deren (1953) depicting her experience of watching Haitian voodoo in *Divine Horseman* stated, "project from the physique to the psyche . . . sucked down and exploded upwards at once" (260).

Despite the time and action gap, however, there is something else that unites these two works. Both depict terpsichorean acts that, while at first appearing to solely originate from the bodies of the dancers, are in fact the result of a complex entangling between human bodies and technical apparatuses that enable and produce the unknown in terms of bodily action. Technology, derived from the Greek *technē*, suggests practical knowledge or skill in the service of the logos—the implementation of order. Yet, from the above descriptions, it is clear that the mathematical rules that enable the first choreography (Trisha Brown's *Accumulation*) or the "algorithmic" systems that generate operations on movement to produce a ballet that swings between order and chaos (the third act of William Forsythe's *Eidos: Telos*) are also technologies. They bring about something else in the makers (choreographers and dancers) and perceivers (their audiences) by enabling a world of acts on stage to unfold in a precariously indeterminate, and thus, lifelike manner. Life, as Georges Canguilhem wrote in his 1947 essay "Machine and Organism," is not the purposive, teleological rigidity of machines but rather that which is spontaneous, improvisational, and subject to transformation, mutation, and alteration (88–90).

What unites these two works is the manner in which such techniques trouble, as Maaike Bleeker in her introduction to this volume argues, the "close connection between practices of capturing and transmitting movement and issues of authority and ownership." They challenge the centralized control of the choreographer inscribing movement on the bodies of dancers like a sculptor by not only deploying *technologies* (i.e., ordering systems) that distance makers from their habitual habits of doing things but also by generating bodily events whose future trajectory is partially unknown. As Forsythe once stated when asked about his approach to choreography, "I only give the dancers my ideas and not the results. I don't tell anyone what they should do, I only say how they should make it" (Odenthal 37).

Whether motion capture, sensor-augmented interaction, or video projection, most of the literature and practice in the field of dance and technology has focused on screen-based, audio-visual driven technologies that toy with, disturb, or exploit problems of choreographic representation. It may therefore seem strange to argue that *Accumulation*, a solo dance constructed by Brown in 1971 and based on a mathematical-like procedure to assist in the generation of the choreography, utilizes technology.

Herein lies the crux of this chapter. Trisha Brown's claim to create "dance machines that take care of certain aspects of dance-making" sets out a particular paradigmatic shift in how we look at the genesis of choreographic action and agency in relationship to techniques. It suggests that choreography (what Forsythe once called "just organizing bodies") is inherently a machinic process—not in the sense of the Descartian part-whole mechanistic body that Canguilhem criticizes for its slavish adherence to the technical objects of Descartes' day (pistons, clocks, artificial fountains), but in Félix Guattari's sense of the machine as a heterogeneous constellation of "multiple components such as material and energy components, semiotic, diagrammatic and algorithmic components (plans, formula, equations and calculations which lead to the fabrication of the machine), components of organs, influx and humours of the human body, individual and collective mental representations and information . . ." (Guattari 34–35).

Similar to Michael Kirby's 1974 statement that in postmodern dance "movement is not pre-selected for its characteristics but results from certain decisions, goals, plans, schemes, rules, concepts, or problems" (3), I want here to explore how such "choreographic" techniques (that is, the spatial and temporal organization of bodies) that intertwine both human and technological agencies (whether these agencies are mathematical schemas, computers or architectural frameworks) influence and have strong repercussions on other kinds of body-based artistic practices.

Processes in which bodily expression, autonomy, and agency operate in the face of technical apparatuses that thwart such assumed bodily "agency" (the fact that movement emerges from a self-autonomous subject), have long crossed over from dance, influencing other disciplines ranging from early cybernetics and cognitive science to the construction of technologically mediated environments in art and design. More specifically, my focus here will be contemporary techno-culturally-driven artistic practice focused on issues of perception. Such practices while not easily qualified as dance do incorporate and borrow (whether consciously or not) technological strategies of the kind I described from Brown and Forsythe in order to organize and steer bodily acts from participants that may no longer be under the centralized control of any single individual but whose actions are determined and executed according to a larger systemic set of forces.

My argument has two parts. The first briefly examines some of the historical interest in system-based approaches for the generation of choreographic action. From a dance historical point of view, these approaches are not only rooted in Cage and Cunningham's aleatoric approach to dance making (starting with *Suite for Changes* in 1953 and culminating in works such as *Variations V* in 1965). They also carry through the work of the core Judson choreographers like Brown, Yvonne Rainer, Lucinda Childs, Alex and Deborah Hay, Simone Forti, and others' interest in rule-based approaches to dance making as well as in experimental music practice and experimental projects involving art and technology (*9 Evenings: Theater and Engineering*) roughly in the same historical period.

These links between Judson choreographers and dancers, experimental musicians, and engineers in *9 Evenings* are certainly not arbitrary given that key Judson members like Childs, Hay, Rainer, Paxton, Forti, and (outside of Judson) Cage were involved in the project. More curious and far less discussed in the literature is the cultural influence between Cage and MIT mathematician and cybernetics founder Norbert Wiener. While it is widely acknowledged that Cage (among others, such as Nam June Paik) read Wiener's mathematically complex treatise on control and feedback systems *Cybernetics: Control and Communication in the Animal and Machine*, it is less clear how cybernetics' interest in feedback models and the behavior of technical systems, in general, entered into performative artistic practices.

Part II of this chapter seeks to transport these concepts into what might appear to be, at first, a radically different context: that of contemporary art practice utilizing new technologies. Here, I want to explore the influence, strategies, and repercussions that such choreographic techniques involving both human and technological agencies have had on a recent performative installation project called *Displace* that I developed in collaboration with a wide range of artists and researchers coming from cultural anthropology, gastronomy, and olfactory-based art history (Salter, *Alien Agency*).

Although the work purposefully does not occupy or qualify in any sense of the word the territory of "dance" (it is more akin to a "participative installation" like Steve Paxton's contribution to *9 Evenings* entitled *Physical Things*), *Displace* utilizes strategies that derive from choreographic composition (the spatial-temporal organizing of the visitors' bodies) and the ways in which the sensing body deals with and processes the operation of multiple sensory modalities, both separately and simultaneously.

Specifically, I will examine the context and framework of *Displace* as an artistic event that explores different degrees of sensorial affects operating on the bodies of the participants (from sensory reduction to overload), and how such sensorial, bodily knowing is catalyzed and shaped by what I call, after Michel Foucault, "technologies of sense." The construction of sensorial environments in which the human body is conceived as part and parcel of a larger set of technologies that produce profound and occasionally consciousness altering affects on the participant-observer may thus be akin to a transformation of choreographic practice using similar strategies of parameterization, schematics, temporal structures, and processes that emerged from the historical path laid out in part I.

Rules, feedback, algorithms and dance machines

It is widely acknowledged that one of the key characteristics of the so-called postmodern dance movement that took place in New York during the mid-1960s was its interest in the exhibition of simple, everyday actions in order to produce dances that moved away from modernist or expressionistic movement. According to dance historian Sally Banes, the period's main chronicler, "whether the prevailing structure is a mathematical system for using space, time, or the body; or arbitrary assemblage; or fragmentation, juxtaposition, the deliberate avoidance of structure by improvisation or the constant shifting of structure by chance methods, there is always the possibility, in post-modern dance, that the underlying form will be bared" (16).

A case in point is Trisha Brown. From early on, Brown's approach to choreography emphasized the use of systems or rules for the generation of movement. In her effort to "find the schemes and structures that organize movement, rather than the invention of movement per se," Brown sought out combinatoric and rule-driven processes (Banes 86). With *Accumulation*, for example, originally a solo created for herself in 1971, Brown developed a simple mathematical procedure by which the dance was propelled forwards by strict adherence to a set of simple rules: adding one gesture to another, one at a time, and repeating the growing phrase with each new movement.

Other earlier choreographies, like *Rulegame 5* (1964) and *Trillium* (1965) also relied on what Brown referred to as "scores" for the creation of movement. Even though these dances appear to be situated within abstract systems, they are certainly not without attention to the complex mechanics of the body. Indeed, part of the choreographic novelty comes from the fact that the body must operate in a highly designed environment, precariously balanced between self-governance and the constraints on this governance generated by the system. In a 1986 interview with Marianne Goldberg, Brown confirmed this much when she argued that the formulation of choreography comes at the nexus of the score meeting the "immediate physical responses of the dancers to it" (Goldberg 7).

If Brown's early works function like a puzzle that the audience has to solve by uncovering the rules that govern the movement, later works like *Locus* (1975) and *Set and Reset* (1983) further stretch complexity of such systems, both in terms of the underlying structures as well as in the physical dynamics of the performers. The notorious *Locus*, for instance, is based around a complex geometric-spatial form: an imaginary cube with 27 sides inside which the performers move, touching and kinesthetically responding to the points based on a score derived from sequences of words (TRISHA BROWN WAS BORN IN ABERDEEN, WASHINGTON . . .) that are then transformed into numbers. The tension between what former Brown dancer Mona Sulzman calls "constraint and freedom" and the immersion of Brown in her own "self-imposed restrictions" within the process of creating and performing *Locus* provides yet another example of how technical systems operate to both restrain the notion of unconstrained bodily agency and, at the same time, make such constraints part of the creative act (Sulzman 122).

The fact that Brown and other Judson Church dancers sought out certain "objective" or rigorous techniques beyond their own knowledge to manipulate, shape, and mold the body also lead some of them towards a more unusual collaboration, this time with Bell Labs engineers under the not yet birthed Experiments in Art and Technology initiative founded by Robert Rauschenberg, Robert Whitman and Bell Labs electrical engineer Billy Klüver. During the period of 18 months between 1965 and 1966, over thirty engineering experts in exotic research areas like speech recognition, solid state physics and signal processing collaborated with core Judson members and other cutting edge performance/musicians like John Cage, Rauschenberg, Öyvind Fahlström, and David Tudor. The aim was to "provide new materials for artists in the form of technology" (Klüver) which resulted in the watershed event *9 Evenings: Theater and Engineering* held before more than 10,000 people at the Park Avenue Armory in October 1966.

Given that the Judson members sought to strip away the *gesamtkunstwerk* attitude and theatrical inauthenticity they perceived in modern dance, it may seem strange that such performers agreed to spend more than ten months collaborating with engineers who had little knowledge (or sometimes interest) of what they were doing and in performances in which new technologies would be center stage. Yet the core Judson dancers involved in *9 Evenings* also saw the potential of far-flung and mostly military derived technologies such as Doppler radar, wireless communication systems, CCTV, robotic actors, and photocell-driven audio to also expand their choreographic process and vocabulary (Salter *Entangled* 241–242).

It should further come as no surprise that Cage was also deeply involved in *9 Evenings*, not only because of his association with Klüver (who had previously designed electronic components for *Variations V*) but also because of the composer's infatuation with the indeterminate possibilities he saw inherent in electronic systems. Cage's interest in chance procedures is, of course, well known, as is his subsequent influence on Merce Cunningham, who started his choreographic career as a proponent of expressionism à la Martha Graham and ended with an extreme formalism that eschewed any kind of fake emotionality. Such Cunningham/Cage collaborations like *Suite for Changes* (1953) whose movement sequences were determined by coin flips using the *I Ching* or later works like *Variations V*, which subjected the dancers to interactive systems that Cunningham once called "not the product of will but of an energy and a law to which one must obey" (Copeland 111), had at their basis the use of systems or technologies that would defer the agency of choreographer and composer from their habitual acts of composition (Copeland) and instead, subject performative events to a rigorous semi-autonomy.

What has been less discussed is the influence of cybernetics—another set of knowledge practices interested in questions of control and autonomy in relation to technical systems—on Cage, Judson, and the larger cultural scene, in general. Historian of science and technology Christina Dunbar-Hester has explored the impact of cybernetics on the experimental music scene of the 1960s, a scene in which Cage had a deep and ongoing influence. Always interested in "the continuum between exactitude and disorder," Cage sought "the curtailment of individual agency in composition and performance" in order to construct musical and artistic events beyond the control of one single individual but instead, derived from a larger set of circumstances (Dunbar-Hester 2010). That Cage was also influenced by the famous Indian art historian Ananda Coomaraswamy's statement that art should "imitate nature in her manner of operation" suggests that Cage's interests in indeterminacy were not just formal concerns but also ontological ones. Art should not attempt to represent nature but rather uncover its underlying structural and operative principles (Coomaraswamy; Crooks).

What then were the major ideas from cybernetics that flowed from the anti-aircraft control theory of MIT mathematician Norbert Wiener into the avant-garde dance, music, and performance scene of downtown New York in the late 1950s–1960s? First, Cage was an avid reader and supporter of Wiener's more than mathematically rigorous 1948 book *Cybernetics*. Second, Wiener's cybernetics revolved around questions emerging in control and communication engineering concerning the *behavior* or "change of an entity with respect to its surroundings" (Wiener et al. 18) manifested in objects or systems. Such change usually included observing the recognizable modification of the *output* of an object or system subjected to some form of internal self-regulation. In an early path-breaking article in collaboration with Mexican cardiologist Arturo Rosenblueth and physicist Julian Bigelow entitled "Behavior, Purpose and Teleology," Wiener defined what he referred to as "goal directed" (that is, purposive) behavior in a system. While purposeful behavior resulted in the system altering itself in order to achieve its set goal, purposeless behavior could be considered stochastic or probabilistic.

For Wiener, however, the central characteristic of a purposeful, goal-driven system is that of feedback. Positive feedback involves the re-circulation of a "fraction of the output of a system" that is literally "fed back" into the input of the system; for example, an acoustic amplifier in which the output signal literally courses back into the input, causing the system to become unstable over time. As Wiener wrote, "positive feedback adds to the input signals, it does not correct them" (Wiener *Cybernetics* 19). Negative feedback, however, involves a kind of self-correcting procedure in which a small portion of the input to the system is derived from the goal and is used to prevent the system from overshooting it—in essence, error correcting it.

The classical example that Wiener gives to articulate such complex engineering concepts is the action of a patient with cerebellar motor disorders drinking a glass of water. As the patient moves the glass of water towards his/her mouth, increasingly amplified movements in the motor system produce a series of undampened oscillations (positive feedback) that cause the patient to overshoot the goal (to bring the glass to the lips) (*Cybernetics* 19–20). The fact that Wiener and his scientific collaborators easily transition between the description of a control principle in engineering and the actions of the human sensorimotor system supports philosopher Jean Pierre Dupuy's argument that early cybernetics saw a fundamental formalist logic governing the behavior of all systems, "whether it was a question of electrical circuits or the brain" (Dupuy 12). Thus, in some way, cybernetics sought a kind of blurring or erasure of the barriers between human and inanimate technical agency.[1]

It does not take much of a stretch in imagination to see how and why cybernetic principles such as feedback could easily enter into and influence (directly in the case of Cage or fellow Cunningham composer David Tudor, who used positive feedback models as a key component of sound generation and composition) the practice of a generation of performing artists interested in how system oriented operations might be used as generative strategies in the production of choreographic or composition events. These events would have outcomes that could not be completely predicted in advance and were subject to the dynamic conditions of the environment in which they took place.

Jumping ahead in time, feedback technologies and organizing systems also found their way into the "improvisational technologies" developed by William Forsythe at the Frankfurt Ballet in the mid-1990s. While Forsythe's work in the late 1980s focused on the continual exploration of what he called "the political histories of observation and perception" by seeking to explode the choreographic and theatrical conventions of classical ballet, beginning with *Limbs Theorem* (1990), continuing with *Slingerland* (1991), *The Loss of Small Detail* (1987 and 1992), *Alie/na(c) tion* (1992), and *As a Garden in This Setting* (1993), and culminating in *Eidos:Telos* (1995), he increasingly shifted towards the construction of fully "systematic" works. Such systems Forsythe claimed "make it impossible for the dancers to know where they are going, when they are going, how long they should stay, what they should do and what intensity it should have . . . I call this alien. I've made a work that is alien to me. I don't know the choreography" (Odenthal 36).

In the three-act ballet *Alie/na(c) tion* to which Forsythe refers to in the above quote, choreographic sequences are, for example, controlled by multiple simultaneous clocks such that the dancers have to respond to several layers of time and information. With the 1995 dance-theater work *Eidos: Telos* on which I collaborated with Forsythe and composers Thom Willems and Joel Ryan, Forsythe also sought to develop operative and iterative/recursive sets of instructions or "algorithms" that when applied to pre-existing movement sequences could generate unthinkable, unknowable choreographic actions. These actions, developed from systems, parameters, and time models, also involved feedback mechanisms that operated according to recursive procedures: actions and movements influenced by external factors are literally fed back into the movement sequences, producing potentially unstable sequences in the future.

This "parametric" approach to choreography not only influenced Forsythe's approach to the dancing body but also his conception of the stage environments within which such acts took place.[2] Indeed, seemingly inanimate objects, machines and other nonhuman stuff for long occupied Forsythe's stage landscapes, transforming such objects into obstacles, entities, and material beings who share space and time with their human interlopers (both dancers as well as audience). In fact, one might argue that the approach that Forsythe has taken to his stage landscapes similarly parallels his systemic approach to the dancing body. "The body is fused into the total aesthetic environment. We develop the parameters for a particular movement vocabulary and with those, the entire environment. Unlike (Robert) Wilson who wants to use the body as part of the image within a stage environment, I conceive of a spatial installation with dancers" (Odenthal 33).

Displace: bodily affects from technologies of the senses

I now want to radically shift context (but not necessarily content) and describe the translation process by which certain choreographic ideas of systemic, constrained agency through technical-corporeal approaches find their way into contemporary artistic projects which, while not classified as dance, strongly focus on the production of bodily affect by way of technological instruments. Concretely, I briefly discuss the performative sensory environment called *Displace*, one of the artistic outcomes of a larger three-year research project conducted by myself, cultural anthropologist David Howes, and computer musician and media artist Maurizio Martinucci (TeZ) exploring the relationship between the anthropology of the senses and the design of new kinds of multi-sensory experiences.

Displace is the name for an ongoing series of sensorial environments, the first of which took place in Montreal, Canada at the Hexagram Concordia Centre for Research-Creation in Media Art and Technology at Concordia University in 2011 as part of the American Anthropological Association's annual meeting.[3] As the visitors (six in total during a 30-minute time period) move through a series of specially designed environments, they are confronted with different sensory experiences ranging from being "baptized" on the forehead with Tiger Balm ointment and tasting liquids whose colors serve to hide what are revealed to be extreme tastes (bitter, sour, cloyingly sweet) to navigating a darkened tunnel alone, whose walls are bathed in infra-red heat and scents.

The experience culminates in the six visitors sitting atop of a raised 5-meter diameter, hexagonally shaped platform whose outer rim and top (suspended three meters above the base) is rung in strips of computer controlled, color changing LEDs (light emitting diodes). In addition, this hexagonal form is surrounded by a cluster of multiple loudspeakers. Within the installation, the participants experience a 10-minute composition of light and sound which borders on the hallucinogenic due to the use of generative algorithmic processes which produce extremely fast rates of colored flicker with the lights as well as the spatial repositioning of the sound achieved through ambisonic-techniques.[4]

Working with while contextually transforming ethnographic accounts of the synesthetic cosmology of the Tucano (Desana) Indians of Colombia and other core examples from the anthropology of the senses (e.g., historian Doreen Kondo's discussion of the sequencing of sensations in the Japanese tea ceremony, see Howes), myself, Martinucci, and Howes designed a dramaturgy that aimed to directly implicate the bodies of the visitors through the totalizing multi-sensory mesh (in this sense, reversing Clifford Geertz's dictum of "webs of meaning" into "webs of sensation") while at the same time created a Benjaminian "gymnasium of the senses" in which the body could gain a renewed sensory awareness.[5]

As Howes articulates, *Displace* functions like a "flight simulator" to enable anthropologists to be more sensorially acute so that during fieldwork they would consider different sensory registers over and beyond the visual (traditionally captured through the genre of ethnographic film or photography).[6] At the same time, however, the sensorial inundation of the installation brought visitors to certain experiences of vertigo, extreme disorientation, and, in some instances, a brief loss of self-awareness and self-consciousness. This tension between sensorial heightening and liminal distortion was highlighted through group interview sessions with many of the anthropologists who attended the installation along with the general public.

Within these collective enunciations, participants expressed a wide range of conflicting emotional and physical responses, ranging from confusion ("what is the difference between this and taking drugs") to enjoyment ("the flashing of the lights . . . I experimented with closing my eyes and having my eyes open and . . . you know, it wasn't a whole . . . it was different, it would have been easier to go on and meditate with your eyes closed cause you had patterns forming on the inside of your lids, eyelids . . . just the color of the lights, it was not unpleasant") to more extreme experiences of disorientation ("the experience . . . it was like a heavenly dance hall . . . the experience of death, limbo and then heaven down the hall") (Salter, *Alien Agency* 246–250).

Based on feedback in Montreal garnered through more than 200 such group interviews, a radically reconceived second version of *Displace (2.0)* took place in The Hague, Netherlands in September 2012 as part of the TodaysArt festival of contemporary art. In contrast to the first iteration, *Displace 2.0* sought to work further with the so-called "lower senses" of touch, taste, and smell—senses that are integral to human perception but rarely brought together within artistic work. In contrast to the Montreal version, visitors to the installation were free to move at will through the different floors with no explicitly dictated time frame.

The Hague iteration was spread across three floors of a closed but newly refurbished gallery, making site-specific use of the space's unique architectural and spatial features. For example, upon entering the installation, visitors exchange their shoes for surgical shoe covers and are given salted sugar crystals which they are told to place in their mouths after they descend into a long, 11 m x 5 m wide room. The space lies in darkness and the floor is completely covered with a thin layer of rock salt creating a tactile sensation beneath the feet of the visitors. In time intervals of 20–25 seconds, the room is pulsed with two stroboscopic lights at such short durations (25 milliseconds) that visitors never actually "see" the real room but only its afterimage. Similarly, we explore further spatial and proprioceptive distortion by utilizing sound projected by way of parabolic reflectors. A parabolic reflector produces the illusion of a direct and narrow beam of sound that can only be perceived when walking into its path, creating the illusion that the sound is closer to the ear than it really is.

As the visitors exit the space, they cross through a 1-meter long, double curtained threshold chamber thick with a sweetened smell concocted by olfactory art historian Caro Verbeek and aroma jockey Jorg Hempinius. Ascending another short flight of stairs, visitors arrive in a smaller room outfitted with a large 5 × 4 m sized rear projection screen saturated in colored light and suspended 2 meters parallel from the floor and under which they can lie on their backs on memory foam mattresses. With pulsing binaural sounds, a shifting olfactory combination of citrus and smoke scents, and the saturated color fields above them, sensorial blurring begins to take place between vision, audition, and olfaction. The visitors' bodies drift between suspension and the borders of trance as they lay (mostly motionless) underneath this continually changing colored plane of light akin to a kind of colored *ganzfeld*.[7]

Finally, as the visitors leave this environment, they ascend a third flight of stairs, wind their way through a darkened hallway which is also permeated with scent and eventually find themselves in a white room in which the hexagonal platform from *Displace 1.0* makes its reappearance. Utilizing techniques such as flicker, spatialized audio, and changing smell, the atmosphere shifts over time through different states, from a kind of meditative quality to one of complete audio-visual-olfactory over-inundation of the visitors' perceptual limits. Furthermore, the gustatory elements that were present with the salt/sugar crystals in room one find their ultimate apotheosis in this final chamber: individual taste stations with edible solid and liquid materials that are extreme variations on the standard tastebud structures of salty, sweet, bitter, sour, and umami.

How then does such an environment intersect with the questions of choreographic and bodily agency discussed earlier? *Displace* clearly sets out to probe how the sensing body "makes sense" of such a barrage of input, examining from a somatic point of view how our bodies navigate specific technical-architectural conditions that attempt to thwart our habitual patterns of perception. As designers, we too have constructed specified sets of parameters (e.g., different qualities of intensity in light or smell or the duration of the flicker rate of the LEDs) and spatial-temporal structures that might catalyze certain kinds of perceptual/kinesthetic forms of sensation in the visitors' bodies. In other words, we have designed a spatial installation integrated with perceiving bodies whose orientation, spatial trajectories, and kinesthetic encounters with themselves, others, and the environment is not wholly determined in advance but subjected to the particular technical (read: ordering principles) strategies the environment employs.

In this way, *Displace* operates close to the kinds of choreographic stage environments described earlier. If as Claire Bishop argues, installation-based art is defined by "addressing the viewer as a literal presence in the space" in which the visitor's senses of "touch, smell and sound are as heightened as much as their sense of vision" (Bishop 6), *Displace* does not take the visitors' body as a passive given but rather, as Alva Noë has argued, engaged in a process of "skillful probing and movement" within an environment whose sensorial structures are in flux (Noë 1). The parameters of how bodies might move and respond are thus part and parcel of the overall conceptual choreographic and technical strategies in creating the event.

What is critical in both versions of *Displace* is the role of *knowing*. The deliberate use of *technologies*, that is, strategies of parameterization within media and architectural systems and processes, place the bodies of the visitors (like the dancers described in part I of this chapter) into a certain state that they cannot know a priori. As Foucault claimed, *technē* involves a "practical rationality governed by a conscious goal" ("Practices and Knowledge" 255). In his later work, Foucault defined four different kinds of technologies, from technologies of production which enable us to make and transform things and technologies of signs where we use signs and symbols to construct meaning, to disciplinary technologies which control and shape bodies into docile subjects and, finally, "technologies of the self," "which permit individuals to effect by their own means or with the help of others a certain number of operations on their own bodies and souls, thoughts, conduct and way of being so as to transform themselves in order to attain a certain state of happiness, purity, wisdom, perfection or immortality" ("Technologies of Self" 17).

Just like the choreographic technologies of rules, games, procedures, and models that shift performers and their audiences from habitual ways of making and understanding what the dancing body is, *Displace* too plays with such technologies—these "political frameworks of observation and perception" (Odenthal 33). Instruments, such as the strobe lights, LEDs or computational algorithms that generate the varying flicker frequencies or position generative sound in the ambisonic field so that it completely surrounds the body without the illusion of a sweet spot, all act to both shape and discipline the bodily agency of the visitors while, at the same time, open up other kinds of perceptual possibilities that may have previously been closed off. In this manner, I claim another kind of technology—a "technology of sense"—which, like the rule-based routines of Brown and Judson or Forsythe's improvisational technologies that produce estranged choreographies, operate in tandem with bodies to produce other kinds of perceptions—perceptions that may at first be alien to the experiencer but that nevertheless produce an altered sense of the world.

Notes

1 See Dupuy and Hayles for further discussion.
2 Forsythe's interest in such parametric models has gone on to influence a generation of computer-based architects, such as Mark Goulthorpe. See Salter *Entangled* 101–102.
3 http://hexagram.concordia.ca, accessed May 25, 2016.
4 http://www.ambisonic.net/, accessed May 25, 2016.
5 I want to emphasize that *Displace* by no means resembles or attempts to replay Victor Turner's NYU experiments in the 1980s attempting to stage ethnographic accounts of Ndembu rituals detailed in *From Ritual to Theater: The Human Seriousness of Play*. See Turner.
6 Personal conversation.
7 See Massumi for a description of *ganzfeld* experiences.

References

Banes, Sally. *Terpsichore in Sneakers*. Wesleyan, Mass.: Wesleyan University Press, 1987.
Bishop, Claire. *Installation Art*. London: Tate Publishing, 2011.

Canguilhem, Georges. *Knowledge of Life (Forms of Living)*. Trans. Stephanos Geroulanos. New York: Fordam University Press, 2008.

Coomaraswamy, Ananda K. *The Transformation of Nature in Art*. New York: Dover Publishing, 1937.

Copeland, Roger. *Merce Cunningham: The Modernization of Modern Dance*. New York: Routledge, 2004.

Crooks, Edward. "John Cage's Entanglement with the Ideas of Coomaraswamy." Diss. University of York, 2011.

Deren, Maya. *Divine Horseman: The Living Gods of Haiti*. New York: McPherson, 1953.

Dunbar-Hester, Christina. "Listening to Cybernetics: Music, Machines and Nervous Systems, 1950–1980." *Science, Technology and Human Values* 35 (2010): 113–139.

Dupuy, Jean-Pierre. *The Mechanization of the Mind: The Origins of Cognitive Science*. Trans. M.B. DeBevoise. Cambridge, Mass.: The MIT Press, 2009.

Foucault, Michel. "Practices and Knowledge." *The Foucault Reader*. Ed. Paul Rabinow. New York: Pantheon, 1984. 121–380.

—— "Technologies of the Self." *Technologies of the Self: A Seminar with Michel Foucault*. Ed. Luther H. Martin et al. London: Tavistock, 1988. 16–49.

Goldberg, Marianne. "Trisha Brown: All of the Person's Person Arriving." *TDR* 30.1 (1986): 149–170.

Guattari, Félix. *Chaosmosis: An Ethico-Aesthetic Paradigm*. Trans. Paul Bains and Julian Pefanis. Bloomington: Indiana University Press, 1995.

Hayles, N. Katherine. *How We Became Post-Human: Virtual Bodies in Cybernetics, Literature and Informatics*. Chicago: University of Chicago Press, 1999.

Howes, David, ed. *Empire of the Senses: The Sensual Culture Reader*. Oxford: Berg Publishing, 2005.

Kirby, Michael. "Post Modern Dance Issue: An Introduction." *TDR* 19.1 (1975): 3–4.

Massumi, Brian. *Parables for the Virtual: Movement, Affect, Sensation*. Durham, NC: Duke University Press, 2004.

Noë, Alva. *Action in Perception*. Cambridge, Mass.: The MIT Press, 2006.

Odenthal, Johannes. "Der Raum vor Seiner Zeit: Ein Gespräch mit William Forsythe über Asethetik, Trance und das Ballett." *Ballett International/Tanz Aktuell*. 2.94 (1994): 33–37.

Salter, Chris. *Alien Agency: Experimental Encounters with Art in the Making*. Cambridge, Mass.: The MIT Press, 2015.

—— *Entangled: Technology and the Transformation of Performance*. Cambridge, Mass.: The MIT Press, 2010.

Sulzman, Mona. "Choice/Form in Trisha Brown's Locus: A View from inside the Cube." *Dance Chronicle* 2.2 (1978): 117–130.

Turner, Victor. *From Ritual to Theater: The Human Seriousness of Play*. New York: PAJ Books, 2001.

Wiener, Norbert. *Cybernetics: Control and Communication in the Animal and the Machine*. Cambridge, Mass.: The MIT Press, 1965.

Wiener, Norbert, Arturo Rosenblueth and Julian Bigelow. "Behavior, Purpose and Teleology." *Philosophy of Science* 10 (1943): 18–24.

20

NEWMAN'S NOTE, ENTANGLEMENT AND THE DEMANDS OF CHOREOGRAPHY

Letter to a choreographer

Alva Noë

In *Action In Perception*, I argued that perception is the embodied activity of making access to the world.[1] Conscious experience, on this view, isn't something that happens inside us, not in our brains, or anywhere else. It is something we do. To pay attention to your experience, then, you need to look not inward, but outward, to your situation, to your context, to the performance we are always carrying out jointly with others.

This enactive approach to perception that I presented in that book prompted you, and other artists, to seek me out; you invited me to join you in the laboratory. In the years since, we have spent many hours dancing and talking, performing, and thinking about performance. We have jointly undertaken research together. I write now, not as a dance scholar—I have no training in performance studies, or dance studies, or cultural studies, nor am I a trained dancer—but as a friend and as your guest. I claim no other authority than that.[2]

Our shared investigations of choreography have led me to understand my own earlier work in new ways. For one thing, it has led me to rethink, or better articulate, what it means to say that perception is an "activity," or that we "achieve" access to the world. The questions that preoccupy me here, though, and that have arisen for me in the context of my work with you over these years, are: if you are conducting research in the form of choreography, what sort of research is this? And if consciousness experience is itself, as I have indicated, a kind of performance, something enacted and composed, an activity whereby we achieve presence, then what is the difference between conscious experience itself and the work of choreography?

Although I was not clear about this when we first began, I now think that there is all the difference in the world between consciousness and choreography, life and art. As Robert Filliou put it—Deborah Hay taught me this—art is what makes life more interesting than art. But the complex entanglement of the two, we might aptly say, is itself one of the facts of life. And I want to understand this. This is the focus of my recent work (*Strange Tools*), and it makes up the subject of this letter.

One final thought before jumping in. Technology, however broadly or narrowly you choose to understand this, is the stuff of life, not of art. In my terminology, it belongs to the ways we find ourselves organized and sets, if you like, our existential agenda. For what we want, what we need, is not more organization. We aim to reorganize ourselves.

***

Barnett Newman, the painter, tacked a note on the wall at the entrance to the Betty Parsons Gallery on the occasion of his first solo show in New York City in 1950.[3] With this note he invited visitors to the gallery to step into the paintings, to look at them close to, rather than from afar. This act of Newman's, this direction, is a choreographic act. But the source of its choreographic nature is not the fact that he sought to guide or govern the movements or attitude of his audience. The choreography in Newman's direction consists rather in the way it sought to upset, or interrupt, or disrupt, what visitors to the gallery would otherwise have been spontaneously inclined to do.

I do not know what Newman's intention was. Perhaps he wanted people to experience something they could only experience up close. But what he did, in effect, was incite visitors to act contrary to habit. Habit dictates that we step back to inspect the large object on the wall, that we adjust ourselves so that we take up an optimal viewing distance, one that would let us view what interests us as a whole. Ordinary perceiving is made up of just this kind of unthought activity, these silent adjustments that are necessary if we are to bring the world in to focus, to cope with what engages us. We peer, squint, turn, we draw close or step back. The stamp collector bends close. When two people talk they position themselves so they can see each other. Not too close, not too far. There is no need to take out a tape measure. In each context we *feel* the tension that indicates that we have not yet found the optimal position and we naturally, that is to say, unthinkingly but with the greatest of skill, adjust and negotiate until the tension is released. Again, not too close, not too far, just right for the situation at hand. Seeing, like other modes of perceptual exploration, is embodied in skills such as these. We bring the world into focus. We achieve access to it. We don't contemplate pictures in the head when we see. We work to see and the seeing is the working itself; the ground of that working, what makes it possible, is our bodily know-how, our understanding, our curiosity, our need, our sensitivity to context.

The effect of Newman's urging, as I understand it, is not to organize our movements in the gallery, but rather to disorganize them; to disturb our predisposition so as to be orchestrated and moved by the object on the wall. He created a new situation, a choreographic situation, in which we are made to do precisely what our understanding and our competence leads us not to do. He asks us not to take up the optimal viewing point, but to resist doing so. He forces us, in this way, to respond to his paintings not as objects to be inspected, but as situations, or occasions, to unmake us, to unorganize us, to unhabituate us. This is the choreography in Newman's note.

It is important to recognize that habit, unthinking engagement, skillful attunement with the world drawing on what we know and can do, is a good thing. It is our achievement and without it there would be no human, indeed no animal life. In Dewey's image, life is the circular making of oneself and one's experience through doing and undergoing and intelligently coping with effects of one's own doings on oneself. We are, in the fullest sense, creatures of habit.

But it is also critical that we admit that because we are, in this sense, creatures of habit, we are also confined and constrained. We are like Gregor Samsa, who wakes up to find he is now an insect. We wake up and find that we are governed by the manner of our organization. Organization enables, but it also disables. Organization is an existential, a biological necessity, but it is a problem for all that.

The effect of Newman's direction is not so as to produce a new or different experience, whatever he may have aimed at; it is the upsetting of that which makes ordinary experience possible. What is upset, really, is the very basis of our competence as perceivers, that is to say, as conscious human being. And what this upsetting of our nature (all our natures) affords is not so much a new experience, or a new seeing, as an unveiling to ourselves of the myriad ways in which our ordinary, habitual modes of coping and engaging make us what we are.

I offer Newman's example as a glimpse into the choreographic. Choreography disorganizes. In doing so it sets the stage for letting us reorganize. Choreography, in this sense, is a reorganizational project.

***

The idea that choreography is tied to organization is, in a way, a commonplace. I have heard you say that we are all choreographed all the time. This gets something right, to be sure.

It gets right the fact that, as we have already noticed, we human beings are organized, by habit and body schema and learning and nature, by our environments. It is when we think of choreography in this way as tied to the ever-present fact of our organization that we say, correctly, that a military general is a choreographer, or that traffic patterns in a city are a choreographic phenomenon. In this sense it is right that every object, by dint of what it affords or solicits, is a choreographic object (Forsythe). Objects—door knobs, paintings on the wall, whatever—these solicit us and make us move. And so in this sense what we call design, in whatever domain—furniture, manufacturing, architecture—is always a kind of choreographic engineering. In this vein, we are entitled to think of stage craft itself as aiming at the choreographing of an audience's looks and attention, or of architecture as the choreography of our active living in human devised structures. And it is in this sense that evolution itself, or rather, the co-evolution of animal and environment, is a choreographic event or process.

When we think of a choreographer as the one who is in charge, the one who decides, for example, on the dancer's steps, and when we think of a good dancer as one who has been trained to do what the choreographer demands, to do the moves, to follow the score, to enact the plan, when we think and talk in this way, we are thinking of choreography as tied to organization in this familiar way.

This conception also captures beautifully the somewhat surprising fact that choreography, really, is more general than dancing. Choreography is organization; it is planning and control. It is counterpoint, the alignment of events of a kind in space and time, as you have put it. And, to repeat, it also captures the fact that organization is, simply put, important. It is the pervasive and abiding condition of human beings that we are organized, that human beings, and all living beings, are by their very nature, governed by situation and habit.

But for all this, I am recommending a different conception.

Yes, you are right, choreography is tied to organization, but not in the way this familiar picture would have us think. Choreography is not, not really, in the organization business. It is not the most general discipline of imposing organization. Choreographers are not engineers of behavior or movement in the way that designers, like evolution itself, may very well be.

Choreography takes organization for granted. It makes this fundamental and indeed biological fact that we are governed by habit and situation, or by other forms of social control, its presupposition. And its aim, its project, is not to tune us up, or organize us better, but rather, to interrupt or disrupt or, more bluntly, to fuck up these inherited, invisible, unnoticed, familiar, conditioning forms of organization. Choreography aims at disorganizing us. Choreography unveils the sometimes lovely, sometimes ugly ways in which we are always already organized and does so in a ways that must change us.

And this is the source of its value, I think. Choreography is important not because we crave better dancing, or better forms of organized engagement. Choreography is important because, given that we are dancers, given that we are moving embodiments of organization and habit, we need to free ourselves from all that.

Choreography is slack and weak and insignificant to the extent that it fails to take up this demand, to the degree to which it fails to try to free us.

***

Choreography, then, has nothing and at the same time everything to do with dancing, or with other forms of human habitual activity. We can understand this better by turning our attention to another reorganizational practice, philosophy.

I have heard it said of philosophy that it begins in conversation. I think people have Socrates in mind when they say this. Socrates is one of the most revered philosophers and this despite the fact that there are no Socratic theses or theories and there are no Socratic writings. Socrates was not an author. Socrates is famous not for books, but for engaging people in dialog or dialectic. It is debate that is his main device.

These facts notwithstanding, I think we misunderstand Socrates' achievement, indeed, we misunderstand not only philosophy but also the nature of conversation, if we hold that Socrates' method was a conversational one.

Socrates' philosophy has about as much to do with conversation as choreography has to do with dancing. Which is to say nothing, and everything, at the same time.

I will try to explain.

Socrates didn't talk to people. He only pretended to. He didn't so much converse, as put a stop to conversation. He disrupted conversation by challenging people to reflect on what they took for granted, namely, the very habits of thought and talk that make conversation possible in the first place. Socrates' method was not conversation, but interrogation (in Greek: *elenchus*).

Socrates' aim, like Newman's, was to disturb the fundament of habit and ease that makes the ordinary continuities of talking (or in Newman's case, looking) possible. Socrates, in my sense, was in the choreography business. He aimed at fucking things up.

And not just for the fun of it. By fucking things up, he brings out the vast delicate thicket of tendency, skill, behavioral force, and automaticity that makes thought and talk possible and that holds it captive at the same time. What is talking but a kind of dancing between or among people, a sort of moving and engaged mutual attuning of each to the other. Talking is organized behavior. Bodily posture, word choice, volume, attitude, eye movements, orientation in relation to the whole scene, and also, at the level of what we say, truisms, assumptions, biases, definitions, values—all this needs to be in place, a dense and imperceptible background presence, if we are to meet each other and engage our oral fluency.

To disrupt that fluency is to dislodge that dark background. And it is to bring the multiple ways we are shaped and made up by it into consciousness. It is to expose us to ourselves.

Every Socratic dialog is the same. One or another interlocutor claims to know. Socrates gets him to see, by appeal to nothing more than what everyone who is present feels compelled to admit, that he does not know. Certainties become uncertainties and the end is not discovery, finding, realization, insight. It is puzzlement and, in a sense, confusion. But the confusion, or *aporia*, is a thing of positive value, even if it is also irritating. Who wants to be interrupted? Or told prevented from carrying on as one is, so to speak, brought up to carry on. It is worth remembering that Socrates was actually put to death for insisting with so much determination on disabling people. And yet the resulting condition of getting fucked up in this way is a positive one. For we were lost before and didn't know it; captured by modes of organization that were never of our own devising and of which we are only dimly aware. We were venting false certainties, offering intuitions, thought-impulses, as if they were verities. Now, at the dialog's end, we are openly confused and so more truly aware of our situation. The dialog ends not with discovery or agreement.

Not with knowledge of this proposition or that. Rather, it concludes with a kind of re-orientation. The practice of philosophy, which consisted, for Socrates, in the disruption of the activities of just carrying on with familiar landlines of thought and talk, affords us a new sense of where we are. It does not give new knowledge, but it radically changes our relationship to everything we know.

James Baldwin is said to have said that art aims at uncovering the questions that have been occluded by the answers. The same is true of philosophy.

Far from just talking, then, Socrates makes us think about our talking. Socrates requires of us that we frame what Wittgenstein called a perspicuous representation *(übersichtliche Darstellung)*, a representation that makes what is otherwise hidden—the manner of our organization—perspicuous. In a way what Socrates demands—and this is the demand of all philosophy down to the present time—is that we stop talking and start representing, that is to say, start *writing*. But to do this we need to invent the means to write ourselves, what we are saying, what we are doing. This is the work of philosophy.

Now Socrates never did actually, literally, put pen to paper (as far as we know). We know Socrates' dialogs through Plato's writing. Plato's texts, like those of Kant and Descartes and all the rest (including *this* text), are scores. They do not score the right conduct of reason or the path to a conclusion. They are scores for fucking things up, scores for disrupting, disorganizing, and so, finally, for reorganizing. They are scores for the making and remaking of representations of ourselves, scores for making us perspicuous to ourselves.

Plato's dialogs of Socrates are not dialogs, but writings of dialogs. They are a triumph over orality, no more just talking than true choreography is ever just dancing. By abandoning talking, looking, dancing, respectively, Plato, Newman, and the choreographer, free us from habit, from culture as well as biology.

Choreography too aims at the invention of writing. It aims at affording us a perspicuous representation of our moving, dancing selves.

***

Actually, you can't be free of culture or biology. Genuine revolution—a willful decision to be different—is not possible for us, not anymore than it is for ants. You can't decide not to sneeze, as Deborah Hay found out.[4] You can't decide not to turn in the direction of what captures your attention. Nor can you choose to be free of ideology, prejudice, bias, lust, or perversion.

But we can change. Not all at once. Not in one fell swoop. We don't achieve a state of being habit free. But we can come to have new habits. We can't do away with organization. But we can reorganize. Art and philosophy, reorganizational practices both, aim at this.

This is why choreography, even if it has nothing essentially to do with dancing and movement, because it is more general than that, has everything to do with dancing and movement. For one thing, choreography, in the proper sense, aims at just those habits and restrictions and limitations in what is possible that reside precisely in the neighborhood of dancing and the moving body. Choreography is concerned with dancing because dancing is important, not in itself exactly, but because, well, it is one of the modes of our habitual, ordinary, mundane, down-to-earth organization. We, we human beings, are, as a matter of fact, dancers. We love to dance! And we use dancing to so many ends (celebration, love, seduction, play, self-display, and on and on.) And so we are creatures of dancerly habit and dancerly organization and dancerly enslavement. Choreography never just makes more dancing. In fact, you can't make dancing. It is a spontaneous, natural/cultural mode of human wandering, human play, and human celebration. But you can put us on display, and you can put us dancing on display. And so you can create, in Wittgenstein's sense, a perspicuous representation of us dancing, one that can, just maybe, if it fits our need just right, change the way we dance. That is, choreography can have the power to change, to permanently alter that which, in a way, it presupposes, namely, our primal, spontaneous, pre-given engagement with dancing. And this is how reorganization happens. Not by a revolutionary act of freeing ourselves once and for all from being organized. But by a remaking that is an inevitable by-product of trying to know ourselves.

I name this looping down *entanglement*. Philosophy is entangled with the habits of thought and talk that it presupposes in the same way. Consider: Socrates attacked conversation and replaced it with something like writing, as I have explained. But in a way Socrates is just the personification—perhaps only in Plato's mind—of the moment in every conversation, or in every engaged life, when talking and thinking turns on itself and reflects and wonders and second guesses. Socrates took aim at unreflective habit, and the automaticities and continuities and unchallenged presuppositions of thought and talk that make conversation possible. But is there ever conversation entirely in the absence of critical, evaluative, normative reflection? Could there ever be? Could conversation truly survive in a reflective vacuum, that is, in a condition of pure flow, unaffected by considerations of how or why or what we are doing, unshaped by normativity? Doesn't conversation already presuppose philosophy? That is, doesn't ordinary thought and talk presuppose and require just the subversive disruptive attitude to thought and talk that is its mortal enemy?

I want to take seriously the idea that talk and criticism, that is to say, talk and philosophy, are entangled in such a way that there can never be one without the other. Existential phenomenologists like Dreyfus, Heidegger, and Merleau-Ponty perhaps have a different picture. For them, there is flow, engaged coping. And the interruption or disruption of flow is, for them, always breakdown, and the effect of breakdown is always detachment (as opposed to engagement), ejection from one's near-to involvement with things. But I think this is just a fantasy of flow. Flow is more resilient than that. Skillful activities always contain within them the resources for coping with the ready-to-hand possibility of accident or disruption. To give a clear example: we don't stop using language just because we find that we do not understand each other. *Not* understanding is something we accomplish, like understanding itself, within language, and language contains the resources we need to let us make new meaning and communicate without, as it were, and *per impossibile*, going outself of language. Similarly, my walk doesn't end when I trip. A competent walker is one who regains his or her balance even on slippery or uneven ground.[5]

One reason why this is important is that that *there is no outside*, no outside of language, and no outside of any of the multiple and nested structures of organized activity in which we find ourselves. We are forced always to adjust and remake and reorganize, from within.

Every language user, however native and unschooled, is always a grammarian, every conversationalist a philosopher, and every dancer also a choreographer. And likewise, as the example of Newman can serve to remind us, every perceiver is always also concerned with seeing differently and seeing what was hitherto invisible. The act of looking presupposes a sensitivity to the possibility of reflecting on our own perspective. We are never simply captured and controlled by our situation, however much we must admit that we are threatened thus to be captured.

And so with choreography and dancing. Granted dancing is one thing, a kind of habitual expression, and choreography another, for the latter is concerned to put the former and its constitutive place in our lives on display. And yet just as choreography presupposes dancing, maybe, however paradoxical this may sound, dancing presupposes choreography too. What is presupposed, at least, is this: that dancing is a problem to itself and does not require a choreographer who stands *outside* of dancing and looks on, to confer its status as problematic on it. Dancing generates the need for choreography *from the inside*. And then, on top of that, once there is a choreographic representation on offer—and, if I am right, there is always a choreographic representation on offer—then how we dance is shaped by that image. Just as pictures of the dressed human body change how it feels to be dressed—as described by Anne Hollander—so representations of dancing (choreography) change how we feel when we dance and so how we dance.

***

Conscious human being is an organized activity. It is skillful, habitual, situated. Experience is not something that happens inside us. It is something we enact or perform. To the degree to which we act out of the confinement of our organization, then to that degree we are human animals at home in the world. To the degree to which our confinement is a problem to ourselves, and it always is a problem, we are philosophers, or artists. What you call choreography is one of the names we give to what is required of us if we are to flourish and survive. Plato understood this.

Notes

1 See also my *Out of Our Heads* and *Varieties of Presence*.
2 I am grateful to Scott deLahunta, William Forsythe, Deborah Hay, Fabrice Mazliah, Lisa Nelson, and Nicole Peisl. I would never have written this letter without you. Thanks also to Maaike Bleeker, Horst Bredekamp, Katye Coe, Claire Cunnningham, Jess Curtis,

Blake Gopnik, Robert Lazzarini, Alexander Nagel, Michelle Steinwald, Rebecca Todd, and Hilary Putnam. See my *Strange Tools: Art and Human Nature* for a further development of the ideas in this letter.
3 I learned this anecdote about Newman from the wall text in the Barnett Newman room at the Abstract Expressionism New York exhibition at the Museum of Modern Art in New York, October 3, 2010—April 25, 2011.
4 Hay describes the disastrous consequences of trying to unlearn sneezing in *Reorganizing Ourselves*, a joint lecture performance she and I undertook with Michelle Steinwald during 2015–2016. See also her *Using the Sky: A Dance* (2015).
5 See my *Varieties of Presence* for more on the fragile resilience of engagement.

References

Dewey, John. *Art As Experience*. Reprint. New York: Penguin, 1980.
Dreyfus, Hubert. "The Myth of the Pervasiveness of the Mental". *The McDowell-Dreyfus Debate*. Ed. Joseph K Schearer. Oxford: Oxford University Press, 2013.
Forsythe, William. "Choreographic Objects," available at http://www.williamforsythe.de/essay.html, accessed February 9, 2016.
Hay, Deborah. *Using the Sky: A Dance*. London: Routledge, 2015.
Heidegger, Martin. *Being and Time*. Trans. John Macquarrie and Edward Robinson. New York: Harper, 1962.
Hollander, Anne. *Seeing Through Clothes*. New York: Viking, 1978.
Merleau-Ponty, Maurice *Phenomenology of Perception*. Trans. Donald A. Landes. New York: Routledge, 2012.
Noë, Alva. *Action in Perception*. Cambridge, Mass.: The MIT Press, 2004.
—— *Out of Our Heads: Why You Are Not Your Brain and Other Lessons From The Biology of Consciousness*. New York: Hill and Wang/Farrar, Straus, and Giroux, 2009.
—— *Varieties of Presence*. Cambridge, Mass.: Harvard University Press, 2012.
—— *Strange Tools: Art and Human Nature*. New York: Hill and Wang/Farrar, Straus, and Giroux, 2015.
Wittgenstein, Ludwig. *Philosophical Investigations*. Trans. G.E.M. Anscombe. Oxford: Blackwell, 1954.

INDEX

3DS Max 19
9 Evenings: Theater and Engineering 220
50 Link Dodecahedral Space Grid 73

A Choreographer's Score 6–7, 14, 52–61
AARON 109
abstracted identities 18–19, 23
abstraction xxii, 148–9, 200–1
Accumulation 215, 216, 217, 219
Achterland 166
Adobe Flash 105
Advanced Computing Center for the Arts and Design (ACCAD) 104
agent, archive as 203–5
agent-based approach 109–10
algorithms 218–23
Alie/na(c) tion 222
alignments 101–2
analogue archives 204
Andrien, B. 37, 38, 39
Animal a l'esquena, L' 36–7
Animazoo motion capture system 194
annotation 195
anthropology of the senses 223–6
'Apache Dance' 163–4
Appear/Disappear 119, 121
appropriation 164
Apps4festivals 88
Arbeau, T. (J. Tabouret) 157, 188–9
archaeological sites 194
archival dynamics 199
archives xxii, 199–214; archive as agent 203–5; archive as pedagogue 163–6; digital *see* digital archives; enacting the archive 209–12; *Siobhan Davies Replay see* *Siobhan Davies Replay*; theorizations of the archive 157–60; twenty-first-century archival logics 212–13
archivization 155–6
art 229–30; installations *see* installations
artificial intelligence (AI) 109
artificial logic 122
artistic response 134
Arts and Humanities Research Council (AHRC) 63, 129
Arts Council of England 174
arts funding 145–6, 151
asymbolic mediation 191
Athenian ceramics 185–6
atlases 190
attribute data 102, 205
augmented reality (AR) 88–9; app 88
Auroux, S. 186, 196
Auslander, P. 157, 158, 159
authorship 168–9, 174–5; authorial input 176–7; *see also* copyright
Ave Nue 32

BADco. xx, 5; *Whatever Dance Toolbox* 9, 11, 15, 118–27
Badiou, A. 54
bag of visual words (BOVW) 76
Baldassarino di Belgiojosa (Balthazar de Beaujoyeux) 187
Baldwin, J. 233
Banes, S. 219

238 Index

Barnard, P. 114
Bartók/Mikrokosmos 52
basic mode of *Double Skin/Double Mind* 94, 97
Bateson, G. 161
Bausch, P. 54
Bay-Cheng, S. 203
Beauchamp, P. 188
Bell Labs 219–20
Ben Ari, A. 75
Benesh notation system 176
Benveniste, E. 197
Berne Convention 176
Beyoncé Knowles 162, 166, 174
Bharatanatyam dance 10, 47–50
BIPED 18–19, 21
Bird Song 65, 74
Bishop, C. 225
Black and Forth 122
Blackwell, A. 110–11, 114
Blake, J. 172
blogging 67
blogging humanities 71
Boden, M. 109
bodily affects xxii, 215–27; from technologies of sense 223–6
Boggia, R. 87
Bonachela, R. 165
books 188, 192
Brandstetter, G. 89
British Black Dance Archives project 77
Brown, M. 179
Brown, T. 57, 215, 216, 217, 219
Bürkle, C. 46
Burrows, J. 132
bystander role 21

Cage, J. 16–17, 25, 218, 220–1
Cage 119, 120, 125
CALM 71
Canguilhem, G. 216
Capture/Replay 119, 121, 125
Capturing Intention research project 97, 98
Caroso, F. 187, 190
Carter, P. 194
categorization 175
cat's cradle 22–3
CD-ROMs 45–6, 50
Centre National de la Danse 37
Cesena 57
Changes 122
Charleroi/Danses 37
ChoreoGraph 110
Choreographer's Score, A 6–7, 14, 52–61

Choreographic Coding Labs 134
choreographic ideas 208–9, 212
choreographic instructions 111–12
choreographic intelligence 146
Choreographic Language Agent (CLA) 8, 11–12, 15, 108–17, 143, 147
choreographic objects 102–3, 129–30, 144, 146–7, 177, 208–9, 212; constitution and circulation of 147–51
Choreographic Objects: Traces and Artifacts of Physical Intelligence network project 63, 129–30, 143, 145
choreographic poetics 56–9
choreographic thinking tools 114–15
Choreographic Thinking Tools (CCT) 114
choreography: demands of xxiii, 228–36; technology, bodily affects and xxii, 215–27
Choreography and Cognition research project 8, 109, 110–11
Choreography of Everyday Movement 192
Choreography or ELSE 87
Church, L. 110
circulation 147–51, 159–60; dance as gift 160–3
cognition 81
Cohen, H. 109
collaboration 177–8
collaborative visualization 99–107
Collomosse, J.P. 76, 77
colour searching 75
commodification 148–50, 162–3
common heritage of mankind 169, 170
community of practice 130, 133
comparative analysis of dance projects 3–15
comparison-actions 26
complexity in exploitation 178
computing humanities 71
consciousness 228–36
Contact Improvisation 32
content-based image retrieval 75–7, 204–5
contextual impulse to transmit knowledge from dance xxi, 141–54
Contredanse 32–3, 37, 39, 40
Convention for the Safeguarding of the Intangible Cultural Heritage 171
Convention on Cultural Diversity of Cultural Expressions 171, 179
conversation 231–3, 234
Coomaraswamy, A. 221
copyright 9, 14, 64–5; challenges for traditional copyright law xxi-xxii, 168–84
Copyright Act 1911 174, 175

Copyright Act 1956 175
Copyright Designs and Patents Act 1988 (CDPA) 175
Cornazzano, A. 187
Countdown 166
counterpoint 58, 102, 107
Court of Justice (CoJ) jurisprudence 175
Coventry University 63, 67
CRDSPCR 20
Creative Commons licences 29, 84
creatures 23–5; sound creatures 26
critical editions 56
cueing 101–2
cultural ecology 26–9
cultural expressions 171
cultural heritage 169–73, 179; culture-specific conventions 170–1, 172, 178–9; relationship with intellectual property rights 172–3; selection and mediation of 173
cultural property 169, 170, 179
cultural spaces 192–3
Cunningham, M. xx, 190, 220; *Loops* 5, 8, 10, 16–31, 211
Cunningham Dance Company 17
curatorial, the 89
customize level of *Double Skin/Double Mind* 95–6
cybernetics 220–3

D-TRACES project 67, 69
Dance Central video games 164
Dance Engaging Science working group 12, 134–5
dance machines 218–23
dance-tech.net 82–4
Dance-tech project 6, 7–8, 9, 80–90, 203–4
dance-tech.tv 84–6
danses à figures 186
dark writing 194–5
Data Fan object 101
Davies, S. xx, 62–9; *Bird Song* 65, 74; *Rushes* 73, 75; Siobhan Davies Replay see Siobhan Davies Replay
De Keersmaeker, A.T. xx, 5, 6–7, 14, 52–61, 166, 174
De Mey, T. 57, 166
decision-making process 121–3
deLahunta, S. 9, 63, 131, 142
Delay/Reverse 119, 120–1
Deleted Messages 122
Deleuze, G. 57
Deren, M. 216
Derrida, J. 155–6

development of projects 6–10
dialogue, Socratic 232–3
dictated by technical requirements 177
difference 107
digital archives xxi, 13, 155–67, 204; Siobhan Davies Replay see Siobhan Davies Replay
Digital Dance Archives (DDA) 5, 6, 9, 13, 14, 67, 70–9, 203–4, 204, 207
digital dance school 43
digital dance score projects 132
digital sustainability 10
digitalization 13, 133, 201–2, 203–4, 207, 211
disciplinary technologies 226
discretization 186, 190, 192, 195, 196
Displace 218, 223–6
dissonance 107
Distributed Choreographic Cognition project 114
distributed cognition 81
divided attention 123
Do It Yourself! workshops 125
Do-Nguyen, T. 166
documentation 54
Doll, The 75
Dorado, J. 87
Double Skin/Double Mind 5, 9, 10, 11, 13, 15, 51, 91–8, 143, 147; glossary 7, 93; shift in archival logics 203–4, 209–12, 212–13
Downie, M. 9, 23–5, 109–10
dramaturgy 59
Drucker, J. 75
Drumming 57, 58
Dublin Core 64
Dunbar-Hester, C. 220
Dunn, S. 193
Dupuy, J.P. 221
DVD-ROMs 10, 32–40, 46–7, 47–50
dynamometer 191

Egyptian tombstone reliefs 185
Eichhorn, K. 156
eido-kinetic intuitions 194–5
Eidos: Telos 44, 215–16, 222
Elena's Aria 52
embodied embedded condition 81
embodiment, double sense of 200
emergent behaviour 23–5
Emio Greco | PC xx, 5, 7, 91–8, 209–10
En Atendant 57
enactment xxii, 209; enacting the archive 209–12; enactive approach to perception 200–1, 228–30, 235

Index

encylopedias 190
engaging users 65–6
entanglement 234–5
ephemerality 145, 157–60, 176, 181, 202
ergograph 191
ergometric instruments 191–2
Ernst, W. xviii, 75, 199, 207, 211
exchange 148–9
existential phenomenologists 234
Experiments in Art and Technology 219–20
external motivation 145–7
Extra Festival 86

Fargion, M. 132
Fase, Four Movements to the Music of Steve Reich 52, 54
feedback 218–23
Feuillet, R.-A. 188
Field 110
Fildes, S. 165
fixation 172, 176
Fleming, R. 75
floor plans 190
Florence, E. 38
flow 234–5
footnotes 56
Forsythe, W. xx, 53, 147; choreographic objects 102–3, 129–30, 144, 208–9, 212; *Eidos: Telos* 44, 215–16, 222; *Improvisation Technologies see Improvisation Technologies; The Loss of Small Detail* 41–2, 43; *Motion Bank see Motion Bank*; *One Flat Thing, reproduced* 99–103, 104, 128, 129, 133, 205–6, 208; *Self Meant to Govern* 41, 43–4; *Synchronous Objects see Synchronous Objects;* systematic approach 222–3
Forsythe Company 128–37
Forsythe Foundation 128, 129
Foucault, M. 226
Frankfurt Ballet 41–3, 222
Frankfurt Lab 130, 131, 132
Franko, M. 160–2
Fresh Prince of Bel-Air 163
funding, public 145–6, 151
Funktionen toolbox 122

GAMA–Gateway 70
gathering together of coordinated materials 156
Gelber, N.D. 45, 46
genesis of movements 58
German Federal Cultural Foundation 130

gestural tablatures 188–90
Gesture Follower 51, 92
gesturo-haptics 195, 196
gesturology 189
gift 148–9, 160–3
Gil, J. 189
Gitelman, L. 203
glossary 7, 93
goal directed behaviour 221
Goethe Institute 106
Graham, M. 174–5
GraindelaVoix 57
grammatization 186, 189, 190, 195, 196
gravity 33, 34, 35
Greco, E. 91, 92, 93, 94
Gregory I 186
Groves, R. 128
Guattari, F. 217
Guilcher, Y. 189
gvadancetraining.org 84

habit 229–30
Haffner, N. 44
hand-drawn line 21
Hand-drawn Spaces 9, 18, 20, 21
Hansen, M. xix-xx, 208, 212–13
Harding, M. 163–4
Hathoric rites 185
Hauert, T. 132
Hay, D. 132, 134, 135, 165
Hayles, N.K. xix, 81, 82, 205–6
heuristic mission 57
historical context 14–15, 185–98
Howes, D. 223, 224
human implicatedness 213
human rights 169
Humphrey, D. 60

ID/entity: portraits for the 21st century 23
If/Then Installed 165
image retrieval 75–7, 204–5
improvisation 82
Improvisation Technologies 10, 12–13, 15, 41, 44–6, 51, 53, 103–4, 128, 142; additional outcomes 11, 46–50; aim 4, 5
In Plain Clothes 65
incorporative donation 161, 165
Indian dance 47–50
inertia 124
Inertia 119, 120, 125
information obsolescence 17, 30, 31, 174
information society 205–6
input, authorial 176–7

inscriptions 144–5
Inside Movement Knowledge research project 9, 11, 53, 97, 98, 210
installations: *Displace* 218, 223–6; interactive 165; *Synchronous Objects* video installations 105–6; *see also Double Skin/Double Mind*
instructions, choreographic 111–12
intangible cultural heritage 171
intellectual creation standard 176
intellectual property (IP) rights 172–3; *see also* copyright
interactive digital notebook 108–17
interactive installations 165; *Double Skin/Double Mind see Double Skin/Double Mind*
interactivity 174
intercesseurs 57, 60
internal motivation 145–7
internet 80, 81
interpretant 192
interpretation 156
intersections 12
ischia 38
Ise Temple, Japan 30
iterative processes 177–8
itinerant searching 72–5, 204–5

Jerwood Bank blog 67
Johns, J. 21
Jonzi D 165
Jose, J.M. 76
Judson Church dancers 218, 219–20
Just Dance video games 164

Kalaripayatthu dance 47, 48, 49, 50
Kern, D. 43, 133, 134
Kirby, M. 217
Kirsh, D. 114
kitchens 65
Klein, G. 141
Kliën, M. 110
Klüver, B. 220
knowledge economy 15, 141–2, 147–51
knowledge production 141–2, 145–6, 147–51
Kühne-Hörmann, E. 146
Kuypers, P. 32–3, 40
kymograph (wave recorder) 191–2
Kyogen 46–7

Laban, R. 70, 72, 73
Laban Movement Choirs 70
Laban notation system 176

language 234–5
L'animal a l'esquena 36–7
Leach, J. 130
learning 86–7; learn level of *Double Skin/Double Mind* 95
Learning Space 67
Learning to Dance in Bali 161
Lem, S. 17
Lepecki, A. 157, 160
licensing 178
LifeForms software program 19, 20
light writing 195
liminal distortion 224
list-actions 26
lived abstraction 200–1
liveness 158
living wills 27–9
location sensing 193
locative media 193
Locus 219
London Inns of Court Manuscripts 188
Loops 5, 8, 10, 16–31, 211
Lorin, A. 188
Loss of Small Detail, The 41–2, 43
Louis XIV 188
Lowenthal, D. 170, 172
Ludwig, K. 191

macrostructural decisions 57–8
Maier, T.-K. 44
main working method 58
Mansaku/Mansai family 47
Manzotti, L. 190
Martinucci, M. 223
Massine v de Basil 175
Massumi, B. xix, 200
masterclass tradition 53
Matching Positions 119–20
material 59
Material for the Spine 6, 7, 10, 13, 14, 32–40, 145
Mauss, M. 161
McGregor, W. xx, 5; *Choreographic Language Agent* 8, 11–12, 15, 108–17, 143, 147
McManus, T. 45, 46
McPherson, K. 165
McPherson, T. 71, 206
Mead, M. 161
mediation 173, 208, 212–13
Memories are Made of This ... Performance Notes 124
memory objects 65
Mereruka, tomb of 185

242 Index

Meskin, A. 181
meta-academy 87, 88
metadata 64, 71–2, 195
metanarrative 59
Mey, T. De 57, 166
Miller, B. 132
Mlada, L. 74
Morrissey, C. 36, 37
MoSys 134
Motion Bank 6, 11, 12, 14, 15, 104, 128–37, 143
Motion Bank Institute (MBI) 135
motion capture 40, 191–2, 192–4, 195, 208; *Loops* 22, 29; *Material for the Spine* 33, 34, 37
motion capture/motion analysis software 123–4
Motion in Place Platform (MiPP) research consortium 193–4
motivation 4–6; internal and external 145–7
Move-Me 165
movement databases 194–5
Movimiento.org 84
Müller, I. 87
multimedia web-based work 174
Museum of Modern Art (MoMA), New York 89
music: critical editions 56; scores 187
'Music Creatures, The' 110
music videos 160, 162
Musso, A. 191

NAGARIKA DVD-ROMs 47–50; *Bharatanatyam* 10, 47–50; *Kalaripayatthu* 47, 48, 49, 50
narrative 59
NASA 17
National Resource Centre for Dance (NRCD) 70, 71, 72, 77, 78
needs, project 4–6
Negri, C. 187
neoliberal market structures 162
networked environment 80–90
Newman, B. 229–30
Nintendo Wii 164
No Time To Fly 135
Nobiltà di Dame 190
Noë, A. xxii, 130, 200, 225
noetic world 192
Nollet, Abbé 191
non-improvised theme 46
notation systems 176; history of 187–90, 192

notebooks 108, 111; interactive digital notebook 108–17
Nowviskie, B. 75

obsolescence 17, 30, 31, 174
Odon of Cluny 186
One Flat Thing, reproduced 99–103, 104, 128, 129, 133, 205–6, 208
Ong, W. xix, 192, 196, 207
online videos 162, 163–4, 165–6, 167; dance-tech.tv 84–6
ontology of performance 157–8
open source code 30
OpenEndedGroup 110
oral-mimetic regime 53
organization 230–1; *see also* reorganization
originality 175–6
outcomes, project 10–12
ownership 64–5, 168–9, 174–5; *see also* copyright

PACT Zollverein 105–6
PAF (Performing Arts Forum) 124, 127
Palazhy, J. 41, 47, 48, 50
parabolic reflectors 224
Parikka, J. 204, 207
passage-actions 26
patterns 205–6; recognition of 75–7
Paxton, S. xx, 144–5, 199; *Material for the Spine* 6, 7, 10, 13, 14, 32–40, 145
pedagogue, archive as 163–6
perception, enactive approach to 200–1, 228–30, 235
performance 149–50, 203; and the archive 156–60; style 59
performed photography 159–60
perishable replaceable materials 30, 211
perspicuous representation 233, 234
Petrucci, O. 187
Phelan, P. 145, 157, 158
Phillips, J. 20
philosophy xxiii, 231–3, 234
Piecemaker 4, 43, 133
Piecemaker2 (PM2) 133–4
Piecemeta (PMa) 134
Pink, A. 74
Pite, C. 46
Plato 233
play level of *Double Skin/Double Mind* 96
Playford, J. 188
poetics, choreographic 56–9
pop-up media labs 86–7
pose-based search 75–7, 204–5

potential of digital technologies xxii, 185–98
preservation 173; *Loops* 16–31
print 188, 192, 207
process: knowledge making 146; phase of projects 6–10
production, technologies of 226
products 10–12
Protopapa, E. 74
public funding 145–6, 151
purposeful behaviour 221

quantification 102

Rain 57
Rainer, Y. 55, 56, 165
randomness 205–6
Rauschenberg, R. 220
Reaccession of Ted Shawn, The 89
readership 186–8
reading aloud 25–6
real-time video analyses 118–27
Recchia, S. 74
reconstructions 58, 61
records 186–8; *see also* archives
Reede, R. 76, 77
reenactment 159
regeneration 207–8, 211
Régnier, E. 191
relationality 201
Relay 66
reorganization xxiii, 230–5
repertoire 159, 202–3, 210–11
Replay see Siobhan Davies Replay
reproducibility 189–90
return-actions 26
rhythmos 195, 197
Rilke, R.M. 16
room writing 46
Rosas 52, 53, 54, 58
Rosas danst Rosas 52, 166
Rosch, E. 81
Rothwell, N. 110
Rotman, B. xix, 186, 196
Royal Academy of Dance 188
rudimentary notation systems 187
Rueb, T. 193
Rulegame 5 219
rules 218–23
Rushes 73, 75

Saxon, D. 7, 64
Schlemmer, O. 190
Schmelzer, B. 57

Schneider, R. 159
Schoenberg, A. 56
Scholten, P.C. 91, 92, 93
score, choreographic 6–7, 14, 52–61
Scott, O. 74
scrapbooks, virtual 65, 67, 73–5
scratch tapes 65, 66
searching 72–5, 204–5
selection of cultural heritage 173
self, technologies of the 226
self-donation 162
Self Meant to Govern 41, 43–4
self-reflective writing 54
sensation 35–6, 38, 39, 145
sense, technologies of xxii, 15, 223–6
Set and Reset 57
Shawcross, C. 72, 73
Shawn, T. 89
shkema 195, 197
Siegal, R. 165
signature practices 64
signs, technologies of 226
Siobhan Davies Replay 13, 14, 62–9, 70, 72, 143, 199–200, 203–4; circulation of choreographic objects 147–8, 150; development 7, 8–9, 62–6; motivation 5, 6; outcomes 11, 66–7
Siobhan Davies Studios 63
situated cognition 81
Slow Arc Inside a Cube III 72
Smith, N. Stark 87
Smith, S. 36
social media: archive as pedagogue 163–4, 165–6; dance-tech.net 82–4; YouTube 73
Socrates 231–3, 234
software systems development 133–4
solar microscope 191
Solo 46
sound creatures 26
spatial data 102, 205
spatial design 57–8, 60–1
stable substrate 156
stage landscapes 222–3
Steele, J. 20
Stiegler, B. 186, 189, 196
Stille, A. 30
Stravinsky, I. 56
Suchman, L. 81
Suite for Changes 220
Sulzman, M. 219
Sunder, M. 180
sustainability 10
sword 16

244 Index

Symmetries: Towards Object Oriented Theatre research project 125
Synchronous Objects 13, 14, 53, 99–107, 128, 143, 208; aim 6; as archive 209, 212–13; choreographic objects 148, 209; development 7, 8, 99–104; outcomes 11, 104–7; patterns and randomness 205–6; as resource 147
syntax 58, 61
system-based approaches 217–18, 218–23

Tabouret, J. (T. Arbeau) 157, 188–9
talking heads 84, 85, 95
Taylor, D. 158–9, 202
technical requirements 177
technogenesis xix
technologies: Foucault's kinds of 226; of sense xxii, 15, 223–6
technologizing of the word xix
TERP interface 44
terrorist acts 161
That's Kyogen! 46–7
themes 101–2
Thinking with the Body 11
Thompson, E. 81
timeline plan 58
timing: Indian dance 50; intricate in *Loops* 22
Tokyo Media Connections (TMC) 11, 46–7
Tomlinson, K. 191
tools determinism 19
training pit 48, 50
Trillium 219
Trio A 165
Tuccaro, A. 187
Turing, D. 9, 118–27
Turnage, M.-A. 114
Turnbull, D. 192
twenty-first-century media xx, 208, 212–13

Ullman, L. 70
UNDANCE 114
United Nations Educational, Scientific and Cultural Organization (UNESCO) 169; Cultural Conventions 170–1, 172, 178–9
Urdimbre.org 84
users 67; engaging 65–6

Van Kerkhoven, M. 57
Varela, F.J. 81
Variable Media Initiative 29
Variations V 220
verb list 114

Vianna, B. 89
Victoria Miro Gallery 72
video analysis, real-time 118–27
video games 160, 162, 163, 164–5
video installations 105–6
video interviews 84, 85
video recordings 55, 65; Frankfurt Ballet 4, 41–2; music videos 160, 162; online videos *see* online videos
Violin Phase 57
virtual scrapbooks 65, 67, 73–5
visual content-based image retrieval 75–7, 204–5
visualizations 99–107, 205–6, 208
voice 25–6
Von Bismarck, B. 89

Wallinger, M. 114
wave recorder (kymograph) 191–2
Web 2.0 73, 80, 81, 90
Weber, A. 134
Weinert, A. 89
Wellcome Collection 11
What the Machine Sees 1-space (WTMS 1-space) 124–5
What the Machine Sees 2-time (WTMS 2-time) 124, 125
Whatever Dance Toolbox (WDT) 9, 11, 15, 118–27
Where the Hell is Matt? videos 163–4
Whitman, R. 220
Wiener, N. 218, 221
William Forsythe: Improvisation Technologies see Improvisation Technologies
Williams, R. 180
Wittgenstein, L. 233
Woolford, K. 193–4
Work 1961–1973 55, 56
workshop mode of *Double Skin/Double Mind* 91, 94–6
World Wide Web: *Digital Dance Archives* web platform 70–9; *Synchronous Objects* 104–5
writing xix, 14, 186, 207, 233; *A Choreographer's Score* 6–7, 14, 52–61; dark 194–5, light 195; self-reflective 54

Xbox 360 Kinect 164

'Youthful Portrait of My Father' (Rilke) 16
YouTube 73

Ziegler, C. 9, 91
ZKM Karlsruhe 41